Touching for Knowing

Cognitive psychology of haptic manual perception

Edited by

Yvette Hatwell

Université Pierre Mendès-France, Grenoble

Arlette Streri

Edouard Gentaz

Université René Descartes and Centre National
de la Recherche Scientifique

John Benjamins Publishing Company
Amsterdam / Philadelphia

™ The paper used in this publication meets the minimum requirements
of American National Standard for Information Sciences – Permanence
of Paper for Printed Library Materials, ANSI z39.48-1984.

Translated (and updated) from: Y. Hatwell, A. Streri and E. Gentaz (2000).
Toucher pour connaître. Paris: Presses Universitaires de France.

Library of Congress Cataloging-in-Publication Data

Touching for knowing : cognitive psychology of haptic manual perception /
edited by Yvette Hatwell, Arlette Streri, Edouard Gentaz.
p.   cm. (Advances in Consciousness Research, ISSN 1381–589X ; v. 53)
Includes bibliographical references and indexes.
1. Touch--Psychological aspects. 2. Visual perception. 3. Perceptual-
motor processes. I. Hatwell, Yvette. II. Streri, Arlette. III. Gentaz, Edouard. IV.
Series.

BF275. T69 2003
152.1′82-dc22   2003056024
ISBN 90 272 5185 1 (Eur.) / 1 58811 423 6 (US) (Hb; alk. paper)
ISBN 90 272 5186 X (Eur.) / 1 58811 424 4 (US) (Pb; alk. paper)

John Benjamins Publishing Co. · P.O. Box 36224 · 1020 ME Amsterdam · The Netherlands
John Benjamins North America · P.O. Box 27519 · Philadelphia PA 19118-0519 · USA

Touching for Knowing

Advances in Consciousness Research

Advances in Consciousness Research provides a forum for scholars from different scientific disciplines and fields of knowledge who study consciousness in its multifaceted aspects. Thus the Series will include (but not be limited to) the various areas of cognitive science, including cognitive psychology, linguistics, brain science and philosophy. The orientation of the Series is toward developing new interdisciplinary and integrative approaches for the investigation, description and theory of consciousness, as well as the practical consequences of this research for the individual and society.

Series B: Research in progress. Experimental, descriptive and clinical research in consciousness.

Volume 53

Touching for Knowing: Cognitive psychology of haptic manual perception
Edited by Yvette Hatwell, Arlette Streri and Edouard Gentaz

Table of contents

5. Some practical applications for visually impaired people

List of Authors

Maryse Badan
Neuropsychologist,
Hôpitaux Universitaires
de Genève (Suisse)
e-mail: Maryse.Badan@hcuge.ch

Dominique Burger
Research Engineer at the INSERM, Creare
University Pierre and Marie Curie,
Paris (France)
e-mail: Dominique.Burger@snv.jussieu.fr

Cesare Cornoldi
Professor of Psychology,
University of Padova (Italy)
e-mail: cesare.cornoldi@unipd.it

Maria Clara Fastame
Research student,
University of Pavia (Italy)

Dorothy Fragaszy
Professor of Psychology,
University of Georgia,
Athens (USA)
e-mail:doree@arches.uga.edu

Olivier Gapenne
Assistant professor,
University of Technology,
Compiègne (France)
e-mail: olivier.gapenne@utc.fr

Christelle Genouëlle[†]
Research student,
University of Technology,
Compiègne (France)

Edouard Gentaz
Researcher at the CNRS,
Laboratory Cognition and Development,
University René Descartes-Paris 5 (France)
e-mail: gentaz@psycho.univ-paris5.fr

John Greaney
Assistant professor in Sciences
of Education,
University of Manchester
(United Kingdom)
e-mail: John.Greaney@man.ac.uk

Sylvain Hanneton
Assistant professor,
Laboratoire de Neurophysique et Physiolo-
gie du Système Moteur (STAPS),
University René Descartes-Paris 5,
Paris (France)

Yvette Hatwell
Emeritus Professor of Psychology,
Laboratory of Psychology
and NeuroCognition,
University Pierre Mendès-France,
Grenoble (France)
e-mail: yvette.hatwell@upmf-grenoble.fr

Morton Heller
Chair and Professor of Psychology,
Eastern Illinois University,
Charleston (USA)
e-mail: cfmah1@eiu.edu

Eileen W. Hill
Research assistant,
University of Birmingham
(United Kingdom)
e-mail: M.J.Tobin@bham.ac.uk

Roberta L. Klatzky
Professor of Psychology,
Carnegie-Mellon University,
Pittsburg (USA)
e-mail: klatzky@andrew.cmu.edu

Agnès Lacreuse
Associate researcher,
Yerkes Regional Research Center,
Emory University, Atlanta (USA)
e-mail: alacreu@rmy.emory.edu

Susan J. Lederman
Professor of Psychology,
Queens University,
Kingston Ontario (Canada)
e-mail: lederman@pavlov.psyc.queensu.ca

Charles Lenay
Assistant professor in History and
Philosophy of Sciences,
COSTECH, University of Technology,
Compiègne (France)
e-mail: charles.lenay@utc.fr

Catherine Marque
Assistant professor,
Department Génie Biomédical,
University of Compiègne (France)
e-mail: catherine.marque@utc.fr

Françoise Martinez-Sarocchi
Researcher at the CNRS,
University of Toulouse-Le Mirail,
Toulouse (France)
e-mail: f.sarocchi@wanadoo.fr

Arlette Streri
Professor of Developmental Psychology,
Laboratory Cognition and Development,
University René Descartes-Paris 5,
Paris (France)
e-mail: streri@psycho.univ-paris5.fr

Michael J. Tobin
Emeritus Professor of Specialized Education, Research Centre for the Education
of the Visually Handicapped, University
of Birmingham (United Kingdom)
e-mail: M.J.Tobin@bham.ac.uk

Tomaso Vecchi
Professor of Psychology,
University of Pavia
(Italy)

CHAPTER 1

Introduction
Touch and cognition

Yvette Hatwell

Is it possible to know something just by touching it? Is it useful, and indeed necessary to do so in certain cases? Touch is a modality whose function, from a cognitive point of view, has given rise to diverse and even contradictory appreciations. Because it is largely redundant with vision for the acquisition of spatial knowledge of the environment and the object properties, it allows blind people to acquire a certain autonomy in their everyday life. Therefore, it is considered as a powerful and effective tool. On the other hand, the dominance of vision seems so complete in normally sighted people that touch appears as a minor sense which usefulness is restricted to some particular domains, such as the control of posture based on corrective insoles or the grasping of objects in order to move or transform them.

The processes at work in the tactile perception have similarly been subjected to diverging evaluations. In the 1960's and 70's, following the work of E. J. Gibson (1969) and of J. J. Gibson (1966), researchers tended to concentrate on those aspects common to all the perceptual modalities, and in particular common to touch and vision. By contrast, more recent studies have emphasized the specific character of this perceptual system. Moreover, progress made in cerebral imagery methods and in neuropsychology today permits a finer approach to how this modality functions and how it is integrated with other sources of information. Some reviews of the works in this field of haptic perception had already been published in the 80's and at the beginning of the 90's (Hatwell 1986; Heller & Schiff 1991; Millar 1994; Streri 1993). But knowledge evolves rapidly and it is our intention to summarize what is currently known about the tactile perceptual processes and the relations that this sense has with the other senses, particularly with vision.

Touch differs from vision and hearing in that it depends on contact and that its receptors are spread over the whole body. This quality of proximal reception has consequences which are at the origin of almost all the problems discussed in the present study. Indeed, because of this property, the tactile perceptual field is limited to the zone of contact with objects. In this passive tactile perception (cutaneous perception) where stimulation is applied to an immobile segment of the body, the perceptual field is drastically reduced and has the exact dimensions of the surface of the skin in contact with the stimulus. While certain discriminations are still possible in this situation, tactile perceptual capacity is limited because of the lack of any exploratory movement (Katz 1925/1989; Gibson 1962, 1966; Revesz 1950).

In most cases, in order to apprehend the whole object, voluntary movements must be made in order to compensate for the smallness of the tactile perceptual field. The size of this field thus varies according to the body parts which are mobilized (a finger, the whole hand, both hands associated to movements of the arms, etc.). The kinesthetic perceptions resulting from these movements are necessarily linked to the purely cutaneous perceptions generated by skin contact, and they form an indissociable whole labeled "haptic" (or tactilo-kinesthetic, or active touch) perception. As a result, object perception is initially incomplete, it may lack coherence and it is highly sequential. This latter property increases the load on working memory and requires, at the end of exploration, a mental integration and synthesis in order to obtain a unified representation of the object (Revesz 1950).

The successive nature of touch has long struck observers and has been opposed to the simultaneous nature of vision. This opposition should however be qualified. Although it is true that the vast visual perceptual field allows a global and immediate apprehension of many aspects of the stimulus, exploratory movements are still necessary in vision to identify the invariants which specify the spatial properties of the environment. However, the magnitude of these ocular and head movements is consistently lower than that of manual movements, especially when hand movements are associated to those of the arms. It seems quite justifiable, therefore, to consider touch as being much more sequential than vision.

This does not mean that touch functioning is more similar to audition than to vision. Audition is specialized in the perception of successive information and it is therefore the most efficient modality for the perception of temporal stimuli (duration, rhythms, speech, etc.), whereas vision excels in space perception. But, although touch is highly sequential, it is nevertheless a spatial modality because it does not explore in a linear way and in an imposed order. In audition, the order of the sequence of stimuli cannot be changed since it carries meaning (in speech, music, etc.). By contrast, touch can explore the stimulus in any order and it can contact several times the same part of the object or set of objects, in the same way as the eyes explore a wide scene or a large picture. Therefore, touch provides information about the spatial properties of the environment and it is largely redundant with vision since it allows the perception of physical and spatial properties (texture, localization, direction, distance, shape, size, etc.). However, the quality of the tactile percept depends both on exploratory movements and the mental synthesis achieved at the end of the perceptual process.

Owing to the central role that these movements play, the regions which are most mobile and best equipped with sensory receptors are also the most effective in the tactile domain. These are the region around and inside the mouth, which is much used by infants because of their motor immaturity, and the hands (or more exactly the arm-hand system). In adults, the latter constitutes, from a cognitive point of view, the real haptic perceptual system. The present study is therefore concerned with manual haptic perception.

But the hands are also, and perhaps especially, the motor organs used to in reaching, holding, transporting and transforming objects in our everyday life. More than in all the other modalities, perception and action are closely linked in the haptic modality. That is why the relation between perception and action is particularly important in the haptic mode.

The present study is concerned both with the development of tactile perception in infants and children and with the functioning of this system in adults. Data taken from pathology and especially from totally blind persons will also be extensively discussed. In the five sections composing this book, specialized authors review the recent studies in their field of research. The questions treated in these sections are presented below.

Part 1. Some anatomical and neurophysiological bases of tactile manual perception

Cutaneous perception and haptic perception can be distinguished by the fact that, in the latter, the motor system is involved in the exploratory activity of the hand which in turn can activate the whole shoulder-arm-hand system. In cutaneous perception, because the corporal segment stimulated is stationary, only the superficial layers of the skin undergo mechanical deformations and are therefore involved in perceptual processing. In haptic perception, the deformations of the muscles, joints and tendons resulting from exploratory movements are added to cutaneous perceptions. Haptic perceptual processing is therefore much more complex because it integrates cutaneous and proprioceptive cues and also corrollary dischanges, cf. Chapter 2. The exploratory movements depend on neural circuits that are partly specific. They are intentional (they are aimed at a goal), auto-initiated (they may be generated internally without external stimulus) and they are generally multi-articular (they activate many corporal segments). Finally, because their speed is relatively slow, they may use the sensory reafferences produced by their execution.

Some selected data concerning the anatomical and neurophysiological bases of cutaneous and haptic perceptions are presented in the two chapters of this Section. In Chapter 2, Gentaz describes some general characteristics of this anatomical and functional organization. Then, in Chapter 3, Gentaz and Badan examine the new insights provided in this domain by the recent data taken from neuropsychology and from functional cerebral imagery methods.

Part 2. Haptic perceptual exploration

As stated earlier, the original characteristic of the haptic system stems from the fact that the hands are both perceptual systems able to explore environment and motor organs performing daily actions controlled by tactile-kinesthetic reafferences. Although it is necessary to distinguish between «action for perception» (exploratory action) and «perception for action» (perception deserving action) (Lederman & Klatzky 1996), perception and action are closely linked in haptic functioning. This link is so strong that very young children use mainly their hands in their motor function and, when they are temporarily deprived of vision, the quality of their manual perceptual exploration is consistently lower than what would be allowed by their motor developmental level (Hatwell 1986, 1987).

The motor system, common to the two functions of the hand, allows independent movements of the hands, arms and fingers. The tactile system is therefore the only one able to modify at will the size of the perceptual field used during exploration, varying it from the pad of a stationary index finger to the entire surface of the two hands in movement. This addresses the question of the distribution of attention on the different activated regions of the hands and that of the relative perceptual efficiency of the right and left hands. However, even when the two hands are used with active exploratory movements, the haptic perceptual field remains greatly reduced compared to the visual field. As a result, the perceptual cues which are pertinent in a task (or useful as a spatial exocentric reference frame) are less available in the haptic than in the visual modes. In addition to the gravitational cues provided by the forces deployed to move the arm, which are present in most cases, other exterior clues must be intentionally sought by the hand.

Of course, the mode of exploration (one or two hands, one or several fingers, the use or not of the palm of the hands, etc.) depends on the properties of the stimulus, in particular its size and volume. The perception of bidimensional material, such as the raised dots of the Braille alphabet (cf. Chapter 14) and the raised lines representing geometrical diagrams or significant drawings, will be examined in Section 5, Chapter 15. Therefore, Section 2 concerns the procedures of manual exploration of volumetric objects, which constitutes the essential part of haptic activity.

As stated earlier, haptic exploration is different from visual exploration in many perceptual-motor aspects. But we know that, in vision, cognitive factors are also involved and they orient the exploratory activity toward one or another property of the stimuli (Piaget & Inhelder 1947; Neisser 1976). In the haptic mode, it is likely that these factors play a role even more determining than in the visual mode (see for example Gentaz & Rossetti 1999). So we can expect to observe a marked evolution of exploratory procedures with age. This is studied first in infants by Streri (Chapter 4) who discusses the relationship between the tactile discriminative capacity of infants and the way in which their hands grasp and explore objects. Then, Hatwell (Chapter 5) pursues this study in children and adults and shows why and how the particularities of manual exploration may modify the mode of processing of object properties.

Finally, in Chapter 6, Streri reviews the recent studies on perceptual lateralization, i.e. the relative perceptual efficiency of the left and right hands. Owing to the strong motor involvement in manual exploration, the question is to know whether superior performances of the right hand will be observed in right-handed subjects or, conversely, if the left hand will be more efficient because it is directly related to the right hemisphere specialized in the processing of spatial information.

Part 3. Haptic perceptions and spatial imaged representations

This section focuses on the haptic processes themselves, although it will be shown that these processes and their perceptual issues depend largely upon the exploratory modes imposed by the properties of the haptic system. The questions discussed are, on the one hand, whether these haptic processes are the same or are very similar to those involved in the visual system and, on the other hand, whether and why the efficiency of the two systems may differ.

The first domain examined is the haptic identification of objects. Klatzky and Lederman, who have made major contributions to the knowledge of haptic functioning, present in Chapter 7 a summary of the questions raised and the answers supplied by their research in this domain. The problem is the following: We know from experimental studies and by everyday experience that the identification by touch alone of common objects is very rapid and precise. In vision, this identification relies mainly on the analysis of the spatial distribution of the edges which constitute object shape (Biederman 1987). But the haptic modality is not very efficient in the perception of spatial properties, especially as concerns complex shapes. Therefore, on what cues does the haptic system rely in the identification process? According to Klatzky and Lederman, this identification is achieved mainly through the apprehension of the material properties of objects (texture, hardness, etc.). These authors show that the haptic efficiency in the perceptual discrimination of material properties and the combination of these perceptions with the spatial cues to which touch has also access (albeit in a less efficient way than in vision) may account for the high level of expertise manifested by this modality in object identification.

The examination of haptic perceptual processes continues in Chapter 8 (Gentaz & Hatwell) with the study of the processing of different spatial and material properties of non-significant and unfamiliar objects. To specify the processing modes involved in each case, the tasks proposed to the subjects concern objects in which the number and values of each dimension are controlled. These experiments confirm the lower general efficiency of haptic perception, as compared to visual one, in the domain of the spatial properties such as shape, location, orientation, length and distance. In addition, they draw attention to certain specific haptic processing modes arising from the particularities of exploration. The picture is very different as concerns the material properties of objects, especially texture. A number of studies show that this property is very salient in young children and that it is very finely discriminated in adults. Finally, the problem of whether haptic perception is analytic or global is discussed in this chapter through the research on perceptual classifications. These studies compare, from a developmental point of view, the salience of "dimensional" classifications (based on the grouping of objects sharing a value on one dimension) versus "overall similarity" classifications (grouping on the basis of similar but non identical values on many dimensions).

A particular case of the perception of size is studied by Heller (Chapter 9) in the area of perceptual illusions. It has long been known (Craig 1931; Revesz 1934) that the illusions labeled in the past as optical-geometrical are not specifically visual and that several of them, but not all, appear too in the haptic mode. The question is to know which ones are common to both modes and which are specific to just one mode. It is also necessary to know the mechanisms which give rise to these deformations, for they are not necessarily the same in vision and touch. Heller also shows in his study that the particular modes of manual perceptual exploration, which differ according to the size of the stimulus, are responsible for the presence or absence of certain haptic illusions.

Finally, the study of Cornoldi and Vecchi (Chapter 10) is concerned with higher levels of processing, those of haptic imaged representations. These representations are examined especially in the congenitally blind, since it is only in this population that the existence of non-visual images could be demonstrated. The authors start from the hypothesis that images are not just simple extensions of perception, and that non-visual images exist and have certain characteristics in common with visual images as well as certain specificities. Using spatial tasks in which the subject is asked to navigate mentally through a path in bi- or tridimensional matrices composed of a set of cubes, Cornoldi and Vecchi show that the congenitally blind have non-visual spatial images. But, as in the domain of spatial perception, they encounter difficulties with the increased complexity of the matrix, the introduction of the third dimension and the production of interactive images.

The conclusions of the different studies presented in this section are therefore relatively consistent. They all underline the efficiency, sometimes underemployed by the sighted, of the haptic perceptual system which can apprehend almost all the properties that vision has access to. But, owing to the particular mode of exploration imposed by its anatomy and by the motor system, this modality is significantly less effective than vision in the spatial domain, whereas it is better adapted to the apprehension of the material properties of objects.

Part 4. Intermodal coordinations

Our everyday activities rely on the simultaneous and interactive involvement of different senses, because the perception of most objects and events activate more than one sensory modality. This is what happens for example when we look for our keys in our bag or when we orient our head toward a sounding source. The exchanges between individuals and environment are therefore multimodal and, as a result, the varied perceptual information they convey need to be coordinated into unified wholes to produce adequate responses to each situation. How is achieved this harmonization between sensory systems that seem to function partly in a modular way? For example, how does one adjust the position of the hand to the size, shape and weight of the object to be grasped? These very usual actions in adults rely on mechanisms still partly unknown.

It may seem paradoxical that so many researchers are interested in the study of a single sensory modality whereas all our everyday activities involve the integration of information coming simultaneously from vision, audition, touch, proprioception, etc. Actually, research on cross-modal coordination is relatively scarce, probably because of its high degree of complexity. Of course, studies on isolated modalities have the advantage of demonstrating the richness of the perceptive function of each sense by stressing its specificity. But they quickly brings up the old question of "common sensitivity", i.e. the origin of cross-modal integration.

Historically, the responses given to these questions were first dichotomous, whereas the contemporary point of view is less clear-cut. An empirical conception has dominated during centuries, especially from the 18th until the end of the first half of the 20th century. In it, our senses were thought to be completely independent at birth and coordinated only through experience and learning (particularly by language mediation). As a result, cross-modal capacities were considered to be very limited in infants and young children and were predicted to improve with age. This explained why, as was anticipated by Locke (1689/1975) in his answer to the famous Molyneux's question (as concerns this question, see Proust 1997), congenital blind people who recover vision late in their life cannot recognize immediately, through vision, the objects that are familiar to them by touch (Jeannerod 1975; von Senden 1960)

By contrast, a nativist conception (having its root in Greek philosophy) has dominated in the early 1960s, when studies on infants, along with observations on animals and with new neurophysiological knowledge, revealed the precocity of intermodal integration and its cortical bases. However, as it will appear in Chapters 11, 12 and 13 devoted respectively to infancy, childhood and primates, both the empirical and the nativist conceptions are now considered as too radical because actually, cross-modal integration depends on the interaction of many neuronal and environmental factors.

In order to examine these factors, it is useful to separate intermodal situations according to the type of functioning they imply (Hatwell 1986). In *intermodal transfer*, an information provided by only one modality is further used by another one. For example, an object felt in darkness may be further recognized visually when the light is switched on. In *bimodal perception*, two modalities are activated simultaneously. When these modalities have access to distinct properties of a single object, a coordination between the different data is required in order to preserve the unity of the object. In this case, the perceptual modalities have complementary functions and they associate signals which are often arbitrary. For example, the visual stimulation provided by the sight of a watch, the tactile stimulation resulting from the grasping of this watch and the auditory stimulation emitted by the functioning of the watch are coordinated so that a single and unitary object is perceived. On the other hand, when the two modalities perceive the same property of the same object (redundant information), an identical value of this property must be assigned by both modalities, although specific sensory stimulations are received by each one. Thus, the shape, size, and texture of an object must remain invariant independently of the perceptual system activated. The cases of decorrelation, as they occur in perceptual conflicts, may reveal the degree of intermodal integration and the relative weight of the modalities in conflict.

These questions are examined first in infants by Streri (Chapter 11). The author relies on the analysis of the coordination between vision and prehension and on studies based on habituation and reaction to novelty to show how precocious these coordinations are. She describes too the kind of constraints limiting them and the difficulties raised by the interpretation of early intermodal transfer. In the next chapter (Chapter 12), similar problems are discussed by Hatwell on school-aged children and adults. The studies on intermodal matching do no support the hypothesis of amodal processing stated by the Gibsons (1966, 1969) and, in perceptual conflict tasks, the visual dominance is not general but limited to the spatial domain. When the task concerns the material properties of the objects, a dominance of the haptic system may sometimes be observed. However, these observations are true only for explicit memory whereas measures on implicit memory do not reveal differences between intramodal and intermodal tasks. Finally, the study of the distribution of attention shows that, because of the strong intermodal links in adults, the orientation of attention toward one modality may disturb the processing of signals provided by the other modality.

Chapter 13 constitutes an opening toward an animal comparative approach. The problems evoked earlier (exploratory manual procedures, tactile discriminations, intermodal transfer, manual laterality) are examined here in non human primates. In this study, Lacreuse and Fragaszy observe that, in spite of some minor differences, the manual exploratory procedures of monkeys are similar to those described in humans by Lederman and Klatzky (1987), and they examine the haptic discriminative capacities of different species of primates. They show also that cross-modal transfer is possible in apes and that the manual skills of these animals are associated with dexterity, although the available studies on manual and hemispheric laterality in primates are not always consistent.

Part 5. Some practical applications for visually impaired people

In many occasions, the characteristics of haptic functioning in totally blind persons and in blindfolded sighted ones have been compared in the preceding chapters. These studies had mainly a theoretical interest allowing, for example, the evaluation of the role of visual representations and of haptic training in the functioning of this modality. Other available works review extensively the state of our knowledge concerning the cognitive consequences of early blindness (for example, Hatwell 2003; Heller 2000; Warren 1994). The last section of this book considers some particular aspects of the visual impairment *per se*. Starting from what we know now about the possibilities and limits of touch, it addresses the practical consequences of blindness or, more exactly, the techniques and devices that have been developed to compensate, as much as possible, for the perceptual handicap generated by permanent visual deprivation.

Obviously, a remediation technique was most acutely needed in the area of reading and writing. During centuries, blind children could not have systematically access to instruction and written culture. Their schooling became much easier when Louis Braille, who was himself a blind pupil attending the Royal Institute for the Blind in Paris (now Institut National des Jeunes Aveugles), proposed in 1829 the raised dot embossed alphabet known all around the world as braille alphabet (cf. Chapter 14, Figure 14.1). This alphabet is remarkably well adapted to the sensory capacities of the internal face of the last phalange of the index finger and it may express punctuation, mathematical signs, musical notation, etc. It has further been adopted in all languages for the transcription of texts for the blind. More recently, the number of points in the braille cell (the unit which defines a letter) has been increased from six to eight so that computer language could be written in braille.

However, the characteristics of the braille alphabet raise particular problems in children and adults when they learn and use it. In the last decades, a number of studies have been conducted on the processes of braille learning and they have concentrated on different problems such as perceptual aspects (sensory discrimination, efficiency of the right and left hands, cooperation between the two hands during bimanual reading), spatial aspects (braille letters are not redundant and can be identified only through the spatial localization of the dots composing them. This is difficult for the young child because no spatial frame of reference is available), phonological and semantic aspects, etc. An original and complete presentation of these studies could be found in Millar (1997). Another trend of research presented here by Tobin, Greaney and Hill (Chapter 14) is centered on the problems of teaching braille to young children and to adults who have recently lost their sight. The introduction of abbreviations and contractions (in Level 2 braille) gains much space and speeds up reading, but it raises multiple difficulties in pupils and teachers. Experimentally tested simplifications are proposed by Tobin et al. who nevertheless stress the users' strong resistance to any modification of the graphic code they are accustomed to.

Whatever it may be, books in braille have long been available to blind people. But, until recently, they had no illustrations, first because there was no technology able to make pictures in relief at a reasonable price, but mainly because it seemed obvious that bidimensional drawings were very difficult to understand by early blind people who have no projective space. The situation has changed over 30 years. There are machines today which can emboss pictures in raised lines or in thermoformed relief allowing the addition of texture to their surfaces. These machines allow now the publication of city maps helping blind people to find their way about their town, their locality or their school, or pictures representing objects, biological and geometrical diagrams, etc. Some observations have revealed that the blind, and even the congenitally blind, are capable of producing pictures which have certain rules of representation in common with the picture production of sighted people (Kennedy 1993, 2000). The use of graphic supports in teaching the blind is thus becoming widespread. In Chapter 15, Hatwell and Martinez-Sarocchi analyze the problems posed by these supports. The study continues with a discussion of the procedures used by publishers of art books and museum curators to make works of art more accessible to the blind.

Another handicap resulting from blindness is the reduction in autonomy with regard to personal mobility, which is a direct consequence of the fact that touch is a sense depending on contact. Only the immediate environment is perceptible, thus making orientation and walking in open spaces (the locality or a town) difficult and dangerous. Devices have thus been developed to transform luminous stimulations in the environment to tactile stimulations perceptible to the blind. The best known of these sensory prosthetic devices is the Tactile-Vision-Substitution-System (TVSS) developed in the 1960's and 1970's by Bach y Rita (1972). The use of this system by early blind people in laboratory research has improved our knowledge of tactile (and, paradoxically, also visual) functioning. Nevertheless, despite many refinements and miniaturizations, it has had little practical success among the blind. In Chapter 16, Lenay, Gapenne, Hanneton, Marque and Genouelle analyze and discuss the psychological processes underlying the use of this device. They explain that the TVSS does not produce a true sensory substitution, but constitutes rather the addition of a particular form of perception.

The final chapter is concerned with the adaptation to the visually impaired people of the new technologies of information so widespread today. While it is fairly easy to transform the texts appearing on a standard computer screen into embossed braille writing, the situation has become more difficult for the blind when icons and graphics have partly replaced the written codes, because these icons are very difficult to distinguish by touch. In Chapter 17, Burger examines the techniques used to adapt the new technologies to visual deficiency and presents the problems arising from this adaptation as well as the solutions proposed.

* * *

This overview of the studies contained in the present book shows that, while retaining the principal aim of studying the psychological processes at work in the cognitive functioning of touch, our attention has also been drawn to the practical consequences that the characteristics of this modality can have, especially in blindness, and to the means of taking these consequences into account. Of course, the book is not exhaustive and many aspects of the cognitive particularities of the tactile functioning of the sighted and the blind could not be examined in its limited framework. We hope however that it may interest not only students and researchers in cognitive psychology, but also practitioners (teachers, psychomotricians, education assistants, etc.) confronted with the problems of visual deficiency. This book may also be useful to the ergonomists who design sensory prostheses and adapt new technologies for the blind, and to the roboticians who need to know the role of tactile reafferences in movement control. In short, this work is for all those who seek to understand how and why "knowing by touching" is possible.

Acknowledgments

The translation of this book from French has been supported by grants from the Centre National de la Recherche Scientifique (CNRS) and by the Minister of Research, "Cognitique" Program. We thank David Hunter for his translation of Chapters 1, 2 and 3, and Andrea Palmer for her translation of Chapters 6, 8, 11, 12 and 15. We thank too Laurence Lévi who kindly helped us to check the proofs and the indexes.

References

Bach y Rita, P. (1972). *Brain mechanisms in sensory substitution.* New York: Academic Press.

Biederman, I. (1987). Recognition by components: A theory of human image understanding. *Psychological Review, 94,* 115–145.

Craig, F. (1931). Variations in the illusion of filled and unfilled tactual space. *American Journal of Psychology, 43,* 112–114.

Gentaz, E. & Rossetti, Y. (1999). Is haptic perception continuous with cognition? *Behavioral and Brain Sciences, 22,* 378–379.

Gibson, E. J. (1969). *Principles of perceptual learning and development.* New York: Academic Press.

Gibson, J. J. (1962). Observation on active touch. *Psychological Review, 69,* 477–491.

Gibson, J. J. (1966). *The senses considered as perceptual systems.* Boston: Houghton Mifflin Compagny.

Hatwell, Y. (1986). *Toucher l'espace. La main et la perception tactile de l'espace.* Lille: Presses Universitaires de Lille.

Hatwell, Y. (1987). Motor and cognitive functions of the hand. *International Journal of Behavioral Development, 10,* 509–526.

Hatwell, Y. (2003). *Psychologie cognitive de la cécité précoce.* Paris: Dunod.

Heller, M. A. (Eds.). (2000). *Touch, representation and blindness.* Oxford: Oxford University Press.

Heller, M. A. & Schiff, W. (Eds.). (1991). *The psychology of touch.* Hillsdale, NJ: Erlbaum.

Jeannerod, M. (1975). Déficit visuel persistant chez les aveugles-nés: données cliniques et expérimentales. *L'Année Psychologique, 75,* 169–196.

Katz, D. (1925/1989). *The world of touch* (translated by L. E. Krueger. 1989). Hillsdale, NJ: Erlbaum.

Kennedy, J. M. (1993). *Drawing and the blind. Pictures to touch.* New Haven: Yale University Press.

Kennedy, J. M. (2000). Recognizing outlines pictures via touch: Alignment theory. In M. A. Heller (Ed.), *Touch, representation and blindness* (pp. 67–98). Oxford: Oxford University Press.

Lederman, S. J. & Klatzky, R. L. (1987). Hand movements: A window into haptic object recognition. *Cognitive Psychology, 19,* 342–368.

Lederman, S. J. & Klatzky, R. L. (1996). Action for perception: Manual exploratory movements for haptically processing objects and their features. In A. M. Wing, P. Hagard, & J. R. Flanagan (Eds.), *Hand and brain: The neurophysiology and psychology of hand movements*. New York: Academic Press.

Locke, J. (1689/1975). *An essay concerning human understanding*. Oxford: Oxford University Press.

Millar, S. (1994). *Understanding and representing space. Theory and evidence from studies with blind and sighted children*. Oxford: Clarendon Press.

Millar, S. (1997). *Reading by touch*. London: Routledge.

Neisser, U. (1976). *Cognition and reality*. San Francisco: Freeman.

Piaget, J. & Inhelder, B. (1947/1967). *The child's conception of space* (translated from: J. Piaget & B. Inhelder (1947), *La représentation de l'espace chez l'enfant*. Paris: Presses Universitaires de France). New York: W.W. Norton.

Proust, J. (Ed.). (1997). *Perception et intermodalité. Approches actuelles de la question de Molyneux*. Paris: Presses Universitaires de France.

Revesz, G. (1950). *Psychology and art of the blind*. London: Longmans Green.

Revesz, G. (1934). System der optischen und haptischen Raumtaüschungen. *Zeitscrift für Psychologie, 131*, 296–375.

Senden von, M. (1960). *Space and sight*. Glencoe: The Free Press.

Streri, A. (1993). *Seeing, reaching, touching. The relations between vision and touch in infancy*. London: Harverster Wheatsheaf.

Warren, D. W. (1994). *Blindness and children. An individual differences approach*. Cambridge: Cambridge University Press.

PART 1

Some anatomical and neurophysiological bases of tactile manual perception

General characteristics of the anatomical and functional organization of cutaneous and haptic perceptions

Edouard Gentaz

The somaesthetic system is not a homogenous entity, for its sensory receptors are widely dispersed and have great functional diversity. However, it is the common neural substrate for the two forms of manual tactile perception, the cutaneous perception (passive tactile perception) and the haptic perception (active tactile perception). It is therefore important to study the characteristics of the somaesthetic system in order to understand the neural bases of the perceptual processes examined in this book (for reviews, cf. Kandel, Schwartz, & Jessel 2000; Massion 1997; Mountcastle 1999; Roll 1994).

1. Available information

1.1 From cutaneous and proprioceptive mechanoreceptors to somaesthetic cortex

In cutaneous perception, information from the mechanical deformation of part of the skin is coded by cutaneous mechanoreceptors situated in the different layers of the skin. At least four types have been identified and are classified on the basis of their adaptive properties (rapid or slow) and of the characteristics of their receptive fields (small and highly localized or large, with indistinct borders). Meissner corpuscles and Merkel disc receptors have small, localized receptive fields, but the first ones have rapid adaptation (they are active during the initial contact with the stimulus) and the second have slow adaptation (they are active during the entire contact with the stimulus). Pacinian corpuscles and Ruffini endings, on the other hand, have large and less localized receptive fields, but the first have rapid, and the second slow, adaptation. It seems that three of these four receptors are involved in cutaneous perception, but each with specific roles depending on their properties (Johnson & Hsiao 1992). Merkel discs seem mainly to code information on the spatial shape and texture of the stimuli (such as raised letters or braille) while Meissner corpuscles mainly code the movements at the surface of the skin (such as a held glass sliding in the hand; Blake, Hsiao, & Johnson 1997; Blake, Johnson, & Hsio 1997). Finally, Pacinian corpuscles seem to be involved in coding the temporal attributes of the stimulus (such as the vibration of a tool manipulated by the hand; Brisben, Hsiao, & Johnson 1999).

In haptic perception, cutaneous information is joined by information from the mechanical deformation of the proprioceptive receptors, resulting from the exploratory movements of the shoulder-hand system. The proprioceptive receptors are situated in muscles (the muscle spindles), tendons (the Golgi tendon organs) and joints (the joint capsule mechanoreceptors). The muscle receptors provide information mainly on the length of the muscles or the speed of change in this length. The tendon receptors provide information on the level of tension of the muscle (the level of force developed) and its variation over time. The role of the joint receptors is still being debated (angle, regulation and/or facilitation of muscle proprioception; cf. Roll 1994).

Roll (1994: 519) remarks that "the information arising from the deformation of muscles (stretching or contraction) are rarely processed by the central nervous system to give rise to sensations concerning the muscles themselves, but they give sensations of position or movement concerning the limb segments stabilized or mobilized by these muscles". So, when a movement is effected, certain active muscles have a motor function (agonist muscles) and others a sensory function (antagonist muscles).

Sensory information coded by cutaneous and proprioceptive mechanoreceptors is transmitted to the central nervous system by two separate major ascending pathways (composed of relays where the initial processing occurs): the dorsal column-medial lemniscal system and the anterolateral (or extralemniscal) system. The latter will not be described here, for it transmits slowly (the small diameter axons transmit signals at speeds from 8 to 40 m/s) a wide range of information (sensitivity to heat, pain and rough touch) which hardly concerns the theme of the present work. The dorsal column-medial lemniscal system interests us more, for it transmits rapidly (the large diameter axons transmit signals at speeds from 30 to 110m/s) and (temporally and topographically) precisely the information involved in fine cutaneous and proprioceptive sensitivity. This pathway (composed of "relay-neurons") ascends ipsilaterally to the medulla (first relay), then crosses the median plane to the middle of the medulla and rises in the cerebral trunk on the opposite side to join the specific nucleus of the thalamus (the group of ventro-posterior nucleus or VP; second relay). Finally, thalamic neurons send their axons principally to the primary and secondary somaesthetic areas, but also to the posterior parietal areas and the motor cortex.

Cutaneous and proprioceptive information are integrated across space and time in complex manner to form a haptic information. The respective contribution of these two types of information in the haptic perception is in debate. It seems that the nature of haptic tasks modify their respective contributions. Thus, a task in which the stimulus (a shape) is mainly explored by the hand over a small space would involve an equivalent contribution of both cutaneous and proprioceptive information (e.g. Voisin, Lamarre, & Chapman 2002). A task in which the stimulus (a rod) needs larger hand movements would entail a greater contribution of the proprioceptive information (e.g. Wydoodt, Gentaz, Gaunet, Chêne, & Streri 2003).

1.2 The hypothesis of corollary discharges

In haptic perception, the peripheral sensory information described previously is not the only information available. Numerous researchers suggested that other information called either corollary discharges (Sperry 1950), or efference copies (in the model described by von Holst & Mittelstaedt 1973), is involved. According to this hypothesis, information from the motor commands generating exploratory movements (the corollary discharges) could participate in haptic perception. The processes by which these discharges would act are still under debate (cf. Jeannerod 1997). Whatever their nature, various arguments support the corollary discharge hypothesis (cf. McClosey 1981). For example, in the absence of peripheral sensory afferences (deafferentation) and with an intact motor capacity, certain persons are capable of making fairly complex movements and seem to be informed of their performance. Also, amputees continue to feel the lost limb (Henderson & Smyth 1948). It seems that the phenomenon of the phantom limb is also present in people born without a limb (Melzack 1992). However, the existence of corollary discharges and their possible role are debated in literature. It is the same for the relative importance of peripheral sensory information and corollary discharges in cognitive and perceptual processes.

2.   General properties of the somaesthetic areas

2.1 Somatotropy, receptive fields and lateral inhibition

Peripheral sensory information is transmitted somatotopically. This means that the information arriving in the primary somaesthetic area (S1, a cortical region situated in the anterior part of the parietal cortex, cf. Figure 2.1) is distributed in this area according to its origin on a somatotopic map. The entire contralateral half of the body is represented in S1: this is the somaesthetic homunculus (Penfield & Rasmussen 1950). For each (spontaneously active) neuron in S1 there is one specific region of the skin whose stimulation modifies (by increasing or decreasing) its level of activity. This region constitutes the receptive field of that cell. The size and density of the receptive fields vary according to the functional importance of the different parts of the body (magnification factor). The most sensitive regions, which have the greatest cortical representation (the lips, tongue and fingers), have the smallest receptive fields and the most numerous receptors per unit of cutaneous surface. Going up the arm, the receptive fields become larger and less dense. Also, each receptive field is made up of a central excitatory region and a peripheral inhibitory region in such a way that the stimulation of a point of the skin provokes the activation of one group of cortical neurons and simultaneously the inhibition of the neighboring neurons, so increasing the contrast and making for perceptive precision: This is the phenomenon of lateral inhibition.

2.2 Neuron sensitivity

Neural coding of a stimulus depends on the cortical neurons' sensitivity to certain properties of the stimulus. Neural coding of a property is estimated by the neuron discharge frequency. For a given neuron, the coding is non-binary: The neuron does not code a property on an all-or-nothing basis, but codes several parameters of the property with different amplitudes. For example, an orientation-sensitive neuron has a maximal response when the orientation of a rod coincides with that of its receptive field. As soon as the stimulus departs from the optimal orientation, the neuron's response diminishes. So, a neuron sensitive to vertical orientation does not only code the vertical orientation of the stimulus, but also the different orientations (with smaller amplitudes) around the vertical. Work done with awake monkeys (macaques) has revealed the sensitivity of neurons in the somaesthetic area S1 (cf. Figure 2.1) to three properties of the stimulus (a rod): Its movement, direction and orientation

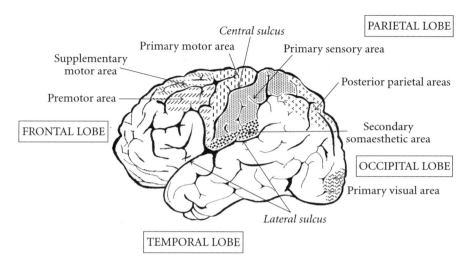

Figure 2.1. Lateral view of the external face of the left hemisphere of the human brain

(Hsiao, Lane, & Fitzgerald 2002; Pubols & Leroy 1977; Warren, Hamalainen, & Gardner 1986).

As well as unimodal somaesthetic neurons, there are bimodal neurons, which respond to tactile and/or visual stimuli. For example, Graziano and Gross (1995) made unitary recordings of neurons in parietal area 7*b* of anaesthetized monkeys. These recordings revealed three types of neuron: Somaesthetic, visual and bimodal visual-tactile neurons. Of the 229 neurons studied in area 7*b*, 22% were somaesthetic, 16% visual, 34% bimodal and 28% gave no response. There are also "multisensory" neurons in the superior colliculus which respond to visual, auditory and tactile stimuli. Certain neurons, found in area 6 and the superior colliculus can be simultaneously sensory and motor (cf. Stein & Meredith 1993; Stein, Meredith, & Wallace 1994). Thus, in the superior colliculus certain neurons respond not only to visual, auditory and tactile stimuli, but are also active during ocular movement. The properties of neurons in the premotor and posterior parietal areas and of the superior colliculus are such that they are considered to be important centers of multisensory and motor-sensory integration (cf. Stein et al. 1994). Although the existence of these multimodal neurons has been known for some considerable time, the comparison of their responses under unimodal and bimodal stimulation, in order to establish their rules of integration, has only been recently undertaken. For example, the effect of bimodal stimulation does not seem to be additive but multiplying: A weak response to visual stimulus can be amplified up to 12 times if it is set off by a bimodal audio-visual stimulus.

Finally, studies show that the property of a stimulus is encoded in the cortex by the pattern of activity of a population of cortical neurons rather than by one single neuron. From a motor point of view, this idea of a "population vector" was shown by Georgopoulos and his colleagues in studying how direction of movements was encoded in the primary motor cortex (Georgopoulos, Kalaska, Caminiti, & Massey 1982). From a sensory point of view, this type of coding has already been observed in the "calculation" of the direction of the visual target relative to the head in the parietal cortex (Andersen 1995). Although coding by an entire population of cortical neurons has not yet been demonstrated in tactile tasks, it is possible that future research will reveal that this type of coding is the rule rather than the exception. Recently, Roll, Bergenheim and Ribot-Ciscar (2000) used this type of coding at a peripheral level. Thus, the authors showed that the parameters of a given drawing trajectory (describing geometrical shapes) imposed on the tip of the foot are encoded by populations of muscles spindles originating from the set of muscles with which a joint is equipped.

2.3 Column organization

The basic module of cortical functioning is the column (with a diameter of about 100 microns). Each column processes signals from different sources according to the general properties and intrinsic connections of the area. The organization of each column is perpendicular to the cortical surface. Their operations are multiple, and are partly determined by their organization. Two neighboring columns are generally structured on two distinct afferences. The column has multiple exits and acts on a large number of cortical and subcortical areas. This column organization permits parallel and simultaneous information processing.

3. Properties of the main cortical areas involved in cutaneous and haptic perception

While it is clear that our brain is the "seat" of permanent activity, some cortical areas are more specialized than others in cutaneous and haptic perception. Because of the motor system's involvement in the exploratory activity of the hand, we present here a selection of the principal properties (excluding connections, which will be described later, in Figure 2.2) of the somaesthetic and motor areas (Figure 2.1). It should be noted that the anatomo-functional organization of the motor areas has similar characteristics to that of the somaesthetic areas (e.g. somatotopy and the organization in columns).

3.1 The primary and secondary somaesthetic areas

The primary (S1) and secondary (S2) somaesthetic areas correspond to the cortical region situated in the anterior part of the parietal cortex. They constitute the two principal areas which process cutaneous and proprioceptive afferences. The area S1 is situated in the postcentral gyrus of the cortex. It is organized in vertical columns and six horizontal layers. Each of the neurons making up one of these columns reacts to the same modality: Some columns are specialized in proprioception and others in tactile sensitivity. Horizontally, the cells of one column are, depending on the layer to which they belong, specialized either in information reception or in the transfer of this information to another structure. The area S1 is divided into four cytoarchitectural areas (Brodmann's areas 1-2-3*a* and 3*b*). The neurons in areas 3*b* and 1 respond mainly to light cutaneous stimulation. Recent research shows that area 3*b* plays an essential role in the neural processing which underlies tactile perception of form and texture (DiCarlo, Johnson, & Hsiao 1998). The neurons of area 3*a* receive muscular afferences and neurons in area 2 receive deep cutaneous and articular afferences. In each of these four areas, the contralateral half of the body is represented: In area S1 there are consequently four juxtaposed representations of the opposite half of the body. It should be noted that we do not know how these four areas in human brain compute somatosensory representation of shape explored by the hand. Area S2 is situated at the base of the postcentral gyrus and has a fairly similar functional organization to that of area S1. Unlike area 1, however, S2 receives afferences from the whole body.

3.2 The primary motor area

The primary motor area (or motor cortex) is the part of the cortex adjacent and immediately anterior to the central sulcus. It is somatotopically organized and representative maps of the musculature have been established. The areas for the hands and the face are very extensive, while those for the trunk, the proximal parts of the limbs and the feet are much more limited (Penfield's motor homunculus). The main projection from the motor cortex is the pyramidal tract leading to the spinal cord. This tract is entirely crossed (unilateral) for the distal musculature and bilateral for the axial and proximal musculature (head, neck, shoulders). The pyramidal terminals at the spinal cord synapse with the different types of neuron (motor neurons, interneurons and pro-priospinal neurons) in order to exert on them actions which are most often excitory but sometimes inhibitory. The primary motor area controls elementary movements rather than muscles. Microstimulation of this area generally provokes contralateral movement with activation of agonist muscles and inhibition of antagonist muscles. The cortical representation of the command of one movement can be multiple.

The neurons of the primary motor area are strongly linked to somaesthetic information. Johansson (1996) demonstrated quite clearly the major role of cutaneous information in such simple tasks as grasping an object, raising it and putting it down. A local anesthetic of the zones of the skin coming into contact with the object to be seized perturbs either the initial force of the act of grasping, increasing it abnormally, or the adjustment of this force to prevent the object slipping in the hand. In a similar vein, Hikosaka, Tanaka, Sakamoto and Iwamura (1985) observed that a temporary lesion of the neurons in S1 results in a diminution of the grasping precision of small objects. Other studies show that the execution of an active movement can reduce, gait or even suppress the transmission of cutaneous afferences (cf. Chapman 1994). For example, Mistlin and Perret (1990) showed that the neurons of a monkey's somaesthetic areas are activated when the experimenter lightly strokes the monkey's hand with a stick, but if it is the monkey that does the stroking, the same neurons do not discharge. This phenomenon (and that of corollary discharge) could partly explain why we are unable to produce on our own body the reactions associated with tickling (Blakemore, Wolpert, & Frith 1998).

Humphrey and Tanji (1991) suggest a "rostral-caudal" organization of the primary motor area, since the neurons in the rostral region (toward the nose) are less afferent than those of the caudal region (toward the back of the head), and their receptive fields are larger. They suggest that the neurons of the rostral region are consequently more involved in the initialization of high amplitude movements, while those of the caudal region are more involved in the maintenance of position, in movements of low amplitude and in manual exploration. Roland and Zilles (1998) and Zilles (1996) proposed dividing the primary motor area into two sub-areas: Areas 4a and 4p (region adjacent to area 3a). The authors show that when the subject has simply to clench his fingers, area 4a, as well as other motor zones, are activated, but that area 4p is silent. Inversely, if the task consists of haptically discriminating an object, area 4a is silent, while area 4p is active. Area 4p seems to intervene during movements triggered by tactile stimulation and area 4*a* during movements triggered by other modalities.

In conclusion, the neurons of the primary motor area and their sensory afferences form sensory-motor modules. However, it should be noted that these sensory-motor modules are influenced by other structures, such as the neocerebellum, the basal nuclei and the parietal, premotor and prefrontal associative areas.

3.3 The posterior parietal and premotor areas

The posterior parietal areas correspond to areas 5 and 7 (for a discussion of this division, cf. Kalaska 1996). They are organized in sub-groups specialized in the processing of one type of information. Area 7 is classically divided into two sub-areas (7*a* and 7*b*) linked to the representation of space. Only the neurons of area 7*b* interest us, for they are both motor and somaesthetic. Among these neurons, some are bimodal visual-tactile and respond, for example, to the same spatial localization of the stimulus. For area 5, the neurons are also somaesthetic and motor. The somaesthetic neurons respond to complex stimuli such as the mobilization of several joints or the simultaneous activation of articular afferences and cutaneous receptive fields. The motor neurons are active during movements involving the extension of the arm, or manipulation. Unlike the premotor cortex (cf. below), area 5 does not seem to participate directly in the process of selection of the type of response to command signals (Kalaska 1996). However, the lesion of this area results in deficits of the coordination of palpatory movements (Stein 1978).

The premotor areas are composed of the premotor area *per se* and the supplementary motor area (SMA), which each correspond to a part of area 6. The premotor area itself, situated on the external face of the cortex, is in relation with the cerebellum and plays an important role in the movements triggered and controlled by exterior signals (visual, tactile): Visually guided movements, manipulation tasks and tasks of food prehension. The SMA, situated on the median face (the median part of area 6), is in relation with the basal nuclei and intervenes in auto-initiated activities, in the preparation and execution of temporal sequences and non-symmetrical bimanual activities. Most of the actions controlled by the SMA are memorized actions.

3.4 The prefrontal cortex and the limbic system

The prefrontal cortex, which occupies most of the frontal lobe (forming a quarter of the cortex surface in the human adult), is just in front of the motor, premotor and supplementary motor areas. The prefrontal cortex also has reciprocal connections with all the areas involved in processing sensory information. Through its afferences to the premotor cortex and the striatum, it participates in motor control. It is also in relation with structures involved in memorization (amygdala-hippocampic complex, thalamus) and the limbic (or motivational) structures. It is in relation with the temporal (21 and 22) and parietal (5 and 7) areas. It plays an important role in the attentional processes of stimulus processing and in the short-term memorization of the sequence of sensory events. It is an important structure in the temporal organization of learned behavior. The subdivisions observed in the posterior parietal areas are also found in the part of the prefrontal associative area specialized in the short-term memorization of spatial targets. However, in the processes of preparation for movement, the prefrontal cortex seems to play an even more important role than the posterior parietal areas. Finally, let us remember that all activity is only possible in the context of motivation dependent on the limbic system.

3.5 The question of general organization

One of the current challenges to the cognitive sciences is to understand how all the cerebral structures mentioned above organize themselves to produce an appropriate response. This difficult question can be apprehended on several levels.

The first level consists in examining the degree of connectivity between the different cortical and sub-cortical structures. Research clearly shows that all the structures are very strongly interconnected (cf. Kaas 1991, 1995). Figure 2.2 is a schematic representation of the principal connections generally presented in the literature between the different structures described in this chapter. The connections between sub-areas of each structure are not represented in this figure, but it is obvious that they are also very numerous.

The second level consists of studying the respective importance of parallel and hierarchical processing in general organization. This question has been debated in the literature (cf. Iwamura 1998; Pons 1996a, 1996b; Rowe, Turman, Murray, & Zhang 1996). Felleman and Van Essen (1991), for example, propose a model based on a hierarchical organization of the motor and somaesthetic areas (the authors distinguish 13 areas). Schematically, in this model area S1

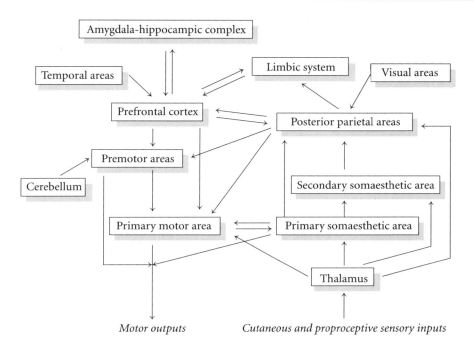

Figure 2.2. Simplified diagram illustrating the principal connections between the cerebral structures involved in haptic perception

occupies the lowest level, S2 an intermediate level and the associated areas the highest level. Relations between the 13 areas are realized by means of 72 connective tracts. The reciprocity of the connections is a general rule and the connections are both horizontal and vertical, with direct links (and no intermediate synapses) able to cross several levels. The great number of connections between the somaesthetic areas makes the system more flexible. These interconnections have several characteristics. The first is that there are many links between the areas of the same processing level. This shows that the system does not function in a strictly sequential, hierarchical way. The second characteristic is that the interconnections of a given area are more numerous if this area occupies a high level in the hierarchical organization. The final characteristic concerns the ascending and descending pathways of the hierarchical organization. Although there are numerous connections between adjacent areas, the majority of the communication lines cross several levels. The ascending tracts seem to be able to cross several levels without synaptic relays whereas the descending tracts rarely cross more than two levels. As we know that the time of cortical information processing increases with the number of synaptic relays, this suggests that the integration of descending information requires more time than does that of ascending information. For Felleman and Van Essen (1991), the processing power of our somaesthetic system depends on this distributed hierarchical organization.

The third level consists of examining the existence of different cortical streams. Physiological research on monkeys and imaging studies on humans have produced evidence for the existence of two cortical visual streams (for recent reviews, cf. Norman 2002; Rossetti & Revonsuo 2000). The dorsal stream is located mainly in the posterior parietal cortex and adjacent areas, and includes areas as such MT (V5), MST (medial superior temporal), LIP (lateral intraparietal) among others. The ventral stream is located mainly in the inferotemporal cortex and adjacent areas, and includes area V4. Regarding the functions of the two visual systems, neuropsychological and psychophysical studies show that the ventral system processes pattern, form and color information and the dorsal system processes motion and spatial information. The question, therefore, is to examine whether it exists also two distinct tactual systems having specific functions similar to those described in vision. Both in passive touch (cutaneous perception), and proprioception, some observations show that a double dissociation may occur (cf. Chapter 3). To our knowledge, no such dissociation has ever been observed in haptic perception (Gentaz, Hatwell, & Streri 2002).

Knowing the degrees of interconnection between the structures, the degrees of parallel/hierarchical processing of the different systems does not, however, explain how the coordination of the different structures involved in a given task is organized. To answer this crucial question, several models have been proposed, such as those integrating a central supervisor or administrator (Shallice 1988). The advantage of the model proposed by Singer (1995, 1999) is that it dispenses with a supra-structure: Faced with a given task, the cerebral structures involved are selected and temporarily linked by a process of temporal synchronization of their electrical activity. A kind of network would thus momentarily emerge, and in it the cognitive resources disposed of by the subject to effect the task would be concentrated. A new network would establish itself for the next task. In this model, the conscious performance of a given task would thus arise from the transitory association of specialized structures, and not from a superior hierarchical structure (for discussions about the binding problem and the neuronal synchrony, see Roskies 1999; Shadlen & Movshon 1999).

References

Andersen, R. A. (1995). Coordinate transformations and motor planning in posterior parietal cortex. In M. S. Gazzaniga (Ed.), *The Cognitive neuroscience* (pp. 519–532). Cambridge: MIT Press.

Blake, D., Hsiao, S., & Johnson, K. (1997). Neural coding mechanisms in tactile pattern recognition: The relative contributions of slowly and rapidly adapting mechanoreceptors to perceived roughness. *Journal of Neuroscience, 17*, 7480–7489.

Blake, D., Johnson, K., & Hsiao, S. (1997). Monkey cutaneous SAI and RA responses to raised and depressed scanned patterns: Effects of width, height, orientation and a raised surround. *Journal of Neurophysiology, 78*, 2503–2517.

Blakemore, S. J., Wolpert, D. M., & Frith, C. D. (1998). Central cancellation of self-produced tickle sensation. *Nature Neuroscience, 1*, 635–640.

Brisben, A., Hsiao, S., & Johnson, K. (1999). Detection of vibration transmitted through an objet grasped in the hand. *Journal of Neurophysiology, 81*, 1548–1558.

Chapman, C. E. (1994). Active versus passive touch: Factors influencing the transmission of somatosensory signals to primary somatosensory cortex. *Canadian Journal of Physiological Pharmacology, 72*, 558–570.

DiCarlo, J., Johnson, K., & Hsiao, S. (1998). Structure of receptive fields in area 3b of primary somatosensory cortex in the alert monkey. *Journal of Neuroscience, 18*, 2626–2645.

Felleman, D. J. & Van Essen, D. C. (1991). Distributed hierarchical processing in the primate cerebral cortex. *Cerebral Cortex, 1*, 1–47.

Gentaz, E., Hatwell, Y., & Streri, A. (2002). Constructivist and ecological approaches in tactual perception. *Behavioral and Brain Sciences, 25,* 106.

Graziano, M. & Gross, C. (1995). The representation of extrapersonal space: A possible role for bimodal, visual-tactile neurons. In M. Gazzanica (Ed.), *The cognitive neurosciences* (pp. 1021–1034). Cambridge: The MIT Press.

Georgopoulos, A. P., Kalaska, J. F., Caminiti, R., & Massey, J. T. (1982). On the relations between the direction of two-dimensional arm movements and cell discharge in primate motor cortex. *Journal of Neuroscience, 2*, 1527–1537.

Henderson, W. R. & Smyth, G. E. (1948). Phantom limbs. *Journal of Neurology, Neurosurgery and Psychiatry, 11*, 88–112.

Hikosaka, O., Tanaka, M., Sakamoto, M., & Iwamura, Y. (1985). Deficits in manipulative behaviors induced by local injections of muscimol in the first somatosensory cortex of the conscious monkey. *Brain Research, 325*, 375–380.

Holst von, E. & Mittelstaedt, H. (1973). The reafference principle. Interaction between the central nervous system and the periphery. In E. von Holst (Ed.), *The Behavioral physiology of animals and man* (pp. 139–173). London: Methuen.

Hsiao, S., Lane, J., & Fitzgerald, P. (2002). Representation of orientation in the somatosensory system. *Behavioural Brain Research, 135*, 93–103.

Humphrey, D. R. & Tanji, J. (1991). What features of voluntary motor control are encoded in the neuronal discharge of different cortical motor areas. In D. R. Humphrey & H.-J. Freund (Eds.), *Motor control: Concepts and issues* (pp. 413–443). New York: John Wiley & Sons.

Iwamura, Y. (1998). Hierarchical somatosensory processing. *Current Opinion in Neurobiology, 8*, 522–528.

Jeannerod, M. (1997). *The cognitive neuroscience of action*. Oxford: Blackwell.

Johansson, R. S. (1996). Sensory control of dexterous manipulation in humans. In A. M. Wing, P. Haggard, & J. R. Flanagan (Eds.), *Hand and brain* (pp. 381–414). San Diego, CA: Academic Press.

Johnson, K. & Hsiao, S. (1992). Tactile form and texture perception. *Annual Review of Neuroscience, 15*, 227–250.

Kandel, E., Schwartz, J., & Jessel, T. (2000). *Principles of neural science*. New York: MacGRaw-Hill.

Kaas, J. (1991). Plasticity of sensory and motor maps in adult mammals. *Annual Review of Neuroscience, 14*, 137–167.

Kaas, J. (1995). The reorganization of sensory and motor maps in adults mammals. In M. Gazzaniga (Ed.), *The Cognitive neurosciences* (pp. 51–71). Cambridge: The MIT Press.

Kalaska, J. (1996). Parietal cortex area 5 and visuomotor behavior. *Canadian Journal of Physiological Pharmacology, 74*, 483–498.

Massion, J. (1997). *Cerveau et motricité*. Paris: Presses Universitaires de France.

McClosey, D. I. (1981). Corollary discharges: Motor commands and perception. In J. M. Brookhart & V. B. Mountcastle (Eds.), *Handbook of physiology – The nervous system Vol. II, Motor control* (pp. 1415–1447). Bethesda: American Physiology Society.

Melzack, R. (1992). Phantom limbs. *Scientific American, 266*, 90–96.

Mistlin, A. J. & Perret, D. I. (1990). Visual and somatosensory processing in the macaque temporal cortex: The role of expectation. *Experimental Brain Research, 82*, 437–450.

Mountcastle, V. B. (1999). *Perceptual neuroscience: The cerebral cortex*. Cambridge: Harvard University Press.

Norman, J. (2002). Two visual systems and two theories of perception: An attempt to reconcile the constructivist and ecological approaches. *Behavioral and Brain Sciences, 25*, 73–144.

Penfield, W. & Rasmussen, T. (1950). *The cerebral cortex of man: A clinical study of localization of function*. New York: MacMillan.

Pons, T. (1996a). Novel sensations in the congenitally blind. *Nature, 380*, 479–480.

Pons, T. (1996b). Serial processing in the somatosensory system of macaques. In O. Franzen, R. Johansson, & L. Terenius (Eds.), *Somesthesis and neurobiology of the somatosensory cortex* (pp. 187–196). Berlin: Birkhäusen Verlag.

Pubols, L. & Leroy, R. (1977). Orientation detectors in the primary somatosensory neocortex of the raccon. *Brain Research, 129*, 61–74.

Roland, P. E. & Zilles, K. (1998). Structural divisions and functional fields in the human cerebral cortex. *Brain Research Review, 26*, 87–105.

Roll, J.-P. (1994). Sensibilités cutanées et musculaires. In M. Richelle, J. Requin, & M. Robert (Eds.), *Traité de Psychologie Expérimentale – Vol. 1* (pp. 483–542). Paris: Presses Universitaires de France.

Roll, J.-P., Bergenheim, M., & Ribot-Ciscar, E. (2000). Proprioceptive population coding of two-dimensional limb movements in humans: Muscle-spindle feedback during "drawing-like" movements. *Experimental Brain Research, 134*, 311–321.

Roskies, A. (1999). The binding problem. *Neuron, 24*, 77–125.

Rossetti, Y. & Revonsuo, A. (2000). *Beyond Dissociation. Interaction between dissociated implicit and explicit processing.* Amsterdam: John Benjamins Publishing Company.

Rowe, M., Turman, A., Murray, G., & Zhang, H. (1996). Parallel processing in the somatosensory areas I and II of the cerebral cortex. In O. Franzen, R. Johansson, & L. Terenius (Eds.), *Somesthesis and the neurobiology of the somatosensory cortex* (pp. 197–212). Berlin: Birkhäuser Verlag.

Shadlen, M. & Movshon, A. (1999). Synchrony unbound: A critical evaluation of the temporal binding hypothesis. *Neuron, 24*, 67–77.

Shallice, T. (1988). *From neuropsychology to mental structure.* Cambridge: Cambridge University Press.

Singer, W. (1995). Time as coding space in neocortical processing: A hypothesis. In M. Gazzaniga (Ed.), *The Cognitive neurosciences* (pp. 91–104). Cambridge: The MIT Press.

Singer, W. (1999). Striving for coherence. *Nature, 397*, 391–393.

Sperry, R. W. (1950). Neural basis of the spontaneous optokinetic response produced by visual neural inversion. *Journal of Computational Physiology and Psychology, 43*, 1737–1344.

Stein, B. E. & Meredith, M. A. (1993). *The merging of the senses.* Cambridge: The MIT Press.

Stein, B. E., Meredith, M. A., & Wallace, M. T. (1994). Development and neural basis of multisensory integration. In D. J. Lewkowicz & R. Lickliter (Eds.), *The development of intersensory perception. Comparative perspectives* (pp. 81–106). Hillsdale, NJ: Erlbaum.

Stein, J. F. (1978). Effects of parietal lobe cooling on manipulation in the monkey. In G. Gordon (Ed.), *Active touch* (pp. 79–90). Oxford: Pergamon.

Voisin, J., Lamarre, Y., & Chapman, C. (2002). Haptic discrimination of object shape in human: Contribution of cutaneous and proprioceptive inputs. *Experimental Brain Research, 145*, 251–260.

Warren, S., Hamalainen, H., & Gardner, E. (1986). Objective classification of motion- and direction sensitive neurons in primary somatosensory cortex of awake monkeys. *Journal of Neurophysiology, 56*, 598–622.

Wydoodt, P., Gentaz, E., Gaunet, F., Chêne, D., & Streri, A. (2003). Haptic estimation of spatial location in virtual and real path completion tasks: Contribution of proprioceptive and cutaneous information on the path effect. In M. A. Heller & S. Ballasteros (Eds.), *Touch, blindness and neurosciences* (pp. 351–361). Madrid (Spain): UNED Publishers.

Zilles, K. (1996). Pour un nouveau découpage du cortex. *La Recherche, 289*, 46–48.

CHAPTER 3

Anatomical and functional organization of cutaneous and haptic perceptions

The contribution of neuropsychology and cerebral functional imagery

Edouard Gentaz and Maryse Badan

1. The contribution of neuropsychology

Following a cerebral lesion (vascular accident, tumor or traumatism), many forms of somaesthetic deficits can occur, depending on the extent and location of the lesion. The neuropsychological investigation of these disorders provides information on the anatomo-functional organization subjacent to cutaneous and haptic perceptions, and also allows the characterization of the different levels of cutaneous and proprioceptive information processing necessary in the identification of the stimuli. The fact that dissociations, even double dissociations, exist in neuropsychological symptomatology is generally admitted as a strong argument in favor of the existence of functional modules of information processing. Efforts are currently being made, with the use of lesion localization, to establish the anatomical substrate of these modules. Here we examine several pathological manifestations of the cutaneous perception and haptic perception, and then we approach the question of the role of the cerebral hemispheres in the control of cutaneous and haptic perceptions.

1.1 Disorders in cutaneous perception

In cutaneous perception, apart from disturbances relating to the perception of temperature or superficial pain, deficits can specifically affect the recognition of more or less complex stimuli: The discrimination of two separate points simultaneously touching the skin, the perception of vibrational stimulations or of a force, the perception of light touch and graphesthesia. Pathological manifestations often appear in the form of negative signs such as diminution, or even extinction, of the perceptual abilities together with the loss of the sense of the position of the limbs. They can also engender troubles of recognition (e.g. digital agnosia, asomatognosia) or of the consciousness of the body itself or a part of the body; they can also take the form of "positive" symptoms, such as hallucinations or sensory illusions.

The disorders of touch observed in patients having lesions of the somaesthetic areas are some of the most severe that can be found. The patients who present symptoms of deafferentation are totally incapable of responding verbally to tactile stimulation. Researchers have sought to know if, in this extreme case, an implicit processing of cutaneous information was nevertheless effected with no conscious access to the stimulation (Paillard 1991; Paillard, Michel, & Stelmach 1983; Rossetti, Rode, & Boisson 1995). Paillard and his colleagues (1983, 1991) showed that a patient, suffering from a left parietal lesion including the somaesthetic areas, could not indicate where she had been touched but could point correctly toward the location of the stimulation. Paillard et al. (1983, 1991) proposed an interpretation of this phenomenon, called "blind-touch", based on the distinction of two pathways of information processing, one responsible for the detection and identification of the stimuli and the other for their location. This can be compared to the analogy with the double path "What" and "Where" of the visual system (Schneider 1969; Ungerleider & Mishkin 1982; cf. Chapter 2). According to the author, the patient was capable of locating but not of identifying the stimuli. This is compatible with the idea of an implicit processing of cutaneous information.

Following up this work, Rossetti et al. (1995) studied patients with complete loss of sensitivity in the right half of the body resulting from a left thalamic lesion. Adopting the method of forced choice, the authors used cutaneous and proprioceptive stimulation (position of the finger) which the patient had to locate under diverse conditions of response. It was observed that the patient could locate stimulations by direct pointing, but he could neither verbally indicate the stimulated places, nor indicate them on a diagram representing an arm. The same results were obtained when these two types of response were solicited simultaneously. These observations show that cutaneous and proprioceptive information can be integrated and used at the sensorimotor level without the elaboration of a representation of the location of the stimuli. They thus confirmed the existence of a dissociation between the "pragmatic" system and the "semantic" system (Jeannerod 1994; Jeannerod, Arbib, Rizzolatti, & Sakata 1995). In addition, the observations suggested the existence of a dissociation between systems specifying the location of the stimuli ("Where") and those which determine the mode of achieving this localization ("How"). As for the anatomical substrate of these residual abilities, the authors think that the ipsilateral somaesthetic pathways could carry out the information transfer necessary to this "localization for action". More recently, the authors, using a neuroanatomical illustration, have proposed that the substrate is the posterior parietal cortex, the same as for blindsight (Rossetti 1998).

Allesthesia is another pathological manifestation of cutaneous perception, in which patients perceive the stimulation applied on one corporal segment, but are unable to locate precisely the point of contact. In general, the stimulation that the patients indicate verbally is displaced towards the same side of the body as that of the cerebral lesion. Although this phenomenon is not fully understood, it again suggests that the processing of cutaneous information allowing detection of this information is disassociated from the processing allowing its precise location in the body space. Finally, the symptomatology known as tactile extinction can be phenomenonologically considered as a reduced form of disturbance in cutaneous perception. Patients with this disorder can only partially relate the tactile stimulation to which they are subjected. Indeed, when stimulation is applied simultaneously at two places, the patients do not perceive the one which is contralateral to the lesion, while if the stimulation is applied successively on the two positions, they are perfectly detected. In the majority of cases, allesthesia and tactile extinction are observed in subjects also presenting the syndrome of hemi-inattention (or hemispatial neglect) which is often the result of a right hemispheric lesion, in particular parietal (cf. Badan 1998).

Moreover, it happens that, in patients with hemispatial neglect, tactile extinction is not limited to a single limb collateral to the lesion. Moscovitch and Behrmann (1994) described the case of patients with left visuo-spatial hemineglect who could not tell if they had been touched on the left during simultaneous stimulation of the left and right parts of the right-hand, ipsilateral to the lesion and irrespective of whether the palm faced up or down. These observations suggest that disturbances in perception can occur independently of any known sensory disorder and most likely depend on perturbations affecting attentional ability and/or the cognitive processes responsible for the elaboration of spatial representation in different systems of coordinates (Vallar 1997).

1.2 Disorders in haptic perception

Disorders in haptic perception deprive patients of a powerful instrument providing knowledge of the environment, for they prevent the identification of manipulated objects in the absence of vision. This perceptual modality can present different types of perturbation. Already at the end of the 19th century, Wernike (1895) distinguished between disturbances in tactile recognition of the characteristics of objects from those related to their integration. Delay (1935) distinguished amorphognosia and ahylognosia (the deficits of recognition of the size and shape of objects or of certain of their properties such as weight and material), from tactile asymbolia (or tactile agnosia) which is a disorder in the identification of objects in the absence of the two preceding conditions.

Tactile agnosia must however be distinguished from tactile aphasia (or anomia) which concerns a disorder in the denomination of perceived objects (Geschwind 1965). Tactile aphasia is generally observed in patients having undergone a surgical or accidental sectioning of the callous body ("split-brain" patients), and concerns primarily the left hand; only a few examples of deficits involving both hands have been identified (Beauvois, Saillant, Meininger, & Lhermitte 1978; Endo, Miyasaka, Makishita, Yanagisawa, & Sugishita 1992). According to the generally accepted interpretation, this disorder in the denomination of objects palpated in the left hand is due to the hemispheric disconnection which prevents the relation between the representation of the tactile object and the corresponding name being made. And indeed, the cortical areas involved in the construction of the spatial representation of the objects palpated in the left-hand are situated in the right hemisphere which, subsequent to the sectioning of the callous body, is no longer in contact with the zones of language situated in the left hemisphere. The results of the study by Baynes, Tramo, Reeves and Gazzaniga (1997) – which stressed the representational capacity of the right hemisphere in split-brain patients – support this proposition. During subsequent investigation of the patient described by Baynes et al. (1997), Badan and Caramazza (1997) showed that in the presence of a material which is more difficult to identify than common objects (letters and shapes with or without signification cut out of glass-paper), the patient also presented disturbances of haptic recognition in the right hand. This result underlines the limits of the left hemisphere concerning the processing of haptic information and stresses the necessity for a contribution from the right hemisphere in the construction of haptic spatial representation.

Finally, as a disorder of haptic spatial perception, tactile agnosia should be differentiated from astereoagnosia, for the latter seems to present in addition a deficit of somaesthetic perception. According to Caselli (1997), astereoagnosia results from a lesion of the sensory system, going from the peripheral nerves to the primary somaesthetic area (S1), via the median lemniscus and the thalamus. The restrictions imposed by these diverse distinctions pose the question of the reality of tactile agnosia and of its interpretation, for in the majority of clinical observations there are disturbances, sometimes only slight, of somaesthetic sensitivity (Bauer 1993; Caselli 1991, 1997; Endo et al. 1992; Nakamura, Endo, Sumida, & Hasegawa 1998; Platz 1996).

On the basis of a detailed analysis of the literature and of the study of two patients presenting troubles of haptic perception, Endo et al. (1992) concluded that tactile agnosia and tactile aphasia existed independently. According to their model, in the case of tactile agnosia, information on the characteristics (shape, material) analyzed by the short-term memory could not reach the semantic memory, while in the case of tactile aphasia, the contents of the semantic memory could not be put into contact with the lexical memory. The authors retain the idea that tactile aphasia results from a tactile-verbal disconnection, and they show that in their patient, tactile agnosia is the consequence of a sub-cortical lesion including the left angular gyrus, disconnecting the associative sensory areas and the areas of the inferior temporal lobe involved in semantic memory (Endo et al. 1992). One of the authors and his collaborators later described a patient with bilateral tactile agnosia due to a bilateral sub-cortical lesion in the region of the angular gyrus (Nakamura et al. 1998).

Another interpretation is proposed by Platz (1996), who studied a patient suffering from right parietal meningioma and presenting the indications of tactile agnosia despite having conserved his basic motor and sensory ability. The author refutes the idea that perception and recognition constitute successive stages of the processing and memorization of information. On the contrary, he interprets the difficulties of the patient as being due to the disconnection of the different systems of analysis of object characterization. These systems are activated in parallel, but they become disconnected and so prevent the constitution of a functional unit (including characteristics and entity), which is essential to the haptic modality.

In a recent study, Valenza et al. (2001) presented a patient with a right hemisphere infarction who showed disorders of tactile recognition of the left hand due to impaired Lederman and Klatzky's (1987) exploratory procedures (cf. Chapter 5) occurring without tactile agnosia. Functional MRI during sensory stimulation of the left hand showed preserved activation of the spared primary sensory cortex in the right hemisphere. This case of pure tactile apraxia was interpreted as a specific inability to use tactile feedback to generate the exploratory procedures necessary for tactile shape recognition.

Other studies found perturbations in the visual and haptic perception of spatial orientations in the fronto-parallel plane of patients with left visuo-

spatial neglect (VSN). Thus, Kerkhoff (1999) observed lower global performance (independently of the orientation value) in neglects patients. Gentaz,
Badan, Luyat and Touil (2002) found also a haptic orientation deficit in the
fronto-parallel plane in neglect patients. The precision of response was lower
in the neglect patients than in the control (young adults and seniors) subjects.
However, the same haptic oblique effect (lower performances in oblique orientations than in vertical-horizontal orientations, cf. Chapter 8) was observed in
the three groups. These results were similar in the left and right hemiespaces of
the participants, even in the neglect patients. Taken together, this means that,
in spite of the global haptic orientation deficit, no specific pattern is observed
in the haptic perception of different orientations in these VSN patients as compared to the two other groups. The haptic orientation deficit of VSN patients
seems to affect in the same way all values and spatial positions of orientations.

1.3 The role of cerebral hemispheres in the control of cutaneous and haptic perceptions

The question of the neuro-anatomical substrate of cutaneous and haptic perceptions must be considered at the level of inter- and intra-hemispheric control of these perceptual modalities, always remembering the role of the corpus
callosum in the transfer and attentional control of tactile information (Gazzaniga 1970; Mayer, Koenig, & Panchaud 1988). Contrary to the situation in
other functions (such as language which is mainly represented in the left hemisphere), the existence of the functional lateralization of tactile perception is
the subject of considerable debate in the literature (see Chapters 6 and 13). It
should be noted that the somaesthetic and motor areas are distributed in an
almost equivalent manner in the two hemispheres. But let us remember that
the organization is crossed, for each hemisphere essentially controls the information relating to the contralateral half of the body. The role devolved to
S1 and S2 is different, and recent papers stress the importance of lesions in
region S2, in particular the parietal operculum and the posterior part of the
insula, in the generation of tactile agnosia (Schnider 1997; Vallar 1997). One
can, then, consider that the intra-hemispheric distribution of lesions engen-
dering tactile perception pathology reveals the preponderant role of S1 in the
region of the postcentral gyrus, and of S2 in the region of the inferior parietal
lobule, the activation of which may be at least partly serial (Bassetti, Bogousslavsky, & Regli 1993; Caselli 1997; Corkin 1970; Critchley 1953; Hécaen &
Albert 1978; Knecht, Kunesch, & Schnitzler 1996; Pause, Kunesch, Binkofsky,
& Freund 1989; Schnider 1997; Vallar 1997).

Paradoxically, and contrary to the predictions based on the almost identical distribution of sensory and motor areas in the two hemispheres (noted above), the consequences of left and right cerebral lesions give rise to an asymmetry which is a determining factor in the incidence of somaesthetic and motor disorders. For example, Sterzi et al. (1993) showed that disturbances in the sense of position are more frequent following a right lesion (37%) than a left lesion (25%). Others symptoms, such as the loss of sensitivity to pain, motor deficits and visual-spatial deficits, also present a certain degree of asymmetry. Thus, the higher frequency of symptoms resulting from right lesions indicates the dominance of the right hemisphere in tactile perception, in the broad sense of the term. This dominance is compatible with the idea, exposed by several authors, of a right hemispheric advantage in the recognition of objects by manual exploration (Bottini, Cappa, & Vignolo 1991; Franco & Sperry 1977; Ledoux, Wilson, & Gazzaniga 1977; Milner & Taylor 1972). Franco and Sperry (1977), for example, asked patients with a partial (anterior) or complete section of the corpus callosum (preventing information transfer from one hemisphere to the other) to distinguish geometrical shapes palpated with the right and left hand. They found that the left hand – right hemisphere had an advantage in this type of task. To interpret the divergences, it is possible to consider that the processing of haptic information brings about the intervention of high-level processes, which are represented more in the right hemisphere and, as suggested above, are spatial or attentional in nature (Bauer 1993; Sterzi et al. 1993; Vallar 1997).

This brief consideration of the consequences of cerebral lesions on the recognition of objects and of the body itself shows that the processes operating at several levels of processing are involved in tactile perception. Certain aspects necessary for the construction of spatial representations are undertaken by high-level mechanisms with asymmetrical hemispheric distribution.

2.   The contribution of cerebral functional imagery

Another way of understanding the cortical organization underlying tactile perception is to examine the neural modifications which occur as a result of over-training or deafferentation. We have long known that cortical organization is characterized by great plasticity (for a review, cf. Buonomano & Merzenich 1998). Hebb (1949) had already proposed a form of plasticity in synaptic connections: "Neurons which discharge together will link together". In addition, if the transmission of sensory information between one part of the body and its cortical representation is interrupted, the corresponding cortical zone does not remain inert, but reorganizes, letting itself be invaded by the adjacent cortical zone. For example, Jenkins, Merzenich, Ochs, Allard and Guic-Robles (1990) showed that in the monkey, the blockage of nervous impulses transmitted from a finger to the somaesthetic areas is not translated by a lasting inactivity of the region which normally processes the information sent by that finger. After a certain lapse of time, the region starts to respond when the adjacent fingers are stimulated. In other words, the fact of modifying the relative importance of synaptic connections by increasing stimulation or deactivating a neural pathway modifies the organization of the cortical areas involved (cf. Elbert et al. 1997).

Recent progress in cerebral functional imagery methods has brought new light onto cerebral plasticity by permitting the *in vivo* examination of cerebral activity (cortical and sub-cortical) of humans as they perform a given task. It may be useful to review some general information on these different methods (cf. Dehaene 1997; Posner & Raichle 1998). We know that the neural mechanisms underlying cognitive and sensory-motor activities give rise to a continuous and considerable metabolic requirement. This demand for energy is principally met by the use of glucose. As the brain has very limited reserves, it is dependent on a continuous supply of oxygen and glucose, and the regional variations correspond fairly exactly to the actual metabolic needs. So, by measuring regional blood deficits or the cerebral consumption of oxygen and glucose, one can estimate the metabolic activity linked to the synaptic activity underlying cognitive and sensory-motor tasks.

Positron emission tomography (PET) and functional magnetic resonance imagery (fMRI) are the two principal methods of measuring the cerebral metabolic activity of the subject as s/he carries out a task. Each method has advantages and disadvantages. PET has good spatial resolution but low temporal resolution. It also has the inconvenience of requiring the injection of a radioactive marker. MRI has better spatial and temporal resolution than PET and it is non-invasive. However, it has still currently the disadvantage of measuring an extremely noisy signal (the signal/noise ratio is not as good as for PET).

Let us now examine the results of research which, using PET and MRI, investigates the effects of overtraining or deafferentation on the reorganization of somaesthetic and visual areas, and especially in completely blind adults. This population is particularly interesting in that it suffers from the complete suppression of visual stimuli associated with the overtraining of the tactile modality.

2.1 Cortical reorganization of somaesthetic areas in musicians and blind people

Elbert et al. (1995) posed this question: Does the intensive use of a limb result in an increase in its cortical representation in the somaesthetic areas? They compared the cortical activity of the somaesthetic areas of non-musicians with those of experienced musicians playing string instruments (violin, cello and guitar). Players of these instruments make great use of the fingers of the left-hand, except for the thumb but including the auricular or little finger. The authors used fMRI to measure the cortical activity of the somaesthetic areas as they responded to light tactile stimuli on the fingertips of both hands. The results revealed that the cortical representation of the left auricular is greater in musicians than in non-musicians. However, representation of the left thumb (less used than the other fingers) and of the fingers of the right hand are similar in musicians and non-musicians.

Sterr et al. (1998) also examined this question in sighted and blind people with different levels of practice in the tactile modality. The authors compared the cortical activity of the somaesthetic areas in blindfolded sighted people to those of blind people who, when reading braille (cf. Chapter 14), use either one or three fingers of both hands simultaneously. The results revealed that cortical representation of the hand is greater in blind people who read braille with three fingers than in the two other groups. It thus seems that the intensive use of one or several parts of the body (such as the expert practice of a string instrument or of reading braille) results in an increase in the cortical representation of that or those parts in the somaesthetic areas.

2.2 Cortical reorganization of the visual areas in blind people

2.2.1 *Cortical hypo- and hyperactivity in the primary and secondary visual areas*

De Volder (1995) and De Volder et al. (1997) examined the effects of early and late blindness on the cortical organization in the primary and secondary visual areas. The authors compared the cerebral activity of three populations: The early-blind (either congenitally blind or blind since before the age of three), the late-blind (blindness occurring in adults subsequent to lesions of peripheral visual pathways) and sighted people. Using PET, they measured the cerebral metabolism at rest and during haptic tasks: The exploration of objects with the right hand, and/or the recognition of three-dimensional patterns using an Optacon (a device which transforms luminous stimulation into tactile stimulation; cf. Chapter 16). The results revealed a clear difference in the metabolism of the primary and secondary visual areas in the three populations, whereas cortical activity of the other areas remained similar in the different groups. Metabolism of the primary and secondary visual areas in the late-blind is lower than that for blindfolded sighted people. Moreover, the cortical activity of visual areas is higher in the early-blind than in sighted and late-blind people. This hypermetabolism of the visual areas is observed in the early-blind whether they are resting or carrying out the various haptic tasks (a similar hyperactivity of visual areas is also present in tasks of auditory location; Wanet-Defalque et al. 1998). All these results are similar in both hemispheres. Taken together, they suggest that early lesions of peripheral visual pathways bring about lasting modifications in the functional organization of the human brain.

In their interpretation, De Volder and her colleagues based their argument on the evolution of synaptic connection density during normal development. This evolution is characterized by an initial overproduction of connections, followed by a reduction of redundant connections. So there would seem to be a "synaptic revision" associated with progressive reduction of synapses per neuron. Synaptic revision, called "functional validation" by Jacobson (1978) and "selective stabilization" by Changeux and Danchin (1976), is thought to be a developmental process favoring the maintenance of the nervous connections activated by exterior stimuli, and eliminating the supernumerary connections less activated by the same stimuli, working progressively towards the cortical organization of the adult. This process would constitute the basis of cerebral plasticity. De Volder and her colleagues used parallel ontogenetic evolution of cerebral metabolism and regional synaptic density in order to explain the hypermetabolism of the visual areas of the early-blind. This, they say, is the result of the absence of "synaptic revision" and therefore of the persistence of an unusually high local concentration of synaptic connections not having undergone the normal selection linked to the functional maturation of the nervous pathways.

2.2.2   The activation of visual areas during tasks of haptic discrimination

According to the research discussed above, it is clear that the level of cortical activity in visual areas is higher in early-blind than in sighted people. Sadato et al. (1996) interpreted this hypermetabolism as showing that the visual areas can assume a non-visual function in certain populations. The authors, therefore, sought to ascertain whether non-visual tasks, such as haptic tasks, could directly activate the primary visual area. It is established that visual areas receive only visual afferences in subjects with no relevant deficiency. Therefore, Sadato and his colleagues used PET to compare the cortical activity of the visual areas of sighted people and early-blind people (who were good readers in braille) in several tasks: Haptic discrimination of spatial properties (angles, width) and of words/non-words in braille (for the blind), and passive stimulation (passive circular movements of the index finger on a homogenous surface of raised points). The results revealed an activation of primary and secondary visual areas (similar in both hemispheres) in the early-blind in all the tasks of haptic discrimination, with a higher level of activation in the task of discrimination of words/non-words in braille than in the other tasks. However, the visual areas did not seem to be activated in the blindfolded sighted people doing the same tasks: The activity of these areas actually diminished in the tasks of haptic discrimination of spatial properties. Moreover, the results showed that the task of passive stimulation (without discrimination) did not result in any significant activation of visual areas in either the blind or sighted groups.

The same team continued the study of the role of the activation of the primary visual area in tasks of haptic discrimination, using a new technique which provokes temporary functional deactivation of the visual areas by magnetic means (*transcranial magnetic stimulation, TMS*). Cohen et al. (1997) could thus make the primary and secondary visual areas unusable for a group of early-blind (good braille readers) and a sighted group during tasks of haptic discrimination (identification of either braille or raised roman letters). The results showed that this "temporary deactivation" of the visual areas brought about a fall in the performance of the early-blind in the two haptic tasks while it had no significant effect on that of the sighted group (which had, moreover, lower performances in the visual tasks).

Recently, Sathian and Zangaladze (2002) extended these results in showing an activation of a region of extrastriate visual cortex, near the parieto-occipital fissure, during cutaneous discrimination of grating orientation in blindfolded sighted adults. TMS over this region interfere with performance in this cutaneous task. Moreover, Pascual-Leone, Theoret and Merabet (2002) observed an activation of the occipital cortex on fMRI by haptic stimulation of the fingers in sighted subjects undergoing 5 days of complete visual deprivation and haptic immersion training. Transient blocking of the visual cortex with TMS at the end of the 5 days, but not at baseline or following removal of the blindfold, disrupts haptic braille symbol discrimination. This establishes the functional role of the visual cortex in haptic processing. None of these changes are seen in non-blindfolded control subjects. The authors suggest that this extremely rapid cross-modal plasticity would mean the existence of masked haptic inputs into visual cortex in normal human subjects that can be unmasked by visual deprivation. Thus, the visually deprived striate and peri-striate cortex would be capable of processing haptic inputs. Further research is needed to confirm these exciting results.

3. Conclusion

The results obtained thanks to cerebral functional imagery thus confirm and put into perspective certain general characteristics established in the literature on cortical organization (cf. Chapter 2). The early-blind seem to use their visual cortex in tasks for which it was not "intended". This result suggests, therefore, that the visual cortex can have a non-visual function under certain conditions. A fuller understanding of this phenomenon could have pedagogical implications for the visually deficient. Also, although the new methods of cerebral imagery are undoubtedly useful, one must remember that they only allow the "visualization" of the regions underlying the cognitive processes: One can only see the container, not what is contained. This is why the behavioral sciences are needed to participate in the establishment of correlates between the neural and perceptive-cognitive processes involved in tactile perception. One can say that the methods of cerebral functional imagery enrich our knowledge by shedding light on the impressive plasticity of the cortical organization of the human brain.

References

Badan, M. (1998). Héminégligences: Le côté manquant du monde. *Sciences et Vie, 204*, 86–94.

Badan, M., & Caramazza, A. (1997). Haptic processing by the left hemisphere in a split-brain patient. *Neuropsychologia, 35*, 1275–1287.

Bassetti, C., Bogousslavsky, J., & Regli, F. (1993). Sensory syndromes in parietal stroke. *Neurology, 43*, 1942–1949.

Bauer, R. M. (1993). *Agnosia*. New York: Oxford University Press.

Baynes, K., Tramo, M. J., Reeves, A. G., & Gazzaniga, M. S. (1997). Isolation of a right hemisphere cognitive system in a patient with anarchic (alien) hand sign. *Neuropsychologia, 35*, 1159–1173.

Beauvois, M. F., Saillant, B., Meininger, V., & Lhermitte, F. (1978). Bilateral tactile aphasia: A tactuo-verbal dysfunction. *Brain, 101*, 381–401.

Bottini, G., Cappa, S. F., & Vignolo, L. A. (1991). Somesthetic-visual matching disorders in right and left hemisphere-damaged patients. *Cortex, 27*, 223–228.

Buonomano, D., & Merzenich, M. (1998). Cortical plasticity: From synapses to maps. *Annual Review of Neuroscience, 21,* 149–186.

Caselli, R. (1991). Bilateral impairment of somesthetically mediated object recognition in humans. *Mayo Clinical Proceedings, 66,* 357–364.

Caselli, R. (1997). Tactile agnosia and disorders of tactile perception. In T. E. Feinberg & M. J. Farah (Eds.), *Behavioral neurology and neuropsychology* (pp. 277–288). New York: McGraw-Hill.

Changeux, J.-P., & Danchin, A. (1976). Selective stabilisation of developing synapses as a mechanism for the specification of neuronal networks. *Nature, 264,* 705–712.

Cohen, L., Celnik, P., Pascual-Leone, A., Corwell, B., Faiz, L., Dambrosia, J., Honda, M., Sadato, N., Gerloff, C., Catala, M., & Hallett, M. (1997). Functional relevance of cross-modal plasticity in blind humans. *Nature, 389,* 180–183.

Corkin, S. (1978). *The role of different cerebral structures in somesthetic perception (Vol. VI B).* New York: Academic Press.

Critchley, M. (1953). *The parietal lobe.* New York: Hafner.

De Volder, A. (1995). *Réorganisation corticale dans la déficience sensorielle précoce chez l'être humain: implications thérapeutiques.* Thèse de Doctorat, Bruxelles.

De Volder, A., Bol, A., Blin, J., Robert, A., Arno, P., Grandin, C., Michel, C., & Veraart, C. (1997). Brain energy metabolism in early blind subjects: Neural activity in the visual cortex. *Brain Research, 750,* 235–244.

Dehaene, S. (1997). *Le cerveau en action. Imagerie cérébrale fonctionnelle en psychologie cognitive.* Paris: Presses Universitaires de France.

Delay, J. (1935). *Les astéréognosies. Pathologie du toucher.* Paris: Masson.

Elbert, T., Pantev, C., Wienbruch, C., Rockstroh, B., & Taub, E. (1995). Increased cortical representation of the fingers of the left hand in string players. *Science, 270,* 305–307.

Elbert, T., Sterr, A., Flor, H., Rockstroh, B., Knecht, S., Pantev, C., Wienbruch, C., & Taub, E. (1997). Input-increase and input-decrease types of cortical reorganization after upper extremity amputation in humans. *Experimental Brain Research, 117,* 161–164.

Endo, K., Miyasaka, M., Makishita, H., Yanagisawa, N., & Sugishita, M. (1992). Tactile agnosia and tactile aphasia: Symptomatological and anatomical differences. *Cortex, 28,* 445–469.

Franco, L., & Sperry, R. (1977). Hemisphere lateralisation for cognitive processing of geometry. *Neuropsychologia, 15,* 107–114.

Gazzaniga, M. S. (1970). *The bisected brain.* New York: Appleton.

Gentaz, E., Badan, M., Luyat, M. & Touil, N. (2002). The manual haptic perception of orientations and the oblique effect in patients with left visuo-spatial neglect. *NeuroReport, 13,* 327–331.

Geschwind, N. (1965). Disconnection syndromes in animals and man. *Brain, 88,* 237–294.

Hebb, D. O. (1949). *The organization of behavior.* New York: Wiley.

Hécaen, H., & Albert, M. L. (1978). *Human neuropsychology.* New York: John Wiley.

Jacobson, M. (1978). *Developmental neurobiology (2nd edition).* New York: Plenum Press.

Jeannerod, M. (1994). *Objects oriented action.* Amsterdam: Elsevier Science.

Jeannerod, M., Arbib, M. A., Rizzolatti, G., & Sakata, H. (1995). Grasping objects: The cortical mechanisms of visuo-motor transformations. *Trends in Neurosciences, 18,* 314–320.

Jenkins, W., Merzenich, M., Ochs, M., Allard, T., & Guic-Robles, E. (1990). Functional reorganization of primary somatosensory cortex in adult owl monkeys after behaviorally controlled tactile stimulation. *Journal of Neurophysiology, 63*, 82–104.

Kerkhoff, G. (1999). Multimodal spatial orientation deficits in left-sided visual neglect. *Neuropsychologia, 37*, 1387–1405.

Knecht, S., Kunesch, E., & Schnitzler, A. (1996). Parallel and serial processing of haptic information in man: Effects of parietal lesions on sensorimotor hand function. *Neuropsychologia, 34*, 669–687.

Lederman, S. J., & Klatzky, R. L. (1987). Hand movements: A window into haptic object recognition. *Cognitive Psychology, 19*, 342–368.

Ledoux, J. E., Wilson, D. H., & Gazzaniga, M. S. (1977). Manipulo-spatial aspects of cerebral lateralization: Clues to the origin of lateralization. *Neuropsychologia, 15*, 743–750.

Mayer, E., Koenig, O., & Panchaud, A. (1988). Tactual extinction without anomia: Evidence of attentional factors in a patient with parietal callosal disconnection. *Neuropsychologia, 26*, 851–868.

Milner, B., & Taylor, L. (1972). Right-hemisphere superiority in tactile pattern-recognition after cerebral commissurectomy: Evidence for nonverbal memory. *Neuropsychologia, 10*, 1–15.

Moscovitch, M., & Behrmann, M. (1994). Coding spatial information in the somatosensory system: Evidence from patients with neglect following parietal lobe damage. *Journal of Cognitive Neuroscience, 6*, 151–155.

Nakamura, J., Endo, K., Sumida, T., & Hasegawa, T. (1998). Bilateral tactile agnosia: A case report. *Cortex, 34*, 375–388.

Paillard, J. (1991). *Brain and space.* New York: Oxford University Press.

Paillard, J., Michel, F., & Stelmach, G. (1983). Localization without content: A tactile analogue of "blind sight". *Archives of Neurology, 40*, 548–551.

Pascual-Leone, A., Theoret, H. & Merabet, L. (2002). Tactile processing in the visual cortex. *Abstract of Touch, Blindness and Neurosciences Congress.* Madrid, Spain.

Pause, M., Kunesch, E., Binkofsky, F., & Freund, H. (1989). Sensorimotor disturbances in patients with lesions of the parietal cortex. *Brain, 112*, 1599–1625.

Platz, T. (1996). Tactile agnosia: Casuistic evidence and theoretical remarks on modality-specific meaning representations and sensorimotor integration. *Brain, 119*, 1565–1574.

Posner, M., & Raichle, M. (1998). *L'esprit en images.* Louvain-la-Neuve, Belgique: De Boeck Université.

Rossetti, Y. (1998). Short-lived motor representation of space in brain-damaged and healthy subjects. *Consciousness and Cognition, 7*, 520–558.

Rossetti, Y., Rode, G., & Boisson, D. (1995). Implicit processing of somesthetic information: A dissociation between Where and How? *NeuroReport, 6*, 506–510.

Sadato, N., Pascual-Leone, A., Grafman, J., Ibanez, V., Deiber, M.-P., Dold, G., & Hallet, M. (1996). Activation of the primary visual cortex by braille reading blind subjects. *Nature, 380*, 526–528.

Sathian, K. & Zangaladze, A. (2002). Feeling with the mind's eye: Contribution of visual cortex to tactile perception. *Behavioural Brain Research, 135*, 127–132.

Schneider, G. F. (1969). Two visual systems. *Science, 163*, 895–902.

Schnider, A. (1997). *Verhaltensneurologie.* Stuttgart: Georg Thieme Verlag.

Sterr, A., Müller, M., Elbert, T., Rockstroh, B., Pantev, C., & Taub, E. (1998). Perceptual correlates of changes in cortical representation of fingers in blind multifinger braille readers. *Journal of Neuroscience, 18*, 4417–4423.

Sterzi, R., Bottini, G., Celani, M., Righetti, E., Lamassa, M., Ricci, S., & Vallar, G. (1993). Hemianopia, hemianeasthesia, and hemiplegia after left and right hemisphere damage. *Journal of Neurology, Neurosurgery, and Psychiatry, 56*, 308–310.

Ungerleider, L. G., & Mishkin, M. (1982). *Two cortical visual systems.* Cambridge: The MIT Press.

Vallar, G. (1997). Spatial frames of reference and somatosensory processing: A neuro-psychological perspective. *Philosophical Transactions of the Royal. Society, London B, 352*, 1401–1409.

Valenza, N., Patk, R., Zimine, I., Badan, M., Lazeyras, F., Schnider, A. (2001). Dissociated active and passive tactile shape recognition: A case study of pure tactile apraxia. *Brain,124*, 2287–2298.

Wanet-Defalque, M. C., Veraart, C., De Volder, A., Metz, R., Michel, C. Dooms, G. & Goffinet, A. (1988). High metabolic activity in the visual cortex of early blind subjects. *Brain Research, 446*, 369–373.

Wernike, C. (1895). Zwei Fälle von Rindenläsion. *Arbeiten aus der psychiatrichen Klinik in Breslau, 2*, 35–52.

PART 2

Haptic perceptual exploration

CHAPTER 4

Manual exploration and haptic perception in infants

Arlette Streri

Interest in the very young infant's haptic modality has grown considerably over the last twenty years. The haptic modality is very primitive – since it is the first modality to be put into practice – and at the same time very original in its ways of working. It has generated a lot of studies into babies, which currently permit a better understanding of its beginnings. A long time before taking an interest in infants' exploratory activity, researchers started by evaluating the organism's reactivity level. They also limited early forms of oral and manual capture to reflex. It is henceforth widely accepted that haptic perception results from an intimate coupling of motricity and sensitivity. Haptic perception, in the context of exploration, is intimately linked to action (e.g. Lederman & Klatzky 1987).

1. The early forms of the haptic exploration

Human beings possess tactile sensitivity from the first weeks of fetal life. Using a fine-haired esthesiometer to stroke the skin, Hooker (1938) and Humphrey (1970, 1964) were able to trigger fetal reactions and describe precisely the tactile sensitivity of the fetus's body. After 7.5 weeks of gestation, the fetus, kept alive for a few minutes after expulsion, responds to a light stimulation of its head by pulling away. Then, the parts of the body which react to tactile stimulation are the area around the mouth (8.5 weeks), a reaction corresponding to an opening of the mouth and swallowing, the genital area (10.5 weeks), the palms of the hands (between 10.5 and 11 weeks), and the soles of the feet (12 weeks). Let us recall (cf. Chapter 2) that these surfaces, although small, are those which possess the greatest number and the widest variety of tactile receptors in adults. Kjaer and Kjaer have only recently shown (1998) that, in the first prenatal period, the size of a fetus's hand can be a good means of predicting the date of its conception, as well as its normal development. This measurement can be regarded as a reliable indicator for the detection and evaluation of fetal pathological development. At birth, tactile sensitivity develops and the organism's reactivity threshold is lower in full-term babies than in premature babies (Rose, Schmidt, & Bridger 1976). This development is fully governed by the maturation of the nervous system. Research into tactile sensitivity reveals that the young infant is able to receive and react to information, in spite of the weak specificity of receptors. However, these first observations focus on the sensorial aspect of the human organism, but say nothing about its manual skills.

Conversely, the observation of babies' motor behavior has contributed considerably to fixing developmental stages (Gesell 1933; McGraw 1935). These studies are flawed by the fact that, contrary to those above, they disregard the newborn's potential, however weak, to gather information about objects and thus to perceive. Already present *in utero* (Erhardt 1973), the grasping reflex in response to a stimulation of the palm of the hand was regarded as the newborn and the infant's dominant behavior that favored a form of interaction with its environment. Pressure exerted on the palm of the hand by an object or even the observer's finger triggers the closing of the fingers around the stimulus. A few weeks later, the avoiding reflex is added to the neonatal grasping reflex. This consists, on the contrary, of the opening wide of the fingers and the rejection of all stimulation (Twitchell 1965, 1970).

The presence of these reflexes during the first five months of the baby's life is regarded as the prelude to more voluntary actions, such as taking and releasing objects. However, for a long time researchers were unaware a third action, between the other two, namely the holding of objects. During holding, manipulation of the objects would allow to gather information about them. In a similar way to the grasping reflex of the palm, oral pressure exerted on a bottle teat or a nipple was rightly regarded as the outward sign of the sucking reflex, whose main function was to allow the baby to feed itself. Extended to non-nutritive sucking situations, the unique function of this reflex was to calm the baby down and stop it crying.

The study of the haptic system, considered in isolation, allows us to answer the question as to the capacities and the means that infant develops to apprehend the environment. This study is generally confined to the first five months of an infant's life. During this period, although oral exploration seems to dominate the baby's exchanges with its environment, manual exploration, still limited, also allows the properties of objects to be apprehended. After the age of five months, the emergence of visual/prehensile coordination breaks off these first forms of interaction. The baby picks up objects within its reach or carries them to its eyes or to its mouth, transfers them from one hand to the other, moves them, etc. The manual system thus fully assures its transporting function, which seems to be exercised to the detriment of the perceptive function.

2. The abilities of the oral haptic mode through the first months after birth

In a similar way to all the activities characterizing a newborn's motor ability, sucking was for a long time regarded as invariable and rigid. Bullinger and Rochat (1985), however, obtain a non-nutritive sucking graph, which shows that the regular sucking pattern is interrupted by an irregular trace of weaker amplitude, corresponding to mechanical deformations exerted on the pacifier. This temporary signal is attributed to active mouth movements which the authors compare to manual palpation and which reveal that the baby is using an expression activity. An evolution of the expression function of oral activity can thus be evaluated objectively. It is thus that Rochat (1983) presents newborns with a series of dummies, varying in shape and in substance (rigid or elastic). He notices that the duration of the regular sucking pattern diminishes according to age, whereas correlatively that of the exploration pattern increases. There is also an interaction between the infants' ages and the type of dummy. The newborns respond differently according to the rigid or elastic substance of the objects, whereas the older babies explore the dummies differently according to variations in shape. Pêcheux, Lepecq and Salzarulo (1988) confirmed the ability of the one to two-month-old infant to tell the difference between dummies of various shapes. Research into intermodal perception also revealed that, between one and twelve months, the infants visually recognize the substance, the texture and the shape of sucked objects (Gibson & Walker 1984; Gottfried, Rose, & Bridger 1977; Meltzoff & Borton 1979; cf. Chapter 11). Although infants' preferred form of exploration is confined to the oral modality in the first months of life, this mode is transitory and will be replaced progressively by manual exploration. A study by Ruff, Saltarelli, Capozzoli and Dubiner (1992) showed that oral exploration or mouthing increases up to the age of seven months and then declines until the age of eleven months, in favor of manual skills, which progress and diversify between the ages of five and eleven months.

3.   Touching by the hands to knowing

There are clear differences between the functioning of the oral and manual modes, and this justifies studying them separately. Thus, Rochat (1987) studied the newborn and the two- to three-month-old baby's capacity to detect information in objects pertinent to setting off oral or manual activity (the affordances). He compares different degrees of pressure applied to both rigid and elastic objects. The objects presented are identical in both modes. Rochat uses a polygraph to record the frequency of the oral and manual pressure exerted on the soft and the hard object. The results indicate behavioral differences according to the baby's age and the consistency of the object explored. Unlike the mouth, the hand exerts more pressure on the hard object than on the soft object. On the other hand, the newborn's oral activity is much greater than its manual activity, and this tendency is reversed at the age of two to three months. Buka and Lipsitt (1991) studied the relation between sucking and grasping responses in 72-hour-old newborns during two periods of sucking activity, with and without sweet water. The grasping reflex is set off when a metal stick is put in the baby's right hand. The results reveal that although the presence or absence of the grasping response has no effect on sucking, the latter, on the other hand, affects grasping strength. The newborn holds the stick more firmly during sucking activities than without sucking activity, and even more firmly when the sugar solution is administered. Thus, the relation between sucking and grasping is not reversible and the two modes of exploration present clear specificities.

From this research, one must not conclude that a newborn's manual capacities are limited to a simple pressure exerted on an object. Recently, Streri, Lhote and Dutilleul (2000) showed that newborns (the youngest was 16-hour-old) were able to detect differences in the contours of two small objects (a prism and a cylinder), with both the right and the left hand (Figure 4.1). The habituation/dishabituation procedure, carried out without visual control, is an effective method for revealing babies' manual perceptive abilities. The habituation method, currently used in visual research, and adapted to the haptic modality (Streri & Pêcheux 1986) can be used from birth (Streri et al. 2000). Tactile space is separated from visual space by a cloth screen that prevents the baby from seeing his/her hands and the object, but allowing complete freedom of exploration. The experimenter puts an object into the baby's right hand and records holding time. If the holding times decrease with the repeated presentation of the object, habituation is observed. When the habituation criteria set by the experimenter are fulfilled, the test phase starts and a new object is presented

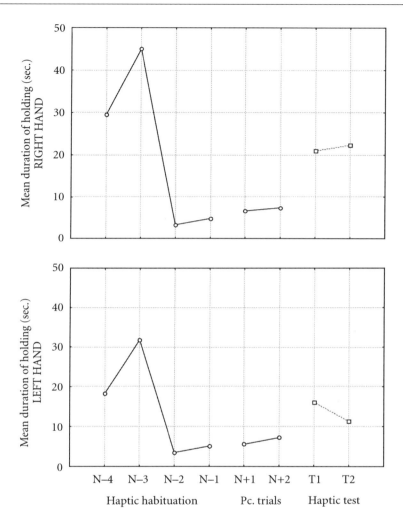

Figure 4.1. Mean duration of holding (in seconds) during haptic habituation (last four trials before criterium) and test phases of discrimination for the right and the left hands. Pc.trials = two post-criterium trials with the familiar object; T1 and T2 = two test trials with the novel object (adapted from Streri, Lhote, & Dutilleul 2000).

to the baby. The increase in holding time means that the baby has detected a change and differentiated between the two objects. This procedure, controlled by the infant, is very effective for attesting to the early discriminatory capacities of young babies. With older babies, the habituation phase is often replaced with a fixed time familiarization phase, in order to test encoding and information processing speed.

In the first semester after birth, the young baby is capable of quite good performances in the detection of object properties. Thus, Molina and Jouen (1998) showed that newborns modulate pressure on objects differing according to their texture, therefore suggesting that they detect differences between the smooth or rough aspects of surfaces. Moreover, neonates are able to compare objects varying in texture properties between hands (Molina & Jouen 2003).

Shapes – curvilinear or rectilinear, full or pierced with a hole – are well differentiated from the age of two months (Streri 1987; Streri & Milhet 1988). At this age, the baby is also capable to discriminate a volumetric object (in the shape of a reel) from a flat object (a cross) (Streri & Molina 1993). However, this does not mean that presenting different shaped objects triggers an exploratory activity that allows the baby to have a clear representation of what is being held in the hand. Probably, shape perception is global or limited to the detection of clues such as points, curves, hole or without hole, etc. The information gathered is the result of the enclosure of the object, which is an effective exploratory procedure for such a performance (Lederman & Klatzky 1987; cf. Chapter 5). When two-handed exploration is possible, from the age of four months, the baby can hold a voluminous or large-sized object. Streri and Spelke (1988) put into babies' hands an object with a ring at each end. The rings were connected in a rigid or a flexible manner (by a wooden bar or elastic). In an exploration using the shoulder-arm-hand system, the babies discriminate between the objects manipulated according to their rigid/flexible properties. In a similar way, it is possible to demonstrate that, at the same age, the baby is capable of detecting differences in the weight (13g or 47g) of objects (cf. Streri 1991, 1993).

Curiously, little research has been done during the first semester of life to examine the evolution of young infants' manual skills regarding the exploration of textures (cf. Bushnell & Boudreau 1991, 1993). Newborns exert pressure differently according to the texture of the object (Molina & Jouen 1998) and an oral exploration allows them, at the age of one month, to discriminate between a smooth and a rough pacifier (Meltzoff & Borton 1979). However, it is only at the end of the second semester that exploratory strategies specific to object texture emerge. Thus, Schellingerhout, Smitsman and van Galen (1997) showed that, from the age of eight months, blind babies use specific exploration procedures such as fingering and rubbing to examine different textures. Nevertheless, it is only at around the age of 21 months that the frequency of these skills is modulated according to different textures. Landau (1991) also showed that blind 18-month-olds use fingering when presented with textured surfaces, but use rotating movements when perceiving shapes. This behavior, as we shall see, is therefore not specific to sighted babies.

Are babies able to gather information manually concerning two properties presented simultaneously in the same object without visual control? Catherwood (1993a) examined this question in infants aged from seven to nine months. During a 30-second period, the infants explored an object characterized by shape (sphere or cube) and texture (rough or smooth). In the test phase, the infant successively manipulated two novel objects, one different in shape and the other in shape and texture. The results showed that babies are capable of considering both the shape and texture presented in objects at the same time.

Young infants are not only able to discriminate different properties of objects such as shape, texture, thickness, etc. by the hands, they can explore the space and be sensitive to different orientations of a rod. Five-month-old infants were familiarized with a vertical (or a 45°-oblique) rod held in their right hand without visual control. Then, in the haptic test phase, they were stimulated with the novel and familiar orientations in alternation. Results reveal that infants detect the discrepancies between orientations of the rod (Gentaz & Streri 2002). This result allows to investigate whether an "oblique effect", i.e. a better discrimination of the vertical orientation than of the 45° oblique orientation (cf. Chapter 8) is observed in the haptic mode as in the visual mode. Indeed, Gentaz and Streri (in press) showed recently that a haptic oblique effect is present at the age of five months.

4.   Haptic memory in infancy

It is now well established that habituation process and memory are narrowly linked revealing a form of mental representation of stimuli (Bornstein 1985, 1988). If such is the case, then the haptic memory in its manual mode is present from birth (Streri et al. 2000). Gottfried and Rose (1980) showed a haptic recognition memory for the first time in one-year-old babies. In this study, the types of manipulation were different according to the degree of familiarity or novelty of an object, and so were the sign of recognition memory. After a two-minute period of haptic familiarization without visual control, the young infants do indeed manipulate novel objects differently from familiar ones. Nevertheless, few studies have insisted on the capacity to retain information from the haptic system in memory. Catherwood (1993b) tested the robustness of the haptic memory concerning shape and texture in eight-month-old babies after a five-minute break or a haptic interference (the presentation of a new object). The babies attested to good texture memory and showed recognition of the shapes of familiar objects after the break, but not after the interference. This failure was interpreted in terms of a too close similarity in the shape of the objects used in the familiar and the interference phases. Furthermore, the duration of the familiarization phase was limited to 30 seconds of manipulation or contact. On the other hand, Lhote and Streri (1998) revealed the baby's capacity to recognize an object manually after a 30-second break at the age of two months, and after two minutes (long term memory) at the age of four months (Lhote & Streri 2003; cf. Chapter 6, §6.2.2). Nevertheless, recognition is sometimes fragile after haptic interference.

To sum up, when the haptic system is studied without visual control, its information gathering skills concerning object properties are relatively wide, both orally and manually. They do not depend on the specific exploratory procedures identified in adults (cf. Chapter 5) as Bushnell and Boudreau's (1993) analysis suggests. Indeed, from birth, the baby is capable of encoding, holding in memory, and recognizing a certain amount of information gathered on shape, substance, weight, size and volume of objects. Non-specific exploratory procedures, such as the enclosure procedure with some light pressures, are enough to explain early abilities. But obviously, it is in bimodal exploration that babies' haptic performances will develop, diversify or, on the contrary, disappear.

5.   Bimodal exploration and haptic abilities

Two important consequences result from the manual exploration of objects under visual control. The baby looks at the object it is holding from different viewpoints, but, more importantly, the baby itself initiates these changes in angle through an active manipulation. Several questions are thus raised. What are the characteristics of both oral and manual haptic exploration under visual control? Are there specific actions for each property of an object?

Ruff (1984, experiment 1) presented infants aged six, nine and twelve months with two series of six objects. Each series consisted of six 30-second familiarization trials. The study of the effects of learning over the course of the trials and their evolution according to age was based on various visual, oral and manual activities. The results revealed that oral exploration and the frequency of alternations between oral and visual exploration decrease between the ages of 9 and 12 months. Manual dexterity increases between the ages of six and nine months, whereas object rotations dominate from this age and up to the age of twelve months. The frequency of these behaviors declines during the familiarization trials, whatever the age studied. Thus, bimodal habituation is possible according to the same principle as a unimodal visual or haptic habituation (cf. also Willats 1983). In a second study, Ruff (1984, experiment 2) evaluated the change in babies' exploratory behavior when, after a period of familiarization, one of the object properties (shape, texture or weight) is modified. Babies do indeed react to changes in object characteristics. A change in weight leads to a reduction in visual exploration, whereas a change in shape triggers an increase in rotating, transferring from one hand to the other and hitting the object. A change in texture stimulates visual exploration more, along with subtler manipulation. Furthermore, Bushnell, Weinberger and Sasseville (1989) showed an increase in the duration of visual or manual exploration when the color or the temperature respectively are modified. Thus, the infants adjust or adapt their activities to object properties in order to extract the most pertinent information.

After gathering the first pieces of information about an object, more specific behavior according to the properties of objects may appear. Thus, the babies hit the floor more readily with hard objects than with soft objects (Lockman & Wright 1988). But their action also depends on the surface (hard or soft) they are playing on. For example, from the age of six months, the babies' actions on a bell are modulated according to the noise it makes, but also depend on the property of the carpet they are sitting on. In order to obtain a same effect, the babies shake the bell when on a soft surface, whereas they bang it when on a hard surface (Palmer 1989). The variability of exploratory behavior is therefore not confined to mere object properties, it also applies to the opportunities presented by the environment.

A series of studies permitted a better understanding of the precision and the efficiency of each modality – visual, oral and manual – in 5-month-old babies' play activities (Ruff et al. 1992). A first study tried to distinguish purely exploratory oral activity from other forms of oral activity. Two forms of behavior specify oral exploration. First, following mouthing, the baby regularly looks at the object. This looking is considered to function as a check on the information the baby has gathered orally. Second, the duration of this "mouthing with look after" behavior decreases in the course of familiarization, whereas non-exploratory oral activity presents fluctuating durations according to tests. A second study attempted to determine the evolution of visual, oral and manual exploratory behavior between the ages of five and eleven months. Manual examining under visual control is used at the same time as oral exploration. It involves different exploratory activities, such as skilled manipulation, applying pressure, transferring from one hand to the other or rotating the object. However, the two modes of functioning of the haptic system evolve differently when they are under visual control. Oral exploration, which performs well at the age of five months, peaks at seven months, then declines until eleven months. On the other hand, the tendency to examine objects manually and visually progresses and supplants oral exploration. After seven months, the baby rediscovers its capacity for subtly manipulating objects and extracting information like shape, texture and substance. According to the authors, this late substitution is explained by the fact that between the ages of five and seven months the visual system is busy checking newly emerging skills like reaching for and grasping objects. The hands can therefore no longer fulfill their exploratory function. Thus, at the prehensile/visual coordination stage, the mouth provisionally takes on the job of exploring objects while the hands are apparently occupied in transporting and moving objects. Streri, Gentaz and Pineau (unpublished manuscript) also showed that at around the age of five months the baby is manually no longer able to detect differences in the shape of objects when occupied in moving them. The perceptive function of the hand is disturbed by the emergence of the transporting function (cf. Streri 1993).

6.   Multimodal exploration and coordination between modalities

In multimodal exploration, it is difficult to isolate and evaluate the effects of a system's activity and its consequences on another system. Indeed, when a baby explores an object with its eyes, its hands and its mouth, the different pieces of information gathered are neither added together nor multiplied. A synthesis or a perceptive reorganization is necessary to give the object some coherence (cf. Ruff 1989). Furthermore, the bimodal exploration of objects has an important consequence: The infant must judge as equivalent certain information gathered simultaneously by the haptic and visual systems, in spite of their structural and functional specificity. How does the baby reorganize information in order to perceive a coherent unit? Do the sensory modalities compete, interfere or participate jointly to achieve a better understanding of objects? Gottfried, Rose and Bridger (1978) tested the hypothesis of cooperation between the sensory modalities for the first time in six-, nine- and twelve-month-old infants. Their aim was to determinate whether the multimodal exploration of objects permitted a better visual discrimination than a unimodal visual exploration. The babies were given three 20-second periods of familiarization, each under different conditions: a unimodal visual presentation, a bimodal presentation and a visual presentation in which the object was placed in a transparent box and thus manipulated without direct contact. The unimodal visual test involved the presentation of a familiar object and a novel object. The results showed that there is a better visual discrimination in the unimodal visual condition at the ages of six and nine months. Bimodal exploration resulted in better visual recognition only at the age of twelve months. The authors concluded from this experiment that before this age the tactile modality interferes with the visual modality regarding the efficient gathering of information about the object. Attention is apparently shared between the modalities (cf. the study of this question in adults, Chapter 12).

Several researchers have questioned this interpretation, as it does not seem very compatible with the results obtained in bimodal exploration (cf. supra). First, the duration of the familiarization period is too short and is identical in all three conditions. Although perfectly suited to the speed of visual information gathering, it is insufficient for efficient manipulation. Next, the baby's task is complicated by a change in context between the familiarization and the test phases which demands a different register of memories. This second hypothesis was put to the test in two studies (Rolfe & Day 1981; Ruff 1981). The first study, involving six-month-olds, used a procedure identical to that of Gottfried et al. (1978) for both the familiarization and the test phases. When the context was not changed, the results showed a good discrimination between the familiar and the novel object for all conditions except the presentation of the object in the transparent box. The second study stipulated the exact information allowing the object to be recognized. The object differed in the two phases, either changing color but keeping the same shape, or on the contrary, changing shape but keeping the same color. Now, color is a specifically visual property, whereas shape can be apprehended by both modalities. The duration of familiarization was six 30-second trials. In the intramodal visual condition no discrimination was observed, whereas in the bimodal exploration condition a novel object preference was apparent. This preference was evidenced more rapidly when it concerned the shape (redundant information) than the color (specific information) of the object. Thus, information gathering is more efficient when carried out jointly by the two modalities. This result was confirmed in another study by Ruff (1982) in which she compared bimodal information gathering on different object properties. She distinguished structural properties, like shape, from non-structural properties, like color. The aim was to know whether object manipulation increased visual attention or, on the contrary, had no effect, according to structural or non-structural object properties. The results showed that manipulating objects under visual control allows a good discrimination concerning texture and shape properties, but not concerning color (cf. also Steele & Pederson 1977). Although the purpose of the experiment was different, a similar result was obtained by Bushnell, Shaw and Strauss (1985). The aim was to find out how six-month-old babies recompose, in a multimodal exploration, the specific properties of the visual modality (color) and the tactual modality (temperature). Amazingly, the infants manipulated the objects longer than they looked at them. They were, as it were, tactually captivated by the temperature of the objects. This is the only case in which a tactile dominance clearly appears, thus organizing the modalities into a hierarchy. Moreover, when the temperature was modified, the duration of tactile and visual exploration changed, whereas there were no clear results when the color was modified. Thus, color is not a pertinent property in babies' bimodal exploration, whereas shape, texture and temperature attract their attention.

7. Conclusion

The whole of this research into manual exploration and tactile perception in infants leads to two conclusions. Firstly, contrary to what one might have thought, when manual activity takes place serving and controlled by vision, its exploratory capacities play a fundamental role. The hand produces visual and tactile sensory changes allowing the simultaneous extraction of perceptive invariants. The dominance of vision from the time prehensile/visual coordination sets in, a hypothesis proposed by Hatwell (1987), is not apparent in game activities, but can appear in other situations such as perceptive conflicts or intermodal transfers (cf. Chapters 11 and 12). Secondly, the baby's exploratory behaviors in the first year of life reveal the extraordinary adaptation of the young infant to its environment, but it is impossible to distinguish whether this adaptation is the cause or the consequence of these behaviors. In this sense, they reinforce Gibson's affordances theory (1979), which stipulates that actions are controlled by perception and that perception depends on the actions possible. But they are also compatible with Piaget's theory (1936/1952, 1937/1954) which proposes that the baby's actions on and in the environment allow it to obtain information which, in turn, feeds organizational action schemes and therefore leads to a greater understanding of the environment.

References

Bornstein, M. H. (1985). Habituation of attention as measure of visual information processing in human infants: Summary, systematization and synthesis. In G. Gottlieb & N. A. Krasnegor (Eds.), *Measurement of audition and vision in the first year of postnatal life: A methodological overview* (pp. 253–300). Norwood, NJ: Ablex.

Bornstein, M. H. (1998). Stability in mental development from early life: Methods, measures, models, meanings and myths. In F. Simion & G. Butterworth (Eds.), *The development of sensory, motor and cognitive capacities in early infancy. From perception to cognition* (pp. 301–332). East Sussex: Psychology Press.

Buka, S. L. & Lipsitt, L. P. (1991). Newborn sucking behavior and its relation to grasping. *Infant Behavior and Development, 14,* 59–67.

Bullinger, A. & Rochat, P. (1985). L'activité orale du nourrisson comme indice du comportement. *Comportements, 2,* 55–68.

Bushnell, E. W. & Boudreau, J. P. (1991). The development of haptic perception during infancy. In M. Heller & W. Schiff (Eds.), *The Psychology of touch* (pp. 139–161). Hillsdale, NJ: Erlbaum.

Bushnell, E. W. & Boudreau, J. P. (1993). Motor development and the mind: The potential role of motor abilities as a determinant of aspects of perceptual development. *Child Development, 64,* 1005–1021.

Bushnell, E. W., Shaw, L., & Strauss, D. (1985). Relationship between visual and tactual exploration by 6-month-olds. *Developmental Psychology, 21,* 591–600.

Bushnell, E. W., Weinberger, N., & Sasseville, A. (1989). *Interactions between vision and touch during infancy: The development of cooperative relations and specializations.* Paper presented at the biennial meeting of the Society for Research in Child Development, Kansas City, MO.

Catherwood, D. (1993a). The haptic processing of texture and shape by 7- to 9-month-old infants. *British Journal of Developmental Psychology, 11,* 299–306.

Catherwood, D. (1993b). The robustness of infant haptic memory: Testing its capacity to withstand delay and haptic interference. *Child Development, 64,* 702–710.

Erhardt, R. P. (1973). Sequential levels in development of prehension. *American Journal of Occupational Therapy, 28,* 592–596.

Gentaz, E. & Streri, A. (2002). Infant's haptic perception of orientations. *Current Psychology Letters. Behaviour, Brain and Cognition, 9,* 61–73.

Gentaz, E. & Streri, A. (in press). An oblique effect in infant's haptic perception of spatial orientations. *Journal of Cognitive Neuroscience.*

Gesell, A. (1933). Maturation and the patterning of behavior. In C. Murchison (Ed.), *A handbook of child psychology* (pp. 209–235). Worcester, MA: Clark University Press.

Gibson, E. J. & Walker, A. (1984). Development of knowledge of visual-tactual affordances of substance. *Child Development, 55,* 453–460.

Gibson, J. J. (1979). *The ecological approach to visual perception.* Boston: Houchton Mifflin Company.

Gottfried, A. W. & Rose, S. A. (1980). Tactile recognition memory in infants. *Child Development, 51,* 69–74.

Gottfried, A. W., Rose, S. A., & Bridger, W. H. (1977). Cross-modal transfer in human infants. *Child Development, 48*, 118–123.

Gottfried, A. W., Rose, S. A., & Bridger, W. H. (1978). Effects of visual, haptic and manipulatory experiences on infants' visual recognition memory of objects. *Developmental Psychology, 14*, 305–312.

Hatwell, Y. (1987). Motor and cognitive functions of the hand in infancy and childhood. *International Journal of Behavioral Development, 10*, 509–526.

Hooker, D. (1938). The origin of the grasping movement in man. *Proceeding of the American Philosophical Society, 79*, 597–606.

Humphrey, T. (1970). The development of human fetal activity and its relation to postnatal behavior. In H. Reese & L. Lipsitt (Eds.), *Advances in child development and behavior, Vol. 5.* New York: Academic Press.

Kjaer, M. & Kjaer, I. (1998). Human fetal hand size and hand maturity in the first half of the prenatal period. *Early Human Development, 50*, 193–207.

Landau, B. (1991). Spatial representation of objects in the young blind child. *Cognition, 38*, 145–178.

Lederman, S. J. & Klatzky, R. L. (1987). Hand movements: A window into haptic object recognition. *Cognitive Psychology, 19*, 342–368.

Lhote, M. & Streri, A. (1998). Haptic memory and handedness in 2-month-old infants. *Laterality, 3*, 173–192.

Lhote, M. & Streri, A. (2003). La mémoire haptique de la forme des objets chez les bébés âgés de 4 mois. *L'Année Psychologique, 103*, 33–50.

Lockman, J. J. & Wright, M. H. (1988). *A longitudinal study of banging.* Paper presented at the International Conference on Infant Studies, Washington, DC.

McGraw, M. B. (1935). *The neuromuscular maturation of the human infant.* New York: Columbia University Press.

Meltzoff, A. N. & Borton, R. W. (1979). Intermodal matching by human neonates. *Nature, 282*, 403–404.

Molina, M. & Jouen, F. (1998). Modulation of the palmar grasp behavior in neonates according to texture property. *Infant Behavior and Development, 21*, 659–666.

Molina, M. & Jouen, F. (2001). Modulation of manual activity by vision in human newborns. *Developmental Psychobiology, 38*, 123–132.

Molina, M. & Jouen, F. (2003). Haptic intramodal comparison of texture in human neonates. *Developmental Psychobiology, 42*, 378–385.

Palmer, C. F. (1989). The discriminating nature of infants' exploratory actions. *Developmental Psychology, 25*, 855–893.

Pêcheux, M.-G., Lepecq, J.-C., & Salzarulo, P. (1988). Oral activity and exploration in 1-2 month-old infants. *British Journal of Developmental Psychology, 6*, 245–256.

Piaget, J. (1936/1952). *The origins of intelligence in children.* (Translated from: J. Piaget, *La naissance de l'intelligence chez l'enfant.* Neuchâtel: Delachaux et Niestlé.). New York: International University Press.

Piaget, J. (1937/1954). *The construction of reality in the child* (Translated from J. Piaget (1954), *La construction du réel chez l'enfant.* Neuchâtel: Delachaux & Niestlé). New York: Basic Books.

Rochat, P. (1983). Oral touch in young infants: Response to variations of nipple characteristics in the first months of life. *International Journal of Behavioral Development, 6*, 123–133.

Rochat, P. (1987). Mouthing and grasping in neonates: Evidence for the early detection of what hard or soft substances afford for action. *Infant Behavior and Development, 10*, 435–449.

Rolfe, A. & Day, R. H. (1981). Effects of the similarity and dissimilarity between familiarization and test objects on recognition memory in infants following unimodal and bimodal familiarization. *Child Development, 52*, 1308–1312.

Rose, S. A., Schmidt, K., & Bridger, W. H. (1976). Changes in tactile responsivity during sleep in the newborn infant. *Developmental Psychology, 12*, 311–320.

Ruff, H. A. (1981). Effect of context on infant's responses to novel objects. *Developmental Psychology, 17*, 87–89.

Ruff, H. A. (1982). Role of manipulation in infants' response to invariant properties of objects. *Developmental Psychology, 18*, 682–691.

Ruff, H. A. (1984). Infants' manipulative exploration of objects: Effects of age and object characteristics. *Developmental Psychology, 20*, 9–20.

Ruff, H. A. (1989). The infant's use of visual and haptic information in the perception and recognition of objects. *Canadian Journal of Psychology, 43*, 302–319.

Ruff, H. A., Saltarelli, L. M., Capozzoli, M., & Dubiner, K. (1992). The differentiation of activity in infants' exploration of objects. *Developmental Psychology, 28*, 851–861.

Schellingerhout, R., Smitsman, A. W., & van Galen, G. P. (1997). Exploration of surface-textures in congenitally blind infants. *Child Care Health Review, 23*, 247–264.

Steele, D. & Pederson, D. R. (1977). Stimulus variables which affect the concordance of visual and manipulative exploration in six-month-olds. *Child Development, 8*, 104–111.

Streri, A. (1987). Tactile discrimination of shape and intermodal transfer in 2- to 3-month-old infants. *British Journal of Developmental Psychology, 5*, 213–220.

Streri, A. (1991). *Voir, atteindre, toucher. Les relations entre la vision et le toucher chez le bébé.* Paris: Presses Universitaires de France.

Streri, A. (1993). *Seeing, reaching, touching. The relations between vision and touch in infancy* (translated from A. Streri (1991), *Voir, atteindre, toucher.* Paris: Presses Universitaires de France). London: Harvester Wheatsheaf.

Streri, A. & Gentaz, E. (2003). Cross-modal recognition of shape from hand to eyes in human newborns. *Somatosensory and Motor Research, 20*, 11–16.

Streri, A., Lhote, M., & Dutilleul, S. (2000). Haptic perception in the newborn. *Developmental Science, 3*, 319–327.

Streri, A. & Milhet, S. (1988). Equivalences intermodales de la forme des objets entre la vision et le toucher chez les bébés de 2 mois. *L'Année Psychologique, 88*, 329–341.

Streri, A. & Molina, M. (1993). Visual-tactual and tactual-visual transfer between objects and pictures in 2-month-old infants. *Perception, 22*, 1299–1318.

Streri, A. & Pêcheux, M. G. (1986). Tactual habituation and discrimination of form in infancy: A comparison with vision. *Child Development, 57*, 100–104.

Streri, A. & Spelke, E. (1988). Haptic perception of objects in infancy. *Cognitive Psychology, 20*, 1–23.

Twitchell, T. E. (1965). The automatic grasping response of infants. *Neuropsychologia, 3,* 247–259.

Twitchell, T. E. (1970). Reflex mechanisms and the development of prehension. In K. Connolly (Ed.), *Mechanisms of motor skill development* (pp. 25–38). New York: Academic Press.

Willats, P. (1983). Effects of object novelty on the visual and manual exploration of infants. *Infant Behavior and Development, 6,* 145–149.

CHAPTER 5

Manual exploratory procedures in children and adults

Yvette Hatwell

The previous chapter examined manual exploration in young babies and the haptic discriminations they can perform. It is difficult to study intramodal tactile perception in infants and toddlers from the second semester of life until the age of 3–4 years, because these babies hardly tolerate that a screen prevents them from seeing what they are manipulating. Thus, we lack data concerning the evolution of manual exploration during this period. The present chapter therefore takes up this study from preschool age until adulthood.

1. Manual exploratory procedures and their consequences

1.1 Changes with age

The difficulties of young sighted children whose vision is masked and who must use their hands in a uniquely perceptive function were already reported by Piaget and Inhelder (1947) and by soviet researchers in the sixties (Zaporozhets 1965). Manual exploration is indeed partial, not very active, stereotyped and unsuitable for the task. At 3–4 years of age, in a shape discrimination task, the hand often remains immobile on the object (exploratory procedures labeled Static Contact and Enclosure by Lederman & Klatzky 1987; cf. Figure 4.1) or scratches the object discreetly. These procedures are not optimal in this case. In addition, the young child produces the same movements to evaluate the length of a rod as to discriminate shape (Abravanel 1968). Even older children do not use the most suitable procedures. Cirillo, Wapner and Rand (1967) presented 8–11-year olds with two rods attached to form an angle. One instruction asked them to indicate the longer branch of the angle, and another the type of angle (acute or obtuse). The difference in the instructions had no effect. This means that the children explored too the branches' length when the instruction concerned the angle, and the size of the angle when the branches were concerned. The adults, on the other hand, adapted their movements to the task.

In blind children, Simpkins (1979) and Simpkins and Siegel (1979) observed an improvement in haptic exploration between 4 and 7 years of age and, correlatively, an improvement in performances, and no difference was found between blindfolded sighted and congenitally blind children. Berlà and Butterfield (1977) studied the effects of training on the exploratory behavior of blind children aged 6 to 17 years. Raised drawings of simple geographical maps were presented during 30 seconds, then the participants were asked to point to the same stimulus among 4. An experimental group had three training sessions in which attention was focused on the critical parts of the figure, whereas another group had no training. As predicted, the performances of the trained group were higher than those of the untrained one. In another study, blind participants aged 11 to 19 years explored raised geographic maps (Berlà & Murr 1974). During a four minutes period training, the observers were instructed to perform only unimanual vertical exploratory movements, or only bimanual horizontal movements, or to explore freely the stimulus. A control group had no training. Performances improved after training, especially with the vertical exploration. Finally, Berlà (1981) observed that training had positive effects in 11-year-old children but not in 15-year-old ones because, at this latter age, it interferes with the proper exploratory habits already build up by these adolescents.

In adults, Davidson (1972) and Davidson and Whitson (1974) observed that the blindfolded sighted had less efficient modes of exploration than the early blind in the evaluation of the curve (concave or convex) of a vertical metal plate. The blind favored procedures implying the whole hand (enclosure and hand span) whereas the sighted used only one or two fingers (sweeping and tracing). The sighted adults thus decreased the size of their perceptual field as much as possible, whereas the blind ones enlarged it by using all their fingers. This difference was associated with unequal discrimination performances, since the blind were here more accurate than the sighted. After training and when the sighted were forced to use the same mode of exploration as the blind, the two groups gave similar results. Because they lack practice in the haptic modality, the sighted thus have a weaker capacity to process tactile data simultaneously, and they prefer a sequential mode of exploration. This is confirmed by Russier (1999) who observed the superiority of the congenitally blind over the sighted in a haptic discrimination task involving two-

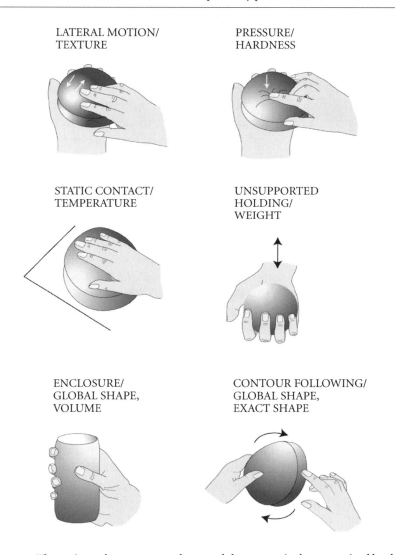

LATERAL MOTION/
TEXTURE

PRESSURE/
HARDNESS

STATIC CONTACT/
TEMPERATURE

UNSUPPORTED
HOLDING/
WEIGHT

ENCLOSURE/
GLOBAL SHAPE,
VOLUME

CONTOUR FOLLOWING/
GLOBAL SHAPE,
EXACT SHAPE

Figure 5.1. The main exploratory procedures and the properties best perceived by these procedures (adapted from Lederman & Klatzky 1987).

dimensional shapes (relief contours) when exploration was two-handed. With one-handed exploration, visual status had no significant effect.

Lederman and Klatzky (1987, 1993, 1996) asked adults to classify objects according to a given criterion, and they identified "exploratory procedures" (EPs), i.e. specific unities of movements (Figure 5.1) characterized by the quantity and the nature of the information they can provide, and therefore by the range of properties they are adapted to. Some procedures are very specialized, others are more general. Thus, *lateral motion* is uniquely adapted to texture, *unsupported holding* to weight, *pressure* to the hardness of the material. *Static contact* principally gives information on temperature and, more approximately, on shape, size, texture and hardness. *Enclosure* also gives global information on these properties, while *contour following* provides precise knowledge about shape and size, and a vaguer idea of texture and hardness. These different procedures are either necessary (compulsory for a property) or sufficient, and some of them are optimal, i.e. they have maximum efficiency for a property. Thus, lateral motion is optimal for texture, while unsupported holding is necessary and optimal for weight.

It is noteworthy that these EPs cannot be practiced simultaneously, they must be performed successively because they are not compatible motorically. Hence, it is impossible to produce simultaneously lateral motion on a surface and contour following on the edges of the object. Therefore, haptic exploration is consistently more sequential and more time-consuming than visual exploration. In addition, because these movements are intentional, a given property of the stimulus may not be perceived if the observer does not produce the exploratory procedure adapted to its processing.

Lederman and Klatzky (1993) observed two phases in adults' exploratory strategies: First come non-specialized procedures, which mobilize the whole hand and gather quite vague information on several properties. This gives a global knowledge of the unit. Then specific procedures are executed. For example, for shape, adults start by enclosing the object and then trace its contours.

The specialized nature of manual exploratory procedures has consequences on the processing of object properties, especially in children. In this book, and especially in Chapter 8, we will discuss some examples showing the effect of exploratory procedures on the processing modes of different properties. Thus, this specialization reduces incidental learning possibilities, because if an instruction does not expressly ask for a particular property to be perceived, subjects do not produce the appropriate exploratory modes and the property is not (or poorly) processed (Hatwell 1995a).

In the same way, Berger and Hatwell (1993, 1995, 1996) attributed to the characteristics of the manual exploration of children aged 5 years the fact that, in a task of free classification of objects varying by their texture and size, the results observed in the haptic modality differed from those reported in vision by different authors. When the task is performed visually, young children tend to group objects according to their "overall similarity" (holistic classification taking into account all the dimensions of the stimulus; Evans & Smith 1988; Shepp & Swartz 1976; Smith 1989). By contrast, in older children and adults, dimensional (analytic) classifications are dominant (grouping together objects sharing a value on one dimension and differing on all the others). According to Berger and Hatwell (1993, 1995, 1996), the early dominance of haptic dimensional classification in 5-year-old children stems from the fact that the different properties of the stimulus are apprehended separately by the child through specific exploratory movements. "Lateral motion", which is well adapted to perceive texture, was the most frequently exploratory procedure observed by Berger and Hatwell (1996) in young children, whereas the procedures adapted to apprehend size (enclosure and contour following) were scarcely used. Therefore, these children produced a dimensional classification taking into account the only property (texture) that their very partial exploratory movements had allowed them to perceive.

However, different observations were reported by Schwarzer, Küfer and Wilkening (1999) who did not find in children aged 4–5 years the dominance of the "lateral motion" procedure observed by Berger and Hatwell at this age. In this research studying category learning by touch, the participants were asked to categorize haptic exemplars of objects which varied in four attributes (size, shape, texture and weight) and this categorization could be either dimensional (analytic) or by overall similarity (holistic). In vision, Ward and his associates (Ward 1989; Ward & Scott 1987; Ward, Vela & Hass 1990) showed that in this condition, dimensional classification dominated even in very young children. In the haptic mode, Schwarzer et al. (1999) obtained similar results, i.e. they observed haptic dimensional responses even at 4 years of age, and these dimensional responses were predominantly based on texture. These results were consistent with those of Berger and Hatwell (1993, 1996). The inconsistencies concerned the analyses of haptic exploration. Contrary to Berger and Hatwell, Schwarzer et al. (1999) did not find a dominance of lateral motion in the young children, even in those who focused on texture in their dimensional classification. Enclosure, lateral motion and rotation (85%, 80% and 80% approximately, respectively) were the most frequently used procedures at age 4. Even contour following (60% approximately), which is well adapted to shape perception, was observed at this age. Therefore, the authors concluded that the preference for dimensional texture classification in very young children did not stem from their tendency to use predominantly the lateral motion procedure leading to a correct perception of texture only.

But many differences in the nature of the task, in the stimuli and the procedure used by Schwarzer et al. (1999) may explain why the exploratory procedures observed in the young children were not the same as those reported by Berger and Hatwell. First, Berger and Hatwell presented a free classification task whereas the participants in Schwarzer et al.'s study were asked to discover a criterion of classification already defined by the experimenter. In the first case, there were no true or false responses and no feedback, whereas in the second, a feedback was given by the experimenter after each trial during the presentation phase. It is likely that when the child was informed that his/her answer was wrong, he/she tried another criterion of classification and therefore modified the way the stimulus was explored haptically. Another major difference between Schwarzer et al.'s and Berger and Hatwell's studies concerns the nature of the stimuli and the way they are presented. Berger and Hatwell proposed wooden flat squares glued on a board whereas the objects used by Schwarzer et al. were volumetric (3D) and free, and were directly put in the hand of the child. Therefore, the occurrence of the enclosure and contour following procedures was much more probable in this latter case than when the stimuli could not be completely grasped by the hand in the air. Finally, the stimuli in Schwarzer et al.'s study varied by their size, shape, texture and weight, whereas those in Berger and Hatwell's studies varied only by their size and texture. It may be that the variations of shape, which is a much more salient property than size at age 4–5, induced exploratory procedures adapted to its apprehension. Further research should clarify these interpretations but, whatever it may be, the above discussion shows that many factors may act on haptic manual exploration.

1.2 The size of the haptic perceptual field and "field effects"

The small size of the tactile perceptual field and the voluntary modulation of its size by the observer consistently reduce "field effects", that is the interactions between the elements of a figure. Thus, certain optical illusions are not present in touch (Delboeuf illusion) as the finger can exclude error-inducing elements from its field (Gentaz & Hatwell, in press; Hatwell 1986).

This possibility of decomposing the figure into its different elements also explains why, at the age of 5, the Gestalt law of proximity does not have the "grouping" effect present in the visual modality. With their small hands, their very fine fingers and their partial and poorly active exploration, young children perceive in isolation the elements which in vision are grouped into a structured unit difficult to divide up. On the contrary, adults explore the figure as a whole and therefore the proximity of its elements has the same structural effects as in vision (Hatwell 1995b; Hatwell, Orliaguet & Brouty 1990).

1.3 Manual exploration in spatial localization tasks

The narrowness of the tactile perceptual field also has marked effects in localization tasks using large portions of the prehensile space, because it is difficult haptically to refer to an exocentric reference system based on stable external cues. When the hand is in contact with the target object, it does not benefit from a "peripheral field" having an appeal value and offering numerous perceptual cues, as it is the case in the ocular system. Thus the observer must intentionally carry out exploratory movements within the working space in order to find exterior landmarks (if there are any).

Hatwell, Osiek and Jeanneret (1973) asked four and five-year-olds to explore 12 identical small cubes, randomly fixed on the surface of a horizontal board (45 x 25 cm), in order to find those which pivoted on their vertical axis. They observed that exploratory movements were disorganized (the children apparently moved at random from one cube to another), partial (on average, only 7 or 8 cubes were actually touched) and concerned the parts of the board closest to the body. By the age of 7–9 years, the size of the area explored grows, but hand movements between cubes remain disorganized. Only adults systematically use markers allowing a structured exploration of the whole board and avoiding passing over the same point several times. However, in this experiment, neither the children nor the adults started with an overall and superficial exploration indicating the limits of the spatial field to be explored and the overall arrangement of the cubes in space. This would have allowed them to plan their exploration. All subjects proceeded from one cube to the next and, at best, they discovered the cubes on the board as they went along. When, in another experimental condition, the subjects could see the board, success was total from the age of 4 onwards. Also, from the age of four, the hand's movement between the objects (guided by vision) was very structured (along reading-type lines, or back and forth, etc.) Finally, when the same subjects performed the haptic task after the task where they could see the board, performances improved consistently, both qualitatively and quantitatively. This demonstrates that it is the lack of perception or representation of the whole of the field to be explored haptically which makes systematic exploration in the prehensile field difficult for the child.

In totally early blind children and children with residual vision aged 7 and 10 years, Ungar, Blades and Spencer (1995) analyzed manual haptic exploration in a task in which the observers were asked to explore a circular disc where 1, 3 or 5 objects were placed, and then to replace the same objects at the same place on another identical disc. Five modes of exploration were identified: 1. A mixed exploration in which the fingers and/or the palms of the hands both explored the edges of the disc and gained relative cues, i.e. an impression of the overall arrangement of each shape relative to the others; 2. Relative exploration alone; 3. Edges exploration alone; 4. Pointing and touching each shape in turn, separately; this was apparently an attempt to localize the shape in a egocentric frame of reference, since no external cues were available; 5. Vision alone, i.e. use of residual vision only without any manual exploration. Results revealed links between mode of exploration and accuracy of reproduction. Errors were lower with the mixed strategy 1 (edge and relative) than with strategies 3 (edge only) and 4 (pointing). This latter strategy leads to the poorest performances and was however dominant (75%) in the younger totally blind children. Strategy 5, in which the task was performed only with residual vision, was observed in all the younger visually impaired children and in 62% of the older ones. This exclusive use of vision was associated with a rate of errors higher than with strategies 1 and 2 (unfortunately, the authors of this research did not indicate the visual acuity of the visually impaired children. However, because all of them attended a specialized institution, it is likely that this acuity was relatively low). This shows that, even when it is seriously impaired, vision is still dominant in spatial tasks. As a result, visually impaired children should be systematically trained to use haptic exploration in addition to visual exploration.

In adults, the trajectory of the hand when exploring four objects placed in the prehensile field was studied in blindfolded sighted, early and late blind participants by Gaunet, Martinez and Thinus-Blanc (1997). The localization of five objects on a circular plate was to be memorized and, in a second phase, the subject was asked to say if one of the objects had been moved by the experimenter. Two exploratory modes were identified: A "cyclical" exploration, in which successive visits to the five different objects ended with a return to the first one visited, and a "back and forth" exploration in which the subject made repeated trajectories between the same two objects, and then explored other two objects, and so on (Figure 5.2). The percentage of correct answers was greater with the second method than with the first, as if the "back and forth" procedure consisted of firmly coding the position of two objects before going on to explore others, whereas the "cyclical" procedure leads to an overall, but approximate, apprehension of the position of the objects. Finally, it is noteworthy that early blind subjects produced more "cyclical" procedures than the late blind and the sighted and, correlatively, they were less efficient in this task than the other two groups.

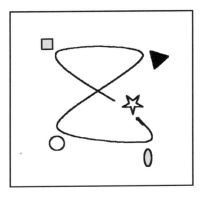

Figure 5.2. An example of "cyclic" travel (adapted from Gaunet, Martinez & Thinus-Blanc 1997).

1.4 The use of gravitational cues

When the magnitude of exploratory movements improve because of the size of the objects to be perceived, the whole hand-arm-shoulder system is involved in exploration. Whereas fingers are slightly sensible to gravitational constraints, the arms and the shoulders are considerably affected by it. Antigravitational forces must therefore be deployed to move the arm and/or to hold it in the air during exploration. The observer receives therefore proprioceptive cues resulting from the stretching or the contracting of the muscles, tendons and articulations. These cues specify the direction of the gravitational vertical and they are used to code haptically the spatial orientations in an exocentric reference frame, in which the vertical axis and the orthogonal horizontal axis act as Cartesian co-ordinates.

This was shown by Gentaz and Hatwell (1995, 1996, 1998; cf. Chapter 8) in research into the "oblique effect", i.e. the fact that the perception of the horizontal and the vertical orientations is more accurate than that of oblique orientations. This phenomenon evidences a Cartesian co-ordinate reference frame which makes the processing of oblique orientations costly, as it requires two co-ordinates to be taken into account, whereas the processing of the vertical and the horizontal is directly based on one single reference axis. This oblique effect, which is very systematically observed in vision, is present haptically only in certain conditions, precisely those in which the gravitational cues provided by exploratory movements are available and prominent. This is another example showing that, in the haptic modality, the mode of exploration determines the type of coding carried out.

1.5 Kinetic effects: "Dynamic touch"

A particular type of haptic perception concerns the activity of the hand when it grasps an object at one end and rotates it in space. The lifting of the object necessitates the production of forces to oppose the resistance caused by the object's mass, and these forces modify the state of the muscles, tendons and articulations of the active limb. Turvey, Solomon and their associates (Solomon & Turvey 1988; Turvey 1996; Turvey & Carello 1995) showed that several properties, such as the length and orientation of a bar, may be perceived via these wielding movements and they analyzed the information provided by kinetics, that is by the association of forces and movements. Referring to Gibson (1966), they looked for the invariant which would account for this perception, and identified it in the moment of inertia. The moment of inertia is a measure of an object resistance to its rotation and it decreases as the axis of rotation approaches the center of the mass. As the rotational forces on an object can be exerted in several possible directions, there are several moments of inertia, the combination of which, under certain conditions, allows an "inertia tensor" to be calculated. This tensor quantifies the rotational inertia of an object (Solomon 1988; Solomon & Turvey 1988) and determines the observer's perceptual estimations. A long series of experiments led by Turvey and Solomon validate this point of view. In the simplest one, for example, a bar held at one end seems longer if a weight is added to the other end, and this overestimation decreases when the weight is placed closer to the held end, because the value of the inertia tensor in the wrist is changed in this condition.

Wielding is a very particular form of haptic perception which will not be studied in the present book. In this perception, the kinesthetic element dominates and the cutaneous element is greatly reduced. In addition, it requires that an object be small enough to be lifted by one hand. It is likely that this form of perception is used in daily life without awareness.

2. Haptic exploration in bimodal situations

In most daily situations, vision and touch function simultaneously. How, then, are tasks shared out? Does manual exploration provide supplementary data to vision? Does the redundancy of visual and haptic information constitute a protection against perceptive errors?

Numerous studies show that when vision allows access to information about geometric properties (size, shape, etc.), the haptic system is not spontaneously activated. The hand simply assures the functions of grasping and transporting the object, so that all its faces are presented to the eye (Abravanel 1972, 1973; cf. Hatwell 1986, 1987). This is true both in children and in adults when the test which follows presentation is a visual one. When this test is tactile, children continue to explore in a visual mode only, whereas adults also explore the object manually and apply adequate exploratory procedures to it. These observations emphasize the dominance of vision in the spatial domain, which will often be apparent in this book. On the other hand, when texture has to be perceived, the spontaneous mobilization of the haptic system is far more systematic (Klatzky, Lederman & Matula 1993).

The question is whether bimodal exploration (simultaneous visual and haptic exploration), when used, is more efficient than unimodal object exploration. In the spatial domain (geometric shapes) and when the test is visual, performances following a bimodal V + H presentation are not different from those following a unimodal visual V presentation. This suggests that the haptic system does not provide additional data as compared to what is available by vision. In a study comparing unimodal and bimodal shape presentation followed by a unimodal or bimodal test, Walsh (1973) found for example that the weakest performances were in the unimodal H – H condition (haptic presentation and haptic test), and that when vision was possible during the test, the bimodal V + H presentation was not different from the unimodal visual V presentation. Conversely, when the test was a unimodal haptic H one, a bimodal V + H presentation of the stimulus considerably improved recognition. We once again observe the superiority of vision over touch in the spatial domain. The situation is different for texture discrimination, since Heller (1982) and Jones and O'Neil (1985) found no differences between the visual and haptic unimodal conditions and the bimodal conditions.

In the above mentioned studies, the observers were asked to explore objects both visually and haptically, but there was no check on what they actually did. Klatzky, Lederman and Matula (1993) studied this question and proposed three possible models of working. The first, called "visual dominance", proposes that visual analysis is exhausted before any attempt to initiate haptic exploration. Haptic exploration occurs only when the visual analysis fails to allow decision. In the other case, the object is left untouched. In the second model, called "visual preview", an initial brief visual analysis serves to produce a response if enough information is obtained. If an immediate response is not possible, the observer selects visual or haptic exploratory procedures to provide further information. These two models are serial since haptic exploration is initiated only after a preliminary visual analysis. The third model is a parallel model. In it, the two modalities are activated separately and function as independent modules. If visual exploration allows the necessary information to be gathered before the haptic exploratory procedure has been selected, then the haptic modality will not be used.

In order to find out a subject's way of working, the latency between the visual presentation of the stimulus and the initiation of haptic exploration is measured. In the visual dominance model, this latency is equal to that observed in a unimodal visual inspection condition, as the subject does not use haptic exploration in the bimodal condition. In the preview model, as well as in the parallel model, the preview time is lower than the response time observed in the unimodal visual condition. In accordance with Klatzky et al.'s predictions (1993), results showed that, for geometric properties, the haptic system is scarcely used as predicted by the visual dominance model. But for material properties (texture, hardness) the preview model best accounts for observations.

This shows that both modalities are complementary: According to the domain considered and because the modalities are not equally efficient in the perception of the different properties of objects, the haptic system is mobilized only if the unimodal visual information, generally richer and more economical, proves insufficient for resolving the problem posed.

3.   Conclusion

In examining the characteristics of children's and adults' manual exploration, we have insisted on the specialization of exploratory procedures according to the property to be apprehended, the motor incompatibility of these procedures, the exiguity of the tactual perceptive field affecting the structural organization of the configurations, and finally the use by the haptic system of gravitational and kinetic cues provided by arm movements. We have also observed that in a bimodal situation, i.e. when vision and touch are simultaneously available, the haptic system is scarcely used in spatial tasks, but that it is activated far more often in the discrimination of material object properties (texture, hardness).

These analyses showed that perception and action are narrowly linked in the haptic function because, more than in other modalities, exploratory actions determine what is perceived and how it is perceived. Haptic perception is therefore strongly dependent on the development of the sensory and motor organs involved in exploration which mature slowly. It relies too on the capacities of working memory, as data picked up successively and laboriously by the hand must be stored and then integrated into a relational whole. It is also tributary to the subject's general cognitive organization, which partially determines the quality of the exploration (adaptation, coherence, etc.). The evolution of this exploration with age is therefore more marked in touch than in vision.

Section 3 of this book will examine in detail the perceptual efficiency of touch. It will show that touch is very efficient in the perception of the texture and the hardness of materials, whereas it is less so in the perception of space. Pick and Pick (1966), Pick (1974), Freides (1974) and Hatwell (1986) insisted on the functional specialization of the modalities: Each modality excels in the processing of certain properties and is less efficient in others. Lederman and Klatzky (1993, 1996) developed this idea and showed that, because of its exploratory mode, touch is not specialized in spatial perception (vision excels in this domain) but rather in the perception of material properties. This specialization is doubtless explained by the simplicity of the optimal exploratory procedures necessary to perceive texture and hardness. This simplicity is confirmed by the fact that adapted manual exploration of texture was observed from the age of 4–6 months by Morhange-Majoux, Cougnot and Bloch (1997). In addition, studies of Molina and Jouen (1998, 2001, 2003), already described in Chapter 4, showed that even newborns modify their grasping according to the texture of the grasped object and can discriminate between soft and rough textures. By contrast, the optimal exploratory procedures allowing the perception of geometric properties require time coordinated and complex movements. The rest of this book will confirm the role of exploratory procedures in haptic functioning.

References

Abravanel, E. (1968). The development of intersensory patterning with regard to selected spatial dimensions. *Monographs of the Society for Research in Child Development, 33,* 1–52.

Abravanel, E. (1972). How children combine vision and touch when perceiving the shape of objects. *Perception and Psychophysics, 12,* 171–175.

Abravanel, E. (1973). Division of labor between eye and hand when perceiving shape. *Neuropsychologia, 11,* 207–211.

Berger, C. & Hatwell, Y. (1993). Dimensional and overall similarity classifications in haptics: A developmental study. *Cognitive Development, 8,* 495–516.

Berger, C. & Hatwell, Y. (1995). Development of analytic vs. global processing in haptics: The perceptual and decisional determinants of classification skills. *British Journal of Developmental Psychology, 13*, 143–162.

Berger, C. & Hatwell, Y. (1996). Developmental trends in haptic and visual free classifications: Influence of stimulus structure and exploration on decisional processes. *Journal of Experimental Child Psychology, 63*, 447–465.

Berlà, E. P. (1981).Tactile scanning and memory for a spatial display by blind students. *Journal of Special Education, 15*, 341–350.

Berlà, E. P. & Butterfield, L. H. (1977). Tactual distinctive feature analysis: Training blind students in shape recognition and locating shapes on a map. *Journal of Special Education, 11*, 335–346.

Berlà, E. P. & Murr, M. J. (1974). Searching tactual space. *Education of Visually Handicapped, 6*, 49–58.

Cirillo, L., Wapner, S., & Rand, G. (1967). Differentiation of haptic exploration in two age groups. *Psychonomic Science, 9*, 467–468.

Davidson, P. W. (1972). Haptic judgments of curvature by blind and sighed humans. *Journal of Experimental Psychology, 93*, 43–55.

Davidson, P. W. & Whitson, T. T. (1974). Haptic equivalence matching of curvature by blind and sighted humans. *Journal of Experimental Psychology, 102*, 687–690.

Evans, P. M. & Smith, L. B. (1988). The development of identity as a privilege relation in classification: Why similar is not similar enough. *Cognitive Development, 3*, 265–284.

Freides, D. (1974). Human information processing and sensory modality: Crossmodal functions, information complexity, memory and deficit. *Psychological Bulletin, 81*, 284–310.

Gaunet, F., Martinez, & Thinus-Blanc, C. (1997). Early-blind subjects' spatial representation of manipulatory space: Exploratory strategies and reaction to change. *Perception, 26*, 345–366.

Gentaz, E. & Hatwell, Y. (1995). The haptic "oblique effect" in children's and adults' perception of orientation. *Perception, 24*, 631–646.

Gentaz, E. & Hatwell, Y. (1996). Role of gravitational cues in the haptic perception of orientation. *Perception and Psychophysics, 58*, 1278–1292.

Gentaz, E. & Hatwell, Y. (1998). The haptic oblique effect in the perception of rod orientation by blind adults. *Perception and Psychophysics, 60*, 157–167.

Gentaz, E. & Hatwell, Y. (in press). Geometrical haptic illusions: Role of exploratory movements in the Müller-Lyer, Vertical-Horizontal and Delboeuf illusions. *Psychonomic Bulletin and Review.*

Gibson, J. J. (1966). *The senses considered as perceptual systems.* Boston: Houghton Mifflin Compagny.

Hatwell, Y. (1986). *Toucher l'espace. La main et la perception tactile de l'espace.* Lille: Presses Universitaires de Lille.

Hatwell, Y. (1987). Motor and cognitive functions of the hand in infancy and childhood. *International Journal of Behavioral Development, 10*, 509–526.

Hatwell, Y. (1995a). Children's memory for location and object properties in vision and haptics: Automatic or attentional processing? *CPC – Current Psychology of Cognition, 14*, 47–71.

Hatwell, Y. (1995b). Le développement des relations entre la vision et le toucher chez l'enfant et l'adulte: implications pédagogiques pour le déficient visuel. In A. Safran & A. Assimacopoulos (Eds.), *Le déficit visuel* (pp. 45–54). Paris: Masson.

Hatwell, Y., Orliaguet, J. P., & Brouty, G. (1990). Effects of object properties, attentional constraints and manual exploratory procedures on haptic perceptual organization: A developmental study. In H. Bloch & B. Bertenthal (Eds.), *Sensory-motor organization and development in infancy and early childhood* (pp. 315–335). Dordrecht: Klumer Academic Publishers.

Hatwell, Y., Osiek, C., & Jeanneret, V. (1973). L'exploration perceptive tactile d'un ensemble d'objets chez l'enfant et chez l'adulte. *L'Année Psychologique, 73*, 419–441.

Heller, M. A. (1982). Visual and tactual texture perception: Intersensory cooperation. *Perception and Psychophysics, 31*, 339–344.

Jones, B. & O'Neil, S. (1985). Combining vision and touch in texture perception. *Perception and Psychophysics, 37*, 66–72.

Klatzky, R. L., Lederman, S. J., & Matula, D. E. (1993). Haptic exploration in the presence of vision. *Journal of Experimental Psychology: Human Perception and Performance, 19*, 726–743.

Lederman, S. J. & Klatzky, R. L. (1987). Hand movements: A window into haptic object recognition. *Cognitive Psychology, 19*, 342–368.

Lederman, S. J. & Klatzky, R. L. (1993). Extracting object properties through haptic exploration. *Acta Psychologica, 84*, 29–40.

Lederman, S. J. & Klatzky, R. (1996). Action for perception: Manual exploratory movements for haptically processing objects and their features. In A. M. Wing, P. Haggard, & J. R. Flanagan (Eds.), *Hand and brain. The neurophysiology and psychology of hand movements* (pp. 431–446). New York: Academic Press.

Morhange-Majoux, F., Cougnot, P., & Bloch, H. (1997). Hand tactual exploration of textures in infants from 4 to 6 months. *Journal of Early Development and Parenting, 6*, 127–135.

Piaget, J. & Inhelder, B. (1947/1967). The child's conception of space. (Translated from: *La représentation de l'espace chez l'enfant*. Paris: Presses Universitaires de France). New York: W.W. Norton.

Pick, A. D. & Pick, H. L. (1966). A developmental study of tactual discrimination in blind and sighted children and adults. *Psychonomic Science, 6*, 367–368.

Pick, H. L. (1974). Visual coding of non-visual spatial information. In R. B. MacLeod & H. L. Pick (Eds.), *Perception* (pp. 153–165). Ithaca, NY: Cornell University Press.

Russier, S. (1999). Haptic discrimination of two-dimensional raised-line shapes by blind and sighted adults. *Journal of Visual Impairment and Blindness, 93*, 421–426.

Shepp, L. B. & Swartz, K. B. (1976). Selective attention and the processing of integral and nonintegral dimensions: A developmental study. *Journal of Experimental Child Psychology, 22*, 73–85.

Simpkins, K. E. (1979). Tactual discrimination of shapes. *Journal of Visual Impairment and Blindness, 73*, 93–101.

Simpkins, K. E. & Siegel, A. J. (1979). The blind's child construction of the projective straight line. *Journal of Visual Impairment and Blindness, 73*, 233–238.

Smith, L. B. (1989). A model of perceptual classification in children and adults. *Psychological Review, 7*, 811–824.

Schwarzer, G., Küfer, I., & Wilkening, F. (1999). Learning categories by touch: On the development of holistic and analytic processing. *Memory and Cognition, 27,* 868–877.

Solomon, H. Y. (1988). Movement produced invariants in haptic exploration: An example of self-organizing information-driven, intentional system. *Human Movement Science, 7,* 201–223.

Solomon, H. Y. & Turvey, M. T. (1988). Haptically perceiving the distances reachable with hand-held objects. *Journal of Experimental Psychology: Human Perception and Performance, 14,* 404–427.

Turvey, M. T. (1996). Dynamic touch. *American Psychologist, 51,* 1134–1152.

Turvey, M. T. & Carello, C. (1995). Dynamic touch. In W. Epstein & S. Rogers (Eds.), *Handbook of perception and cognition: Perception of space and motion* (pp. 401–490). San Diego, CA: Academic Press.

Ungar, S. Blades, M., & Spencer, C. (1995). Mental rotation of a tactile layout by young visually impaired children. *Perception, 24,* 891–900.

Walsh, J. K. (1973). Effect of visual and tactual stimulation on learning abstract forms: A replication. *Bulletin of Psychonomic Science, 2,* 357–359.

Ward, T. B. (1989). Analytic and holistic modes of processing in category learning. In B. E. Shepp & S. Ballasteros (Eds.), *Object perception: Structure and process* (pp. 387–419). Hillsdale, NJ: Erlbaum

Ward, T. B. & Scott, J. (1987). Analytic and holistic modes of learning family-resemblance concepts. *Memory and Cognition, 15,* 42–54.

Ward, T. B., Vela, E. & Hass, S. D. (1990). Children and adults learn family-resemblance categories analytically. *Child Development, 61,* 593–605.

Zaporozhets, A. V. (1965). The development of perception in the preschool child. *Monographs of the Society for Research on Child Development, 30,* 82–102.

CHAPTER 6

Handedness and manual exploration

Arlette Streri

1. Introduction

Since human beings have two hands which do not interact in the same way with the environment, the emergence and evolution of manual skill in children has always been a controversial topic in philosophers, anatomists, biologists and psychologists for centuries (cf. Harris 1983). The question as to why the great majority of humans (between 85% and 95%) show a right-handed preference in numerous activities, such as writing, drawing, teeth brushing, etc. and, conversely, a left-handed preference in perceptive activities, remains a polemical subject today.

Given the interest in manual skill that has been shown over the years, it is surprising to note that the question of its origin in babies was first studied only two decades ago (cf. Young, Segalowitz, Corter, & Trehub 1983). One of the main reasons for this is that the emergence of manual skill was examined as an epiphenomenona linked to language acquisition, and not really studied as a behavior in its own right. Yet the question is important because behavioral asymmetries are regarded as a reflection of the asymmetries in the working of the two hemispheres. The demonstration of these asymmetrical behaviors in babies, and indeed fetuses, would be a sign of an early functional specialization of the brain hemispheres. However, the nature of the relationship between functional asymmetries, brain morphology and behaviors at the beginning of a child's development are still not widely known. But, thanks to recent methods in functional brain imagery (cf. Chapter 3), this relationship has become visible directly and is no longer inferred from clinical or experimental observations. There are two main approaches to brain dissymmetry or hemispherical specialization (cf. Bradshaw & Nettleton 1981). In the first, brain dissymmetry is based on the type of material to be handled. In this case, it seems that the left hemisphere is specialized in the sequential handling of information, and more particularly in linguistic data, whereas the right hemisphere is specialized in the handling of spatial data. This dichotomy has principally been studied via two sensory systems, vision for spatial data, and hearing for linguistic data. In the second approach, brain dissymmetry is based on the way the information is handled, globally or analytically. The left hemisphere works in a more analytical, sequential, serial and focal way and uses this skill to handle verbal data. The right hemisphere works in a more global, simultaneous, parallel and holistic way and is thus better adapted to the handling of spatial data. The study of the visual and hearing modalities has also provided answers in this second approach.

The haptic modality has a different status from the visual and hearing modalities, and certain difficulties arise when faced with these two dichotomous approaches (Verjat 1988). On the one hand, the arm-hand system fulfils two functions, the first one is perceptive and the second is instrumental in transporting objects in space. On the other hand, the manual exploration of objects involves a perception/motor coupling difficult to dissociate. Thus, for the majority of people, the motor and sequential skills which emerge during writing activities, and also during exploration tasks, are achieved better by the right hand. These activities, in a similar way to the auditory perception of word sounds, should be taken care of by the left hemisphere. Otherwise, the haptic modality apprehends spatial properties of objects (shape, orientation, localization; cf. Chapter 8) in the same way as vision, and this function should be taken care of by the right hemisphere. The study of the haptic system is also contradictory regarding the global *vs.* analytical handling of data. The arm-hand system apprehends the subject's near external space (localization and object taking) and the space of the object (shape and orientation). The right hemisphere should play a dominant role in these activities. But as a contact modality, the hand apprehends spatial data sequentially, and hardly in a holistic way. The left hemisphere should therefore also intervene in this function. How can the moment when the hand is treating information globally be distinguished from the moment when it is detecting more local information? How can spatial data handling be distinguished from sequential handling? Is one hand more skilled in the haptic perception of shape and orientation, whereas the other is more skilled in fine motor activities?

Healey, Liederman and Geschwind (1986) proposed that the adult manual skill be characterized according to the musculature involved in carrying out a task (distal or proximal muscles). With regard to the arm-hand complex, the distal musculature, limited to the hand, is involved in fine manipulation movements and is strongly lateralized. Steenhuis and Bryden (1989) and Bryden,

Singh, Steenhuis and Clarkson (1994) contest this classification, suggesting that it is the complexity of the gesture which should be considered, rather than the muscles involved in its organization. For example, fewer motor skills are necessary to pick up an object than to manipulate or use it. The picking up of an object is also characterized by a less lateralized hand preference than using or manipulating tools. If we are interested in hemispherical specialization in haptic activities, and if we want to know when it emerges, we must direct ourselves towards the study of the fine perceptive/motor performances of the hand, and not towards those mobilizing the global arm-hand motor system.

2.   Handedness in infancy

2.1 Motor asymmetries in infancy

Researchers into early childhood were at first interested in motor and posture asymmetries because they are easily observable and quantifiable – take for example head orientation preference, hand-mouth coordination, postural asymmetry such as A.T.R.N., etc. Moreover, a large range of manual motor responses are possible for a single visual target. The reaching for and the picking up of objects have also led to numerous observations. Looking at all of these behaviors, it emerges that babies tend to prefer their right hand for picking up an object and for putting their thumb in their mouth, and tend to orient their head to the right. However, up to the age of one year this tendency is not very stable and changes in preference are often observed. These fluctuations are partly dependent on the transversal studies carried out, and serious longitudinal studies would clear up this question. Authors opinions diverge widely as to the age that handedness in its adult form sets in. The markers proposed range from 13 months (Bates, O'Connell, Vaid, Sledge, & Oakes 1986) to eight years (Gesell & Ames 1947). Factors linked to the diversity of activities, postures, object properties and other variables linked to the subject and his/her culture account for such a difference in estimations (cf. Hopkins & Rönnqvist 1998; Young 1990).

Studies focusing on fine manual skills in young babies are rare, and can easily be summed up (cf. Table 6.1). They generally involve recording the object holding duration according to two conditions. In the one-handed condition, an object is put into one of the baby's hands, and then into the other, and the holding time is recorded for each presentation. Each hand is mobilized alternately during two or three sequences according to studies. This alternating procedure, initiated by Caplan and Kinsbourne (1976), differs from the tactile habituation procedure in which the object is successively presented to the same hand (Streri & Pêcheux 1986; cf. Chapter 4). In the two-handed condition, two identical objects are put simultaneously into each hand, and the holding time is recorded for each hand.

The results reveal that in the one-handed condition the holding time is longer for the right hand than for the left hand (Caplan & Kinsbourne 1976; Hawn & Harris 1983; Petrie & Peters 1980; Streri & Gouarir 1996). Such a difference does not seem to be observed at birth (Strauss 1982). However, grasping strength is also greater on the right than on the left, and this from the age of two weeks (Petrie & Peters 1980). Thus, an asymmetry favoring the right hand is observed from the first weeks of life. This asymmetry may reflect an early dominance of the left hemisphere (Lockman & Wright 1988). In the two-handed condition, the difference in holding times between the two hands is no longer so great. The right hand holds the object for a shorter time than in the one-handed condition, as if it were disturbed by the left hand's simultaneous activity. This difference in the object holding times only becomes significant from the age of five or six months (Hawn & Harris 1983; Streri & Gouarir 1996). Caplan & Kinsbourne (1976) accounted for these results by suggesting the existence of an inhibition process between the two hemispheres. The left hemisphere may inhibit the right hemisphere when they are activated simultaneously or are competing in the same task.

2.2   Perceptual haptic asymmetries in infancy

The study of haptic perceptual asymmetries in babies presents serious limits. It may seem easy to study the relative efficiency of the left hand/right hemisphere and right hand/left hemisphere complex as each hand is in liaison with the contralateral hemisphere and insofar as the maturation of the *corpus callosum* (which acts as an exchange route between the hemispheres) is immature in infants and that the myelinization of this weft of fibers does not occur until late in childhood (Yakolev & Lecours 1967). However, subcortical structures may nevertheless play a role in the inter-hemispherical transfer of information. Constraints in experimental conditions also limit the interpretation of observations. The immobilization of the hands would be too great a discomfort for the baby, and therefore arm movements must be taken into account during manual exploration of objects. Moreover, not knowing whether the baby will be a right or left-handed adult, the experimenter unavoidably introduces a bias into the constitution of samples, which can mask important phenomena. Finally,

Table 6.1. One or two-handed holding time in seconds for the left and/or the right hand

Authors' names	Objet	Number of Trials (max. duration)	Age	One handed holding		Two handed holding	
				Right hand	Left hand	Right hand	Left hand
Caplan & Kinsbourne (1976)	Rattle	4 × 2 (150 sec)	2.7 months	*61.88 sec*	*40.71 sec*	44.58 sec	35.64 sec
Petrie & Peters (1980)							
– grasp force	Ball	3 × 2 (150 sec)	17/105 days	R > L			
– holding duration	Rattle	4 sessions		*36.6 sec*	29 sec	25.5 sec	25.2 sec
Strauss (1982)	Tongue depressor	3 × 2 (180 sec)	3.3 days	10.7 sec	13.3 sec	—	—
			9.5 weeks	26.2 sec	29.5 sec		29 sec
Hawn & Harris (1983)	Doll	4 × 2 (150 sec)	2 months	*54 sec*	35 sec	35 sec	
Streri & Gouarir (1996)	Doll	3 × 2 (120 sec)	5 months	*110 sec*	*67 sec*	*85 sec*	*55 sec*
	Cube vs. Tétrahedron	10 × 2	6 months	*129 sec*	*82 sec*	*108 sec*	*81 sec*
			6 months	*330 sec*	*156 sec*	—	—

The numbers in *italic* type show a difference between right hand-left hand holding times which is significant at p < .05

during the object exploration activities, how can motor actions be dissociated from perceptive actions?

In previous research, the accent was placed on the motor aspect of grasping rather than the perceptive aspect. It is towards the latter that Streri and Gouarir (1996, Experiment 2) directed their research. Indeed, the authors remarked that in the one-handed task (Experiment 1) there was a reduction in holding time comparable to that obtained during haptic habituation, and this after just three alternated presentation trials. This result suggests that information is gathered concerning object shape. In the second experiment, six-month-old babies were presented with the same object up to twenty times according to an alternating procedure. In order to find out whether the reduction in holding time was due or not to motor fatigue, a novel object was presented to each hand after the familiarization phase. An increase in holding time for the novel object allows us to draw the conclusion that there is discrimination and therefore a manual perceptive activity. The results showed that the right hand presented longer holding times than the left hand in all trials, confirming the results already given. But habituation was noted after the second trial for the left hand, whereas it was evidenced more slowly for the right hand. When a novel object was presented, discrimination was observed for the left hand, but not for the right hand. Finally, a qualitative analysis of the baby's actions showed that it is often the right hand that transports the object in space. Thus, the results seem to reveal the more perceptive aspects of the left hand (right hemisphere). At the age of six months, the right hand (left hemisphere) is preferred for the durable holding of objects and carrying out instrumental tasks.

The alternating procedure favors the right-handed holding of the objects and thus the motor aspect of grasping. But this procedure could also weaken the left hand and make it less skilled in holding objects. If a habituation procedure is applied, are differences observed in the way the objects are manipulated? Segond and Streri (1994) showed that in a habituation procedure without visual control applied to both hands, babies from the age of two months collect information about object shape and detect changes in shape with both the right and the left hand. The perceptive performances of both hands are thus equivalent. Recently, Streri, Lhote and Dutilleul (2000) found an analogous result in newborns. On the other hand, the development of these perceptual capacities diverges according to the hand solicited. A reduction in handling time is observed for the left hand in four and six-month-old babies, whereas older babies seem to lose the capacity to discriminate objects with their right hand (Segond & Streri 1996). Therefore, the left hand progresses in its capacity to treat the surface of objects (right hemisphere), whereas the right hand tends to lose this skill to the benefit of the function of localization and transporting objects in space (left hemisphere).

If, in addition to discrimination, important cognitive skills such as the baby's haptic memory are examined, signs of laterality are evidenced from the age of two months (Lhote & Streri 1998). In this experiment, after the manual habituation of an object, memory is evaluated according to three conditions: After haptic interference (the presentation of a novel object), after a thirty-second break, and without a break. Generally, the babies retain information better after left-handed handling than after right-handed handling. Nevertheless, a gender effect is observed. Haptic memory is present only in boys, both after a break and under certain conditions after interference. In girls, recognition memory is established after interference, but only for the left hand. This result is ascribable to the speed of information handling, which is particularly slow in girls when the left hand is solicited. Two months later, in 4-month-old infants, these discrepancies between hands and between gender are less clear (Lhote & Streri 2003). Asymmetrical performances in haptic memory seems transient in the course of development.

Pineau and Streri (1990) found that 5-month-old infants detect an unseemly element inside a complex object. In consequence, infants are able to process the contour of an object and also the details inside it. In order to demonstrate a manual specialization in the global versus analytical information processing, four-month-old babies carried out a tactile discrimination task between two objects: a square with concave or raised details and a disc with the same type of details. The "global" group had to differentiate the contour (the details remaining invariant), whereas the "detail" group had to differentiate the concave or raised aspect of the elements situated on the surface of the objects (the contour remaining identical). The right and left hands of each baby were stimulated. The babies seem to detect rather the difference of details with their right hand and detect rather the change of contours with their left hand (Streri 2002). Thus, when infants are haptically presented with complex objects, a manual specialization in the global vs. analytical processing of shapes may be shown.

3.   Manual exploration and handedness in children

3.1 Motor skills and manual laterality

In the same way as for research concerning babies, the motor or instrumental aspect of manual skills has been the subject of much research in children. The lateralization process stands out and becomes more and more evident in the course of development. However, faced with great variations and even contradictions in the results obtained, the dichotomy between manual preference and manual performance has become prominent in the literature. Manual preference is revealed through the use of the dominant hand for carrying out simple and current tasks and allows a distinction to be made between right-handed, left-handed and ambidextrous people, whereas manual performance permits the study of hemispherical laterality and the advantages taken by one or the other of the hemispheres in more complex or unusual tasks. Manual preference and manual performance are two separate dimensions of manual skills (Porac & Coren 1981). This dichotomy is justified insofar as, in an adult population, performance scores are distributed according to a normal curve, whereas preference scores present a j-shaped distribution. Moreover, preference and performance indexes are not always perfectly correlated. This dichotomy, which is not suitable for studies of babies (what constitutes a simple or current task for a baby?), clears up certain results concerning children and adults.

Manual preference is evaluated in children via about ten activities such as drawing with a pencil, brushing the teeth, doing one's hair, hitting with a hammer, throwing a ball, etc. Bimanual tasks are also proposed, such as cutting with scissors or opening a bottle. These tests reveal a manual preference from the age of one year and up to the age of four years. Nevertheless, this asymmetry in favor of one hand or the other is more or less pronounced according to the activity proposed. The using of a pencil or the throwing of a ball are very asymmetrical activities and allow the classification of children as well as adults as left- or right-handed. It is even possible to calculate a laterality index from the results obtained for the different items, taking into account the number of activities carried out by the right or the left hand. One simply has to relate the difference between the number of items carried out by one hand or the other to the total number of items ($LI = R - L/R + L$). The laterality index obtained can also be associated with measures of eye laterality and footedness. There are standard handedness tests for children, such as that of Auzias (1975) and of Porac and Coren (1981) (see for a review Fagard 2001).

Performance laterality is revealed in children in peg-moving situations (Annett 1970a). From the age of three and a half, children carry out this type of task more quickly with their right hand. Other situations require the children to tap out a rhythm given by a metronome (Wolff 1977) and evaluate the children's handedness. If the preferred hand is not the best performer in all tasks, one can question whether preference asymmetry is also revealed in performance. In the peg-moving task, Annett observed that right and left-handed subjects are quicker with their preferred hand, whereas the ambidextrous are as quick with one hand as with the other (Annett 1970a, 1970b, 1985). In a tapping task, Carlier, Dumont, Beau and Michel (1993) showed that right-handed girls are more lateralized in this test than left-handed boys. The left and right-handed are more clearly differentiated in the tapping speed than in variability. Thus, the different measures of laterality seem to be quite well correlated in children (cf. Fagard 2001).

3.2 Perception and handedness

Haptic perception tasks can be sorted into two categories: the identification of two or three-dimensional forms and somaesthetic sensitivity. This dichotomy corresponds to the distinction usually made between active and passive touching. Perceptive laterality has been studied in children in intra- and intermodal transfer situations, known to reveal important perceptive-cognitive skills (cf. Chapter 12). The basic experimental outline consists of a tactile presentation of a stimulus followed by a recognition via the tactile channel, or more often via the visual channel. The stimuli may be presented successively to each hand (monohaptic condition) or simultaneously to both hands (dichaptic condition). Finally, the duration of the presentation may vary from one to thirty seconds, the number of objects to be compared from one (identical/different) to 40 and the subject's response may be manual or verbal. The type of stimuli may also vary widely according to studies (cf. Summers & Lederman 1990).

Originally, the hypothesis was that the simultaneous manual presentation of different stimuli (dichaptic procedure) would create a competition between the hemispheres and would provoke perceptive asymmetries revealing which one is the most efficient for the processing carried out. But Flanery and Balling (1979) showed that successive intramodal stimulation caused similar asymmetries. The following logic underlies these experiments: If the children (or the adults) show a superior tactile or visual recognition of stimuli after manipulating them with the left hand rather than the right hand, then one can conclude that the right hemisphere predominates for the spatial processing of haptic data. The subjects' motor skills are generally controlled by means of a questionnaire or a manual preference test which strengthens the asymmetric character of the situation and guarantees the homogeneity of the studied population. We will limit our discussion to shape perception (for orientation and dot configurations, cf. Verjat 1988).

Witelson (1974, 1976) was the first to reveal right hemisphere specialization for the haptic processing of spatial data. According to the dichaptic procedure, which she initiated and tested, the children simultaneously felt two differently shaped objects, one object in each hand, with the index and middle fingers and without seeing the objects. The exploration duration was limited to ten seconds. The subjects were then asked to pick out these two forms from among several others, presented visually. The results showed that the boys aged from six to twelve years more accurately identified shapes previously explored by their left hand than their right hand. However, the girls showed no difference between the two hands. Other research found a left hand advantage for both sexes at the same age (Coiffi & Kandel 1979), whereas Verjat (1988) observed a manual perceptive dissymmetry favoring the left hand from the age of eleven, in both boys and girls. These results throw light on the divergences already brought up. Rose (1984) adapted this experimental situation for younger children, aged 1, 2 and 3 years. The children manipulated an object with one or the other of their hands for 25 seconds, then they were visually presented with the familiar object and a novel object for ten seconds. Although the children looked significantly longer at the novel object than at the familiar one, thus attesting to an intermodal transfer from touch to vision, their performances were nevertheless better when the object was manipulated by the left hand than by the right hand, but only from the age of two years. Hemispheric specialization regarding the haptic processing of shape apparently sets in its adult aspect during the child's second year.

The dichaptic procedure, essentially used with children aged between five and thirteen years, reveals a left hand advantage when the explored shapes are geometrical. When letters are used as a stimulus the results are less clear and the above performance asymmetry is no longer present (Gibson & Bryden 1983; Witelson 1974). The explanation often put forward is that the spatial processing demanded in haptic letter perception and carried out by the right hemisphere may be weakened, or even eliminated, by the linguistic processing carried out by the left hemisphere (Witelson 1977). Coiffi and Kandel (1979) broadened the identification task from geometrical shapes and one letter shapes to bigrammes and two-letter words. They observed a classic left hand/right hemisphere advantage for geometrical shapes in all subjects. But the boys showed a left hand superiority for the bigrammes, whereas girls showed no asymmetry before the age of thirteen. At this age, the right hand proves more efficient than the left hand. Both boys and girls are better at recognizing meaningful words explored with the right hand. These results reveal not only a left laterality for the spatial processing of forms, but also a right laterality for the processing of linguistic data, even when this is carried out via the haptic channel. The concrete object shapes used as a stimulus (a tree, a house, a cow, etc.) favor the left hand in ten and twelve-year-old boys, but not in girls. These results indicate a right hemisphere specialization for treating spatial information haptically, which develops earlier in boys than in girls (Hatta, Yamamoto, Kawabata, & Tsutui 1981). The problem linked to the use of concrete objects is that they are easily identifiable by their name and, as for letter shapes, a verbal mediation may weaken the right hemisphere's capacity to handle the data.

An analysis of all the literature about perceptive laterality in children reveals a left hand advantage for the manual exploration of shapes, which varies according to age, sex and the type of stimulus, but no coherence can be discerned in this asymmetry (cf. Hahn 1987; Koenig 1990; Summers & Lederman 1990; Verjat 1988). It appears that the divergence of results is caused by the influence of the cognitive strategies linked to the dichaptic procedure. For example, one cannot be sure that the subjects manipulate the two shapes in a truly synchronous way. A long palpation (ten seconds in Witelson's (1974) study), different procedures, and varied material favor the emergence of contradictory results. In order to test the hypothesis that changes linked to age depend on cognitive strategies underlying performance, and are not uniquely the result of a simple lateralization process, Koenig and Hauert (1986), using the classic dichaptic procedure, studied the effect of felt geometrical shapes in children aged between 5 and 10 years. The stimuli were placed in the palm of each hand and some of them varied in texture or in their center of gravity. This second property tended to distort shape recognition. The asymmetrical fluctuations observed with age seemed to reflect evolutions in cognitive strategies rather than a reorganization of brain functions.

Nor does research into somaesthetic identification of stimulations give clear evidence regarding asymmetries according to the age or the sex of subjects. Ghent (1961) examined sensitivity to pressure applied to a single point on the thumbs of children aged 5, 6, 7, 8, 9 and 11 years. Differences linked to gender were observed. Five-year-old girls' right thumbs are more sensitive, but the adult pattern of strong right thumb sensitivity only appears towards the ages of seven and nine. On the other hand, the boys show a strong left thumb sensitivity at the age of eleven. Similar results were found by Kimura (1963). These two studies reveal that the asymmetry in somaesthetic sensitivity appears in the course of development, but at different ages according to the gender of the children. A third study found no difference according to gender in the perception of a tactile stimulation applied to five-year-old children's hands. All subjects were more accurate in perceiving a stimulation in the left hand than in the right hand (Moreau & Milner 1981). Thus, except in this study, somaesthetic sensitivity is shown to develop with age in favor of the left hand. A convergence of results nevertheless appears regarding left hand superiority for boys aged around eleven years. It is revealed both in tactile sensitivity to pressure and in shape identification (Flanery & Balling 1979; Hatta et al. 1981).

4. Handedness in adults

4.1 Motor skills and handedness

Adult hand preference is measured either by a questionnaire asking subjects which hand they use for usual activities (Oldfield 1971; Annett 1970b; Bryden, Singh, Steenhuis, & Clarkson 1994), or by a battery of tests (Porac & Coren 1981). As for children, a laterality index is calculated. Using a hammer, a racket, a toothbrush, lighting a match, throwing a ball, and of course writing and drawing are all activities which are strongly associated with a hand preference.

But it is evident that some manual activities are amply influenced by culture. For example, asking the question "Which hand do you write with?" is different from asking "Which hand do you hold your fork in?". The answer to the first question immediately shows the subject's hand preference whereas the answer to the second is ambiguous, as it is influenced by a country's social customs. A manual skill questionnaire filled in by different oriental and occidental populations revealed that left-handedness is discouraged in the East and it is thus not surprising to note that there are fewer left-handed people in India or Japan than in Canada (cf. Bryden, Roy, McManus, & Bulman-Fleming 1997). Nevertheless, if hand skill is genetically controlled, as suggest the models proposed by Annett (1985), McManus and Bryden (1992, 1993), and Yeo and Gangestad (1993), then it is possible that the left-handed gene is rarer in some populations than in others.

Performance laterality, as for children, is evaluated via the speed and accuracy of execution of certain tasks, such as peg-moving (Annett, Hudson, & Turner 1974), repeatedly tapping a surface with the index finger (Todor &

Smiley 1985), dot-marking or drawing squares (Bishop 1980). Generally, the tests show that performances, are better with the preferred hand. More exactly, the right hand of the right-handed excels when carrying out a rapid sequence of gestures, such as tapping, or when spatial and temporal resolution are fine (Bryden et al. 1997). The left hand of the right-handed is more skilled at carrying out certain individual finger movements or dotting, notably in the absence of visual control. Thus, we visually control our preferred hand. The planning of an action is also a differentiating factor between the two hands and shows itself to be more important than the execution of an action (cf. Fagard 2001).

4.2 Perceptual skills and handedness

The literature is saturated with inconsistencies and experimental difficulties regarding the perceptive laterality question. When differences are found, the results suggest that men are more strongly lateralized than women, with the general hemispherical dichotomy that verbal functions are taken on by the left hemisphere and non-verbal or spatial functions are more effectively carried out by the right hemisphere (McGlone 1980). The data gathered on subjects having left or right damages or split-brain patients clearly reveal a right hemisphere superiority in the haptic processing of geometrical shapes, whereas healthy subjects (the control group) show no difference in skill between the two hands (Nebes 1971; Ledoux et al. 1977; Franco & Sperry 1977; cf. Chapter 3). More specifically, Nebes's 1971 study suggests that right hemisphere superiority is the result of its capacity to treat information more globally than the left hemisphere.

In healthy subjects, whether the situation be intramodal monohaptic (H-H condition) or intermodal (H-V condition), the results often show a superiority in the performance of the left hand (cf. Lacreuse, Fagot, & Vauclair 1996). Other work has led to contradictory results and no difference is observed in the skills of each hand (Yamamoto & Hatta 1980; Webster & Thurber 1978) or a right hand advantage is observed (Cranney & Ashton 1982). In the dichaptic intermodal situation (H-V), although the classic left hand advantage is observed in research by Dawson (1981) and Fagot, Hopkins and Vauclair (1993), contradictory data have also been observed. In the same way, gender effects on asymmetrical strength and direction in manual perception are not clearly established. A global effect favoring the left hand seems to emerge in the tactile processing of geometrical shapes (cf. Fagot, Lacreuse, & Vauclair 1997; Verjat 1989).

According to Lacreuse et al. (1996), the lack of homogeneity in these results may be explained by the exclusive choice of just one type of measure. The differences in the competence of each hemisphere are inferred from the comparison of the scores of each hand, and not from the analysis of the processes underlying these performances. These authors tested the hypothesis that exploration strategies (the duration and spatial distribution of finger contact), rather than performance, would better display underlying cognitive operations and their lateralization. Their aim consisted of looking for asymmetries both during the initial exploration phase and during the recognition phase of geometrical shapes, and this according to the mode of manual exploration (mono- or dichaptic). The left hand advantage only appears in dichaptic exploration situations. The strategies are especially used during the learning phase and not during the recognition phase. The dichaptic mode favors the appearance of differences in inter-manual performances. Finally, according to the authors, these differences are imputable more to the cognitive constraints of the task (shared attention, memory load) and less to the emergence of an inter-hemispherical competition.

Currently, research is oriented towards the relation between certain cognitive and manual skills. For example, using a monohaptic procedure with stimuli made up of dots which become more and more complex, Ernest (1988) examined manual asymmetry in male and female subjects having weak or strong visuospatial and verbal skills. The results reveal a close relation between cognitive abilities, manual lateralization, and the subjects' gender (cf. Benoit-Dubrocard, Liégois, & Harlay 1997; Halpern, Haviland, & Killian 1998).

5. Conclusion

We need to re-examine two problems which come out of this ontogenetic evolution (from infancy to adulthood): Firstly, the contradictions in the results obtained on gender difference and on the age that perceptive-motor asymmetries appear; and secondly, the central and peripheral processes in play in two-handed and dichaptic situations.

Firstly, information on infants reveals a very early lateralization process since a manual and a postural bias favoring the right (left hemisphere) is observed and a more efficient perceptive activity develops for the left hand (right hemisphere). But this lateralization process, confirming Kinsbourne and Hiscock's hypotheses (1983), must not mask changes observed in the course of development and not linked to experimental artifacts. If boy/girl differences are not always observed in a stable way, this is because the rhythm and the speed of maturation differ between the two genders, and probably from one child to another. It is generally thought that maturation occurs earlier in girls than in boys and that, from the fetal stage, testosterone is responsible for this difference (Tanner 1974). Moreover, the process of maturation does not occur harmoniously in all parts of the brain. On the one hand, there is a discrepancy in the maturation of the brain hemispheres, and on the other hand, the events related to brain maturation do not happen in a synchronous way in the course of development. For example, the primary 17 visual area reaches its adult size at around the age of four months, while the whole brain is only half its adult size. The question remains as to whether anatomical asymmetries are correlated to a functional asymmetry present, or are the anatomical substratum of later specializations (cf. Dehaene-Lambertz 1997).

Secondly, the dichaptic procedure, inspired by the dichotic listening procedure, is based on the principle of an inter-hemispherical competition process which should bring out the more specific perceptive capacities of the left hand. This hypothesis seems to have been left to the benefit of an interpretation in terms of strategies or cognitive constraints (Koenig & Hauert 1986; Lacreuse et al. 1996). The rejection of this hypothesis is based on the observation that in dichaptic situations information gathering is not simultaneous, even if it seems independent, and that an analogous advantage is revealed in the monohaptic condition (Flanery & Balling 1979). Consequently, left hand superiority, observed in numerous spatial tasks, may not be the result of a true competition between the two brain hemispheres (cf. Verjat 1989). The reasoning is different for two-handed procedure used with young babies. It weakens the right hand's motor performances regarding the holding of an object, whereas the left hand's performances hardly vary with those seen in the one-handed situation. The conclusion in terms of an inhibition process between hemispheres, proposed by Caplan and Kinsbourne (1976), seems plausible insofar as conditions of simultaneousness are required. The fact that both hands are simultaneously occupied may disturb the young babies. They cannot use the right hand to transport the object. Thus, they let go of the object since this hand cannot fulfill its instrumental function. However, the left hand is not hampered in its perceptual function. Such a scenario is nevertheless plausible only if the designated behaviors reflect the hemispherical asymmetries.

The complexity of skills shared by one hand or the other reveal the complexity of the human haptic system and its originality with regard to the other sensory systems. One must therefore be prudent when drawing conclusions from the results of studies. Sergent (1987) suggested that the contribution of each hemisphere to a function may vary according to factors such as the type of task, the context it is carried out in, the strategies adopted to accomplish it, etc. This suggestion is now confirmed by the results obtained with brain imagery techniques. They reveal that cognitive activities, like language or manual skills, are not localized in one hemisphere, but in view of their complexity, involve several sub-systems and it is they which are lateralized (cf. Heilige 1993).

References

Annett, M. (1970a). A classification of hand preference by association analysis. *British Journal of Psychology, 61*, 303–321.

Annett, M. (1970b). The growth of manual performance and speed. *British Journal of Psychology, 61*, 545–548.

Annett, M. (1985). *Left, right, hand and brain: The right shift theory.* London: Lawrence Erlbaum Associates.

Annett, M., Hudson, P. T., & Turner, A. (1974). The reliability of differences between the hands in motor skills. *Neuropsychologia, 12*, 527–531.

Auzias, M. (1975). *Enfants gauchers, enfants droitiers: une épreuve de latéralité usuelle.* Neuchâtel: Delachaux & Niestlé.

Bates, E., O'Connell, B., Vaid, J., Sledge, P., & Oakes, L. (1986). Language and hand preference in early development. *Developmental Neuropsychology, 2*, 1–15.

Benoit-Dubrocard, S., Liégeois, F., & Harlay, F. (1997). What does the haptic modality do during cognitive activities on letter shapes? A study with left- and right-handers. *Cortex, 33*, 301–312.

Bishop, D. V. (1980). Measuring familial sinistrality. *Cortex, 16*, 311–314.

Bradshaw, J. L. & Nettleton, N. C. (1981). The nature of hemispheric specialization in man. *Behavioral and Brain Sciences, 4*, 51–91.

Bryden, M., Singh, M., Steenhuis, R., & Clarkson, K. (1994). A behavioral measure of hand preference as opposed to hand skill. *Neuropsychologia, 32*, 991–999.

Bryden, M. P., Roy, E. A., McManus, I. C., & Bulman-Fleming, M. B. (1997). On the genetics and measurements of human handedness. *Laterality, 2*, 317–336.

Caplan, P. J. & Kinsbourne, M. (1976). Baby drops the rattle: Asymmetry of duration of grasp by infants. *Child Development, 47*, 532–534.

Carlier, M., Dumont, A. M., Beau, J., & Michel, F. (1993). Hand performance of french children on a finger-tapping test in relation to handedness, sex and ange. *Perceptual and Motor skills, 76*, 931–940.

Coiffi, J. & Kandel, G. (1979). Laterality of stereognostic accuracy of children for words, shapes and bigrams: Sex differences for bigrams. *Science, 204*, 1432–1434.

Cranney, J. & Ashton, R. (1982). Tactile spatial ability: Lateralized performance of deaf and hearing age groups. *Journal of Experimental Child Psychology, 34*, 123–134.

Dawson, G. D. (1981). Hemispheric differences in tactuo-spatial processing. *Perceptual and Motor skills, 53*, 935–944.

Dehaene-Lambertz, G. (1997). Image du développement cérébral. In S. Dehaene (Ed.), *Le cerveau en action: Imagerie cérébrale fonctionnelle en psychologie cognitive* (pp. 185–204). Paris: Presses Universitaires de France.

Ernest, C. H. (1988). Spatial ability and lateralization in the haptic modality. *Brain and Cognition, 36,* 1–20.

Fagard, J. (2001). *Le développement des habiletés de l'enfant. Coordination bimanuelle et latéralité.* Paris: Editions du CNRS.

Fagot, J., Hopkins, W. D., & Vauclair, J. (1993). Hand movements and hemispheric specialization in dichaptic explorations. *Perception, 22,* 847–853.

Fagot, J., Lacreuse, A., & Vauclair, J. (1997). Role of sensory and post-sensory factors on hemispheric asymmetries in tactual perception. In S. Christman (Ed.), *Cerebral asymmetries in sensory and perceptual processing* (pp. 469–494). Amsterdam: Elsevier.

Flanery, R. C. & Balling, J. D. (1979). Developmental changes in hemispheric specialization for tactile spatial ability. *Developmental Psychology, 15,* 364–372.

Franco, L. & Sperry, R. (1977). Hemisphere lateralisation for cognitive processing of geometry. *Neuropsychologia, 15,* 107–114.

Gesell, A. & Ames, L. (1947). The development of handedness. *Journal of Genetic Psychology, 70,* 155–175.

Ghent, L. (1961). Developmental changes in tactual thresholds on dominant and non-dominant sides. *Journal of Comparative and Physiological Psychology, 54,* 670–673.

Gibson, C. & Bryden, M. P. (1983). Dichaptic recognition of shapes and letters in children. *Canadian Journal of Psychology, 37,* 132–143.

Hahn, W. K. (1987). Cerebral lateralization of function: From infancy through childhood. *Psychological Bulletin, 101,* 376–392.

Halpern, D. F., Haviland, M. G., & Killian, C. D. (1998). Handedness and sex differences in intelligence: Evidence from the Medical College Admission Test. *Brain and Cognition, 38,* 87–101.

Harris, L. J. (1983). Laterality of function in the infant: Historical and contemporary trends in theory and research. In G. Young, S. J. Segalowitz, C. M. Corter, & S. E. Trehub (Eds.), *Manual specialization and developing brain, 10* (pp. 177–239.). New York: Academic Press.

Hatta, T., Yamamoto, M., Kawabata, V., & Tsutui, K. (1981). Development of hemispheric specialization for tactile recognition in normal children. *Cortex, 17,* 611–616.

Hawn, P. R. & Harris, L. J. (1983). Hand differences in grasp duration and reaching in two- and five-month-old infants. In G. Young, S. J. Segalowitz, C. M. Corter, & S. E. Trehub (Eds.), *Manual specialization and developing brain* (pp. 331–348). New York: Academic Press.

Healey, J. M., Liederman, J., & Geschwind, N. (1986). Handedness is not a unidimensional trait. *Cortex, 22,* 33–53.

Hellige, J. B. (1993). *Hemispheric asymmetry. What's right and what's left.* Cambridge: Harvard University Press.

Hopkins, B. & Rönnqvist, L. (1998). Human handedness: Developmental and evolutionary perspectives. In F. Simion & G. Butterworth (Eds.), *The development of sensory, motor and cognitive capacities in early infancy. From perception to cognition* (pp. 191–236). East Sussex: Psychology Press.

Kimura, D. (1963). Speech lateralization in young children determined by an auditory test. *Journal of Comparative and Physiological Psychology, 56,* 899–902.

Kinsbourne, M. & Hiscock, M. (1983). The normal and deviant development of functional lateralization of the brain. In P. Mussen (Ed.), *Handbook of child psychology, infancy and developmental psychobiology* (pp. 158–280). New York: John Wiley & Sons.

Koenig, O. (1990). Child neuropsychological development: Lateralization of function – hemispheric specialization. In C. A. Hauert (Ed.), *Developmental psychology. Cognitive, perceptuo-motor and neuropsychological perspectives* (pp. 357–388). North-Holland: Elsevier Science Publishers.

Koenig, O. & Hauert, C. A. (1986). Construction de l'objet chez l'enfant de 5 à 9 ans: Approche dichhaptique. *CPC-Current Psychology of Cognition, 6,* 21–39.

Lacreuse, A., Fagot, J., & Vauclair, J. (1996). Latéralisation hémisphérique et stratégies d'exploration dans des tâches de perception tactilo-kinesthésique. *L'Année Psychologique, 96,* 131–145.

Ledoux, J. E., Wilson, D. H., & Gazzaniga, M. S. (1977). Manipulo-spatial aspects of cerebral lateralization: Clues to the origin of lateralization. *Neuropsychologia, 15,* 743–750.

Lhote, M. & Streri, A. (1998). Haptic memory and handedness in 2-month-old infants, *Laterality, 3,* 173–192.

Lhote, M. & Streri, A. (2003). La mémoire haptique de la forme des objets chez les bébés âgés de 4 mois. *L'Année Psychologique, 103,* 33–50.

Lockman, J. J. & Wright, M. H. (1988). *A longitudinal study of banging.* Paper presented at the International Conference on Infant Studies, Washington, DC.

McGlone, J. (1980). Sex differences in human brain asymmetry: A critical survey. *Behavioral and brain sciences, 3,* 215–263.

McManus, I. C. & Bryden, M. P. (1992). The genetics of handedness and cerebral lateralization. In I. Rapin & S. J. Segalowitz (Eds.), *Handbook of Neuropsychology, Vol. 6* (pp. 115–144). Amsterdam: Elsevier.

McManus, I. C. & Bryden, M. P. (1993). Handedness on Tristan da Cunha: The genetic consequences of social isolation. *International Journal of Psychology, 28,* 831–843.

Moreau, T. & Milner, P. (1981). Lateral differences in the detection of touched body parts in young children. *Developmental Psychology, 17,* 351–356.

Nebes, N. D. (1971). Superiority of the minor hemisphere in commissurotomized man for the perception of part-whole relations. *Cortex, 7,* 333–349.

Oldfield, R. C. (1971). The assessment and analysis of handedness: The Edinburgh inventory. *Neuropsychologia, 9,* 97–113.

Petrie, B. F. & Peters, M. (1980). Handedness: Left/right differences in intensity of grasp response and duration of rattle holding in infants. *Infant Behavior and Development, 3,* 215–221.

Pineau, A. & Streri, A. (1990). Intermodal transfer of spatial arrangement of the component parts of an object in 4–5- month-old infants. *Perception, 19,* 785–804.

Porac, C. & Coren, S. (1981). *Lateral preferences and human behaviour.* New York: Springer.

Rose, S. A. (1984). Developmental changes in hemispheric specialization for tactual processing in very young children: Evidence from cross-modal transfer. *Developmental Psychology, 20,* 568–574.

Segond, H. & Streri, A. (1994). Mieux percevoir la forme des objets à deux mois: main droite ou main gauche? *Enfance, 2,* 155–164.

Segond, H. & Streri, A. (1996). *Handedness and information processing in 2-, 4-, and 6 month-old infants.* Paper presented at the International Conference on Infant Studies, Providence (USA), April.

Sergent, J. (1987). L'asymétrie fonctionnelle du cerveau. In M. I. Botez (Ed.), *Neuropsychologie clinique et neurologie du comportement* (pp. 205–214). Montréal: Presses de l'Université de Montréal, Masson.

Steenhuis, R. E. & Bryden, M. P. (1989). Different dimensions of hand preference that relate to skilled and unskilled activities. *Cortex, 25,* 289–304.

Strauss, E. (1982). Manual persistence in infancy. *Cortex, 18,* 319–322.

Streri, A. (2002). Hand preference in 4-month-old infants: Global or local processing of objects in the haptic mode. *Current Psychology Letters. Behaviour, Brain and Cognition, 7,* 23–34.

Streri, A. & Gouarir, C. (1996). Handedness: Left-right differences in object holding and motor skills in 6-month-old infants. *CPC – Current Psychology of Cognition, 15,* 209–230.

Streri, A. & Pêcheux, M. G. (1986). Tactual habituation and discrimination of form in infancy: A comparison with vision. *Child Development, 57,* 100–104.

Streri, A., Lhote, M., & Dutilleul, S. (2000). Haptic perception in the newborn. *Developmental Science, 3,* 319–327.

Summers, D. C. & Lederman, S. J. (1990). Perceptual asymmetries in the somatosensory system: A dichhaptic experiment and critical review of the literature from 1929 to 1986. *Cortex, 26,* 201–226.

Tanner, J. (1974). Variability of growth and maturity in newborn infants. In N. Lewis & L. A. Rosemblum (Eds.), *The effects of the infant on its caregiver* (pp. 146–163). New York: Wiley.

Todor, J. I. & Smiley, A. L. (1985). Performance differences between the hands: Implications for studying disruption to limb praxis. In E. A. Roy (Ed.), *Neuropsychological studies of apraxia and related disorders* (pp. 309–344). Elsevier: North-Holland Publishing.

Verjat, I. (1988). La dissymétrie fonctionnelle cérébrale dans la modalité tactilo-kinesthésique manuelle. *L'Année Psychologique, 88,* 83–109.

Verjat, I. (1989). A propos de l'exploration dichaptique. *L'Année Psychologique, 89,* 277–289.

Webster, W. H. & Thurber, A. D. (1978). Problem-solving strategies and manifest brain asymmetry. *Cortex, 14,* 474–484.

Witelson, S. F. (1974). Hemispheric specialization for linguistic and nonlinguistic tactual perception using a dichotomous stimulation technique. *Cortex, 10,* 3–17.

Witelson, S. F. (1976). Sex and the single hemisphere: Right hemisphere specialization for spatial processing. *Science, 193,* 425–427.

Witelson, S. F. (1977). Developmental dyslexia: Two right hemisphere and none left. *Science, 195,* 425–427.

Wolff, P. H. (1977). The development of manual asymmetries in motor sequencing skills. *Annals of the New York Academy of Sciences, 299,* 319–327.

Yakolev, P. I. & Lecours, A. R. (1967). The myelogenetic cycles of regional maturation of the brain. In A. Minkowski (Ed.), *Regional development of the brain in early life* (pp. 3–65). London: Blackwell.

Yamamoto, M. & Hatta, T. (1980). Hemispheric asymmetries in a tactile thought task for normal subjects. *Perceptual and Motor skills, 50,* 467–471.

Yeo, R. & Gangestad, S. W. (1993). Developmental origins of variation in human hand preference. *Genetica, 89,* 281–296.

Young, G. (1990). Early neuropsychological development: Lateralization of functions – hemispheric specialization. In C. A. Hauert (Ed.), *Developmental psychology. Cognitive, perceptivo-motor, and neuropsychological perspectives* (pp. 113–181). North-Holland: Elsevier Science Publishers.

Young, G., Segalowitz, S. J., Corter, C. M., & Trehub, S. E. (1983). *Manual specialization and developing brain.* New York: Academic Press.

PART 3

Haptic perceptions and spatial imaged representations

CHAPTER 7

The haptic identification of everyday life objects

Roberta Klatzky and Susan Lederman

1. General processes of object recognition

Identifying common objects, which surround us every day, is a specific version of the more general perceptual task called pattern recognition. When we recognize a pattern, we assign it to some category of past experience. We may call a visual display a "chair," for example. In general, theories of pattern recognition tend to include a number of assumptions. They assume a process of analysis, in which sensory systems break down incoming stimulation into component features, and a process of synthesis, in which higher-order systems build features into integrated units. They assume that units at one or more of these levels access memory for known categories of patterns, and the best match with memory determines the category to which the incoming stimulus is assigned. Typically, pattern recognition theories assume not only that these processes are driven by sensory stimulation, in a bottom-up fashion, but also that they rely on acquired knowledge and current expectations, in a top-down driven manner.

These theoretical assumptions are sufficiently broad that they can be applied to any sensory modality – vision, touch, audition, or olfaction, for example. But there is no doubt that by far the predominant modality examined in studies of pattern recognition is vision, followed by speech recognition. Relatively little work, in contrast, has been devoted to the study of how we recognize familiar patterns by touch.

Intuitively, one may feel that the emphasis on vision is appropriate, because it is the way we typically recognize objects in the real world. One might believe that there is little role for object recognition by touch in everyday life. We would argue, however, that the importance of touch in everyday object recognition has not been highlighted as it deserves to be; that in fact, we frequently recognize objects by touch. People often interact with and manipulate an object without looking at it; to do this, they must know what the object is. When we dress, we do not have to fixate on buttons to fasten them; we can find the button and buttonhole by touch. When we drive a car, we can shift gears and adjust knobs without bothering to look; indeed it is better not to take our eyes from the road. When we seek an object in our pocket or purse, vision is occluded; yet, we find our keys or wallet with ease. In short, there are ample examples from day-to-day experience indicating that recognizing common objects by touch is not only something that we can do, but that we do do.

We documented the ability to recognize objects by touch in some of our earliest work together (Klatzky, Lederman & Metzger 1985), where we showed that people could name a set of 100 familiar objects with virtually no error, and with a modal response time of 2 seconds or less. This work not only confirmed that people can recognize objects by touch, but it also hinted at the way in which they do so. Before continuing with a discussion of how people perform haptic object recognition, let us first briefly consider how visual object recognition is performed.

2.   The role of spatial information in visual and haptic object recognition

It is now well known that the earliest features that the visual system extracts from objects are spatial, in the form of oriented edges. Not surprisingly, then, theories of visual object recognition assume that low-level features, or primitives, are based on edges. In what is perhaps the most widely known theory, that of Biederman (e.g. 1987; Hummel & Biederman 1992), edges are spatially arranged so as to produce a feature in the form of a regular volume, called a geon. A small number of geons, appropriately arranged in space and relatively sized, is proposed to be sufficient to compose any familiar object. The process of pattern recognition consists in part, then, of extracting edges, determining geons from their spatial layout, combining the geons into an object, and comparing that object to representations in memory corresponding to object categories. There has been much debate recently as to whether a single memory code, or structural description, is used to represent an entire category, or whether multiple representations, reflecting the variety of past experience with perceiving an object from that category, are matched with the input image (e.g., Edelman & Bulthoff 1992; Tarr & Pinker 1989). Nonetheless, the basic ideas of reliance on early edge extraction and synthesis of object images from edges are widely accepted in theories of visual pattern recognition.

At the outset, applying such a model to haptic pattern recognition is problematical, because the haptic system is simply not very good at extracting information about the spatial layout of edges. Note that Lederman and Klatzky (1997) made a distinction between two kinds of information that edges may provide – intensive information, indicating that an edge is present somewhere on an otherwise uniform surface, and spatial information, which specifies the location and orientation of the edge. While intensive information about edges is quickly available through touch, as we discuss below, information about their spatial layout is relatively inaccessible.

It is useful to consider three types of edge layout that might be presented in a haptic display: (i) The edges may form a 2-dimensional pattern within the scale of the fingertip. In elevators in the U.S., for example, one can find embossed symbols representing the alarm bell or the door close button, which are roughly scaled to the finger. (ii) The edges may form a 2-dimensional pattern that extends beyond the scale of the fingertip. Patterns of those sort are exemplified by raised line drawings used as illustrations for the blind. They can also be found in free-standing planar objects, which have varying contours of uniform thickness, like a piece from a puzzle. (iii) The edges may form the contours of a fully three-dimensional object, like a drinking cup.

Each of these cases has been examined in experimental work, and performance tends to be slow and error-prone. The ability to encode edges from patterns lying under the fingertip was systematically investigated by Loomis (1990), who evaluated sighted, blindfolded people's ability to identify small (6 mm on the larger dimension) raised letters and digits. Several sets of these characters were used; they included conventional Braille, a version of Braille in which adjacent dots were connected to form edges, and conventional alphanumeric characters made up of raised lines. Subjects were presented with each display for 2 s. The average percentage correct for these three sets was, respectively, 56%, 66%, and 40%.

With respect to the second category of edge displays considered above, those that vary in two dimensions and that extend beyond the finger, we can consider a study by Klatzky, Lederman and Balakrishnan (1991). This study assessed sighted, blindfolded subjects' ability to determine whether two successively presented planar objects were the same or different. Although the differences were easily detected by eye, the subjects did not perform above chance. In other studies, we have assessed the ability of sighted, blindfolded and blind individuals to recognize drawings of common objects made up of raised lines.

Lederman, Klatzky, Chataway and Summers (1990) found that sighted individuals recognized only 34% of the objects, even when they were allowed up to 2 minutes of exploration. The blind did substantially worse (10% success).

Loomis, Klatzky, and Lederman (1991) and Klatzky, Loomis, Lederman, Wake, and Fujita (1993) showed similar levels of performance with raised drawings of objects. In the latter study, we also examined performance in the third case described above – where edges are found on a three-dimensional object. People were asked to explore real common objects by touch and then to name them. We wished to assess people's ability to do so entirely from edge information. In order to ensure that people only had access to edges, we had them wear a heavy glove and allowed them only to use a single extended finger. All of the objects were rigid, and they were fixed in place, so that they could not be examined for weight. In addition, moving parts of the objects were stabilized. Under these conditions, the percentage correct was about 75%.

It should also be noted that the extraction of edges from free-standing objects, having a size beyond the scale of the fingertip, is a slow process. Subjects in the Klatzky et al. (1993) study, who were exploring an object's edges with a single extended finger, took about 45 s to respond on average. Lederman and Klatzky (1987) found that when attempting to determine the best match for a planar object, subjects took 11 s on average to explore it. They spent this time following the edge with one hand while stabilizing and rotating the object with the other. This particular pattern of exploration, which we call "contour following," turned out to be the only way to achieve accurate performance in the matching task. Thus when attempting to extract relatively precise edge-layout information from objects that extend beyond the scale of the fingertip, there is no substitute for a process that is slow and sequential – that of following the contours with the finger – but that nonetheless does not guarantee a high level of accuracy.

The experiments that have been reviewed in this section point to a basic difficulty with determining the spatial arrangement of edges by touch; they indicate that the ability to encode contours of 2- or 3-dimensional objects is limited to fairly coarse levels that do not produce high levels of accuracy in many tasks. At the same time, theories of visual object recognition emphasize the role of extracting the layout of edges. Other work suggests, moreover, that different regions of a 3-dimensional object's geometry may typically be extracted through vision and touch (Lakatos & Marks 1999; Newell, Ernst, Tian, & Bülthoff 2001). These contrasts make clear that theories from the visual modality cannot be applied to explain how people recognize objects by touch. We have indicated that haptic object recognition is fast and accurate – typically, more fast and accurate than people perform when obtaining edge information alone. This leads to the question of how objects are recognized by touch, if spatial edge processing is not the means of doing so. In the following sections of this chapter, we will consider another type of information that might lead to object recognition – the material from which an object is made.

3.   The availability of material information about objects from haptic exploration

If spatial edge information cannot be extracted quickly enough by the haptic system to account for the efficacy with which people identify objects, how do they do so? The experiment by Klatzky et al. (1985) demonstrating highly accurate identification performance gave some indication of how people arrived at object identity. They reported using a variety of object properties and not just shape. Those properties often pertained to the material from which the object was fabricated. This finding suggests that material properties may play an important role in haptic object recognition.

In general, a material property is an attribute that is independent of geometric structure. Klatzky and Lederman (1993) partitioned object properties into material properties – such as texture, compliance, and apparent temperature (due to heat flow); and geometric properties – including size and shape. (Weight was a hybrid property reflecting density and size.) In order to claim that material properties might be useful cues to haptic object identification, we need to demonstrate that the haptic system can extract information about an object's material.

We conducted studies that directly addressed the availability of material properties under haptic exploration of objects (Lederman & Klatzky 1997). The procedure was based on a paradigm from vision, called visual search, as adapted by Treisman and Gormican (1988). In this task, a subject is given a target value of some object property to detect in a display. For example, the property may be line orientation, and the subject may be told to look for a target consisting of a horizontal line (the value of orientation to be detected). On some trials, there is no horizontal line in the display, and the subject responds negatively. On other trials, there is a horizontal line, and the subject responds affirmatively. When the horizontal line is present, it may be embedded in varying numbers of additional lines, which are vertical rather than horizontal. The vertical lines constitute distractors. The subject's response time is recorded and plotted as a function of the total number of items in the display, including the target – if present – and the distractors. The processes used in the task can be inferred from the resulting response-time function.

If response time is independent of the number of items in the display, that is, if the subject is no slower for determining a target is present when there are many distractors than when there are few or none, then the target is said to "pop out." For example, if subjects who search for a horizontal line are unaffected by the presence of additional, vertical lines, then one can say that the horizontal line pops out. An attribute that pops out of a perceptual display, as defined by a constant yes/no detection time across varying numbers of distractors, was proposed by Treisman and Gormican (1988) to constitute a "primitive" feature to which the perceptual system is tuned. A primitive need not correspond to an entire dimension of variation; it is, rather, a particular value of the property that is detected automatically. For example, considering the property of line orientation, it is possible that horizontal line orientations might be primitives that are detected automatically, but that oblique line orientations might not be.

In a visual display, it is relatively straightforward to vary the number of items by adding distractors to or subtracting them from the field of view. It is less obvious, however, how to vary the number of items in a haptic display. We chose to do so by varying the number of fingers that were stimulated. On each trial, the subject placed the three middle fingers of each hand on finger rests. A haptic display was then raised to contact the fingers. The number of stimuli in the display ranged from one, contacting a single finger, to six, one contacting each finger. The apparatus that accomplished this task has been described in Moore, Broekhoven, Lederman, and Ulug (1991).

The subject's task was to say whether any of the stimulated fingers was in contact with a designated target. One target, for example, was a rough surface, consisting of a fingertip-sized plate with small raised elements. When it was present, the target could be the only stimulus, touching a single finger, or it could be mixed with up to five distractor stimuli (smooth surfaces) simultaneously contacting other fingers. When the rough surface was absent, from one to six fingers were contacted by smooth surfaces.

This task was performed not only with roughness but with a variety of object properties, for each of which we chose two values that would serve as targets or distractors across different trials. The two values were chosen to be as different as the object property allowed, so that the discrimination between targets and distractors was made as easy as possible. For a rough target, then, the distractor was very smooth. Across different blocks of trials, the two values of a property were designated alternately as targets and distractors. Thus some-

Table 7.1. Search discriminations (after Lederman & Klatzky 1997. Reprinted by permission from the American Psychological Association).

Material

SMOOTH	vs.	ROUGH
HARD	vs.	SOFT
COOL	vs.	WARM

Abrupt-surface discontinuities

EDGE (vertical bar)	vs.	NO EDGE
EDGE (horizontal bar)	vs.	NO EDGE
HOLE (cyclindrical)	vs.	NO HOLE
SHALLOW	vs.	DEEP (hole)

Relative orientation

LEFT	vs.	RIGHT (relative position)
HORIZONTAL	vs.	VERTICAL (2-D bar)
LEFT	vs.	RIGHT (2-D bar)
LEFT	vs.	RIGHT (slanted 3-D ramp)

Continuous 3-D surface contours

CURVED	vs.	FLAT
SLANT (3-D ramp)	vs.	FLAT

times the subjects searched for a rough surface among smooth distractors, and sometimes they searched for a smooth surface among rough distractors.

In total, the task was performed with 13 object properties, as described in Table 7.1. They could be divided into four sets: (i) material discriminations, such as rough surface vs. smooth surface or warm vs. cool surface; (ii) discrimination of a flat surface from a surface with an abrupt spatial discontinuity, such as a raised bar; (iii) discrimination of two- or three-dimensional spatial layout, such as whether a raised dot was on the left vs. the right of an indentation, and (iv) discrimination between continuous three-dimensional contours, such as a curved surface vs. a flat surface. For each of these properties, four search functions were obtained, representing the two possible responses (target present vs. target absent) combined with the two values that could serve as target (for example, target = rough and distractors = smooth, or the reverse). Each search function plotted the response time against the total number of items in the display. In general, the search functions were fit well by a linear equation with a slope and an intercept (y-value when x = 0). These two parameters allow us to make inferences about the perceptual availability of the property that is being discriminated, as follows.

Consider first the implications of the slope of the response-time function. If the function is flat, as was noted above, the result is taken as evidence that the target feature pops out of the display. This pattern is generally known as a parallel search process, and in this task the search is in parallel across the fingers. If the response-time function is increasing, a limited-capacity search is indicated, with greater capacity being used as more fingers must be examined. Our interest was not only in whether the functions were flat or increasing, but in the need to define the relative availability of properties to the haptic perceptual system. For this purpose the numerical value of the slope is critical, with greater slopes indicating properties that are less available.

The intercept of the function is also informative about availability. In visual search tasks, Treisman and Gormican (1988) found relatively little variation in the intercept across different properties. However, we found a significant correlation between slope and intercept. That is, properties that led to a higher slope tended also to produce a higher intercept. This suggests that the intercept, like the slope, is measuring the amount of processing that must be done to detect the target feature. In theory, the intercept can include two types of processes: those that occur one time, regardless of the number of fingers stimulated, and those that occur in parallel across the fingers. One–time processes that would affect the intercept include generating the response output and executing it. One-time processes may also include exploratory movements or hand positioning that occur across all fingers simultaneously, not finger by finger.

In addition, the intercept may also include the time to process information in parallel across the individual fingertips. If the search function is flat, then all of the extraction of information about the object property occurs in parallel and is measured by the intercept. But even if the search function is increasing, there may be some computation of the property that occurs in parallel, without capacity limitations, and this would enter the intercept value, with the remaining stimulus processing, which requires limited resources, showing up in the slope.

To summarize our results, both the slope and intercept values of the response-time functions implicated a progression in the availability of haptic object properties, such that material properties were most available and spatial layout information was least available (see Figure 7.1 for example). The slopes of the response-time functions for material properties were small (none was greater than 36 msec, and several were close to zero). In contrast, the slopes for discriminating spatial positions tended to be among the highest of those measured, with a slope of approximately 500 msec being observed for the slowest search process. Similarly, the material properties tended to produce the lowest intercepts. There was one exception to the low intercepts for material properties: the search for a cool surface (copper) among warm distractors (pine).

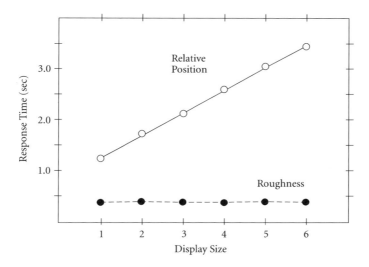

Figure 7.1. Mean response time (in seconds) as a function of the number of items in a search task, in two conditions: when the subjects judged the relative positon of a raised point in relation to an indentation, and when the subjects judged the roughness of a surface. The slope of the upper curve is .44 sec and the intercept value is .82 sec. The slope of the lower curve is .04 sec and the intercept value is .39 sec (after Lederman & Klatzky 1997).

This intercept was relatively high, because detection of the cool surface requires enough time in order to detect heat flow from the fingers into the surface, which occurs in parallel across all the fingers contacting the surface.

In short, this haptic search task clearly indicates that material properties are available relatively early through the sense of touch, earlier than spatial properties such as edge orientation or relative positions of raised elements. The findings from this task are congruent with other work, described above, indicating that information about the spatial layout of edges is not highly available to the haptic perceptual system. Together, these various research findings suggest that the role of material in haptic object identification could contribute substantially to the high level of performance that is observed. But in order for material information about the stimulus object to be important in identification, the representation of objects in memory must also incorporate material information that can be matched with the stimulus. We discuss whether material is part of the memory representation of object categories in the next section.

4. The role of material properties in object representation

While it is conceivable that material properties could be used to represent and identify an object, there is a problem with this idea. The problem arises because object identification involves giving an object its most common name, and it has been demonstrated that the name given to an object primarily depends on its shape, a geometric property. That is, it is well known that people use naming to divide objects into categories whose members share attributes, and that shape is a particularly important attribute when an object is categorized by its most common name.

For any given object, a variety of names are usually available. We can call the object that one sits on a "chair," an "article of furniture", a "desk chair," or even "the desk chair belonging to Roberta Klatzky." In the act of naming, we assign the object to a category shared by other objects, and depending on the name given, the object shares its category with different members. For example, the category of chairs includes more members than the category of desk chairs. In a classic body of research, Rosch (e.g., 1978) demonstrated that when one considers the category corresponding to an object's most common name ("chair"), called the "basic level" category, members of the category are highly similar in terms of shape. If an object is named at a more superordinate level ("furniture"), the members tend not to be so similar in shape. If an object is named at a more subordinate level ("desk chair"), the members are not much more similar than members at the basic level. The basic level is, then, the most abstract level of categorization where the members of a category are shaped very similarly. Objects at the basic level tend to be similar in other respects as well, such as function and associated movements. But perhaps most importantly, when an object is recognized, the category to which it is assigned by pattern-recognition processes appears to be at the basic level. We recognize an object first as a chair, and only later as an article of furniture or desk chair.

It is commonality of shape at the basic level that leads to the problem raised above: How can we use material properties to identify an object, when the category to which we assign it, by virtue of identification, is based on shape, a geometric property? In other words, if shape is the primary property that objects share when they have a common basic-level name, how can we use anything but shape to identify them?

There are two potential answers to this question. One answer may be that shape is not the only thing that is common to a large extent for objects at the basic level. The second answer may be that although shape is most important, material may help to compensate for the limited knowledge about shape that is available from the haptic system. These answers are not, of course, mutually exclusive, and both appear to be correct, at least to a limited degree.

Let us consider first whether shape is the only attribute shared by objects at the basic level. Lederman and Klatzky (1990) addressed the importance of various properties of objects for identification at the basic level. They gave subjects the names of objects and asked them to choose, from a list of properties, those that would be most useful for determining whether an object was from the named category. Object names were given both at the basic and subordinate level (for example, "pencil" and "used pencil," respectively). The list of objects was designed so that a variety of properties might be important for identification at the subordinate level. In the example of "used pencil," which is a subordinate-level name, shape should be important for identification (a used pencil has a rounded tip). But the list also included "stale bread," where texture and hardness should be important. A particularly critical aspect of this experiment was that subjects were asked to indicate the importance of the property for identifying an object by touch alone, *without vision*. From the rank order of subjects' responses, we were able to determine which property was most important for recognizing a given object by touch. As expected from the way the list was constructed, when objects were named at the subordinate level, a variety of properties were noted to be important. But we found that when the same objects were named at the basic level, although shape was important for identifying many objects, there were also a number of objects for which material properties were judged important. Texture, in particular, was cited as being important for identifying objects at the basic level, by touch alone. This study at least supports the possibility that material properties could be used to identify objects by touch.

5.   Contribution of material properties to object identification

Now let us consider the second possibility raised above, namely, that even if material is not sufficient by itself to identify an object, it can still help to compensate for weak shape cues by contributing to object identification. The study of Klatzky et al. (1993), in which people identified real objects from their contours, is relevant to this issue. As was described previously, people could identify objects with about 75% accuracy while wearing a glove that eliminated most cues to material (although coefficient of friction, for example, might still be available), and while being restricted to feeling the objects with an outstretched finger. In the same study, we compared performance when people wore the heavy glove to performance when the fingertip of the glove was cut off, permitting full access to material information. There was a significant improvement in performance when the material information was added. This was mainly for the single finger condition, which enforced sequential exploration and processing. Thus it appears that material can augment coarse shape information from touch, improving the speed and accuracy with which an object can be recognized.

In another study (Klatzky & Lederman 1995), we pushed to its limits the use of material for identifying objects. Subjects in this experiment were allowed only 200 msec of passive fingertip contact with an object in order to identify it. We were interested not only in the level of identification that could be achieved with such limited exposure, but with whether performance would depend on the attributes of the objects that were to be identified. We looked at two attributes: the size of the object, and the property that had been identified (by Lederman & Klatzky 1990) as most important in identifying it by touch alone, called the most diagnostic property. Accordingly, objects in this study were selected so that they represented two levels of *size* and two types of *most diagnostic property*. With respect to size, objects were either small – having at least one axis that could be spanned by the middle fingers – or large – with both the principal axes extending beyond the middle fingers. With respect to diagnostic property, objects were used for which texture was more important to identification than shape, or for which shape was more important than texture. Our prediction was that with such a short duration of exposure, and such a small area of the object being explored (that which touched the fingertips), subjects would be best at identifying objects for which texture was most diagnostic, or objects for which shape was diagnostic but that were small enough to be entirely explored by exposure to the fingertips.

In order to constrain subjects to approximately 200 ms of exploration, we had them guide their hand, with fingers extended, down to the object by following a vertical rod. The object was placed under the descending hand so that if it had a particularly informative region (for example, the pouring lip on a pitcher), that region would be contacted. A force-sensitive board placed under the object sensed initial contact, and a tone was emitted, instructing the subject to lift the arm away, after 100 msec. The subject then attempted to generate the name of the object that had been contacted.

We found that even under such limited exposure, objects could be named at levels above chance. Overall, 15% of objects were named correctly, and as expected, the level of performance depended on the object's size and diagnostic property. People performed worse, identifying only 5% of the objects, when they were large and shape was the most important property for identification. This is predictable, because with a large object, the relevant shape cues would extend beyond the region contacted by the hand. Performance was best (25%) when the object was large and texture was diagnostic. In this case, the large size maximizes the textured region that is so important for identifying the object. It is somewhat surprising that people could name 25% of objects for which texture is a critical cue to identity, with so short an exposure time. This supports the idea that material properties can contribute substantially to the process of object recognition by touch.

Another interesting outcome of this experiment was an analysis of confusion errors, in which we determined the similarity between the object that was presented and the object that people named, when they made an error. An analysis of nearly 600 errors of this type revealed that most confusion errors (75%) matched the original object with respect to material. Again, this indicates the high level of availability of material information to the sense of touch.

6.   Converging contributions of multiple properties

To summarize the arguments being made so far, we have observed first that haptic object identification cannot rely virtually entirely on information about the spatial layout of edges, as appears to be the case in vision, because spatial information is extracted coarsely and slowly by means of touch. Material information was suggested as a potential supplement, if not alternative, to information about spatial layout, and material properties were shown to be more available than spatially coded properties under haptic exploration. However, material is useful in categorization only if object categories can be differentiated by their material properties. We have given evidence that to some extent, at least, this is the case in touch. Further, we have described data indicating that access to material properties can facilitate haptic object identification. In this section, we will consider whether material properties might be combined, or integrated, with one another and with geometric properties to facilitate object identification.

In a number of studies, we investigated the extent to which subjects could integrate information about multiple object properties during object identification. The task we used was a simple classification task, using novel, specially fabricated, objects rather than common objects. Subjects learned to assign objects from the pool into a set of discrete categories. The objects were fabricated to represent all possible combinations of a set of properties. For example, in one study (Klatzky, Lederman, & Reed 1989), the objects were planar and represented all possible combinations of 3 shapes, 3 sizes, 3 surface textures, and 3 levels of compliance, for a total of 81 objects. Subjects learned to assign each object to a designated category, as rapidly as possible.

Depending on the categories designated by the experimenter, the objects could be classified by just one property, or redundantly, by any one of multiple properties. For example, members of the category "A" might all be oval shapes and members of category "B" might all be hourglass shapes, but each of the two categories might include members with varying size, textures, and compliance levels, so that those properties were irrelevant to classification. In this case, only a single property, shape, could be used to assign an object to its category. In another version of the task, categories A and B might be defined redundantly, by both shape and texture. The A members, for example, might be oval and rough, while the B members were hourglass shaped and smooth. Again, both categories would contain members varying in size and compliance, so that those properties could not be used for classification. The question we asked was whether the redundant information would speed classification; that is, whether categorization would be faster when either of two properties defined category members, than when there was only one property that defined the category.

We reasoned in advance that whether people could capitalize on redundant properties for defining category membership would depend on the specific properties involved. The important consideration was whether the two properties could be processed at the same time. Some properties could be processed together and therefore would speed classification when combined; others would not. In particular, we proposed that properties can be processed together when they are found on the same region of an object, and when the hand movements that extract the two properties were motorically compatible, allowing them to be performed together. This proposal drew on our earlier work (Lederman & Klatzky 1987) showing that there are specialized hand movements, or exploratory procedures, for extracting object properties. If the exploratory procedures for two properties that redundantly define a category can be performed together, the two properties can be processed together, and object identification should be faster than if only one property is processed at a time.

Examples of two material properties that can be processed together include texture and hardness. In this case, the exploratory procedure for extracting texture is a lateral or tangential movement across the object, and the exploratory procedure for extracting hardness is the application of force into the object.

These procedures can be executed together in the form of a forceful rubbing motion. Texture and hardness were found to speed classification when they redundantly defined a category (Klatzky et al. 1989).

We also considered whether redundant material and geometric properties can be extracted together. The answer appears to be affirmative; Klatzky et al. (1989) found that objects were classified faster into categories defined by both planar shape and texture than into categories defined by either of the properties alone. In another study, we used a set of three-dimensional objects that varied in surface curvature (Lederman, Klatzky, & Reed 1993). The curvature could be extracted locally, from the pattern of skin deformation under the fingertips; following the object's global contour was not necessary. Classification of these objects showed evidence for integration of texture and curvature. Although both these studies indicated integration between material and geometric properties, one must be careful about concluding that the geometric properties were coded in terms of spatial layout. Although spatial coding seems likely in the case of planar shape, it is not clear whether curvature is processed as a spatial or an intensive property, as Lederman and Klatzky (1997) noted. LaMotte and Srinivasan (1993) have shown that cutaneous mechanoreceptors provide both intensive and spatial information about curvature.

To summarize, it appears that if two properties of an object can be extracted together during exploration, object classification is speeded when the properties provide redundant category cues. Not only is this found when both are material properties, but there is also some evidence that it can occur between material and geometric properties, even when the latter are coded spatially. We argue that such convergent use of properties of objects supports rapid and accurate identification by the haptic system and helps to compensate for the system's limited coding of spatial layout information.

7. Top-down contributions

We should not forget that object identification proceeds not only by extracting information from the stimulus that is presented, but by combining presented information with expectancies based on context or past experience. This is what we call top-down processing. Just as visual object identification makes use of top-down processing, so does touch. We demonstrated this effect, for example, in the experiment in which people had only 200 msec of contact in order to identify an object (Klatzky & Lederman 1995). Although they performed at a 15% correct level overall when they had no advance information about the object, performance improved when they had a cue in advance, such as the name of a superordinate category (for example, "container top" when the object was a cork). And when they were given the basic-level name of an object and asked, "Is this the object you touched?" they performed with an accuracy of 72% (relative to 50% chance) at the 200-ms exposure. It is difficult to compare the accuracy level for different cues, because the levels of performance expected by guessing differ. However, people's confidence in their responses increased significantly with cue informativeness, indicating a facilitatory effect of context and demonstrating the top-down contribution to haptic object recognition.

8. Conclusion

We have described studies demonstrating that people are fast and accurate at identifying common objects by touch. We have also described a process of haptic object recognition that shares some elements with visual recognition, but also departs with respect to others. Shared elements that transcend the modality of object recognition include analysis of the object into component features and comparison with memory, along with the contribution of top-down as well as bottom-up processing. Haptic and visual object recognition diverge, however, when it comes to the nature of the features that are processed, with the haptic system relying far more on material properties. This reflects the greater availability of material than spatial properties to haptic perception. The contribution of material may be limited by the fact that shape is the most important attribute that defines every-day object categories; however, the representation of objects in memory has sufficient information about material to make haptic object recognition reliable and rapid.

References

Biederman, I. (1987). Recognition by components: A theory of image human understanding. *Psychological Review, 94,* 115–145.

Edelman, S. & Bülthoff, H. H. (1992). Orientation dependence in the recognition of familiar and novel views of three-dimensional objects. *Vision Research, 32,* 2385–2400.

Hummel, J. E. & Biederman, I. (1992). Dynamic binding in a neural network for shape recognition. *Psychological Review, 99,* 480–517.

Klatzky, R. L. & Lederman, S. J. (1993). Toward a computational model of constraint-driven exploration and haptic object identification. *Perception, 22,* 597–621.

Klatzky, R. L. & Lederman, S. J. (1995). Identifying objects from a haptic glance. *Perception and Psychophysics, 57,* 1111–1123.

Klatzky, R. L., Lederman, S., & Balakrishnan, J. D. (1991). Task-driven extraction of object contour by human haptics: I. *Robotica, 9,* 43–51.

Klatzky, R., Lederman, S., & Metzger, V. (1985). Identifying objects by touch: An "expert system". *Perception and Psychophysics, 37,* 299–302.

Klatzky, R. L., Lederman, S. J., & Reed, C. L. (1989). Haptic integration of object properties: Texture, hardness, and planar contour. *Journal of Experimental Psychology: Human Perception and Performance, 15,* 45–57.

Klatzky, R. L., Loomis, J., Lederman, S. J., Wake, H., & Fujita, N. (1993). Haptic identification of objects and their depictions. *Perception and Psychophysics, 54,* 170–178.

Lakatos, S. & Marks, L.E. (1999). Haptic form perception: Relative salience of local and global features. *Perception and Psychophysics, 61,* 895–908.

LaMotte, R. H. & Srinivasan, M. A. (1993). Responses of cutaneous mechanoreceptors to the shape of objects applied to the primate fingerpad. *Acta Psychologica, 84,* 41–51.

Lederman, S. J. & Klatzky, R. L. (1987). Hand movements: A window into haptic object recognition. *Cognitive Psychology, 19,* 342–368.

Lederman, S. J. & Klatzky, R. L. (1990). Haptic object classification: Knowledge driven exploration. *Cognitive Psychology, 22,* 421–459.

Lederman, S. J. & Klatzky, R. L. (1997). Relative availability of surface and object properties during early haptic processing. *Journal of Experimental Psychology: Human Perception and Performance, 23,* 1680–1707.

Lederman, S. J., Klatzky, R. L., Chataway, C., & Summers, C. D. (1990). Visual mediation and the haptic recognition of two-dimensional pictures of common objects. *Perception and Psychophysics, 47,* 54–64.

Lederman, S. J., Klatzky, R. L., & Reed, C. L. (1993). Constraints on haptic integration of spatially shared object dimensions. *Perception, 22,* 723–743.

Loomis, J. M. (1990). A model of character recognition and legibility. *Journal of Experimental Psychology: Human Perception and Performance, 16,* 106–120.

Loomis, J., Klatzky, R. L., & Lederman, S. J. (1991). Similarity of tactual and visual picture recognition with limited field of view. *Perception, 20,* 167–177.

Moore, T., Broekhoven, M., Lederman, S., & Ulug, S. (1991). Q'Hand: A fully automated apparatus for studying haptic processing of spatially distributed inputs. *Behavior Research Methods, Instruments, and Computers, 23,* 27–35.

Newell, F. N., Ernst, M. O., Tian, B. S., & Bülthoff H. H. (2001). Viewpoint dependence in visual and haptic object recognition. *Psychological Science, 12,* 37–42.

Reed, C. L., Lederman, S. J., & Klatzky, R. L. (1990). Haptic integration of planar size with hardness, texture and plan contour. *Canadian Journal of Psychology, 44,* 522–545.

Rosch, E. (1978). Principles of categorization. In E. Rosch & B. Lloyd (Eds.), *Cognition and categorization* (pp. 27–48). Hillsdale, NJ: Erlbaum.

Tarr, M. J. & Pinker, S. (1989). Mental rotation and orientation-dependence in shape recognition. *Cognitive Psychology, 21,* 233–282.

Treisman, A. & Gormican, S. (1988). Feature analysis in early vision: Evidence from search asymmetries. *Psychological Review, 95,* 15–48.

CHAPTER 8

Haptic processing of spatial and material object properties

Edouard Gentaz and Yvette Hatwell

In order to find out how the haptic processing of each object property works on an intramodal level, we will examine here the studies in which one or several dimensions of non-significant objects are systematically varied. Are there specific modes of processing in the haptic domain or do the laws known in the visual modality also apply to the haptic modality? Numerous studies have been conducted on this question and they concern various object properties. We will first examine spatial properties, then material properties (especially texture). Finally, we will consider the relations between these properties, i.e. the analytical or global nature of haptic perception and the dimensional preferences of children and adults.

1. The perception of spatial properties

1.1 Shape

Shape is a complex property which is studied either globally or by decomposing its constituting elements (curves, angles, etc.).

1.1.1 *Global shape*
Although the haptic discrimination of shape is very generally less efficient than visual discrimination (speed and number of errors), the processing modes of the haptic and visual modalities appear similar in numerous studies. Thus, both modalities are sensitive to the same dimensions of differentiation (Pick & Pick 1966) and to the same effect of complexity, evaluated by the number of sides of each shape (Brumaghin & Brown 1969; Owen & Brown 1970). This similarity has been confirmed by Garbin and Bernstein (1984) and Garbin

(1990) who, through studies of multidimensional scaling, found that the same shape attributes (size, symmetry and complexity) determine the subjective similarity of shapes in vision and haptics. But only 67% of the stimuli occupy the same position on the visual and haptic scales, in adults and at the age of 6–7 years.

However, in other works, differences appear between the visual and the haptic processing of shape. Thus, due to the sequential nature of manual exploration and the possibility of modifying the size of the tactual perceptual field at will, touch is less sensitive than vision to the Gestalt laws of organization and spatial configuration (cf. for example Hatwell, Orliaguet, & Brouty 1990, for a study of the sensitivity of touch to the law of proximity; Chapter 5). On the other hand, Lakatos and Marks (1999) found that when adults were asked to make either visual or haptic similarity judgments on pairs of geometrical forms differing in local features or global shape, the pairs with comparable global shape but different local features were judged less similar by touch than by vision. This differential effect tended to decrease over time and was not related to the haptic exploratory procedures used by the subjects.

In the same vein, the facilitating effect of symmetry, particularly vertical symmetry, which is always present in vision (e.g., Locher & Wagemans 1993; Wagemans 1995; Walk 1965), is not observed in haptic shape perception. Walk (1965), and more recently Ballasteros, Manga and Reales (1997), found that two-dimensional non-symmetrical shapes were haptically detected more quickly and with fewer errors. On the other hand, with three-dimensional objects, an advantage appeared for symmetrical shapes in touch as well as in vision.

To interpret these results, Ballasteros, Millar and Reales (1998) assumed that the reference frames available in the tasks presented induced a specific spatial organization of the stimulus and were responsible for the facilitating effect of symmetry. Thus, several reference frames are available when manipulating 3-D objects with both hands: The body's median (Z) axis, the gravitational vertical, the reference to the position of the hand itself in relation to the head or trunk, etc. But there are far fewer exterior perceptive cues available for small, drawn figures, which are less well discriminated than 3-D objects without training. Sensory data in this case can only be related to a body-centered reference frame (Millar 1994). As a result, reference to an egocentric Z axis should be easier when the two index fingers are placed on either side of this axis in a two-handed exploration than in a one-handed exploration in which the active index finger is not previously positioned in the body's median axis. If such is the case, we should observe the facilitating effect of symmetry in the two-handed condition and the absence of this effect in the one-handed condition. Ballasteros, Millar and Reales (1998) obtained this result in a task in which the subject was asked to judge if small, drawn figures (2 x 2cm), symmetrical or not according to the vertical, horizontal or oblique axes, are open or closed. Fewer errors and shorter response time were observed when the two index fingers explored than when only one was active. According to the authors, this indirect measure presents the advantage of indicating that, as in vision, the effect of symmetry is primitive and incidental, i.e. it appears in the initial stages of perceptual encoding and without voluntary research.

Thus, the facilitating effect of symmetry depends on the availability of spatial reference systems. Note, however, that Ballasteros et al. (1998) obtained facilitation in the two-handed condition only with open figures and not with closed figures, a result which is difficult to account for.

1.1.2   Curvature

The curvature of a stimulus is defined by the converse of the radius of the corresponding curve. For example, a curvature of $0.8m^{-1}$ is defined by a circle having a radius of 1.25 m (1/0.8). The haptic perception of a shape's curvature is linked to exploratory conditions. Gordon and Morison (1982) showed that the discrimination of curvature in blindfolded sighted adults was better when the stimulus was small enough (smaller than a finger) to involve a digital exploration without moving the shoulder-hand system (the forearm rests on the table). For stimuli (10 x 20 cm) with a curvature varying from $0m^{-1}$ to $3m^{-1}$, the absolute threshold of discrimination was 0.09 mm and the relative threshold 0.11mm. The authors studied stimuli whose curvature varied over one dimension, as for cylindrical surfaces, and over two dimensions, as for spherical surfaces. The advantage of spherical surfaces is that all the lines passing through the center of the stimulus have the same degree of curvature. Nevertheless, performances did not differ according to the two types of stimulus.

However, when the size of the object requires exploration mobilizing the shoulder-hand system, performance was degraded. Davidson (1972) asked blindfolded sighted and blind adults to use one hand to explore stimuli whose curvature varied (over one dimension) from $-1.6m^{-1}$ to $+1.6m^{-1}$, and to classify them as concave (the center of the curvature is the body of the subject), convex or straight. When the stimuli were placed on a horizontal surface (the forearm resting on this surface during the exploration), the sighted and the blind made more errors in the classification of concave curvatures than convex ones. When the stimuli were placed in the subjects' fronto-parallel plane, overall performances improved and there was no longer a difference between concave and convex curvatures.

More recently, Kappers and her colleagues (Kappers, Koenderink, & Licht-enegger 1994; Kappers, Koenderink, & Te Pas 1994; Pont, Kappers, & Koen-derink 1997; 1998; Vogels, Kappers, & Koenderink 1996) more systematically examined the haptic perception of curvature by proposing mathematically well-defined, hand-sized objects (elliptical, hyperbolical, spherical and cylin-drical paraboloid shapes). For example, Pont et al. (1998) showed that the es-timation of the curvature of a stimulus is influenced by its orientation in rela-tion to the hand. The same curvature is deemed to be more curved when the stimulus is parallel to the fingers than when it is perpendicular. The authors explained this phenomenon by the "length of contact" between the hand and the stimulus (i.e. the portion of the stimulus in contact with the skin at a given time). This length differs according to the orientation of the exploration: It is shorter when exploration is perpendicular to the hand than when it is parallel, because of the small width of the palm.

Like Gordon and Morison (1982), Pont, Kappers and Koenderink (1999) concluded that the effective stimulus for curvature perception is the explo-ration difference over the curved surface. Louw, Kappers and Koenderink (2000) investigated haptic curvature detection thresholds over a wide range of spatial scales (the width of the Gaussian profile of the stimulus ranged from 150mm to 240mm). In this range of spatial scales a number of mechanisms, ranging from cutaneous mechanoreception to proprioception in fingers, arm and shoulder, contribute to haptic perception. Interestingly, from 1 mm width on, the dependence of the detection threshold on the spatial width of the stimulus was found to be a power function with an exponent of 1.3.

1.1.3   Angle size

The perception of angle size is more accurate in vision than haptics (Appelle 1971). Lakatos and Marks (1998) asked blindfolded adults to explore (accord-ing to different procedures defined by the experimenter) the angles of wooden plates or of raised lines forming isoscele triangles, and to verbally estimate their size in degrees. The authors proposed different angles (from 20° to 150°) and, furthermore, modified the extent of continuity of the intersection between the two angle branches by inserting portions of "circles" with different curvature radii. The results showed that the angles of both types of stimulus (3-D plates or raised lines) were systematically underestimated in all the exploration pro-cedures proposed. The amplitude of this underestimation varied inversely to that of angle size. This underestimation was also present in vision but to a lesser degree. In addition, the estimation of an angle size increased as the curvature radius increased. This effect, present in the haptic modality, was absent in vision.

Thus, haptic performance in shape perception is always inferior to visual performance, and, although the general processing modes are analogous in both modalities, the particular characteristics of manual exploration (spontaneous or imposed) often have specific effects on haptic perceptual estimations.

1.2 Orientation

The spatial orientation of a stimulus is always relative to a reference axis. The vertical and horizontal axes correspond to the direction of the gravity and of the visual horizon respectively form a reference frame in two-dimensional space, where all other orientations are said to be oblique.

At all ages, the perception of orientation is more accurate in vision than haptically, and this accuracy improves with development. In haptic orientation perception, we do not always observe the anisotropy (a better perception of vertical and horizontal than oblique orientations) systematic in vision. This "oblique effect" (Appelle 1972) is present at all ages in most visual tasks. It is evidenced when the difference is made between the performances observed for vertical and horizontal orientations (which most often do not differ and are grouped together) and those for oblique orientations (also grouped together when they do not differ). As it is a question of difference, this oblique effect may appear whatever the overall accuracy of responses. For example, in a reproduction task, the same subjects make average errors in vision and haptically of 1° and 3.8° respectively for the vertical orientation and of 3.6° and 5.7° for oblique orientations (Gentaz et al. 2001). In vision, the processes responsible for the systematic presence of the oblique effect are influenced by multiple factors which operate on different anatomo-functional levels of the visual system according to the nature of the task (Gentaz & Ballaz 2000; Gentaz & Tshopp 2002). In the haptic modality, as we shall see, the existence *per se* of an oblique effect is debated.

1.2.1 *Does an intrinsic oblique effect exist in haptic perception?*
According to Lechelt and his colleagues (Lechelt, Eliuk, & Tanne 1976; Lechelt & Verenka 1980), an intrinsic oblique effect exists in the haptic system, since such an effect is present when blindfolded sighted adults explore a rod stimulus with one hand and simultaneously or successively reproduce its orientation on a response rod with the other hand. Appelle and Countryman (1986), on the

contrary, find that this effect is not intrinsic to the haptic system, as Lechelt's results may be explained by the fact that particular exploration-reproduction movements were induced by the experimental display. Indeed, in these experiments, both rods were placed in the fronto-parallel plane, on each side of the subject's median plane. Exploration and reproduction movements thus differ according to orientation. When one hand explores the rod and the other reproduces its orientation, the symmetrical organization of the shoulder-hand system imposes non-homologous movement patterns during the exploration and reproduction of oblique orientations (different mobilization of the agonist and antagonist muscles), whereas movements are homologous for vertical and horizontal orientations. In order to validate their hypothesis, Appelle and Countryman (1986) showed that the haptic oblique effect disappeared in an ipsilateral condition (the same hand explores and reproduces), i.e. when exploration and reproduction movement patterns were homologous for all orientations. This absence is the result of a reduction in error in the reproduction of oblique orientations.

However, Gentaz and Hatwell (1994, 1995) invalidated Appelle and Countryman's hypothesis by varying the plane of the space in which the task was carried out. The task was accomplished in the horizontal plane (as for Appelle & Countryman), the frontal plane (as for Lechelt et al.) and the sagittal plane (the median plane, perpendicular to the horizontal and frontal planes), and either with the ipsilateral hand (the same hand) or with the contralateral hand (the other hand). In the sagittal plane, the oblique exploratory movements of one hand become homologous to those necessary to their reproduction by the other hand, and the oblique effect should therefore be absent if Appelle and Countryman's (1986) hypothesis is correct. The results obtained in adults did not confirm these predictions, as the same oblique effect was observed in the frontal and sagittal planes in ipsilateral and contralateral conditions. But the results for the horizontal plane replicated Appelle and Countryman's (1986) results, that is to say that an oblique effect was present in the contralateral condition and absent in the ipsilateral condition. The same qualitative results were observed in 7–9 year-olds, although the children's errors were 2° greater than the adults' (who make errors of 6°). But why, in the ipsilateral condition, were oblique orientations more difficult to process than vertical and horizontal orientations in the frontal and sagittal planes, but not in the horizontal plane?

Gentaz and Hatwell (1996) answered this question by studying the gravitational cues produced during stimulus exploration, which specify the direction of the gravitational vertical. The size of the stimulus rod (25cm) and its position in relation to the subject (40cm) effectively demand a significant participation of the shoulder-hand system during exploration. This system, subject to strong gravitational constraints, must deploy antigravitational forces in order to move. The tissue deformations (cutaneous, muscular and articular), which bring gravitational cues specifying the vertical, depend on specific muscular forces needed to maintain and to move the arm in a gravitational environment. The nature of these cues differs according to exploratory conditions. In a normal situation, their average amplitude is more or less the same in the three planes since the arm is always subject to the same gravitational force. However, the variability of these cues differs with the plane. It is high in the frontal and sagittal planes, as the arm uses more antigravitational forces when moving from bottom to top than from top to bottom. Conversely, the gravitational cues vary less in the horizontal plane as the arm always moves perpendicularly to gravity.

Gentaz and Hatwell (1996) thus found that the oblique effect was absent when adults explored and reproduced rod orientation with the same hand in the horizontal plane while resting the forearm, wrist and hand on the surface supporting the rod ("supported forearm" condition, Figure 8.1A, used in the previous experiments). As gravitational constraints were reduced in this case, subjects used few antigravitational forces to explore the rod and thus received little information concerning the orientation of the gravitational vertical. On the other hand, the oblique effect was present when subjects held the forearm, wrist and hand in the air ("unsupported forearm" condition, Figure 8.1B). In this condition, antigravitational forces must necessarily be produced as the stimulus is 8cm above the support surface. The same qualitative results were observed in 6–10 year-olds (cf. Gentaz 2000).

The role of these gravitational cues also appeared (Gentaz & Hatwell 1996) when subjects were tested in a "lightened forearm" condition, in one of the three planes. This lightening, obtained by holding the arm in a balanced position via a system of pulleys linked to a weight, diminished the gravitational cues present during exploration. The oblique effect was attenuated, as vertical and horizontal estimations became less accurate, whereas oblique estimations remained stable. By contrast, when the forearm was made heavier with bracelets (500g or 1000g), the oblique effect was not modified, perhaps because subjects are used to their arms feeling heavy when they are transporting objects (cf. Marchetti & Lederman's (1983) analogous results in the haptic estimation of length). These results suggest that gravitational cues play a role in the haptic perception of orientations in the blindfolded sighted adults and children, even if the effects of their variations are not symmetrical.

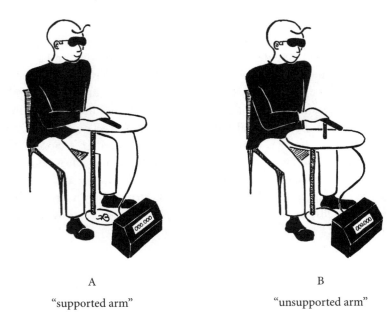

A
"supported arm"

B
"unsupported arm"

Figure 8.1. Experimental displays used to study the reproduction of orientation in the horizontal plane. A: "supported arm" condition (the rod is at 0 cm from the plate). B: "unsupported arm" condition (the rod is 8 cm far from the plate) (adapted from Gentaz & Hatwell 1996).

In order to find out whether visual experience is involved in the presence of the oblique effect, Gentaz and Hatwell (1998) compared the performances of early and late totally blind adults by varying the amplitude (natural or reduced level of gravitational constraints) and the variability of gravitational cues (weak variability in the horizontal plane, strong variability in the frontal plane). No difference was found between the early and late blind in the overall accuracy of reproduction. In the horizontal plane, the oblique effect was absent whatever the gravitational constraints in both the early and the late blind. In the frontal plane, the oblique effect was present in both groups whatever the gravitational constraints. The fact that, according to conditions, this effect was present in the early blind and absent in the late blind invalidates the hypothesis assuming a role of visual experience. Furthermore, these results showed that the totally blind, who have an intensive practice of the haptic system, are above all influenced by the variability of gravitational cues.

In all of these studies, the delay between exploration and reproduction was of five seconds and unfilled. Gentaz and Hatwell (1999) finally showed that when this delay (5 or 30s) was unfilled, the perception of orientation in the horizontal plane in blindfolded sighted subjects depended on the available gravitational cues: The oblique effect was absent when gravitational cues were weak ("supported forearm" condition) and present when these cues were natural. On the other hand, when the 30-second delay was filled with interfering activities, which were either verbal (reciting the alphabet backwards) or haptic (haptically following a sinuous pathway), the oblique effect was present whatever the available gravitational cues. The presence of the oblique effect in the two conditions with interfering activities could be explained by the decrease in accuracy of oblique orientation coding as compared to the performances observed in the two conditions with unfilled delays. To sum up, memorization conditions influence the haptic processing of orientation only when the gravitational cues available during the experiment are weak.

In order to identify the nature of the spatial reference in which orientations were mapped, Luyat, Gentaz, Regia-Corte and Guerraz (2001) examined the effect of body and head tilts on the haptic oblique effect. In natural conditions (like in previous studies), the egocentric (referred to the participant's body) and allocentric (referred to environment cues like the direction of the pull of gravity) reference frames are aligned. Body or head tilts lead to a mismatch between egocentric and gravitational axes and indicate whether the haptic oblique effect is defined in an egocentric or in a gravitational reference frame. The ability to reproduce principal (vertical and horizontal) and +/− 45° oblique orientations was studied in upright and tilted (+/− 45°) postures. Moreover, by controlling the deviation of the haptic subjective vertical provoked by postural tilt, the possible role of a subjective gravitational reference frame was tested. Results showed that the haptic reproduction of orientations was strongly affected both by the position of the whole-body and the position of the head. In particular, the classical haptic oblique effect observed in the upright posture disappeared in tilted conditions, mainly because of a decrease in the accuracy of the vertical and horizontal settings. The subjective vertical appeared to be the orientation reproduced the most accurately. The results showed that the haptic oblique effect is not purely gravitationally or egocentrically defined but rather that it depends on a subjective gravitational reference frame which is tilted in a direction opposite to that of the head in tilted postures. Luyat and Gentaz (2002) observed similar results in the visual modality.

1.2.2   *Discussion*

First, these results confirmed the existence, under certain conditions, of an intrinsic oblique effect in haptic perception, contrary to Appelle and Countryman's assertions (1986), since this effect was observed in the early totally blind. Secondly, these results showed that haptic perception of orientations depended on the conditions of exploration, memorization and reproduction of the stimulus. According to Gentaz (2000), the presence or the absence of the oblique effect attests that different types of processes are involved in each case. Thus, its presence is evidence of encoding in a reference frame in which the vertical and horizontal orientations are used as norms. Within this frame and in a single plane, vertical and horizontal orientations are encoded directly onto one of the norms, whereas oblique orientations are encoded relative to the two norms. Encoding oblique orientation therefore requires more calculations than the direct encoding of the vertical and horizontal orientations, and this difference may partially explain the presence of the haptic oblique effect. This type of process, relatively stable over time, presents the advantage of requiring few attentional resources, but the drawback of generating anisotropic perception.

As for the absence of the oblique effect, there is evidence of the implementation of original haptic processes based on the encoding of orientations via the very dynamics of the exploratory movements accomplished and memorized. Each orientation is encoded through a kinesthetic sequence of movements. In this case, the fact that all orientations are not encoded according to reference norms, but rather according to sequences of movements would explain the absence of anisotropy in the haptic perception of orientations. These haptic processes, also relatively stable over time, present the advantage of not generating an anisotropic perception of orientation, but the disadvantage of requiring considerable attentional resources (sensitivity to interference).

Finally, regarding the selection and the availability of these two types of haptic processes, the absence of the qualitative effects of age and visual experience on the appearance of the haptic oblique effect suggests that they are available at least from the age of six, regardless of visual status. In addition, the existence of several participating factors in the oblique effect reveals that the selection of these two types of processes is multi-determined and not exclusive (they may act together).

1.3   Perception of the line parallelism

Kappers (1999, 2002) and Kappers and Koenderink (1999) investigated the haptic perception of spatial relations in both horizontal and mid-sagittal planes. In a simple task where blindfolded participants were asked to rotate a test bar in such a way that it felt as being parallel (in physical space) to a reference bar, huge systematic subject-dependent deviations were found. Observers systematically produced deviations of up to 90°, thus setting the two bars perpendicular! This effect was very robust and remained even after visual inspection and various ways of feedback. Unimanual and bimanual, and also pointing and collinearity measurements yielded similar results. These results confirmed that haptic space is not Euclidean, contrary to common expectations. The current hypothesis of the authors of these studies is that the deviations reflect the use of a reference frame that is a weighted average of egocentric and allocentric reference frames. Cuijpers, Kappers and Koenderink (2000, 2002) performed similar parallelity and collinearity experiments in vision. That visual space is not Euclidean was already established early in the previous century, but these new studies provided quite some extra evidence. For example, bars at eye height separated by a visual angle of 60° have (depending on the participant) to differ 20° in orientation in order to be perceived as parallel. Conventional explanations fail to account for these facts. Deviations depend on the task used to determine the deviations, suggesting that the concept of a unified "visual space" is mistaken.

1.4 Length

Length perception is more accurate in vision than in haptics, especially in the youngest subjects (cf. Hatwell 1986). In the haptic modality, the results observed in the literature are very variable. To understand them, we will examine the different methodologies used in the various studies.

1.4.1 *Psychophysical function*

The first method involves establishing the psychophysical function linking the physical length of a stimulus (a segment) and its estimated size. In vision and in adults, this function is linear and its exponent is equal to 1: An increase in the physical value of the stimulus produces a proportional increase in the perceived size. In haptics, the response mode influences this psychophysical function. Thus, the function is linear with an exponent of 1 when the estimation is given via the space between the two index fingers actively placed at each end of the stimulus by the participant (Teghtsoonian & Teghtsoonian 1965) or via the movement along the stimulus of just one index finger or the whole hand (Hermelin & O'Connor 1975; Stanley 1966). However, when the estimation is given by the space between the index finger and the thumb in a pincer posture, the exponent is 1.2 (Teghtsoonian & Teghtsoonian 1970). Thus, an increase in the physical value of the stimulus produces a more rapid increase in the size perceived by the hand.

More recently, Lanca and Bryant (1995) presented haptically stimulus-segments made up of raised dots to adults. The stimuli were placed on a horizontal surface and blindfolded participants were asked to rest their forearm and hand on this surface while they explored the stimulus with the index finger. Then, they reproduced the length of the stimulus with the same index finger. Each length was tested in seven orientations (0° to 90°). The length had an effect on the accuracy of reproduction, with increasing underestimation when the physical length of the stimulus increased. The psychophysical function was linear and its exponent was 0.885. Stimulus orientation had no effect on length estimation. The authors pointed out (unfortunately without indicating the numerical value) that the value of this exponent was different according to stimulus orientation when subjects did not rest their forearm on the table during exploration.

In studies not directly concerned with the psychophysical function, Lederman, Klatzky and Barber (1985) also observed the influence of the response mode in the estimation of rectilinear lengths. Thus, when responses were given via the distance between the index fingers ("static" response), overall errors were of 2.45 cm and varied little. When reproduction was carried out by moving the index ("dynamic" response), overall errors were of 1.56 cm and varied more. These performances were not improved when the index finger unused during the experiment remained or did not remain at the starting point of the stimulus. These "dynamic" response results are close to those obtained by Lanca et al. (1995) and Schellingerhout (1998) with the same response mode and other lengths. Lederman et al. (1985) also observed that early blind subjects made consistently higher errors than late blind ones. Lederman, Klatzky, Collins and Wardell (1987) proposed the same task, but with three speeds of stimulus exploration (slow/20s; normal/10s; fast/1.5s) and a verbal response mode. In these conditions, overall errors were similar in the three exploratory speeds and were greater than those obtained in 1985.

Lederman et al. (1985) also examined the perception of the length of sinuous stimuli with static and dynamic response modes. Errors followed one of Weber's laws: There was a systematic overestimation of about 5 cm for short lengths (from 2.1 cm to 20 cm), very weak errors for lengths of around 25 cm and finally an underestimation which increased as physical length increased (from −5 cm for 30 cm to −20 cm for 90 cm). These results were also observed in the late and early blind, and there was no difference between these two populations. In a similar perspective, Lederman et al. (1987) studied the perception of the length (from 7.5 cm to 55 cm) of stimuli composed of two segments forming an angle. The stimulus length estimation (with a verbal response) increased as physical length increased, with a coefficient of 1.17 which differed according to exploratory speed: This coefficient was maximum with the slow speed and minimum with the fast speed. These results are different from those observed in 1985 by the same authors. This difference may stem from the fact that the response modes and the stimuli used were not the same in the two studies.

1.4.2 *Length Bisection*

In length bisection, the subject has to indicate the point which splits a segment into two equal parts. This technique is frequently used in neuropsychology as it evidences the hemineglect phenomenon (i.e. the inattention of the side opposite to a cerebral lesion) in patients suffering from a brain damage generally situated in the right parietal area (cf. Chapters 2 and 3). These patients show a significant deviation to the right of the point of bisection, as if they had not noticed the left part of their perceptual field (the field contralateral to the lesion). This phenomenon, well known in vision, is also present in haptics.

Haptic bisection tasks were first applied to normal subjects by Bowers and Heilman (1980) who observed an error reverse to that of the heminegligent patients, that is a deviation to the left of the point of bisection. According to some authors, this error called "pseudo-neglect" results from the preferential activation of the right hemisphere in spatial processing. This activation would produce an expansion of the contralateral left hemispace. However, in haptics, the existence of this left deviation in normal subjects has been questioned in later research. Pseudoneglect appeared in some studies (Bradshaw et al. 1987; Sampaio & Philip 1991), whereas the overall error was not significant in others (Fisher 1994; Mattingley et al. 1993). Philip and Hatwell (1998) observed, like Chokron and Imbert (1993), that each hand tended to deviate into the contralateral space. When the exploratory direction was imposed (left to right exploration only, or right to left exploration only), the point of bisection was deviated in the direction opposite to the departure point (Philip & Hatwell 1998). All of these results cast a doubt on the interpretation of bisection errors in terms of hemispheric activation, and suggest that exploratory modes once again modify the nature and the direction of errors. It is possible that errors in haptic bisection tasks result from a change in the subject's egocentric reference point, as Jeannerod and Biguer (1989) and Chokron and Imbert (1995) asserted.

1.4.3   *Inferring Euclidian distances*

Another way of studying the haptic perception of length involves examining the estimation of an Euclidean distance inferred between two points. Thus, Lederman et al. (1985) asked blindfolded sighted adults to infer the Euclidean (shortest) distance between two points in a task where the subject's index finger arrived at the second point after following a trajectory including detours. The authors tested several Euclidean distances (from 2.5 cm to 15.2 cm) and proposed winding detours 2, 4, 6 and 8 times longer than these Euclidian distances. Estimations of length were done by positioning a cursor along rectilinear rule. The results revealed an overestimation of the Euclidean distances which increased as the length of the detours increased ("detour effect"). This effect was present even if the subjects did not know in advance whether they should estimate detour length or Euclidean distance, but its amplitude was reduced if the subject was warned of what was to be judged. The detour effect was present with static and dynamic responses, whatever the stimulus orientation. However, it was only observed when the length of the detour was at least twice as long as the Euclidean distance tested. Lederman et al. (1985) also observed this effect in the late and early blind, with greater amplitude in the early blind.

Faineteau, Gentaz and Viviani (in press) studied the same task in the kinesthetic modality. Blindfolded participants followed straight and curvilinear paths with a hand-held stylus (encoding phase). Then, with a straight movement, they estimated the Euclidean distance between the start- and endpoints of the path (response phase; see Figures 8.2 A and B). Signed errors increased as a function of path length. But the detour effect was not homogeneous. The tendency for estimated distances to increase with the length of the detour was much more marked for small paths (A, B and C) than for large paths (D, E and F). Moreover, signed errors were consistently smaller when the path covered a larger surface.

Lederman et al. (1985) explained the detour effect by invoking an encoding heuristics that would (erroneously) take into account the duration of the finger movements. Instead, Faineteau et al. (in press) suggested that the key factor was the extent of the workspace covered by the encoding movements. Tracking the small paths involved hand and arm movements spanning a more limited portion of the workspace than tracking the large paths. Because large errors occurred only in the former case, this suggest that the accuracy with which kinesthetic inputs are able to encode the relevant metric information increases with their range of variation. Thus, the detour effect should not be present if Euclidean estimations were based mainly on positional cues. The very fact that errors depend on the path length suggests instead that the linear extent of the

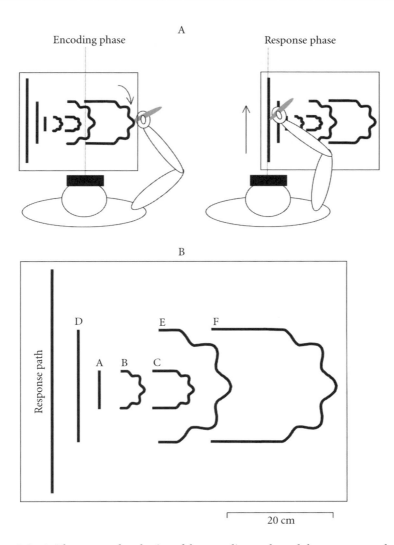

Figure 8.2. A: The start and endpoint of the encoding path, and the response path were both on the mid-sagittal axis of the trunk. B: Outlay of the workplane. Each set of paths (G1: {A, B, C} and G2: {D, E, F}) included one straight, and two variable-curvature paths. The straight paths (A and D) were 7.5 and 22.5 cm long, respectively, and were parallel to the sagittal axis of the participant. The length of the curved paths in the two sets was equal to 2 and 3 times the length of the corresponding straight paths, respectively (B=15 cm; C=22.5 cm; E=45 cm; F=67.5 cm). Responses were given by following the 45 cm vertical path on the left side of the board (adapted from Faineteau et al. in press).

path followed by the hand is also taken into account for estimating Euclidean distance. In principle, linear extent information could be used to derive the true Euclidean distance by decomposing the time-varying displacement vector, and taking into account only the component along the sagittal direction. If so, errors would reflect the inability to filter out the orthogonal (irrelevant) component of the displacement vector. Specifically, separating the components may become increasingly difficult as the points where the balance of the component changes get closer in space and time. Indeed, all the four curved test paths (B, C, E, F) had the same number (8) of points of inflection, in each of which the component balance changed drastically. However, these points were more spatially clustered in small space than in large space. Moreover, because the encoding phase was shorter for paths in small space than for those in large space, these points were also closer in time.

1.4.4   Discussion

In conclusion, these studies revealed a considerable variability in performances which results probably from methodological differences. Nevertheless, they show that haptic length perception depends on exploratory conditions and response modes. Thus, performances are most coherent and accurate when subjects are asked to reproduce the estimated length of a previously explored stimulus in a horizontal plane with the same index finger as used in exploration. These results suggest the implementation of haptic processes based on the encoding of length via the very dynamics of the exploratory movement. Indeed, the length seems to be encoded, at least partially, via a sequence of movements. This "encoding of movements", available regardless of the subject's visual status, is in use when the shoulder-hand system is largely occupied during exploration. It is possible that this type of process is close to that at work in the non-anisotropic perception of orientation. To test this hypothesis, a more systematic study of length perception in adults and children is necessary, manipulating the factors used in orientation studies. Thus, all the studies presented here place the stimulus in the horizontal plane, and only Lanca and Bryant's (1995) study controls whether the forearm rests or not on the table during exploration. And yet orientation studies have shown the importance of controlling this factor (see also Chapter 9), i.e. the available gravitational cues.

1.5   Localization

Localization perception is more accurate in vision than in haptics (cf. Hatwell 1986). As for the study of length perception, the different approaches used for studying this type of haptic perception will be presented.

1.5.1   *Reference frame*

Localizing a stimulus in the environment involves encoding its position in a reference frame. As the haptic system is a contact modality which provides less information about external environment than the visual system, the question is whether an egocentric reference is used more often than an allocentric reference to locate a stimulus haptically, especially in children. In order to answer this question, the frame within which an object position must be estimated is varied, making egocentric reference easy or difficult.

In vision, results showed that, early on, young children can locate objects in an allocentric reference frame (with reference firstly to stable exterior cues present in the visual environment, then later in relation to a gravitational reference frame). In haptics the situation differs according to whether subjects have visual representations or not. In blindfolded sighted and in late blind subjects, the haptic localization of an object is generally accomplished within an allocentric reference frame, especially in older children and adults. However, in the haptic modality, younger blindfolded sighted children favor longer a non-updated egocentric reference frame, that is to say one which has not taken the spatial consequences of the displacement of the subject or the objects into account. This was observed by Hatwell and Sayettat (1991) in four-year-old children in a task involving the localization of a target after the rotation of its supporting surface.

Early blind participants are deprived of most of the various salient cues available to the sighted and the late blind. Even as adults, they tend to localize an object haptically in relation to their own bodies (Millar 1994). Therefore, they most often experience difficulty in inferring the position of an object after the displacement of the object or of the subject himself (Hatwell 1966, 1978; cf. Thinus-Blanc & Gaunet 1997).

This appears, particularly in young children, in "perspective taking" tasks, in which the arrangement of objects must be represented from different points of view. By simplifying Piaget and Inhelder's (1947) "three-mountains" test, Flavell, Flavell, Green and Wilcox (1981) and Salatas and Flavell (1976) described a Level 1 in which a child knows that an object appears in the same way to oneself and to another person if both look at it from the same place. In Level

2, a child knows that an object with heterogeneous faces appears differently to oneself and to another person looking at it from different places. In the sighted using their vision, Level 1 is reached from the age of three years, and Level 2 at around the age of 4 ½, but exact responses revealing a correct representation of the different points of view obviously appear later.

In order to understand the effect of blindness on these acquisitions, Miletic (1995) compared three groups of eight-year-old children: Totally blind from birth, severely visually impaired (residual acuity of about 1/10 to 1/50) and sighted. The latter two groups could use vision during the test. The task consisted of verbally describing and then reproducing the spatial position of a geometrical object, fixed on a circular plate, such as it would appear to a doll placed near the child (0°), then at 45, 90, 135, 180, 225, 270 and 315°. Level 1 was reached by all the children but Level 2 was affected by visual status: The performances of the sighted were at maximum, those of the visually impaired slightly inferior, and those of the early totally blind very weak and revealed an almost total failure (except at 0°). In another study (Miletic 1994), congenitally blind subjects were equipped with the Optacon/TVSS (cf. Chapter 16). This display transforms the visual image provided by a video camera into vibrations stimulating the interior face of the index finger; this allows therefore a kind of "remote" tactile perception of objects. The performances of the blind using the Optacon were consistently higher than those of the blind working in the usual haptic condition.

In these tasks involving the representation of changes in point of view, the late blind do not show the same difficulties as the early blind (Hatwell 1966; Millar 1994; Thinus-Blanc & Gaunet 1997). But some inconsistent results are sometimes noted in the literature. For example, in adults, Klatzky et al. (1995) observed no effect of visual status in adults in spatial tasks, including those involving inference after displacement. However, this difference may be due to the way subjects were selected: In these latter studies (as in many other contemporary ones), the sample includes only those blind people who could travel alone in town and were employed or students. This mode of selection obviously excludes all those whose spatial difficulties have made these acquisitions impossible.

1.5.2   *Automatic or attentionnal processing of localization?*

Another way of studying object's spatial localization involves finding out whether the processes at work in memorizing its position are intentional or automatic. As the haptic system is less efficient in processing space than the visual system, the attentional resources needed to localize a stimulus may be

greater, particularly in children. Hatwell (1995) compared the visual and haptic memorization of the position (to the left or to the right of the subject's
median plane) of an object in 7 to 9-year-old children in an intentional or incidental learning task. In the incidental learning condition, the subjects were
asked to explore haptically or visually a geometrical form in order to memorize its shape only. During the test, they were asked to recognize the studied
shape and, in addition, to indicate whether this object appeared on the left or
the right side of the board during presentation. In the intentional learning condition, the children were asked to memorize both the shape and the left-right
localization of the object. In the visual modality, object localization was very
well memorized in both conditions, intentional and incidental (with slightly
lower performances in the incidental condition), which suggests an automatic
processing at least from the age of 7. These results are coherent with those reported in the literature concerning vision. However, in haptics, and contrary
to what would be observed if processing was completely automatic, performances were clearly better in the intentional condition than in the incidental
condition. This means that attention improved performances. The amplitude
of this difference was smaller in children aged 9 because performances in the
incidental condition improved at this age. These latter results suggest that haptic localization processing becomes automatic during development, although
this automatic functioning is reached later in haptics than in vision.

1.5.3   *Inferring localization*

A final way of studying haptic localization is to find out if, haptically, the inference of stimulus position is linked to the exploratory movements needed to
reach it, as is the case for Euclidean distance. In order to study this question, Lederman et al. (1985) proposed a paradigm similar to that proposed to examine
the inference of Euclidean distances. The authors fixed an Euclidean distance of
6.7 cm between a departure and an arrival point, and changed the orientation
and the length of the detours between these two points. After freely exploring
the detour with their index finger, subjects were asked to position a pointer
reproducing the direction linking the departure and arrival points. The results
showed that direction estimations were not influenced by the different detours.

Klatzky (1999) proposed a completion task, in which blindfolded sighted
adults depart from the end of one branch of a triangle and cover two sides
with their index finger. Then, at the end of the second side, they were asked to
go back to the starting point with the same finger. The paths were formed by
the combination of three variables: Length of the first leg, length of the second
leg and angle between legs. Each path was made of raised dots 2 mm in dia-

meter. Two parameters of the completing leg traced were measured: Its length and the internal angle formed by the second and completing leg. The results showed that the length of the completing leg was increasingly underestimated as a function of the actual length. It is likely that the discrepancy between these results (underestimation) as compared to those obtained in 1987 (overestimation) can be explained by the response mode used (a motor response in the 1999 experiment and a verbal response in 1987). In contrast, the direction of the leg was estimated accurately, whatever the explored paths. Taken together, the presence of a path effect on the distance errors and its absence on the direction errors suggests that these two parameters were computed by separate processes (Klatzky 1999).

Wydoodt et al. (2003) proposed the same completion task but the paths were made of 3D metal rods. Regarding the distance response, the results showed a path effect. These results are consistent with Klatzky's findings (1999) in which the distance errors were also affected by the variations of paths. Regarding the direction response, the results also showed a path effect. This is not consistent with Klatzky's findings (1999) in which the direction errors were not affected by the variations of paths. Taken together, the results of Wydoodt et al. suggest that the two parameters (distance and direction) are not computed by separate processes. A tentative interpretation of the discrepancies between Wydoodt et al.'s results (2003) and those of Klatzky (1999) was to take into account one difference concerning the nature of stimulus. The paths were made of raised dots in Klatzky's study (1999) whereas the paths were made of 3D metal rods in Wydoodt et al.'s study. Some studies showed that information concerning texture may be taken into account in the haptic perception of length in some conditions (Corsini & Pick 1969; Schellingerhourt, Smitsman, & Van Galen 1998).

1.5.4   Discussion

In conclusion, these results in the simple task of perception suggest that localization encoding operates in a spatial reference frame (egocentric or allocentric) depending on the visual status and the age of the subjects. The position of a stimulus seems to be encoded in relation to the axes of the reference frame used, whatever the movements produced to reach it. This type of process would need limited or no attentional resources and could be close to the anisotropic orientation perception. By contrast, the results in the complex task of localization inference (completion task) reveal variability in performances which results probably from experimental differences. As indicated above, new research is necessary to test both these discrepancies and the hypothesis concerning the similarity of the processes at work in the haptic perception of different spatial properties.

2. The perception of material properties: Texture

In a wider sense, all physical properties defining a surface's micro-structure are included in the term "texture": Roughness, hardness, elasticity, etc. (Lederman & Klatzky 1997). However, only roughness, and to a lesser extent hardness, have been studied.

In order to vary roughness in experiments, different fabrics, abrasive papers of varied grain density, or rectilinear grooves with varied depth and spacing have been used. Katz (1925/1989) was the first to insist on the necessity of movement in order to perceive texture. However, this movement may arise indifferently from the subjects rubbing the object with their fingers or the object being moved under the subjects' immobile fingers. Indeed, contrary to what is found in other domains, Heller (1989) and Lederman (1974) observed no difference between these active and passive conditions and suggested that texture perception was less the result of kinetics than of cutaneous information. This was confirmed by Srinivasan and La Motte (1996) but only regarding the texture of slightly supple surfaces like an eraser. When surfaces are very rigid, these authors observed better performances in the active condition than in the passive one. According to Lederman (1974, 1981; cf. Hughes & Jansson 1994), texture perception is hardly sensitive to variations in the speed of movement. It depends on the force of pressure on the surface and on the width of grooves, if there are any. However, these factors linked to exploration account for only 1% of the estimated variance (Lederman 1974, 1981; cf. Hughes & Jansson 1994). Furthermore, using the valid or non-valid priming procedure, Sathian and Burton (1991) observed that selective attention is not needed for the detection of an abrupt change in texture, while attention improves performances when the task is to detect an absence of texture or to discriminate two textures. Finally, using a multidimensional scaling analysis, Hollins, Faldowski, Rao and Young (1993) found that, in adults, a three-dimensional space accounts for results with a roughness factor (rough-smooth), a hardness factor (hard-soft) and an unspecified third factor.

Tactile texture perception is as efficient as visual perception, and sometimes, for the extremely fine textures of abrasive papers (ranging from n° 1000 to 6000, according to standard norms), tactile perception surpasses visual. This was found by Heller (1989) in blindfolded sighted adults and in early blind and late blind people (visual status had no effect on performances). The question of whether bimodal visual and tactile (V + T) perception improves discrimination is under discussion. Heller (1982) found a superiority of the bimodal condition as compared to the unimodal one (V only and T only). However, this superiority was not due to the perception of texture itself, but to the vision of the hands exploratory movements. In other studies (Heller 1985; Jones & O'Neil 1985), there was no difference between unimodal and bimodal stimulus presentations: Both modalities participated equally in the bimodal presentation, but responses were faster with visual presentation.

The fact that touch is well adapted to texture perception is also apparent in perceptual conflict situations. Whereas, in the spatial domain, a visual capture generally occurs (cf. Hatwell 1986, 1994; Welch 1978; cf. Chapter 12), in texture conflict compromise responses are often observed (Lederman & Abbott 1981) or a tendency towards tactile capture when instructions explicitly ask for an evaluation of roughness. On the other hand, when instructions ask for an evaluation of the spatial density of the grain of abrasive paper, a tendency towards visual capture is observed (Lederman, Thorne, & Jones 1986). The haptic modality thus seems to be well specialized in the apprehension of objects material properties, whereas vision is specialized in the spatial domain.

Information concerning texture is moreover taken into account in the perception of other properties, which sometimes causes interference and sometimes helps. Thus, Corsini and Pick (1969) observed an overestimation of length when stimuli had very rough textures (abrasive paper from 24 to 50) and an underestimation when their texture was finer (120 and 320). Schellingerhout, Smitsman and Van Galen (1998) studied the effect of three different surfaces (smooth, evenly rough and graded rough) on the estimation of the distance and the localization of the arrival point either of an active movement or of a passive movement of a surface over an immobile index finger. They obtained a texture effect only when the movement was passive and when displacement speed was not the same in the presentation and reproduction phases: Absolute errors were maximum with the smooth texture (underestimation) and minimum with the graded texture. In the other conditions (passive movement/same speed, active movement/different speed, active movement/same speed), the texture effect was not significant. This shows that when the main kinesthetic cues (on which haptic evaluations of distance and localization are based: Amplitude and speed of movement) are absent, the cues linked to texture are used and these lead to biased judgments. These cues intervene even more markedly in early blind 8 to 12-year-old children. In these children, texture variations lead to variations in distance and localization judgments, even in the active movement condition (Schellingerhout 1998; Smitsman & Schellingerhout 2000). In other situations, the tactile/haptic perception of the texture gradient of a raised-line drawing allow a three-dimensional property such as slant to be apprehended. This is apparent in Holmes, Hughes and Jansson's (1998) study, in which blindfolded adults demonstrated good ability in discriminating texture gradients. After they have received explanations concerning the spatial signification of gradients, they were able to reproduce the slant of a panel from the graphic representation of its gradient. A group of early blind produced analogous performances, which led the authors to discuss the usefulness of introducing such texture gradients in tactile drawings and maps for the blind.

3.   Relations between properties

Up until now, we have examined the haptic processing of different properties taken in isolation. We will now look at the relations maintained by these different properties and the way in which they interact when they are apprehended by the subject.

3.1 Analytic or global perception?

Because objects are multi-dimensional, they have values in several dimensions: Texture, localization, orientation, size, shape, etc. In vision, all dimensions are perceived practically simultaneously (a question of milliseconds) in a single glance. This is not the case in the haptic modality, due to the mode of exploration and motor incompatibilities which make perception very sequential (cf. Chapter 5). That is why this form of perception seems to be less "global" and more "analytic" than visual perception (Revesz 1950). More recent works allows now a better understanding of what that means.

These works began with Garner (1974) who distinguished "integrated" and "separated" dimensions in vision. The former are seen globally, that is to say that they are not dissociated from each other, even in adults: This is the case for the elements which make up color, namely hue (wave length), saturation (the quantity of pure color) and brightness (the quantity of reflected light). Any change in saturation alters the perception of hue and brightness. On the other hand, the "separated" dimensions are dissociable and independent. Thus, in adults, changing size does not affect shape perception and vice versa. In order to understand the integrated or separated nature of dimensions,

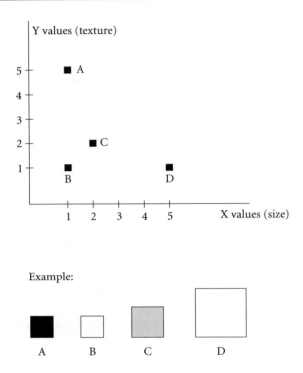

Figure 8.3. Properties of the objects used by Berger and Hatwell (1993, 1995, 1996) in their studies of free haptic classification tasks. In the above example, the most granular texture appears in the darkest color.

Garner used free and rapid classification tasks according to imposed criteria. In the free classification task, 3 objects (or 4 in more recent studies, cf. Figure 8.3) are varied according to two dimensions, each one varying along five values. Object B, taken as standard, has the same value as objects A and D in one dimension, but is very different from them in the other dimension. On the other hand, object C shares no value with B, but is only slightly different from C in both dimensions. The subject is asked to indicate which object "goes best with B". If C is chosen, it means that the two dimensions have been processed, whereas if A or D are chosen, only one dimension has been taken into consideration and the other has been ignored ("filtered"). In the first case, the classification is based on "overall similarity" (it reveals therefore integrated dimensions), and in the second case the classification is "dimensional" (it reveals separated dimensions).

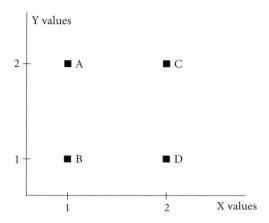

Figure 8.4. Properties of the objects used by Berger and Hatwell (1995, 1996) in their studies of rapid imposed haptic classification tasks.

In the method of "imposed rapid classification", Garner used four objects taking two values in two dimensions (Figure 8.4). The subject had to classify each objects as quickly as possible according to a particular criteria (size, color, etc.) given by the experimenter. Thus, only one of the dimensions should be taken into consideration and the other ignored. In a Control condition, only one dimension varied (for example, the size) and the other was constant (the color). This corresponded to the presentation of objects A and B only, or of B and D only of Figure 8.4. In a Correlated condition, the pertinent dimension was correlated with the non-pertinent dimension. Thus, in a size classification task, the small objects were all red, and the large objects were all blue (objects B and C, or objects A and D). If size and color dimensions are separated, color will be ignored and performances (correct responses and response time RT) will not be different from those in the Control Condition, where color does not vary. However, if benefit is drawn from the redundancy of information, i.e. if the Correlated Condition appears easier than the Control one, this would mean that the two dimensions have been processed and thus have not been dissociated (integrated dimensions). Finally, in an Orthogonal condition, the two dimensions varied independently of each other: The objects, large or small, were red or blue (the 4 objects A, B, C and D were used). If filtering is successful (separated dimensions), performances in this condition will be similar to those in the Control condition. If on the contrary interferences occur (increase in RTs and errors), it would mean that the non-pertinent dimension has been processed (integrated dimensions) and caused disturbance.

In vision, it has been shown that the separated or integrated nature of the dimensions is dependent not only on stimulus characteristics, but also on age: Young children tend to classify objects by overall similarity and adults by dimension (Evans & Smith 1988; Shepp & Swartz 1976; Smith 1989; Smith & Kemler 1977). This classification also depends on the experimental situation: If objects are very complex and if there is a strict speed constraint, even adults classify by similarity in an integrated way (Ward 1983).

These methods proposed by Garner (1974) in vision were further applied to the haptic modality. The question was to find out whether, because of the sequential nature of tactile apprehension, dimensional separation and/or integration took place according to the same laws as in vision.

3.1.1   Changes in relation to age

In the visual modality, many dimensions are processed globally (in an integrated way) by children (4–5 years old) and then become separated in adults (Evans & Smith 1988; Shepp & Swartz 1976; Smith 1989; Smith & Kemler 1977). This has been attributed to the selective attention difficulties of the young, which prevent them from dissociating properties, and to the fact that children, unlike adults, do not favor identity criteria in their classifications (Smith 1989). Is the same true in the haptic modality where access to the different properties of an object is sequential and incomplete, due to the specialization of exploratory procedures and the sometimes partial nature of children's exploration (cf. Chapter 5)?

Berger and Hatwell (1993, 1995, 1996) obtained different results in the haptic modality than those found in vision. In free classification tasks, classification by similarity did not predominate over dimensional classification in children. At the ages of 5 and 9 years, the majority of responses were dimensional, and this seemed to be the result of exploratory characteristics. Thus, for flat objects (squares glued on a board) varying in size and texture (five levels in each dimension), 5-year-olds used mainly lateral motion and produced predominantly dimensional classifications based on texture. For objects varying in texture and hardness, the most frequently used procedure was enclosure/pressure and they were associated with predominant dimensional classification by hardness. The absence of overall similarity responses seemed therefore due to the fact that the two properties were not equally well perceived during exploration because exploratory movements were adapted only for one of them. In Chapter 5, we discussed this interpretation in reference to the study of Schwarzer et al. (1999) concerning haptic category learning (i.e. imposed classification, and not free classification as in Berger & Hatwell's research). As stated in Chapter 5, Schwarzer et al. did not find a prevalence of the lateral motion procedure in children aged 4–5. Differences in the task, the stimuli and the procedures were proposed to explain this discrepancy.

In their studies, Berger and Hatwell (1993, 1995, 1996) found in addition that in adults, and contrary to what happens in vision, haptic dimensional classifications were not always dominant and could be replaced by overall similarity classifications. Contrary to children whose responses were based on what was perceived in the initial stages of the perceptual process, adults privileged the information taken from the ultimate perceptual stages. In haptics, the dimensions are primarily perceived separately and then are integrated into a whole. Conversely, in vision, the first phases of the process are global, then the dimensions are extracted and analyzed separately. This may explain why, in haptics, classifications were in majority dimensional in children, and by similarity in adults, whereas the reverse was observed in vision. Berger and Hatwell (1996) confirmed this interpretation by showing that when adults were forced to carry out a global haptic exploration and a sequential visual exploration, results were modified: There was an increase in the number of dimensional classifications in haptic, and an increase in the number of classifications by similarity in vision.

These conclusions of Berger and Hatwell were questioned by Schwarzer et al. (1999) in a research studying not haptic free classification, but haptic category learning, i.e. the learning of a grouping principle determined by the experimenter. The reasoning of these authors was the following. The cognitive demands of category learning are consistently higher than those of free classification because, in the latter, there is no true and false answers and, therefore, the task requires simple perceptual classification. By contrast, in category learning, the child has to find the correct answer, that is to discover the category criterion governing a pre-established classification. According to Schwarzer et al., "Berger and Hatwell stated that the processing of haptic stimuli on a higher cognitive level seems to induce holistic processing" (1999: 869). Since category learning requires such an elaborate processing, these authors predicted, on the bases of the assumptions attributed to Berger and Hatwell, that category learning would increase the number of holistic responses, even in children.

Schwarzer et al. presented therefore to children aged 4–5 and 9 years and to adults an imposed classification task (with no time limits, however) in which volumetric objects varied by their size, shape, texture and weight (3 values in each dimension). The stimuli and procedures were directly taken from the studies of Ward and his associates in the visual modality (Ward & Scott 1987; Ward, Vela, & Hass 1990). During the presentation phase, the participants were presented with pairs of stimuli and were asked to assign each stimulus either to a red or a blue puppet. Feedback about the correctness of the categorization was given after each trial. The stimuli in each category were constructed in such a way that two modes of classification were possible, either holistic (by overall similarity) or analytic (dimensional). A subsequent test allowed to know which type of categorization had been used in the presentation phase. Schwarzer et al. (1999) found that dimensional classification based on texture predominated in children, and this was consistent with the results of Berger and Hatwell (1993, 1996). But, contrary to what was observed in these latter studies, Schwarzer et al. did not find in haptics a preference for similarity classification in adults. They concluded therefore that the predictions based on Berger and Hatwell's arguments were not supported and that analytical processing was dominant both in vision (as demonstrated by Ward and his associates) and haptics, and both in children and adults.

The question is that Schwarzer et al. (1999) interpretation of the studies of Berger and Hatwell is wrong because Berger and Hatwell did not relate analytic and holistic processing to the level of cognitive complexity of the task. Instead, they related these modes of categorization to the phases of perceptual processing in free classification tasks. In these tasks, children seemed to base their answer on the data collected in the early phases of processing and, in haptics, separate dimensions are perceived during these early phases. By contrast, adults seemed to base their choice on the ultimate phase of processing where the object is reconstructed into a unified whole. Because they attribute a high value to the integrated object, adults tend therefore to group objects by overall similarity in haptics. However, this analysis holds only for free classification, where the subject is "free" to externalize his/her spontaneous mode of processing. In category learning tasks, the situation is very different, as was noted by Schwarzer et al., because a feedback is given after each trial during the presentation phase. This feedback induces constant modifications of the subject's hypotheses about the grouping principle in order to find the correct one as soon as possible. Therefore, this task orients attention toward each variable dimension of the stimuli and, therefore, it is not surprising to observe in it predominant dimensional (analytic) haptic responses, even in adults.

Whatever it may be, this discussion shows how important is the analysis of the cognitive requirements of each task when comparing different studies on haptic functioning.

3.1.2   *Other research on adults*

Reed, Lederman and Klatzky (1990) studied the integration of the properties of size, shape, texture and hardness with two-dimensional material in imposed rapid classification tasks. The first two properties are spatial, the last two are material. A redundancy gain was observed in size and shape, as with texture and hardness, but the effect was less clear in size-texture and size-hardness combinations. For the authors, this may be explained by exploratory procedures. Indeed, the procedures optimum for texture and hardness are incompatible with those adapted to size, whereas those peculiar to the two material properties suffice to give the information required. Reed (1994) demonstrated the importance of exploratory procedures. She used either three-dimensional curvilinear shapes (without edges) for which lateral rubbing also gave information about shape, or two-dimensional shapes with edges and surfaces, for which the procedures relative to shape and texture were incompatible. A redundancy gain was observed with the 3D shapes, but also with the 2D shapes, which was unexpected and showed that redundant information, even partial, leads to the integration of haptic properties.

In adults, this integration occurs at a very early stage in the perceptual process when intensive properties such as texture and hardness are concerned, probably because these properties do not require an external reference frame in order to be encoded. This was shown by Lederman and Klatzky (1997) using Treisman and Gormican's (1988) research paradigm. In a target detection task, the number of distractors was varied. If response times increased when the number of distractors increased, this would mean that selective attention was at work. Conversely, if response times remained stable, then the target "popped out" and did not require attention (cf. Chapter 7). Lederman and Klatzky (1997) thus found that material properties were accessible very early on, whereas spatial orientation and continuous contour properties were accessible later, maybe even much later.

3.2 Dimensional preferences

It is known that in vision the different properties of objects have not the same prominence at different ages. At the age of 2–3 years, color dominates shape as a classification criterion, and this relation further reverses to the benefit of shape. In haptics, Klein (1966) observed a preference for texture before the age of 6–8 years, and for shape after this age, whereas for Gliner, Pick, Pick and Hales (1969) and for Siegel and Vance (1970) this inversion appeared at around the age of 5–6 years. Berger and Hatwell (1993, 1996) and Schwarzer et al. (1999) also found a massive preference for texture classification at the expense of size or shape at the age of 5, whereas adults preferred size or shape classification. Although the discriminability of the different dimensions was rarely controlled, these dimensional preferences do not originate in such differences (Gliner 1967). Functionally, texture thus behaves like color in the visual modality. This is not surprising because it is accessible via a simple and partial exploration of the object and does not require external reference frame. On the contrary, the spatial properties of shape and size require elaborate exploratory procedures and a spatial reference system which adults master far better than young children.

4. Conclusion

We successively examined the nature of the haptic processing of spatial properties (shape, orientation, length, location), then the texture properties of objects and finally, we discussed the relations between properties during perceptual processing (overall vs. analytical decomposition of properties, dimensional preferences). The specificity of haptic functioning appeared clearly in the spatial domain. Not only are the discriminatory capacities of touch inferior to those of vision, but some original processing modes are manifested. These are often linked to the spatial reference systems used by touch and the nature of the perceptive cues on which estimations are based (gravitational cues, movement encoding, etc.). In all cases, the importance of exploratory procedures has been underlined, as these procedures generally determine reference systems, available cues and therefore the encoding mode of spatial properties.

Differences between vision and touch are however weak, or even inexistent, in the processing of texture, which is said to be a "material" property (Lederman & Klatzky 1993). Numerous studies have shown the very good discriminatory capacities of touch in this field, in children and in adults. In children, a dimensional preference for texture has even been observed as compared to other spatial properties such as shape or size. This preference is later reversed and resembles the color preference present in the visual modality in very young children.

As concerns the study of analytical processes and the integration of different object properties into a unified whole, the works which take up Garner's (1974) classification research paradigms in the haptic modality have evidenced some specificities of the haptic system, mainly due to the nature of haptic exploration. Because of partial and poorly organized exploratory procedures, young children accede to certain properties very sequentially (if at all), and their classifications are thus based on the dimension they perceived well. That is why, in free classification tasks, changes due to age seem to operate in the opposite direction to what is usually observed in vision, since the young preferentially make dimensional classifications and not classifications by overall similarity. Adults also have reversed results. They classify more by overall similarity than by dimension in haptics, contrary to what is done in vision, because they privilege the ultimate step of perceptive processing which, in haptics, is the reconstruction of the total object from its elements. By contrast, in category learning tasks where a feedback is given after each trial, attention seems to be oriented towards the analysis of dimensions and, therefore, dimensional categorization is observed both in young children and adults.

References

Appelle, S. (1971). Visual and haptic angle perception in the matching task. *American Journal of Psychology, 84*, 487–499.

Appelle, S. (1972). Perception and discrimination as a function of stimulus orientation: The "oblique effect" in man and animals. *Psychological Bulletin, 78*, 266–278.

Appelle, S. & Countryman, M. (1986). Eliminating the haptic oblique effect: Influence of scanning incongruity and prior knowledge of the standards. *Perception, 15*, 365–369.

Ballasteros, S., Manga, D., & Reales, J. M. (1997). Haptic discrimination of bilateral symmetry in 2-dimensional and 3-dimensional unfamiliar displays. *Perception and Psychophysics, 59*, 37–50.

Ballesteros, S., Millar, S., & Reales, J. (1998). Symmetry in haptic and in visual shape perception. *Perception and Psychophysics, 60*, 389–404.

Berger, C. & Hatwell, Y. (1993). Dimensional and overall similarity classifications in haptics: A developmental study. *Cognitive Development, 8*, 495–516.

Berger, C. & Hatwell, Y. (1995). Development of analytic vs. global processing in haptics: The perceptual and decisional determinants of classification skills. *British Journal of Developmental Psychology, 13*, 143–162.

Berger, C. & Hatwell, Y. (1996). Developmental trends in haptic and visual free classifications: Influence of stimulus structure and exploration on decisional processes. *Journal of Experimental Child Psychology, 63*, 447–465.

Bowers, D. & Heilman, K. M. (1980). Pseudoneglect: Effects of hemispace on a tactile line bisection task. *Neuropsychologia, 18*, 491–498.

Bradshaw, J. L., Nathan, G., Nettleton, N. C., Wilson, L., & Pierson, J. (1987). Why is there a left side underestimation in rod bisection? *Neuropsychologia, 18*, 491–498.

Brumaghin, S. H. & Brown, D. R. (1969). Perceptual equivalence between visual and tactual stimuli: An anchoring study. *Perception and Psychophysics, 4*, 175–179.

Chokron, S. & Imbert, M. (1993). Egocentric reference and asymmetric perception of space. *Neuropsychologia, 31*, 267–275.

Chokron, S. & Imbert, M. (1995). Variations of the egocentric reference among normal subjects and one unilateral neglect patient. *Neuropsychologia, 33*, 703–711.

Corsini, D. & Pick, H. L. (1969). The effect of texture on tactually perceived length. *Perception and Psychophysics, 5*, 352–356.

Cuijpers, R. H., Kappers, A. M. L., & Koenderink, J. J. (2000). Large systematic deviations in visual parallelism. *Perception, 29*, 1467–1482.

Cuijpers, R. H., Kappers, A. M. L., & Koenderink, J. J. (2002). Visual perception of collinearity. *Perception and Psychophysics, 64*, 392–404.

Davidson, P. W. (1972). Haptic judgments of curvature by blind and sighted humans. *Journal of Experimental Psychology, 93*, 43–55.

Evans, P. M. & Smith, L. B. (1988). The development of identity as a privileged relation in classification: When very similar is not similar enough. *Cognitive Development, 3*, 265–284.

Faineteau, H., Gentaz, E., & Viviani, P. (in press). The kinaesthetic perception of Euclidean distance: A study on the detour effect. *Experimental Brain Research.*

Fisher, M. H. (1994). Less attention and more perception in cued line bisection. *Brain and Cognition, 25*, 24–33.

Flavell, J. H., Flavell, E. R., Green, F. L., & Wilcox, S. A. (1981). The development of three spatial perspective-taking rules. *Child Development, 52*, 356–358.

Garbin, C. P. (1990). Visual-touch perceptual equivalence for shape information in children and adults. *Perception and Psychophysics, 48*, 271–279.

Garbin, C. P. & Bernstein, I. H. (1984). Visual and haptic perception of tri-dimensional solid forms. *Perception and Psychophysics, 36*, 104–110.

Garner, W. R. (1974). *The processing of information and structure.* Potomac, MD: Erlbaum.

Gentaz, E. (2000). Existe-t-il un "effet de l'oblique" dans la perception tactile des orientations? *L'Année Pschologique, 100*, 111–140.

Gentaz, E. & Ballaz, C. (2000). La perception visuelle des orientations et l'effet de l'oblique. *L'Année Psychologique, 100*, 715–744.

Gentaz, E. & Hatwell, Y. (1994). L'effet de l'oblique. *Pour la Science, 198*, 20–21.

Gentaz, E. & Hatwell, Y. (1995). The haptic "oblique effect" in children's and adults' perception of orientation. *Perception, 24*, 631–646.

Gentaz, E. & Hatwell, Y. (1996). Role of gravitational cues in the haptic perception of orientation. *Perception and Psychophysics, 58*, 1278–1292.

Gentaz, E. & Hatwell, Y. (1998). The haptic oblique effect in the perception of rod orientation by blind adults. *Perception and Psychophysics, 60*, 157–167.

Gentaz, E. & Hatwell, Y. (1999). Role of memorisation conditions in the haptic processing of orientations and the "oblique effect". *British Journal of Psychology, 90*, 373–388.

Gentaz, E. & Tshopp, C. (2002). The oblique effect in the visual perception of orientations. In P. Shovoh (Ed), *Advances in Psychology Research* (pp. 137–163). New York: Nova Sciences Publishers.

Gentaz, E., Luyat, M., Cian, C., Hatwell, Y., Barraud, P.-A., & Raphel, C. (2001). The reproduction of vertical and oblique orientations in the visual, haptic, and somato-vestibular system. *Quarterly Journal of Experimental Psychology, 54*, 513–526.

Gliner, C. (1967). Tactual discrimination thresholds for shape and texture in young children. *Journal of Experimental Child Psychology, 5*, 536–547.

Gliner, C. R., Pick, A. D., Pick, H. L., & Hales, J. A. (1969). A developmental investigation of visual and haptic preferences for shape and texture. *Monographs of the Society for Research on Child Development, 34, n° 6* (serial number 130), 1–40.

Gordon, I. & Morison, V. (1982). The haptic perception of curvature. *Perception and Psychophysics, 31,* 446–450.

Hatwell, Y. (1966/1985). *Piagetian reasoning and the blind* (Translated from Y. Hatwell (1966), *Privation sensorielle et intelligence*. Paris: Presses Universitaires de France). New York: American Foundation for the Blind

Hatwell, Y. (1978). Form perception and related issues in blind humans. In R. Held, H. W. Leibowitz, & H. L. Teuber (Eds.), *Handbook of sensory physiology, VII: Perception* (pp. 489–519). New York and Berlin: Springer Verlag.

Hatwell, Y. (1986). *Toucher l'espace*. Lille: Presses Universitaires de Lille.

Hatwell, Y. (1994). Transferts intermodaux et intégration intermodale. In M. Richelle, J. Requin, & M. Robert (Eds.), *Traité de Psychologie Expérimentale, Vol. 1* (pp. 543–584). Paris: Presses Universitaires de France.

Hatwell, Y. (1995). Children's memory for location and object properties in vision and haptics: Automatic or attentional processing? *CPC – Current Psychology of Cognition, 14,* 47–71.

Hatwell, Y., Orliaguet, J. P., & Brouty, G. (1990). Effects of object properties, attentional constraints and manual exploratory procedures on haptic perceptual organization: A developmental study. In H. Bloch & B. Bertenthal (Eds.), *Sensory-motor organization and development in infancy and early childhood* (pp. 315–335). Dordrecht: Klumer Academic Publishers.

Hatwell, Y. & Sayettat, G. (1991). Visual and haptic spatial coding in young children. *British Journal of Developmental Psychology, 9,* 445–470.

Heller, M. A. (1982). Visual and tactual texture perception: Intersensory cooperation. *Perception and Psychophysics, 31,* 339–344.

Heller, M. A. (1985). Combining vision and touch in texture perception. *Perception and Psychophysics, 37,* 66–72.

Heller, M. A. (1989). Texture perception in sighted and blind observers. *Perception and Psychophysics, 45,* 49–54.

Hermelin, H. & O'Connor, N. (1975). Location and distance estimates by blind and sighted children. *Quarterly Journal of Experimental Psychology, 27,* 295–301.

Hollins, M., Faldowski, R., Rao, S., & Young, F. (1993). Perceptual dimensions of tactile surface texture: A multidimensional scaling analysis. *Perception and Psychophysics, 54,* 697–705.

Holmes, E., Hughes, B., & Jansson, G. (1998). Haptic perception of texture gradients. *Perception, 27,* 993–1008.

Hughes, B. & Jansson. (1994). Texture perception via active touch. *Human Movement Science, 13,* 301–333.

Jeannerod, M. & Biguer, B. (1989). Référence égocentrique et espace représenté. *Revue Neurologique, 145,* 635–639.

Jones, B. & O'Neil, S. (1985). Combining vision and touch in texture perception. *Perception and Psychophysics, 37,* 66–72.

Kappers, A. M. L., Koenderink, J. J., & Lichtenegger, I. (1994). Haptic identification of curved surfaces. *Perception and Psychophysics, 56*, 53–61.

Kappers, A. M. L., Koenderink, J. J., & Te Pas, S. F. (1994). Haptic discrimination of doubly curved surfaces. *Perception, 23*, 1483–1490.

Kappers, A. M. L. (1999). Large systematic deviations in the haptic perception of parallelity. *Perception, 28*, 1001–1012.

Kappers, A. M. L. (2002). Haptic perception of parallelity in the midsagittal plane. *Acta Psychologica, 109*, 25–40.

Kappers, A. M. L. & Koenderink, J. J. (1999). Haptic perception of spatial relations. *Perception, 28*, 781–795.

Katz, D. (1925/1989). *The world of touch* (translated by L. E. Krueger. 1989). Hillsdale, N.J.: Erlbaum.

Klatzky, R. L. (1999). Path completion after haptic exploration without vision: Implications for haptic spatial representations. *Perception and Psychophysics, 61*, 220–235.

Klatzky, R. L., Golledge, R. G., Loomis, J. M., Cicinelli, J. G., & Pellegrino, J. W. (1995). Performance of blind and sighted persons on spatial tasks. *Journal of Visual Impairment and Blindness, 89*, 70–82.

Klein, S. D. (1966). The development of tactual perception: Processes and achievements. In S. Wapner & B. Kaplan (Eds.), *Heinz Werner: Papers in memorium*. Worcester, Mass: Clark University Press.

Lakatos, S. & Marks, L. (1998). Haptic underestimation of angular extent. *Perception, 27*, 737–754.

Lakatos, S. & Marks, L. (1999). Haptic form perception. Relative salience of global and local features. *Perception and Psychophysics, 61*, 895–908.

Lanca, M. & Bryant, D. (1995). Effect of orientation in haptic reproduction of line length. *Perceptual and Motor Skills, 80*, 1291–1298.

Lechelt, E. C., Eliuk, J., & Tanne, G. (1976). Perceptual orientational asymmetries: A comparison of visual and haptic space. *Perception and Psychophysics, 20*, 463–469.

Lechelt, E. C. & Verenka, A. (1980). Spatial anisotropy in intramodal and cross-modal judgements of stimulus orientations: The stability of the oblique effect. *Perception, 9*, 581–589.

Lederman, S. J. (1974). Tactile roughness of grooved surfaces: The touching processes and effects of macro and microsurface structure. *Perception and Psychophysics, 16*, 385–396.

Lederman, S. J. (1981). The perception of texture by touch. In W. Schiff & E. Foulke (Eds.), *Tactual perception* (pp. 130–167). Cambridge: Cambridge University Press.

Lederman, S. J. & Abbott, S. G. (1981). Texture perception: Studies of intersensory organization using a discrepancy paradigm and visual vs tactual psychophysics. *Journal of Experimental Psychology: Human Perception and Performance, 7*, 902–915.

Lederman, S. J. & Klatzky, R. L. (1993). Extracting object properties through haptic exploration. *Acta Psychologica, 84*, 29–40.

Lederman, S. J. & Klatzky, R. L. (1997). Relative availability of surface and object properties during early haptic processing. *Journal of Experimental Psychology: Human Perception and Performance, 23*, 1680–1707.

Lederman, S. J., Klatzky, R. L., & Barber, P. O. (1985). Spatial and movement-based heuristics for encoding pattern information through touch. *Journal of Experimental Psychology: General, 114*, 33–49.

Lederman, S. J., Klatzky, R. L., Collins, A., & Wardell, J. (1987). Exploring environments by hand or foot: Time-based heuristics for encoding distance in movement space. *Journal of Experimental Psychology: Memory, Language and Cognition, 16*, 606–614.

Lederman, S. J., Thorne, G., & Jones, B. (1986). Perception of texture by vision and touch: Multidimensionality and intersensory integration. *Journal of Experimental Psychology: Human Perception and Performance, 12*, 169–180.

Locher, P. J. & Wagemans, J. (1993). Effects of element type and spatial grouping on symmetry detection. *Perception, 22*, 565–587.

Louw, S., Kappers, A. M. L., & Koenderink, J. J. (2000). Haptic detection thresholds of Gaussian profiles over the whole range of spatial scales. *Experimental Brain Research, 132*, 369–374.

Luyat, M., Gentaz, E., Regia-Corte, T., & Guerraz, M. (2001). Reference frames and haptic perception of orientation: Body and head tilt effects on the oblique effect. *Perception and Psychophysics, 63*, 541–554.

Luyat, M. & Gentaz, E. (2002). Body tilt effect on the reproduction of orientations: Studies on the visual oblique effect and subjective orientations. *Journal of Experimental Psychology: Human Perception and Performances, 28,* 1002–1011.

Marchetti, F. M. & Lederman, S. J. (1983). The haptic radial-tangential effect: Two tests of Wong's "moment-of-inertia" hypothesis. *Bulletin of Psychonomic Society, 21*, 43–46.

Mattingley, J. B., Pierson, J. M., Bradshaw, J. L., Philips, J. G., & Bradshaw, J. A. (1993). To see or not to see: The effects of visible and invisible cues on line bisection judgements in unilateral neglect. *Neuropsychologia, 31*, 1201–1215.

Miletic, G. (1994). Vibrotactile perception: Perspective taking by children who are visually impaired. *Journal of Visual Impairement and Blindness, 88,* 550–563.

Miletic, G. (1995). Perspective taking: Knowledge of Level 1 and Level 2 rules by congenitally blind, low vision and sighted children. *Journal of Visual Impairement and Blindness, 89*, 514–523.

Millar, S. (1994). *Understanding and representing space. Theory and evidence from studies with blind and sighted children.* Oxford: Clarendon Press.

Owen, D. & Brown, D. (1970). Visual and tactual form discrimination: A psychophysical comparison within and between modalities. *Perception and Psychophysics, 7*, 302–306.

Philip, J. & Hatwell, Y. (1998). Effects of cueing and of the direction of scanning on the tactile line bisection of normal adults. *CPC – Current Psychology of Cognition, 17*, 31–51.

Piaget, J. & Inhelder, B. (1947/1967). *The child's conception of space* (translated from: J. Piaget & B. Inhelder (1947), *La représentation de l'espace chez l'enfant.* Paris: Presses Universitaires de France). New York: W. W. Norton

Pick, A. D. & Pick, H. L. (1966). A developmental study of tactual discrimination in blind and sighted children and adults. *Psychonomic Science, 6*, 367–368.

Pont, S. C., Kappers, A. M. L., & Koenderink, J. J. (1997). Haptic curvature discrimination at several regions of the hand. *Perception and Psychophysics, 59*, 1225–1240.

Pont, S. C., Kappers, A. M. L., & Koenderink, J. J. (1998). Anisotropy in haptic curvature and shape perception. *Perception, 27*, 573–589.

Pont, S. C., Kappers, A. M. L., & Koenderink, J. J. (1999). Similar mechanisms underlie curvature comparison by static and by dynamic touch, *Perception and Psychophysics, 61*, 874–894.

Reed, C. L. (1994). Perceptual dependance for shape and texture during haptic processing. *Perception, 23*, 349–366.

Reed, C. L., Lederman, S. J., & Klatzky, R. L. (1990). Haptic integration of planar size with hardness, texture, and planar contour. *Canadian Journal of Psychology, 44*, 522–545.

Revesz, G. (1950). *Psychology and Art of the Blind*. London: Longmans Green.

Salatas, H. & Flavell, J. H. (1976). Perspective taking: The development of two components of knowledge. *Child Development, 47*, 103–109.

Sampaio, E. & Philip, J. (1991). Sensory and motor aspects of pseudoneglect, hemifield and hemispace in the tactile modality. *Brain and Cognition, 16*, 74–82.

Sathian, K. & Burton, H. (1991). The role of spatially selective attention in the tactile perception of texture. *Perception and Psychophysics, 50*, 237–248.

Schellingerhout, R. (1998). *Surface texture as a source of haptic spatial information for blind children*. Ph.D Thesis, Nijmegen, NL.

Schellingerhout, R., Smitsman, A. W., & Van Galen, G. P. (1998). Texture information in tactual space perception. *Acta Psychologica, 99*, 93–114.

Schwarzer, G., Küfer, I., & Wilkening, F. (1999). Learning categories by touch: On the development of holistic and analytic processing. *Memory and Cognition, 27*, 868–877.

Shepp, B. E. & Swartz, K. B. (1976). Selective attention and the processing of integral and nonintegral dimensions: A developmental study. *Journal of Experimental Child Psychology, 22*, 73–85.

Siegel, A. W. & Vance, B. J. (1970). Visual and haptic dimensional preference: A developmental study. *Developmental Psychology, 3*, 264–266.

Smith, L. B. (1989). A model of perceptual classification in children and adults. *Psychological Review, 7*, 811–824.

Smith, L. B. & Kemler, D. G. (1977). Developmental trends in free classification: Evidence for a new conceptualization of perceptual development. *Journal of Experimental Child Psychology, 24*, 279–298.

Smitsman, A. W. & Schellingerhout, R. (2000). Exploratyory behavior in blind infants: how to improve touch? *Infant Behavior and Development, 23*, 485–511.

Srinivasan, M. & LaMotte, R. (1996). Tactual discrimination of softness: Abilities and mechanisms. In O. Franzen, R. Johansson, & L. Terenius (Eds.), *Somesthesis and the neurobiology of the somatosensory cortex* (pp. 123–136). Berlin: Birkhäuser Verlag.

Stanley, G. (1966). Haptic and kinesthetic estimates of length. *Psychonomic Science, 5*, 377–378.

Teghtsoonian, M. & Teghtsoonian, R. (1965). Seen and felt length. *Psychonomic Science, 3*, 463–464.

Teghtsoonian, R. & Teghtsoonian, M. (1970). Two varieties of perceived length. *Perception and Psychophysics, 8*, 389–392.

Thinus-Blanc, C. & Gaunet, F. (1997). Representation of space in the blind: Vision as a spatial sense? *Psychological Bulletin, 121*, 20–42.

Treisman, A. & Gormican, S. (1988). Feature analysis in early vision: Evidence from search asymmetries. *Psychological Review, 95*, 15–48.

Vogels, I. M. L., Kappers, A. M. L., & Koenderink, J. J. (1996). Haptic aftereffect of curved surfaces. *Perception, 25,* 109–119.

Wagemans, J. (1995). Detection of visual symmetries. *Spatial Vision, 9,* 9–32.

Walk, R. D. (1965). Tactual and visual learning of forms differing in degrees of symmetry. *Psychonomic Science, 2,* 93–94.

Ward, T. B. (1983). Response tempo and separable-integral responding: Evidence for an integral to separable processing sequence in visual perception. *Journal of Experimental Psychology: Human Perception and Performance, 42,* 273–302.

Ward, T. B. & Scott, (1987). Analytic and holistic modes of learning family-resemblance concepts. *Memory and Cognition, 15,* 42–54.

Ward, T. B., Vela, E., & Hass, S. D. (1990). Children and adults learn family-resemblance categories analytically. *Child Development, 61,* 593–605.

Welch, R. B. (1978). *Perceptual modification.* New York: Academic Press.

Wydoodt, P., Gentaz, E., Gaunet, F., Chêne, D., & Streri, A. (2003). Haptic estimation of spatial location in virtual and real path completion tasks: Contribution of proprioceptive and cutaneous information on the path effect. In M. A. Heller & S. Ballasteros (Eds.), *Touch, blindness and neurosciences* (pp. 351–361). Madrid (Spain): UNED Publishers.

CHAPTER 9

Haptic perceptual illusions

Morton A. Heller

1. Introduction and history

Illusions are not merely optical, they occur in touch as well (Revesz 1950). This makes one question whether touch is invariably a "reality sense" and is used to calibrate vision. The problem of error is a fundamental one in psychology. It is relevant to general issues about how we obtain an understanding of reality, and helps us distinguish psychology from some of the other scientific fields (O'Neil 1958). I have studied the question of whether metric judgments of extent are subject to similar illusions in vision and touch.

My interests in touch stem from a number of theoretical issues and some practical problems as well. The theoretical questions of particular interest concern issues about intersensory equivalence. One wonders if information derived from different senses translate directly from one sense to the other, or if they vary in important ways (cf. Section 4). The alternative, radical view is that information from vision and touch are never the same, despite the use of similar words to label very different ideas (e.g. Berkeley 1732/1996). It is also possible to assume that the senses of vision and touch may sometimes provide redundant information. However, they may also serve very different functions, and might function in a cooperative manner. Thus, vision has multiple functions, and can pickup information about patterns, but can also serve to guide the hand as it explores stimuli (Heller 1982). Note too that while similar illusions may occur in both vision and touch, they could occur for very different reasons.

There are practical reasons for studying illusions in touch. Blind people are dependent upon touch for obtaining spatial and graphical information. If touch operates very differently from vision, then pictorial devices should be tailored to touch, and different forms of depiction may be called for. Illusions in touch seem a perfect vehicle for the study of these questions. I use the term "haptic" to refer to the active use of touch to explore objects or patterns.

Haptic illusions may take a number of forms. They may involve perception of movement where no real motion over the skin exists, as in apparent movement (Burtt 1917; Geldard & Sherrick 1972). Other haptic illusions involve distortions in judgments of extent, or in curvature. Kappers, Koenderink and their colleagues report that people tend to misperceive curvature (also see Edington 1956), and that touch is subject to curvature aftereffects (Vogels, Kappers, & Koenderink 1996). Aristotle's illusion involves a doubling of sensation that occurs when crossed fingers contact a single curved object (Robertson, 1876). Illusions of extent and area have been studied most extensively in touch, and researchers have been concerned with the factors that influence illusory misperception.

The size-weight illusion has been studied, frequently with an attempt to determine if the illusion is linked to visualization. In this illusion, people tend to overestimate the weight of a smaller object. One frequently reported explanation is cognitive, and assumes that the size-weight illusion may be the result of expectations. However, Masin and Crestoni (1988) argued for a sensory explanation, while Ellis and Lederman (1993) showed that the illusion is haptic, and is not dependent upon visual imagery. Ellis and Lederman found the illusion in congenitally blind subjects.

Tsai (1967) found that the haptic version of the Müller-Lyer illusion is influenced by visual experience and by hand. The haptic illusion was present in blind as well as blindfolded sighted subjects. However, Tsai reported a stronger illusion in the congenitally blind participants. The illusion was also affected by hand, with stronger illusory misperception when the preferred (right) hand examined the tangible stimuli. This is understandable, if the left hemisphere is better suited for verbal skills, and the right is superior for making accurate spatial judgments (cf. Chapter 5). This follows, on the assumption that illusions are the result of poor spatial judgments, and misperception would be more likely if information is processed by a hemisphere, that is ill-suited for spatial analysis. Unfortunately, Tsai's report suffers from a problem affecting most research in this area, that is, excessively small samples of blind subjects.

Over (1966, 1968) has reported that illusions in touch do not always respond to experimental manipulations in quite the same manner as visual illusions. For example, he found that extent of finger movement matters, but only when contextual tactual stimulation was present (Over 1966a). Tangible illusions were not influenced by instructions to attend to "apparent size" or "objective size." In vision, however, directions to report apparent size resulted in a larger illusion (Over 1968). It should be noted, however, that the haptic and visual Müller-Lyer illusions are both influenced by the angles of the arrows (Heller, Brackett, Wilson, Yoneyama, Boyer & Steffen 2002; Over 1966b).

There is some evidence that practice may influence haptic illusory misperception. Over (1967) reported a reduction in the strength of the horizontal-vertical illusion over trials. Rudel and Teuber (1963) also found a reduced haptic Muller-Lyer illusion with practice.

Considerable effort has been directed toward the study of optical illusions, but Coren and Girgus (1978) devote merely one page to a discussion of haptic illusions. Researchers have investigated the Muller-Lyer illusion, and many other illusions in touch. Perhaps, the largest research efforts have been focused on the horizontal-vertical illusion, probably because it is so robust (see Fry 1975).

2. The haptic horizontal-vertical illusion

In the horizontal-vertical illusion, vertical extents are overestimated when compared to horizontal extents, in both vision and touch (see Coren & Girgus 1978; Hatwell 1960). Thus, people may report that the vertical segment of an inverted "T" shape is longer than the horizontal segment. The illusion is powerful, and some researchers report overestimation by as much as 30% in vision. The haptic illusion is not quite as powerful, and has been related to the influence of radial/tangential scanning effects. Radial motions refer to motions that are directed toward the body, while tangential scanning motions do not converge on the body. People tend to overestimate radial motions compared with tangential motions. Wong (1977) argued that overestimation of radial motion occurs because these movements are executed at a different rate than tangential motions. Wong reported that judgments of movement extent are altered by time cues, and that radial motions are executed more slowly than tangential motions. An alternative explanation, of course, is that the horizontal segment may be underestimated because it is bisected by the vertical (Coren & Girgus 1978). However, the illusion also occurs with L-shaped figures, but is not nearly as strong as with inverted T-shapes. In addition, subjects do not overestimate continual versus bisected lines in touch (Heller, Calcaterra, Burson, & Green 1997). It is possible that the illusion is linked to the fact that inverted Ts and Ls are "letter-like." Thus, we do not normally write the horizontal segment of a normal T as large as the vertical segment, and it is possible that this contributes to the illusion.

Hatwell (1960) reported that the horizontal-vertical and Muller-Lyer illusions were weaker in touch than in vision. Furthermore, she found a total lack of a haptic version of illusory effects in the Delboeuf and Halteres figures. It is noteworthy that Hatwell used rather small stimuli, and touch may yield more accurate percepts when motions are limited in scale. In addition, Hatwell's subjects included a mixed-group of early and late blind children, ranging in age from 8–17 years of age. There is a delay in the development of haptics, and so it is unlikely that one may generalize from data derived from children directly to adults.

Results with the haptic horizontal-vertical illusion vary as a function of hand and manner of exploration (Heller, Joyner, & Dan-Fodio 1993). No illusion was found when stimuli were examined with the left thumb. This was interpreted as demonstrating the superiority of the right hemisphere for spatial processing. Involvement of the right hemisphere promoted veridical perception, and a lack of illusory overestimation of the vertical. However, later research has not supported these results (Heller et al. 1997), and suggests that it may be important to control for hemispace as well as hand. Heller et al. (1993) did not control for hemispace, that is, whether the hand making judgments was kept at the body midline, or was presented to the left or right of the midline. It is very possible that subjects may have allowed the "judging hands" to stray to one or the other side of the body. Heller et al. (1997) reported an interaction between hand and hemispace, with judgments made by the left hand affected by hemispace. In addition, it is important to control for the, gender factor in this research area, since females tended to make smaller size estimates than males. Also, males showed different size estimates as a function of hemispace. Note that the illusion was obtained in one experiment, even when the same hand feeling stimuli made judgments. This was found with judgments in the same orientation as the vertical and horizontal lines being touched.

According to Day and Avery (1970), the haptic horizontal-vertical illusion is configurational since the illusion was linked to orientation of the stimuli (also see Kunnapas 1955). They failed to find illusory overestimation of verticals when subjects felt an L shape in the frontal orientation, but did find this for the inverted T shape. Most prior demonstrations of the haptic illusion occurred with the stimuli flat on a table surface. This shows that the haptic illusion may derive, in part, from a poor vantage point. Heller (1992) noted that the accuracy of perceptual identification may vary with touching position, and some positions are not optimal for touch, just as some conditions of visual observation are nonoptimal (see Kennedy & Portal 1990). Orienting stimuli in the frontal plane improves tactual identification of a variety of tangible stimuli.

Heller and Joyner (1993) investigated the influence of visual experience on the haptic horizontal-vertical illusion. We used a Swedish raised-line drawing kit for the production of stimuli. A durable and tangible line is produced when a normal ballpoint pen is pressed and drawn over the surface of a plastic sleeve. The purpose of the study was to evaluate the necessity of visual imagery for illusory misperception of extent in the illusion. Thus, congenitally blind people are thought to lack visual imagery, while adventitiously (late) blind people may remember how things "looked" and make use of visual imagery. Illusory misperception in late blind individuals could reflect visual imagery, and not the influence of touch per se. Blindfolded sighted subjects in a first experiment made size judgments about line lengths of L and inverted T shapes that were 2.54, 5.1, 7.6, and 10.2 cm in extent. Size estimates were obtained by having subjects make a pincer's posture of the index finger and thumb of the hand that was not used to touch the stimuli. The span between the tip of the index finger and thumb was measured with a ruler. The illusion was not found for smaller stimuli (< 5.2 cm long). It is possible, however, that blindfolded sighted people are influenced by visualization when they touch stimuli.

A second experiment explicitly examined the influence of visual experience. Independent groups of congenitally blind and late blind subjects examined raised-line L and inverted T figures, and made size estimates using the finger span method. Perhaps the late blind perceived these shapes differently because of their prior exposure to pictures, or because of the presence of visual imagery. Congenitally blind subjects showed no illusion with the smallest stimuli, either with L or inverted T shapes. It was surprising, though, that the congenitally blind subjects showed stronger overestimation of verticals in the L figure than the inverted T shape. This pattern was the opposite of that for the late blind subjects, who showed minimal or no overestimation of verticals in the figure.

These results support explanations of the horizontal-vertical illusion that ascribe illusory overestimation of the vertical to radial/tangential scanning effects. Visual imagery explanations would not predict a lack of the illusion in the figure the late blind. These data are also consistent with the idea that the nature of stimulus presentation conditions, and perhaps, the choice of scanning strategies, could explain the presence of illusory effects in haptics.

It is very possible that misperception, and haptic illusions, derive from nonoptimal haptic exploration of stimuli. Thus, people may sometimes choose poor methods for exploring stimuli, and that could explain perceptual errors and illusory misperception. Heller, Calcaterra, Burson and Green (1997) studied the effect of the type of movement and the involvement of motion of the entire arm on the presence of the horizontal-vertical illusion. Small forms, for example, can be examined with a tracing motion of the index finger. Larger patterns may induce larger movements, including radial motion of the entire arm, and this could contribute to misperception and the horizontal-vertical illusion. Much earlier research did not consider the impact of arm extension, or involvement of whole-arm motion on the presence of the illusion.

Conditions of stimulus presentation can often determine whether subjects are likely to rest their elbows on the table surface, or suspend their elbows in the air. For example, if stimuli are presented near the edge of a table, subjects are unable to rest their wrists or elbows on a tabletop. The distance that stimuli are from the subject's body may then significantly alter the geometry of the arm, even when this is unintended by the experimenter.

Heller et al. (1997) studied the effect of elevating the elbow off of the table surface. They noticed that in uncontrolled conditions, subjects adopted different exploratory strategies when examining large and small forms. Subjects were likely to rest their arms and wrists on the tabletop when feeling smaller stimuli, since they could be scanned with finger motion alone. Larger forms induced motion of the entire arm, and subjects typically elevated their arms off of the tabletop when feeling these stimuli with flexion at the elbow. The presence of the illusion was diminished or absent when subjects were instructed to keep their elbows down on the table surface. Moreover, a strong illusion was present when the subjects were told to elevate the stimuli off of the tabletop.

These results were confirmed in a further experiment (Heller et al. 1997, Experiment 4) that more effectively controlled motion of the arm. Some subjects were forced to engage in whole arm motion, since the arm and hand were splinted to prevent any possibility of tracing with the fingertip (Figure 9.1c). Other subjects were restricted to finger tracing, since their arms were "clamped" rigidly between foam-covered blocks, and motion of the elbow or arm was eliminated (Figures 9.1a, b and d). The results were consistent with the idea that illusory spatial distortion is more likely when motion of the entire arm is permitted.

These results show the importance of scale for haptic perception. When stimuli are small enough, they can be explored with the fingertip, or perhaps with the hand and multiple fingers. However, larger stimuli prompt motions of the entire arm for exploration. It is in these instances that illusory misperception is more likely.

Motion of the entire arm is likely to magnify the impact of gravitational cues, and Gentaz and Hatwell (1998) have stressed the importance of gravitational cues for haptic perception. Moreover, use of the entire arm prompts

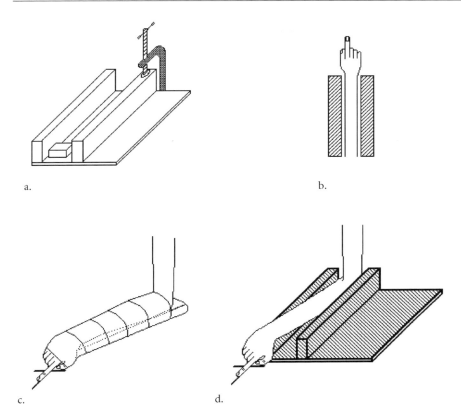

Figure 9.1. Displays used to clamp the arm and prevent motion of elbow and arm (a, b and d), and splints preventing tracing with the fingertip (c). The foam-covered wooden blocks (a, b and d) were adjustable to restrict arm motion for individuals with arms of different sizes (from Heller, Calcaterra, Burson, & Green 1997).

involvement of a different representational space, that of the arm and torso, than exploration that is limited to the hand (see Paillard 1991). The arm or reach space is served by different cortical mechanisms than the space that is accessed by the hand. Thus, according to Paillard, reach space attempts some localization with reference to the body and a body-centered coordinate system (see Klein & Schilder 1929). The hand space is concerned with an attempt to know the properties of an object. Whole arm motion, therefore, is thus far more likely to induce misperception and illusion.

The present argument is that touch is best suited for manipulation of object characteristics within a far smaller spatial domain than vision. Thus, haptic perception is more likely to suffer illusory distortion when scale is magnified.

At the very least, a larger scale places more of a memory burden upon touch. Smaller stimuli, however, are understood faster, and are more likely to yield veridical haptic percepts. Thus, Katz (1989/1925) viewed the hand as the organ of touch, and one might then expect that perceptual error is more likely when we force an individual to employ less efficient methods for obtaining information.

3.   Conclusion and future directions

The study of haptic perceptual illusions indicates that the causes of illusory misperception may not be identical to those in vision. In addition, visual and haptic illusions may occur for different reasons. Illusory misperception in haptics may derive from the use of poor exploratory strategies, and this can come from lack of skill or poor choice of exploratory strategy because of lack of experience with the use of touch for pattern perception. In addition, illusion can be diminished with practice in touch. This suggests that touch may differ in very important ways from vision, and we should be cautious about blanket generalization from one sense to the other.

The previous comments also suggest caution when attempting to generalize from our knowledge base derived from the study of blindfolded, sighted people to blind individuals (Heller, Brackett, Wilson, Yoneyama, & Boyer 2002). Blind people may have increased haptic skills, but diminished or minimal experience with graphics. Thus, their reactions to raised-line illusory configurations could be variable, perhaps as a function of the presence or absence of visual experience.

Note that skillful exploration may allow individuals to perceive stimuli accurately in touch. Whether or not illusions appear apparently depends upon the scale and size of the stimuli, and the choice of exploratory strategies by the observer. Even rather potent illusions may disappear when stimuli are small enough, and are within the scale of the hand. On this interpretation of the results of a number of studies, illusory misperception in haptics may derive from the use of larger stimuli that prompt whole-arm motion. Thus, the hand may be the appropriate organ of touch for some forms of stimuli, and use of the arm-shoulder system promotes illusory misperception

It is also possible that information derived from raised-line drawings may not always generalize to naturalistic, three-dimensional solids. Certainly, most researchers have assumed that the study of geometrical illusions will tell us about naturalistic stimuli. Coren and Girgus, for example, argued that the horizontal-vertical illusion occurs in the natural environment, and gave the St. Louis Arch as an example. However, the St. Louis Arch (in Missouri) is a human construction, and while it occurs in normal 3-Dimensional space, it is not natural. Quantification of the horizontal-vertical illusion is certainly difficult, and one does not invariably see overestimation of the vertical in haptics. When the vertical is gravitationally vertical, one may see overestimation of horizontals, that is, a negative haptic illusion may be found with 3-D objects (Heller, Brackett, Salik, Scroggs. & Green, in press).

Acknowledgement

Some of the research reported here and the preparation of this chapter were supported by NIH grant RO1 EY 12040.

References

Berkeley, G. (1732/1996). An essay towards a new theory of vision. In M. R. Ayers (Ed.). *George Berkeley: Philosophical works*. London: Everyman vision.

Burtt, H. E. (1917). Tactual illusions of movement. *Journal of Experimental Psychology, 2,* 317–385.

Coren, S. & Girgus, J. S. (1978). *Seeing is deceiving: The psychology of visual illusions.* Hillsdale, N. J.: Lawrence Erlbaum Associates.

Day, R. H. & Avery, G. C. (1970). Absence of the horizontal-vertical illusion in haptic space. *Journal of Experimental Psychology, 83,* 172–173.

Edington, E. (1956). A tactual-kinesthetic curvature illusion. *The Journal of Psychology, 41,* 271–272.

Ellis, R. R. & Lederman, S. J. (1993). The role of haptic versus visual volume cues in the size-weight illusion. *Perception and Psychophysics, 53,* 315–324.

Fry, C. L. (1975). Tactual illusions. *Perceptual and Motor Skills, 40,* 955–960.

Geldard, F. A. & Sherrick, C. E. (1972). The cutaneous rabbit: A perceptual illusion. *Science, 178,* 178–179.

Gentaz, E. & Hatwell, Y. (1998). The haptic oblique effect in the perception of rod orientation by blind adults. *Perception and Psychophysics, 60,* 157–167.

Hatwell, Y. (1960). Etude de quelques illusions géométriques tactiles chez les aveugles. *L'Année Psychologique, 60,*11–27.

Heller, M. A. (1982). Visual and tactual texture perception: Intersensory cooperation. *Perception and Psychophysics, 31,* 339–344.

Heller, M. A. (1992). The effect of orientation on tactual braille recognition: Optimal "touching positions." *Perception and Psychophysics, 51,* 549–556.

Heller, M. A., Brackett, D. D., Salik, S. S., Scroggs, E., & Green, S. (in press). Objects raised-lines and the haptic horizontal-vertical illusion. *Quarterly Journal of Experimental Psychology: A.*

Heller, M. A., Brackett, D. D., Wilson, K., Yoneyama, K., & Boyer, A. (2002). Visual experience and the haptic horizontal-vertical illusion. *British Journal of Visual Impairment, 20,* 105–109.

Heller, M. A., Brackett, D. D., Wilson, K., Yoneyama, K., Boyer, A., & Steffen, H. (2002). The haptic Muller-Lyer illusion in sighted and blind people. *Perception, 31,* 1263–1274.

Heller, M. A. & Joyner, T. D. (1993). Mechanisms in the tactile horizontal/vertical illusion: Evidence from sighted and blind subjects. *Perception and Psychophysics, 53,* 422–428.

Heller, M. A., Joyner, T. D., & Dan-Fodio, H. (1993). Laterality effects in the haptic horizontal/vertical illusion. *Bulletin of the Psychonomic Society, 31,* 440–443.

Heller, M. A., Calcaterra, J. A., Burson, L. L., & Green, S., L. (1997). The tactual horizontal-vertical illusion depends on radial motion of the entire arm. *Perception and Psychophysics, 59,* 1297–1311.

Katz, D. (1989/1925). *The world of touch* (L. E. Krueger, Ed. & Trans.). Hillsdale: Lawrence Erlbaum.

Kennedy, J. M. & Portal, A. (1990). Illusions: Can change of vantage point and invariant impressions remove deception? *Ecological Psychology, 2,* 37–53.

Klein, E. & Schilder, P. (1929). The Japanese illusion and the postural model of the body. *The Journal of Nervous and Mental Disease, 70,* 241–263.

Kunnapas, T. M. (1955). An analysis of the "vertical-horizontal illusion." *Journal of Experimental Psychology, 49,* 134–140.

Masin, S. C. & Crestoni, L. (1988). Experimental demonstration of the sensory basis of the size-weight illusion. *Perception and Psychophysics, 44,* 309–312.

O'Neil, W. M. (1958). Basic issues in perceptual theory. *Psychological Review, 65,* 348–361.

Over, R. (1966a). Context and movement as factors influencing haptic illusions. *Australian Journal of Psychology, 3,* 262–265.

Over, R. (1966b). A comparison of haptic and visual judgments of some illusions. *American Journal of Psychology, 79,* 590–595.

Over, R. (1967). Intermanual transfer of practice decrements with a haptic illusion. *Quarterly Journal of Experimental Psychology, 19,* 215–218.

Over, R. (1968). The effect of instructions on visual and haptic judgment of the Müller-Lyer illusion. *Australian Journal of Psychology, 3,* 161–164.

Paillard, J. (1991). Motor and representational space. In J. Paillard (Ed.), *Brain and space* (pp. 163–182). New York: Oxford University Press.

Revesz, G. (1950). *The psychology and art of the blind.* London: Longmans Green.

Robertson, C. (1876). Notes: Sense of doubleness with crossed fingers. *Mind, 1,* 145–146.

Rudel, R. G. & Teuber, H.-L. (1963). Decrement of visual and haptic illusion on repeated trials: A study of crossmodal transfer. *Quarterly Journal of Experimental Psychology, 15,* 125–131.

Tsai, L. S. (1967). Müller-Lyer illusion by the blind. *Perceptual and Motor Skills, 25,* 641–644.

Vogels, I. M. L., Kappers, A. M. L., & Koenderink, J. J. (1996). Haptic after-effect of curved surfaces. *Perception, 25,* 109–119.

Wong, T. S. (1977). Dynamic properties of radial and tangential movements as determinants of the haptic horizontal-vertical illusion with an L figure. *Journal of Experimental Psychology: Human Perception and Performance, 3,* 151–164.

CHAPTER 10

Congenitally blindness and spatial mental imagery

Cesare Cornoldi, Maria-Chiara Fastame and Tomaso Vecchi

1. Introduction

The interest in studying mental imagery in totally congenitally blind people is motivated by different goals. Firstly, it allows to establish the contribution of visual perception in the generation of mental images. Secondly, it shows whether and how it is possible to use mental imagery in order to improve memory performance in congenitally totally blind people. Third, if, on one hand, a series of tools is sensible for discriminating performances between sighted and blind individuals, on the other hand, the same tasks can be used in the assessment of individual differences in order to highlight the different nature of the Working Memory processes, in particular the distinction between the passive maintenance and the active manipulation and transformation of information.

It is necessary to clarify that, in this chapter, visuospatial mental images refer to a specific type of mental representations, which are different from sensory traces and that are created on the basis of different sources. According to our theory (Cornoldi, De Beni, Giusberti, & Massironi 1988; Cornoldi & Vecchi 2000, 2003), visuospatial mental images are the result of a complex cognitive process that relies on different information sources: Visual, spatial, tactile, conceptual. These information are processed within the visuospatial working memory (VSWM) system in a format that shows specific properties which are only partially identical to those of visual traces and, more in general, to those of the original sources.

In our opinion, and empirical data support this view, the congenital absence of visual perception does not prevent from processing or using visuospatial mental images. Congenital blindness does not prevent from generating mental images, although they should be differently organized. This difference should be caused by the type of stimuli that elicits the creation and use of mental images. It is intuitive to argue that mental imagery in congenitally blindness relies mainly on tactile and spatial information sources and does not derive, from visual experiences. Conversely, in the daily life of sighted people it is difficult to distinguish spatial mental images coming from visual experiences and mental representations generated on the basis of spatial information coming from other types of external or internal stimuli. It follows that we cannot radically discriminate the influence of those different information sources in mental imagery of sighted people. For this reason, in this context, we prefer to consider visuospatial mental representations without any differentiation. In this chapter, we will show how blind people can use mental imagery and then we will focus our attention on the specific characteristics of their mental representations.

With regard to the nature of mental images in absence of visual experience, a wide range of investigations showed that totally congenitally blind people may process and use mental images in a partially different way. For instance, one interesting finding is that blind people show a selective difficulty in processing different information simultaneously. In turn, this determines that the time needed to generate mental images can be longer in blind individuals. However, the pattern of performance of blind people seems to be more complex: longer delays are present even when a limited range of information resources contribute to create mental representations. Thus, it does not seem correct to identify blind people limitations in relation with a limited capacity to process large amount of information at the same time.

In the remaining part of this chapter, we will present a series of investigations, carried out within the last ten years, in which we demonstrated that blind people can generate and use visuo-spatial images, at the same time indicating that specific limitation can be present. Hence, we will consider the implication raised by our empirical results within a larger theoretical framework. In particular we will argue that it is important to redefine the nature of VSWM with respect to the working memory system originally developed by Baddeley and collaborators (see Baddeley 1986; Baddeley & Hitch 1974).

A debate that in the past thirty years encouraged the investigations on mental imagery concerns the nature of mental images: Two different theoretical approaches, namely the pictorial and the propositional ones, have been proposed. In our view, they both seem too simplicistic and reductive. According to the pictorialist approach (e.g. Paivio 1971), mental images are internal representations coming from perceptual experiences. On the contrary, from a propositional point of view (e.g. Pylyshyn 1973), all of the mental representations –

such as the propositions – represent objects in the same format following arbitrary rules. The pure analogical approach, according to which visuospatial mental image is identical to the represented object, argues that totally congenitally blind people cannot process any type of mental images. On the contrary, propositionalists argue that non-sighted people can have mental images functionally equivalent to those of sighted people, as the so-called mental images may not require a specific type of mental representation, neither in the blind, nor in the sighted people (Zimler & Keenan 1983).

We believe that both blind and sighted people use mental imagery. We also think that the former group can process a specific type of mental representations which may suffer of specific limitations. This idea is consistent with the opinion of the researchers that, for the first time, recognized that mental representations of sighted people are similar to those generated in absence of visual perception. However, this idea was not empirically supported by experimental data and one of the goals of this chapter is to show evidence that mental representations sharing visuo-spatial properties can be processed by blind people. In addition, these images may be partially different from the ones generated from visual perception of sighted people.

A wide range of studies showed that the functioning in tasks involving mental imagery in total congenital blindness is similar to that of sighted people. For instance, Jonides, Kahn and Rozin (1975) found that memory performance in blind people improves with the use of mental imagery strategies. This position has been further supported by Kerr (1983) who administered different mental imagery tasks to blind and sighted participants and discovered that they both showed an identical pattern of behavior. Marmor (1978) argued that even when visual experience is absent at all, people can represent color similarly to sighted individuals. More recently, we carried out specific investigations focused on the distinction between active processes and passive maintenance within visuospatial working memory (VSWM). On the basis of our results, we can argue that passive storage is well preserved in totally congenitally blind people, whereas their active processes seem partially compromised (e.g. Vecchi 1998; Vecchi, Monticelli, & Cornoldi 1995).

2. The use of mental images in congenital blindness

If we consider mental imagery as a subjective experience that is defined by specific phenomenological properties, then it is necessary to establish how our naive theory of mental imagery can influence the creation of our mental representations (e.g. Cornoldi, De Beni, & Giusberti 1997; Pylyshyn 1973). Indeed, in order to demonstrate that blind people process and use mental images, it is not sufficient to believe in their assertions, even if these are detailed descriptions on what they can mentally represent. Hence, in order to argue that congenital blindness does not prevent from using mental imagery, it is necessary that mental representations generated in absence of visual experience share the same properties with mental images created by sighted people. On the basis of our experience, we argue that mental imagery represents a complex function that is not bound by the modality in which information is presented, but it depends on different types of short and long term information coming from different sensory sources.

One of the first objectives that cognitive psychologists had to achieve was to design memory tasks requiring mental imagery strategies in which congenitally blind people could be compared with sighted individuals. This issue has been tackled by several researchers. For instance, it has been found that blind people can use interactive mental images in order to retrieve paired words (e.g. Zimler & Keenan 1983), although it seems that they need a longer time in order to create their mental images (Kerr 1983) (we think that it is necessary to be cautious in generalizing these results, because the slowness in creating mental images in blindness condition can be due to the individual characteristics of that experimental sample rather than to the general lack of visual knowledge).

Other research investigated the qualitative differences characterizing mental images processed by blind and sighted people. Those studies highlighted a large amount of similarities in the mental representations created with and without visual knowledge, pointing out that some properties are not necessarily due to the visual experience (Marmor 1978; Zimler & Keenan 1983). For instance, it was found that in carrying out mental rotation tasks, performance of blind people is subject to the same characteristics to that of the sighted ones: The time taken in order to judge the identity of two spatial configurations differently oriented in the third dimension depends on their rotation angle. According to Marmor and Zaback (1976) this result is an effect of the use of mental images. This position has been also confirmed by Carpenter and Eisenberg (1978). In their study, it was requested to identify the stimulus (e.g. a letter) located in the center of a geometrical configuration. Although congenitally blind participants were slower and made more errors than controls, the authors argued that performance of non-sighted could be improved by a more accurate knowledge of that experimental material. Indeed, in recent years, it was found that blind people did better than the sighted in a task in which they had to recognize a series of letters written in braille code but presented in a right/left inverted format (Heller & Kennedy 1990).

According to other results, an important difference between blind and sighted people is that the former seem to ignore the rules of perspective (Arditi, Holtzam, & Kosslyn 1988; Heller, Calcaterra, Tyler, & Burson 1996), although in different studies it was found that drawings carried out by a blind sample contained unexpected spatial perspective notions (Kennedy 1982, 1993; cf. Chapter 15).

The development of new specific experimental tasks largely contributed to the investigation of mental imagery in congenital blindness. For instance, a relevant contribution came from a methodology that firstly requires a tactile exploration of stimuli and then the creation of a mental representation that is stored in visuo-spatial working memory. By using this experimental procedure many authors have showed that tactile exploration of a pattern of stimuli is sufficient to generate mental images in congenitally blind people (e.g. Carreiras & Codina 1992; Klatzky, Golledge, Loomis, Cicinelli, & Pellegrino 1995).

Further investigations showed that a common characteristic of mental imagery in blind and sighted people is that mental imagery is particularly useful in geographical orientation (Loomis et al. 1993), although mental images in congenital blind people proved to be less effective (e.g. Rieser et al. 1992). These results are supported by Juurmaa and Lehtinen-Railo (1994) and by Rieser, Guth and Hill (1986), according to whom blind people are slower in those tasks requiring a modification of their spatial mental representations and also when it is required a judgment on orientation and distance. Different causes can explain these data. According to some authors the slowness is due to the lack of suitable exploration strategies useful in carrying out the different tasks (Thinus-Blanc & Gaunet 1997). Conversely, other researchers (e.g. Stuart 1995) hypothesized a different cerebral organization that regulates the generation and the use of mental images in the blind.

In our studies we have investigated the nature of mental images and of visuo-spatial processes in blind people by evaluating the effects of different stimulus types and experimental instructions. One of our goals was to investigate the role played by subjective experience in mental imagery and the effect of imagery value in recalling three different categories of nouns. We used 1) concrete words evoking some mental image of objects experienced by the blind (HI, High Imagery value); 2) abstract stimuli for which it was harder to create a link with personal knowledge of the world both for blind and sighted people (LI, Low Imagery value); 3) stimuli that could evoke a mental image but that could not be associated with a direct personal experience, such as for the item 'spaceship' (HINE, High Imagery Not Experienced) (Cornoldi, Calore, & Pra Baldi 1979). Blind people judged HINE stimuli as having a low imagery value. However, data on their memory performance were not so clear. Indeed non-sighted participants recalled a greater amount of LI names, whereas in other conditions their performance was poorer than sighted. Furthermore, the accuracy of performance in blind people depended on whether the recall was intentional or incidental.

The pattern of results found in HINE condition was further on investigated by De Beni and Cornoldi (1988) and Tinti and colleagues (1999). These researchers replicated the early findings confirming that blind people have difficulty in recalling HINE words, but if we take into account their limited knowledge of the world, their performance was less impaired than it could be hypothesized.

A debate is still open on the role played by imagery value in recalling verbal information such as names. According to Marschark and Cornoldi (1990) it is not necessary that the effect of imagery value on memory tasks depend upon mental imagery abilities. However, we cannot exclude that in order to recall concrete words, blind people generate mental images on the basis of their knowledge of the world, even if this is partial and potentially incomplete. It follows that in absence of a direct experience, it is likely that also blind people create mental images of unknown stimuli by using their memories of similar situations using a process of assimilation. For instance, if we consider a HINE word such as 'volcano', blind people can process a mental image of this object defining its characteristics on the basis of their experience of a mountain, of their recall of a "fire" experience and assembling these informations in a mental representation together with all other available data on this object. The same mechanism based on assimilation is also used by sighted people when they are required to create a mental image of an object that they never touched or saw or smelt, such as for the word 'paradise'.

In another series of studies, differences between sighted and blind participants in using mental imagery were investigated by comparing their performance in recalling sequences of verbal information. In a study by De Beni and Cornoldi (1985), we asked sighted and blind participants to use the loci mnemonics – that consists in imaging to locate a series of stimuli along a well known pathway – in order to retrieve a list of twenty single, pairs and triplets of words. We found that also non-sighted people took advantage in this task from imagery instructions, because they preferred to use mental representations instead of using the rehearsal strategy in order to recall the items list. Moreover, congenitally blind participants could generate complex interactive mental im-

ages, but they had difficulty in creating a single mental representation containing different stimuli. The difficulty met by the blind in memorizing triplets
was not due to a generic increase in the memory request. In fact, according to
Tinti and colleagues (1999), when complex mental images are processed and
used in an auditory format, non-sighted people are not impaired.

In two further investigations (Cornoldi et al. 1989; De Beni & Cornoldi
1988) we confirmed that congenitally blind participants could generate an interactive mental representation in which a word was associated to a given location, but their performance was inadequate when ther were asked to create
a more complex mental image in which many words and locations had to be
represented. An overall effect of complexity seems to influence blind people's
performance, although the specific characteristics of this effect are still not well
specified.

3. Active and passive functions in mental images created in totally blindness condition

A series of our own studies that we carried out in the last decade is based on
the administration of an experimental task that was already used in a visual
modality by other researchers in the eighties (Attneave & Curlee 1983; Kerr
1987). It is a mental imagery task that is organized in a series of steps. Firstly it
requires the haptic exploration of a matrix composed of blocks; then, participants have to imagine they are following a pathway within that configuration
on the basis of statements of direction given by the examiner; and finally they
have to point to the block corresponding to the last position of the pathway.
This tool represents an active spatial mental imagery task, because in order to
carry it out, it is necessary to generate and update a mental representation of
the pathway on the basis of the sequential information (e.g. the number of
statements of directions) that are progressively given. According to our original procedure, the level of complexity can be manipulated by the experimenter,
respectively varying three aspects which have partially different cognitive implications: 1) (memory load) the size of the configuration, that is the number
of blocks comprising the matrix (e.g. 2×2, 3×3, 4×4, etc.); 2) (updating request) the length of the pathway, that is the number of direction changes (e.g.
left/right, forwards/backwards); 3) (degree of spatial involvement) the number of dimensions that composes the configuration (2D or 3D). These tools
proved to be very useful in evaluating visuo-spatial abilities of both blind and
sighted individuals: It does not require any particular expertise or knowledge,

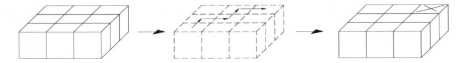

Figure 10.1. Example of the method used to evaluate active processes: The subject is asked to imagine a matrix, to follow the spatial instructions (for example, up, right, up, right, etc.) and then indicate the final position.

it is easy to use and very flexible in experimental practice. In addition, the implicated set of tasks allowed us to investigate different aspects of visuo-spatial processing and to evaluate several theoretical assumptions related to the characteristics of the Working Memory system. In particular, it was possible to address the distinction between passive and active processes in VSWM and to investigate the characteristics of several central/integration processes that can be involved in the execution of mental imagery task. In most cases, the performance on the active, mental pathway, task has been combined with a passive storage task requiring to memorize target positions within matrices of different dimensions.

One of the most interesting results that we reported in several studies concerned the role of dimensions. We noticed that both blind and sighted people can generate and process a sequence of positions within a matrix. However, blind people experience a selective difficulty in manipulating 3D information. Performances between the two groups were often comparable when using 2D matrices but differences, favoring sighted individuals, merged in 3D tasks (e.g. Cornoldi, Cortesi, & Preti 1991; Cornoldi, Bertuccelli, Rocchi, & Sbrana 1993). This result was found both when the number of units per side and the number of statements of direction of the pathway was identical in 2D and 3D matrices and when the number of blocks composing the two types of matrices was equated (e.g. 3 × 3 matched with 2 × 2 × 2 matrices, 9 vs. 8 blocks).

Subsequent Cornoldi et al.'s data (1993) have been obtained manipulating the number of dimensions in which the matrices were presented – at the same time controlling that the level of complexity was equivalent (e.g. 3 × 3 and 2 × 2 × 2 matrices) – and the length of the pathway, and varying the rate at which instructions of direction were delivered (one instruction per second or every two seconds). Totally congenitally blind people showed again a poorer performance than controls in recalling the last positions of the pathways, and differences were emphasized in 3D matrices when compared to 2D ones. Moreover, it was found that blind people were more impaired in the faster conditions.

In a further experiment (Cornoldi et al. 1993) we investigated whether blindness determine a reduction in active spatial working memory functions only or the deficit concerned also the passive – more visual – functions. Congenitally blind and sighted participants were asked to carried out two different active mental imagery tasks. In order to carry out the spatial task participants had to recall the last position of a mental pathway on a matrix, whereas the visual task required to recognize the shape of that pathway. Although blind participants once again had more difficulty in processing information presented in the third dimension, their performance was more impaired in carrying out the spatial task than the visual, passive one.

However the tasks that we used in the studies previously described raised some concerns. In particular, they had the limits that they did not allow us to investigate the passive functions of visuo-spatial working memory in congenitally blind people by using a task completely comparable to the active ones. For this reason, Vecchi, Monticelli and Cornoldi (1995) designed two tasks that respectively gave a measure of active and passive VSWM processes, and that were adapted to a presentation to both blind and sighted individuals. In this study we maintained constant the level of complexity of the matrix, by using only 5×5 two-dimensional configurations. In order to assess active working memory functions, participants (congenitally blind and sighted) had to imagine to follow a pathway on a matrix and then they had to indicate the final position on the configuration. The length of the pathway was manipulated requiring six or ten statements of direction. We expected that greater difficulty were found in generating a mental image of a longer pathway, because in this case it was necessary to take into account a greater number of movements and a greater amount of cognitive resources were necessary in order to update the mental representation.

Moreover, we hypothesized that this difficulty should be more evident in the totally congenitally blind group. In order to design the passive task, we prepared a series of 5×5 matrices in which the target-positions were covered with sandpaper to be easily recognized by touch. Participants tactually explored the configuration and then had to recall the targets by pointing to the positions previously occupied on a neutral matrix. The results showed that non-sighted participants were not impaired (with respect to the sighted participants) in retrieving passive matrices, both when the target-positions were four and when they were eight. On the contrary, and in agreement with our previous findings, the active task was very difficult for the non-sighted participants, especially when they had to imagine longer pathways.

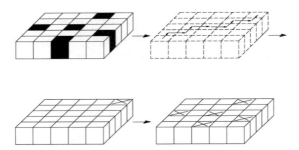

Figure 10.2. Example of the method used by Vecchi et al. (1995) to evaluate the active and passive processes. In this example, there are five passive positions and a trajectory including eight changes of position.

In the same study, a second experiment was carried out in order to have at a time a measure of passive and active visuo-spatial working memory functions in blind and sighted people. The active task was equivalent to that of the previous experiment but in this case the length of the pathway was fixed (8 statements of direction). Moreover, the passive tasks consisted in remembering 2, 3, 4 or 5 positions. Both tasks had to be carried out within a single trial. The experimental procedure firstly required the tactile exploration of the matrix in order to memorize the target positions (e.g. passive task); then the participant had to generate the mental representation of the pathway on the basis of the instructions (e.g. active task), hence the final position of the pathway had to be pointed at; and finally the target-positions of the first configuration had to be recalled. We again found that blind participants had no difficulty in carrying out the passive task. At the highest level of complexity (i.e., five to-be-remembered positions) differences were negligible and, in some cases, blind people performed better than the sighted. However, blind participants' performance was poorer in the active task, showing once again a deficit in generating and updating the mental representation of a sequence of spatial information.

Overall, these data are consistent in indicating the capacity to generate and process mental images even in the absence of visual perception. At the same time, they are consistent in indicating a selective impairment associated with congenital blindness in active tasks. This problem seems to be maximized when tasks involve three-dimensional material. It is then necessary to explain the reason why totally congenitally blind showed difficulty in generating and using mental imagery with 3D materials. One possible explanation is that the creation of a mental representation concerning a pattern of positions on a 3D configuration requires the simultaneous treatment and maybe also the integration of different images (a series of 2D representations) of the same spatial context which are processed and maintained in working memory. It follows that a possible consequence is that for blind people it is more difficult to generate complex and interactive spatial mental images, although the capacity to maintain a series of information can be preserved. In other words, a possible deficit in active working memory functions, involved in simultaneous treatment and integration in 3D representations, can be dissociated by an impairment in passive recall.

In order to investigate these issues, a very recent line of studies has been carried out by Cornoldi, Tinti and Vecchi (in preparation). The aim of the first experiment was to explore whether passive recall was preserved in totally congenitally blindness when blind participants were requested to carry out an imagery task based on the creation of multiple representations. Blind people had to recall a number of positions tactually presented: the overall number of targets could be presented either within a single 5 × 5 matrix (e.g., 6 positions) or divided into two 5 × 5 matrices (e.g. three positions showed in one and three positions presented in the other configuration). In order to recall information, participants used respectively a single (for the single-matrix condition) or two blank matrices (for the two-matrices condition) in which the positions-target had to be pointed to. Results indicated that two-matrices task were more difficult for all participants: however, performance of congenitally blind people was less accurate than controls in the two-matrices condition, whereas no significant differences between the groups emerged in the single-matrix condition. This result implies that in order to recall the sequence of positions, blind people had more difficulty in contemporarily generating more than one mental image at the same time.

It is also possible that blind people could have difficulty in shifting from one mental representation to another in order to update and rearrange the information flow. On the basis of these results, it is not clear whether in congenital blindness there is not only a difficulty in manipulating simultaneously two or more mental representations but also an impairment in integrating more than one image at a time. Hence, a second experiment was carried out by Cornoldi et al. (in preparation) in order to investigate the specific effects of integration compared with the difficulty in remembering multiple matrices. In one condition congenitally totally blind and sighted people were asked to remember two series of positions showed in two different matrices and then to recall them by providing the answers on two separate blank configurations (multiple images condition). In the other condition, participants had to store a series of positions respectively presented on two separate matrices and then they had to recall all of the targets on a single blank configuration (integrated condition). We hypothesized that, if blind people have a difficulty in assembling different information sources in a unique representation, then their performance should have been poorer in the integrated condition. The results showed that integration capacity was preserved in blind people. Moreover, blind people tended to be facilitated in the integration condition, possibly an effect due to the reduction of the overall to-be-memorized material. The patterns of performance were very clear and provided empirical evidence that visuo-spatial deficit in blind people cannot be associated to the capacity of integrating different information but rather to a selective impairment in maintaining and processing more than a single image at a time.

Although further data are necessary to support our findings on mental imagery in totally congenitally people, our results allowed us to suggest that different causal factors are implicated in the difficulty to manipulate at a time complex mental images representing 3D stimuli. It seems evident that blind people are mainly impaired in the contemporary maintenance of more than one mental representation rather than in the organization of different information sources in a single 3D visuo-spatial configuration. However, other factors may have an influence on the difficulty met by the blind with the third dimension, including the involvement of verticality, an aspect which is now also under study.

4. Conclusion

The results of the studies previously described allow to conclude that the generation and use of visuo-spatial mental images have a positive effect on memory performance even in totally congenitally blind people. It is plausible to hypothesize that the non-sighted people process these mental representations in a specific format – not necessarily verbal – which is partially similar and partially different from that of mental images based on the visual experience. Differences do not necessarily involve a greater use of verbal strategies by the blind: Previous studies have also showed that the use of verbal strategies is not larger in blind than in sighted individuals (Vecchi 1998).

It is important to underline that the characteristics of mental images also in blind people are partially similar to those generated on the basis of sensorial, perceptual experiences. At the same time, some limitations may affect blind people's images. It has been showed that congenital blindness may influence the generation and use of mental images in different ways. The required speed of processing, the level of complexity of the representation, the selective involvement of passive or active visuo-spatial working memory functions are all factors possibly playing a role in determining subjects' capacity. In particular, our studies demonstrated the importance of considering the nature of the task, passive *vs.* active, as a key variable in interpreting blind people limitations. (At the same time, we also highlighted that active tasks cannot be considered as a homogeneous set of abilities. For example, blind people did not show any impairment in integrating different information and, in some cases, they performed such tasks better than the sighted). From a theoretical perspective, the observation of the performance of blind people in tasks assumed to involve the use of mental imagery is of great importance since it gives specific indications on the organization of VSWM functions and, in particular, on the relationship between more peripheral modality-specific structures and more central abilities.

References

Arditi, A., Holtzam, J., & Kosslyn, S. (1988). Mental imagery and sensory experience in congenital blindness. *Neuropsychologia, 26*, 1–12.

Attneave, F. & Curlee, T. E. (1983). Locational representation in imagery: A moving spot task. *Journal of Experimental Psychology: Human Perception and Performance, 9*, 20–30.

Baddeley, A. D. (1986). *Working memory.* Oxford: Oxford University Press.

Baddeley, A. D. & Hitch, G. J. (1974). Working memory. In G. Bower (Ed.), *The psychology of learning and motivation, Vol. VIII*, (pp. 47–90). New York: Academic Press.

Carreiras, M. & Codina, M. (1992). Spatial cognition of the blind and the sighted: Visual and amodal hypotheses, *CPC – Current Psychology of Cognition, 12*, 51–78.

Carpenter, P. A. & Eisenberg, P. (1978). Mental rotation and the frame of reference in blind and sighted individuals. *Perception and Psychophysics, 23*, 117–124.

Cornoldi, C., Bertuccelli, B., Rocchi, P., & Sbrana, B. (1993). Processing capacity limitations in pictorial and spatial representations in the totally congenitally blind. *Cortex, 29*, 675–689.

Cornoldi, C., Calore, D., & Pra Baldi, A. (1979). Imagery ratings and recall in congenitally blind subjects. *Perceptual and Motor Skills, 48*, 627–629.

Cornoldi, C., Cortesi, A., & Preti, D. (1991). Individual differences in the capacity limitations of visuospatial short-term memory: Research on sighted and totally congenitally blind people. *Memory and Cognition, 19*, 459–468.

Cornoldi, C., De Beni, R., & Giusberti, F. (1997). Meta-imagery: Conceptualization of mental imagery and its relationship with cognitive behavior. *Psychologische Beitrage, 38*, 484–499.

Cornoldi, C., De Beni, R., Giusberti, F., & Massironi, M. (1988). Memory and imagery: A visual trace is not a mental image. In M. Conway, S. Gathercole, & C. Cornoldi (Eds), *Theories of memory, Vol. 2* (pp. 87–110). Hove: Psychology Press.

Cornoldi, C., De Beni, R., Roncari, S., & Romano, S. (1989). The effects of imagery instructions on totally congenitally blind recall. *European Journal of Cognitive Psychology, 1*, 321–331.

Cornoldi, C., Tinti, C., & Vecchi, T. (in preparation). Memory and integration processes in congenital blindness.

Cornoldi, C. & Vecchi, T. (2000). Mental imagery in blind people: The role of passive and active visuo-spatial processes. In M. A. Heller (Ed.), *Touch, representation, and blindness* (pp. 143–181). New York: Oxford University Press.

Cornoldi, C. & Vecchi, T. (2003). *Visuo-spatial working memory and individual differences.* Hove: Psychology Press.

De Beni, R. & Cornoldi, C. (1985). The effects of imaginal mnemonics on congenitally totally blind and on normal subjects. In D. Marks and D. Russel (Eds.), *Imagery, Vol. 1* (pp. 54–59). Dunedin: Human Performance Associates.

De Beni, R. & Cornoldi, C. (1988). Imagery limitation in totally congenitally blind subjects. *Journal of Experimental Psychology: Learning, Memory and Cognition, 14*, 650–655.

Heller, M. A., Calcaterra, J. A., Tyler, L. A., & Burson, L. L. (1996). Production and interpretation of perspective drawings by blind and sighted people. *Perception, 25*, 321–334.

Heller, M. A. & Kennedy, J. M. (1990). Perspective taking, pictures, and the blind. *Perception and Psychophysics, 48*, 459–466.

Jonides, J., Kahn, R., & Rozin, P. (1975). Imagery instructions improve memory in blind subjects. *Bulletin of the Psychonomic Society, 5*, 424–426.

Juurmaa, J. & Lehtinen-Railo, S. (1994). Visual experience and access to spatial knowledge. *Journal of Visual Impairment and Blindness, 88*, 157–170.

Kennedy, J. (1982). Haptic pictures. In W. Schiff & E. Foulke (Eds.), *Tactual perception* (pp. 303–333). New York: Academic Press.

Kennedy, J. (1993). *Drawing and the blind: Pictures to touch.* New Haven: Yale University Press.

Kerr, N. H. (1983). The role of vision in "visual imagery" experiments: Evidence from congenitally blind. *Journal of Experimental Psychology: General, 112*, 265–267.

Kerr, N. H. (1987). Locational representation in imagery: The third dimention. *Memory and Cognition, 15*, 521–530.

Klatzky, R. L., Golledge, R. G., Loomis, J. M., Cicinelli, J. G., & Pellegrino, J. W. (1995). Performance of blind and sighted persons on spatial tasks. *Journal of Visual Impairment and Blindness, 89*, 70–82.

Loomis, J. M., Klatzky, R. L., Golledge, R. G., Cicinelli, J. G., Pellegrino, J. W., & Fry, P. A. (1993). Nonvisual navigation by blind and sighted: Assessment of path integration ability. *Journal of Experimental Psychology: General, 122*, 73–91.

Marmor, G. S. (1978). Age at onset of blindness and the development of the semantics of color names. *Journal of Experimental Child Psychology, 25*, 267–278.

Marmor, G. S. & Zaback, L. A. (1976). Mental rotation by the blind: Does mental rotation depends on visual imagery? *Journal of Experimental Psychology: Human Perception and Performance, 2*, 515–521.

Marschark, M. & Cornoldi, C. (1990). Imagery and verbal memory, in C. Cornoldi & M. Mc. Daniel (Eds.), *Imagery and cognition* (pp. 133–182). New York: Springer.

Paivio, A. (1971). *Imagery and verbal processes.* New York: Holt Rinehart & Wiston.

Pylyshyn, Z. W. (1973). What the mind's eye tells the mind's brain: A critique of mental imagery. *Psychological Bulletin, 80*, 1–24.

Rieser, J. J., Guth, D. A., & Hill, E. W. (1986). Sensitivity to perspective structure while walking without vision. *Perception, 15*, 173–188.

Rieser, J. J., Hill, E. W., Taylor, C. R., Bradfield, A., & Rosen, S. (1992). Visual experience, visual field size, and the development of nonvisual sensitivity to the spatial structure of outdoor neighborhoods explored by walking. *Journal of Experimental Psychology: General, 121*, 210–221.

Stuart, I. (1995). Spatial orientation and congenital blindness: A neuropsychological approach. *Journal of Visual Impairment and Blindness, 89*, 129–141.

Thinus-Blanc, C. & Gaunet, F. (1997). Representation of space in the blind: Vision as a spatial sense? *Psychological Bulletin, 121*, 20–42.

Tinti, C., Galati, D., Vecchio, M. G., De Beni, R., & Cornoldi, C. (1999). Interactive auditory and visual images in the blind. *Journal of Visual Impairment and Blindness, 93*, 579–583.

Vecchi, T. (1998). Visuo-spatial limitations in congenitally totally blind people. *Memory, 6*, 91–102.

Vecchi, T., Monticelli, M. L., & Cornoldi, C. (1995). Visuo-spatial working memory: Structures and variables affecting a capacity measure. *Neuropsychologia, 33*, 1549–1564.

Zimler, J. & Keenan, J. M. (1983). Imagery in the congenitally blind: How visual are visual images? *Journal of Experimental Psychology: Learning, Memory and Cognition, 9*, 269–282.

PART 4

Intermodal coordinations

Chapter 11

Intermodal relations in infancy

Arlette Streri

Human adults know how to take an object they desire, and adapt their hand to size, shape, volume and orientation of the object in order to grip it suitably. Conversely, when they manipulate a non-visible object, they visually recognize its shape, its size and its volume without difficulty when the object becomes visible. These two types of intermodal coordination are evidence of the abstraction of several pieces of information common to vision and touch which appear in the course of development. This chapter examines the earliest forms of intermodal coordination, as they appear in infants.

1. Visual-tactile coordination showing an intermodal relationship

1.1 The formation of reaching trajectory

Adult reaching trajectory may be divided into two functionally different phases: The longer reaching phase, which takes up about three-quarters of the time, and the shorter grasping phase (cf. Jeannerod 1981). In babies' motor expressions, one must distinguish between the disorderly gestures arising from the organism's natural motility and those which are goal-oriented. In this case, the stimulus triggers the gesture and provides its goal, or even its meaning. However, newborns show an intentional coordination, in which proprioceptive information guides the newborn in its movements. For example, the baby often opens its mouth to put its hand in, whereas the contact of the hand with other parts of the body does not triggers the opening of the mouth (Butterworth & Hopkins 1988; Gallagher, Butterworth, Lew, & Cole 1988). Curiously, this first form of hand-to-mouth coordination directed towards the body itself and without visual control, does not take place when the newborn is holding an object in its hand (Streri, Lhote, & Dutilleul 2000). Yet we have seen the importance of exploring objects with the mouth at this age (Chapter 3).

Prehension-vision coordination appears towards the age of 5–6 months, at a period when the baby starts to maintain a sitting position. The baby catches all the objects within its reach and brings the held objects to its eyes. The first stages of this reversible hand-eye coordination are to be found when the newborn reaches for a visual target, which, according to the authors, may evidence a reflex or an intentional ballistic movement (Bower, Broughton, & Moore 1970). In von Hofsten's observations (1982), infants a few days old were firmly sat in 50° tilting chair, which supported the head and trunk and thus freed the arms. Stabilizing the head diminished disorderly arm movements, and the reaching for an object could be observed. The movement was triggered visually. In this study the frequency of arm and hand movements were also compared in two conditions: With a target and without (control condition). When the target object was present, the reaching movements were analyzed according to the baby's visual attention (the fixing or non-fixing of the object, closed eyes, indeterminable looking). As the object was rarely reached and grasped, it is difficult to conclude that there was visual-tactile coordination. Nevertheless, a joint orientation of the eye and the hand showed the baby's capacity to link visual and proprioceptive information on certain spatial characteristics such as the direction and the distance of the object. This joint orientation is not frequent but nevertheless exists. Taking a perception/action approach, von Hofsten (1993) regards this movement as an action for which the tool (the arm-hand system) is not yet fully controlled by the baby and depends on neural maturation. This primitive action is the base of the mature movement.

A decline in this movement is reported towards 7–8 weeks of age (von Hofsten & Fazel-Zandy 1984). The baby's activity does not return to its initial level before 12–14 weeks. Reaching for objects reappears, but is slow and discontinued. This disorganization also affects the form taken by the hand. The arm is projected towards the object with a closed fist and not with the palm open, and is not followed by grasping. When reaching is carried out with the palm open in order to grasp an object, the whole action is controlled visually and the eyes come and go between the hand and the object to be grasped. The hand opens progressively, in an anticipated way. When the hand reaches the object, it gropes about before grasping the object. The movement therefore has some of the characteristics of the adult system (cf. von Hofsten 1993). In a longitudinal study, during which the babies were observed every week from 8 to 24 weeks, Wimmers, Savelsbergh, Beek and Hopkins (1997) analyzed the relationships between two types of reaching: Reaching without grasping and reaching followed by grasping. Their analysis, carried out within the framework of the theory of dynamic systems, reveals that the transition between the two types of reaching is very sudden, and it is interpreted as attesting to a phase of discontinuity in development. Less dependent on the baby's posture at six months, the prehension movement, exercised intensively, reaches its objectives absolutely efficiently and possesses most of the characteristics of the adult movement (Jeannerod 1984).

1.2 Visual information interpreted by the hand

In looking for which visual information is interpreted by the hand, we will consider only those studies which concern the intrinsic properties of stationary or moving objects. The study of the spatial relationship between objects needs a two-handed coordination, and the grasping of an object behind a screen calls on cognitive requirements of another sort. Visually gathered information about object properties must be taken into account by the hand for an object to be grasped correctly. The anticipated opening of the hand reveals that the grasping action is planned and integrated into the reaching phase. This preparation is influenced by several of the target's properties. A photograph of an object does not trigger the reaching movement in newborns, contrary to the three-dimensional object (Bower 1972). But a difference in the way the hand takes into account the convex, concave or flat properties of objects is not observed in babies until the age of nine months (Piéraut-Le Bonniec 1985, 1986). Object size has been the subject of several studies. Bruner and Koslowski (1972) had observed that 8–21 week-old babies reached for an object differently, according to the smallness (3.12 cm) or largeness (25 cm) of the object. These first observations have not been conclusively replicated, as the finesse of a movement during reaching necessitates a more complex recording material than just an observer's eyes. Von Hofsten and Rönnqvist (1988) placed two infrared diodes on the thumb and index finger of the dominant hand of each child in order to evaluate the precise moment the gesture took place and how far the fingers were open. Three objects of 1.5 cm, 2.5 cm and 3.5 cm in diameter were presented at chin-height to babies aged 5–6, 9 and 13 months. The results showed that, from the age of five months, reaching behavior and hand presentation are well-mastered regarding different object sizes. At all the ages studied the actions of reaching for and grasping an object are strongly integrated. Nevertheless, Fontaine and Piéraut-Le Bonniec (1988) showed that the capacity to anticipate object size is also linked to 5-month-old babies' mastery of the sitting posture. This mastery is decisive in the grasping of big objects (5.5

cm) but hardly plays a role for small objects (1.5 cm). Finally, taking into account both the properties of the objects to be grasped (size and shape) and the constraints of the organism, Newell, Scully, McDonald and Baillargeon (1989) revealed that, from the age of four months, babies present different grasping configurations according to object properties, notably size, and do so thanks to their analysis of visual and tactile information. At eight months, visual information is enough for an object to be suitably grasped (cf. also Butterworth, Verweij, & Hopkins 1997; Newell & McDonald 1997).

Object orientation is more difficult for babies. At the age of five months babies do not orient their hand according to visual information, but after contact with a stick. Only at the age of nine months do babies adjust their hand before contact according to the horizontal or vertical orientation of the stick (Lockman, Ashmead, & Bushnell 1984; von Hofsten & Fazel-Zandy 1984). If the orientation of the object is changed just after the reaching movement has started, the five-month-old babies are disoriented. Only from seven months do they change their strategy and make the necessary adjustments to grasp the newly-oriented object (Morrongiello & Rocca 1989). When anticipating the trajectory of a moving object, the baby must consider not only spatial references but also an important time dimension. From the age of 18 weeks, the baby develops predictive reaching strategies when faced with a moving target. These strategies are efficient, since most of the reaching movements programmed from the beginning are successful (von Hofsten 1980). At the slowest speed of 3.4 cm/s, the ipsilateral arm is preferred and in faster speeds of 15 or 30 cm/s the contralateral arm is mostly mobilized.

Studies on visual perception have revealed the early capacity of young babies to discriminate surfaces and objects differing in size, volume and orientation. This perceptive skill appears before babies' ability to exert action upon objects. This gap between perception and action reveals the difficulty in taking object properties into account in the organization of reaching movements. It underlines the nature of control and movement planning which might involve a greater cognitive cost than a simple perceptive discrimination.

2. Intermodal transfer tasks

Intermodal transfer between vision and touch in babies has been considered as a way of answering Molyneux's famous question: Will a person born blind who recovers his/her sight as an adult immediately differentiate visually between a cube and a sphere (cf. Proust 1997)? The historical and philosophical debate that this question gave rise to three centuries ago has been revived in recent years, as difficulties in the methodology of studying perception in babies were overcome. Regarding infants, the answer to Molyneux's question makes sense only if it is given in the first semester after birth. Indeed, from the age of six months, during a bimodal object exploration, the baby can easily confront visual and tactile information and develop strategies favoring their integration. Studies carried out after the age of six months have tried to establish the conditions and limits within which intermodal transfer between touch and vision can be obtained. Examples of such research include modulating the length of familiarization, creating perceptual conflicts or evaluating the impact of certain pathologies or of premature birth (cf. Kellman & Arterberry 1998).

2.1 Intermodal transfer during the first semester after birth

Meltzoff and Borton's (1979) experiment provided the first evidence of intermodal transfer in very young infants. For 90 seconds, babies aged nearly one month explored a rough or a smooth pacifier in their mouth without possibility seeing it. After this familiarization phase, the babies saw two large orange balls, one smooth and the other with spikes. The visual fixation duration was recorded for each ball. The babies who had explored the smooth pacifier looked preferentially (longer) at the smooth ball, and those who had explored the rough pacifier looked longer at the spiked ball. In other words, the babies match the objects perceived successively in the oral and visual modes using information on texture, thus revealing their capacity to abstract and recognize this information.

This research was very skeptically received and these results are indeed weak, since they have always not been reproduced (see Maurer, Stager, & Mondloch 1999). Arguing that the babies in Meltzoff' s experiment looked preferentially at the familiar object and not at the novel one, as is the case in most transfer experiments, Turkewitz and Mellon (1989) suggested that the young baby's organism is sensitive only to the quantity of stimulation brought by the objects and that intermodal equivalence is based on this response modality. The logic behind their interpretation is as follows: certain aspects of intersensory functioning appear to demand low level treatments, physiologically mediated by receptors, whereas others, conversely, require more elaborate psychological processes. The results obtained in Meltzoff and Borton's (1979) experiment may be the result of the first mechanism. The babies who explored the smooth dummy had a weak vigilance level and thus react favorably on seeing the smooth ball. Conversely, the babies who explored the spiked dummy had a high vigilance level, due to the stimulation of receptors by the spikes, and later are oriented preferentially towards the spiked ball. This interpretation comes down to postulating that each sensory system interacts with an object property and that matching is based on this form of interaction. Thus, it is not a question of information transfer, in the sense of the transcription of perceived elements into a new code, readable by a second system.

If this interpretation allows us to account for Meltzoff and Borton's (1979) results, how should those based on substance obtained by Gibson and Walker (1984) be interpreted? In this experiment, the babies, also aged one month, orally explored a hard or soft object for sixty seconds. They then saw two sticks, one which moved like a rigid object and the other like a flexible object. The babies looked longer at the visual object which did not correspond to the property of the object previously explored. Turkewitz's reasoning, given to explain the experience of Meltzoff et al., is not suitable here, as the babies react to the novel object. According to Maurer et al. (1999), these differences observed in oral-visual transfer might be explained by the complex interactions between sucking, arousal and visual attention.

Recently, intermodal transfer from hand to eyes has been studied in newborns (Streri & Gentaz 2003). After manual habituation to an object (a prism or a cylinder) without visual control, 3-day-old neonates were visually presented simultaneously with the familiar and unfamiliar objects. Looking duration at each visual object and gaze shifts were recorded and compared to a control group performances that looked at the same objects but without previously haptic habituation. The findings revealed that, in transfer group, neonates looked longer at the novel object than the familiar one. Moreover, the number of looks at the novel object were significantly higher than the familiar object. In the control group, such results were not observed. This experiment may be considered as a genuine positive answer from newborn to Molyneux's question.

Other research were performed in two-month-old babies (Streri 1987, exp. 2) and in 4 to 5-month-olds (Streri & Pêcheux 1986a). The aim was to find out whether babies are capable of visually recognizing the shape of an object that they have previously manipulated without seeing. But one must bring up the question of reversible transfer from vision to touch. It may be difficult to understand why only tactile familiarization is apparently able to influence the babies' visual response, thus indicating that "touch educates vision", as Berkeley (1732/1996) thought about the third spatial dimension. Recent research on the visual capacities of babies and even of newborns tends to show that a visual influence on tactile behavior is also possible. In these studies, age factor is also important. At two months the action of reaching for a visual object, which is present at birth, declines and then reappears at the age of around 4–5 months: Is information transfer nevertheless observed? At five months prehension-vision coordination comes into being and starts playing a linking role between the two modalities.

It must be ensured that the objects are well differentiated in each of the modalities concerned (Streri 1987, exp. 1; Streri & Pêcheux 1986b). Thus an intermodal transfer failure cannot be attributed to the modalities' failure to differentiate two shapes. The equivalence of intramodal capacities constitutes a prerequisite for obtaining a reversible transfer between touch and vision. The results of transfer experiments have revealed that two-month-old babies visually recognize an object they have previously held (Streri 1987, exp. 2), but the reverse relationship, that is a tactile recognition of an already seen object, is not observed. At five months, the asymmetrical relationship is the opposite. For the first time, the baby becomes capable of tactually recognizing an object already looked at, but the reciprocal touch-vision relationship temporarily disappears (Streri & Pêcheux 1986b). At six months and over, touch-to-vision transfer is once again observed (Ruff & Kohler 1978; Rose, Gottfried, & Bridger 1981a).

Thus, at two months, a period during which prehension-vision coordination is absent, an information transfer from touch to vision is observed. At five months, when object grasping is intensive, touch-vision transfer disappears. The conditions which favor the setting up of transfer are thus far from constant. They are strictly dependent on the speed of maturation of the peripheral systems. Indeed, the perceptive development of different modalities is not synchronous from the beginning of conception. The primitive tactile system and its slow maturation opposes the visual system, which appears later but evolves more quickly. How can the non-reversible transfers of the first semester be explained? The answers differ according to the age looked at.

Let us first of all underline two important differences between the haptic and visual systems (Hatwell 1986; cf. Chapters 4 and 8). The first concerns the way in which object information is gathered: Haptic perception is fragmented and successive whereas visual perception is holistic. In order to obtain a coherent representation of manipulated objects partially gathered information must be re-combined (Revesz 1950). The second difference regards the relationships between the perceptive and motor aspects of the studied modalities. Indeed, at the time of the organs' functioning, the two systems include a closely linked perceptive-motor element. The fundamental difference is to be found in the motor aspect. The visual system is based on several motor mechanisms which increase the quality of sensory information projected onto the retina.

The motor element of the manual system is implicated in both functions. In the perceptive function, manual exploration consists in moving the hand over the surface of an object, which produces deformations of the skin and the articulatory and muscular layers of the hand (haptic perception). Fine manual motor skill increases the accuracy of tactually gathered information. The second function is instrumental and involves moving objects in space. The perceptive function ensures contact with and knowledge of the environment whereas the instrumental function modifies and transforms it. These two functions of the hand do not appear at the same time during development.

At the age of two months, the perceptive function dominates the infant's exchanges with its environment, but does not become efficient for the hand until freed from the strong motor element that is reflex. The infant's fingers then exert light pressure on the held object, sliding across the object surface and picking out heterogeneousness of contour and surface. Manual and digital skills will thus allow the infant to represent the manipulated object better. Intermodal transfer in young babies is thus dependent on the weakness of the hand's perceptive function. A plausible hypothesis would be that the levels of representation reached by each modality are not equivalent in order for exchanges of information to take place. When the baby is tactually familiarized with an object, s/he builds up a representation of its parts from pressure exerted on its surface and contour but does not have the capacity to reconstruct a structured whole from this partial information. The infant's perception is situated on Revesz's (1950) first level of construction, where partial information is gathered. When the infant then sees the object, s/he is capable of recognizing it as the transfer is from a partial level to a higher level of representation. On the other hand, when the child is visually familiarized with an object, s/he builds up a relatively complete representation of it as visual perception is holistic. However, s/he then fails to tactually recognize the object because the transfer must go from a global to a partial representation of the object. It is more difficult to go down to a low level of representation when situated at a higher level than to reach a high level from a lower level of treatment, as the perceptive process proceeds from the most elementary levels to the most elevated (Marr 1982; Pinker 1984). This interpretation is validated by the fact that, if a two-month-old baby is presented with a degenerated visual stimulation, i.e. a sketch of an object emphasizing its contour, tactile recognition is possible (Streri & Molina 1993, 1994). Contour is thus a property which is tactually apprehended by the subject (cf. Chapter 7).

Well established at birth and two months of age, touch-to-vision transfer disappears at five months, whereas the baby manually recognizes an object already looked at (Streri & Pêcheux 1986a). This absence of reversibility cannot be explained in the same way as above. The baby is at a stage when the function of transporting objects dominates exchanges with the environment. A plausible explanation would be that the object is no longer there to be tactually explored, but to be looked at. If the object is looked at, then it is to be taken. One hypothesis would be that the transporting function temporarily interferes with the perceptive function of the hand.

Although other experiments must to be performed to test the reversible transfer between touch and vision, our findings suggest that, in very young infants, the foundations of intermodal transfer of object shape has to be find between the haptic and visual systems.

2.2 Thinking with the hands: The unity of object partially occluded

Our hands are tools acting on the world but also perceiving and thinking the world. In this second function, some similarities with the visual mode are possible. We investigated the infant's haptic mode, asking how it "understands" the physical world in the perception of the unity of partially occluded objects. Intermodal transfer of shape needs the handling of an object with only one hand. At about 4 months, infants are able to hold large objects with both their hands simultaneously and to explore vigorously.

Four-month-old infants perceive the two ends of a visually presented, center-occluded object as one connected unit when the ends undergo a common translation and they perceive two adjacent objects as separate units when the ends undergo independent motion (Kellman & Spelke 1983). By using intermodal transfer tasks, similarly, we found that 4-month infants, who explore without visual control the two ends of a haptic assembly with one end in each hand, perceive the display as a connected unit when they undergo a common rigid motion and as two distinct units when they undergo different, independent translatory motions (Streri & Spelke 1988). These observations are consistent with the hypothesis that translatory motion specifies object unity and boundaries for infants in both the modalities. Although the ends of the rigid device differed in texture, weight and shape (Streri & Spelke 1989), thus destroying object unity, the movement exerted on the object nevertheless allowed it to be recognized as one single object. Movement thus trumps the analysis of surface properties of the elements held in the hands. These studies underline the importance of arm movement and action in general in the perceptive organization of the world into distinct or related surfaces in 4 to 5-month-old babies (cf. also Streri, Spelke, & Rameix 1993).

More recently, we have found that young infants perceive object unity from rotary motion patterns in the haptic mode earlier than in the visual mode (Streri, Gentaz, Spelke, & Van de Walle 2003). These results suggest that all rigid displacements-rotations as well as translations- are potentially informative to infants, at least in the haptic mode. These findings provide evidence that young infants are sensitive to motion patterns and can identify object boundaries from only handling the ends of a haptic assembly. Thus, perception of object unity depends on amodal processes that group surfaces into objects whenever those surfaces are spatially connected and undergo common rigid motion, regardless of the perceptual mode through which the objects are perceived.

2.3   Intermodal transfer during the second semester after birth

In order to test the solidity of the links between the sensory modalities during the second semester of life, the most frequently manipulated variable is that of the familiarization duration. Thus, touch-vision (T-V) intermodal transfers concerning object substance reveal an improvement in the speed of the treatment of haptic information between the ages of 1 and 12 months. Walker-Andrews and Gibson (1986) showed that the six-month-old baby does not recognize the substance (hardness) of an object manipulated after twenty seconds of familiarization, whereas at 12 months s/he does. The development of the intermodal transfer of object shape during the second semester confirms the complexity of the results obtained in very young babies and insists on the highly cognitive character of this form of relation between the two modalities. For example, Ruff and Kohler (1978) obtained a touch-vision transfer (T-V) in six-month-olds after a thirty-second manual familiarization period with simple objects like a sphere and a cube. On the other hand, at the same age, Rose et al. (1981a) tested three T-V transfer tasks with more complex objects explored either orally (1 test) or manually (2 tests). The tactile familiarization duration phase was also 30 seconds. The six-month-old babies failed to visually recognize the sucked or palpated objects. This failure, attributable to the short duration of haptic familiarization, is also linked to the complexity of the objects. If the babies explore the objects for sixty seconds visual recognition is observed after manual exploration, but not after oral exploration. The three transfer tasks are successfully completed only at about the age of twelve months (Gottfried, Rose, & Bridger 1977). At the same age, however, the reverse transfer – from vision to touch (V-T) – is not obtained after 30 seconds of familiarization but is obtained after sixty seconds in a two-minute tactile test (Rose, Gottfried, & Bridger 1981b). This research once again brings up the question as to the non-reversibility of transfers. The question was re-examined by Rose and Orlian (1991), who compared intramodal visual (V-V) and tactile (T-T) performances with intermodal V-T and T-V tasks in twelve-month-olds. The familiarization phases lasted fifteen, thirty or sixty seconds according to groups. The results revealed that the V-V condition is the easiest, whatever the duration of familiarization. The T-T and T-V conditions are intermediate since recognition is obtained after thirty and sixty seconds, but not after fifteen seconds of familiarization. However, the babies fail to tactually recognize objects already looked at, whatever the duration of the familiarization period. These results recall those found with two-month-old babies, but Rose and Orlian (1991) offer another interpretation and explain the V-T transfer failure as attributable to a difference in the information gathered on the characteristics of the objects by the two modalities (cf. Rose 1994). However, after 45 seconds of familiarization 12-month-old babies can visually recognize in a photo or a sketch an object they have previously held (Rose, Gottfried, & Bridger 1983). The transfer between the two modalities is thus based on the abstraction of the contour of the objects, which is invariant.

With different paradigms Bushnell and Weinberg (1987) showed that eleven-month-old babies are sensitive to the difference between a smooth egg and a furry cube on the one hand, and a smooth cross and a furry cube on the other hand. However, the babies do not react to the presentation of the cube and the smooth cross whereas they make the difference between the cube and the smooth egg. Intermodal matching is thus easier when the objects differ in more than one dimension (shape + texture). The fact that babies fail to discriminate between the cube and the cross suggests that they are not yet very sensitive to linear breaks in shape, thus confirming the oldest Bryant, Jones, Claxton and Perkins (1972) intermodal transfer study. Conflict situations are an interesting way of testing the degree of integration of the two systems. Bushnell (1982) put 8, 9 ½ and 11-month-old babies in a situation in which they saw an object different from the one they manipulated. An integration of visual and tactile space is obtained only from the age of nine months, thus confirming the weakness of transfers before this age.

This weakness also appears in studies examining the risks linked to populations of children presenting mental handicaps, neuronal damage or learning difficulties (cf. Freides 1974). Rose, Gottfried and Bridger (1978) studied the influence of social and biological factors on intermodal transfer in twelve-month-old babies born prematurely (at birth the gestational age was 32.6 weeks, the weight was 1650g) and full term twelve-month-olds, from a low socio-economic class. The authors re-used the three transfer tasks already mentioned, for a 30-second period of haptic familiarization. No intermodal transfer was obtained, contrary to experiments carried out on babies of the same age but from a middle socio-economic class. These experiments were repeated on baby monkeys (macaca nemestrina) by Gunderson, Rose and Grant-Webster (1990). The baby monkeys were aged 13.5 weeks on average at the time of the experiment (biological maturation was thus comparable to that of twelve-month-old human babies). Twelve were regarded as capable of normal development from a cognitive point of view, whereas 15 were classed as "high-risk" due to their light birth weight, difficult development, a traumatic birth, or pre-natal exposition to ethanol. The babies were orally and manually familiarized with objects for thirty seconds, then the visual recognition task lasted twenty seconds. The monkeys which presented deficits failed the visual recognition test, whereas those born normally succeeded. This similarity in performance with human babies suggests that processes underlying intermodal transfers are shared by different species (cf. Lewkowicz 2000; Lewkowicz & Lickliter 1994). But the fact that intermodal transfer is sensible to clinical factors or depends on the speed of treatment of information casts a doubt on its stability in older children.

3.   Conclusion

The visual and haptic modalities function in a similar way in detecting the invariants in shape, texture, unity of object, etc., necessary for obtaining a primitive unity of senses. However, each system has its own biological or behavioral constraints, which give each its specificity and which limit the possibilities of information exchange between sensory modalities. The type of intermodal relationships examined reveals early integration behaviors between modalities. These integration behaviors, the neurological bases of which are beginning to be known (Stein et al. 1994; cf. Chapters 1 and 2), evolve according to the biological and functional constraints of each system. Notably, the non-synchronous maturation speed of the perceptive systems are one possible cause of the intermodal transfer asymmetries observed during the first year of life. If transfer cannot be explained by an amodal perception, as Gibson suggests, the mediator or the coding method (other than the symbolic – linguistic or image – method) constituting the link between the two modalities still needs to be determined. In other words, if sense unity is a primitive datum in newborns, it is not immutable. The fluctuations observed during development suggest that it is a matter of perpetual construction and conquest for the child, either to maintain or to re-establish the relationship.

References

Berkeley, G. (1732/1996). An essay towards a new theory of vision. In M. R. Ayers (Ed.), *George Berkeley: Philosophical works*. London: Everyman vision (originally published in 1732).

Bower, T. G. R. (1972). Object perception in infants. *Perception, 1*, 15–30.

Bower, T. G. R., Broughton, J. M., & Moore, M. K. (1970). The coordination of visual and tactual input in infants. *Perception and Psychophysics, 8*, 51–53.

Bruner, J. S. & Koslowski, B. (1972). Visually preadapted constituents of manipulatory action. *Perception, 1*, 3–14.

Bryant, P. E., Jones, P., Claxton, V., & Perkins, G. H. (1972). Recognition of shapes across modalities by infants. *Nature, 240*, 303–304.

Bushnell, E. W. (1982). Visual-tactual knowledge in 8-, 9 ½,- and 11-month-old infants. *Infant Behavior and Development, 5*, 63–75.

Bushnell, E. W. & Weinberg, N. (1987). Infants' detection of visual-tactual discrepancies: Asymmetries that indicate a directive role of visual information. *Journal of Experimental Psychology: Human Perception and Performance, 13*, 601–608.

Butterworth, G. E. & Hopkins, B. (1988). Hand-mouth coordination in the newborn human infant. *British Journal of Developmental Psychology, 6*, 303–314.

Butterworth, G. E., Verweij, E., & Hopkins, B. (1997). The development of prehension in infants: Halverson revisited. *British Journal of Developmental Psychology, 15*, 223–236.

Fontaine, R. & Piéraut-Le Bonniec, G. (1988). Postural evolution and integration of the prehension gesture in children aged 4 to 10 months. *British Journal of Developmental Psychology, 6*, 223–233.

Freides, D. (1974). Human information processing and sensory modality: Crossmodal functions, information complexity, memory and deficit. *Psychological Bulletin, 81*, 284–310.

Gallagher, S., Butterworth, G. E., Lew, A., & Cole, J. (1988). Hand-mouth coordination, congenital absence of limb and evidence for innate body schemas. *Brain and Cognition, 38*, 53–65.

Gibson, E. J. & Walker, A. (1984). Development of knowledge of visual-tactual affordances of substance. *Child Development, 55*, 453–460.

Gottfried, A. W., Rose, S. A., & Bridger, W. H. (1977). Cross-modal transfer in human infants. *Child Development, 48*, 118–123.

Gunderson, V. M., Rose, S. A., & Grant-Webster, K. S. (1990). Cross-modal transfer in high- and low-risk infant pigtailed macaque monkeys. *Developmental Psychology, 25*, 576–581.

Hatwell, Y. (1986). *Toucher l'espace*. Lille: Presses Universitaires de Lille.

Hofsten von, C. (1980). Predictive reaching for moving objects by human infants. *Journal of Experimental Child Psychology, 30*, 369–382.

Hofsten von, C. (1982). Eye-hand coordination in the newborn. *Developmental Psychology, 18*, 450–461.

Hofsten von, C. (1993). Prospective control: A basic aspect of action development. *Human Development, 36*, 253–270.

Hofsten von, C. & Fazel-Zandy, S. (1984). Development of visually guided hand orientation in reaching. *Journal of Experimental Child Psychology, 38*, 208–219.

Hofsten von, C. & Rönnqvist, L. (1988). Preparation for grasping an object: A developmental study. Paper presented at the *International Conference on Infant Studies*, Washington, DC.

Jeannerod, M. (1981). Intersegmental coordination during reaching at natural visual objects. In J. Long & A. Baddeley (Eds.), *Attention and performance IX* (pp. 153–168). Hillsdale NJ: Erlbaum.

Jeannerod, M. (1984). The timing of natural prehension movements. *Journal of Motor Behavior, 16*, 235–254.

Kellman, P. K. & Arterberry, M. E. (1998). *Cradle of knowledge: Development of perception in infancy*. Cambridge: MIT Press.

Kellman, P. K. & Spelke, E. S. (1983). Perception of partly occluded object in infancy. *Cognitive Psychology, 15*, 483–524.

Lewkowicz, D. J. (2000). The development of intersensory temporal perception: An epigenitic systems/limitations view. *Psychological Bulletin, 126*, 281–308.

Lewkowicz, D. J. & Lickliter, R. (1994). *Development of intersensory perception. Comparatives perspectives*. Hillsdale, NJ: Erlbaum.

Lockman, J. J., Ashmead, D. H., & Bushnell, E. W. (1984). The development of anticipatory hand orientation during infancy. *Journal of Experimental Child Psychology, 37*, 176–186.

Marr, D. C. (1982). *Vision: A computational investigation into the human representation and processing of visual information*. San Francisco: Freeman.

Maurer, D., Stager, C. L., & Mondloch, J. E. (1999). Cross-modal transfer of shape is difficult to demonstrate in one-month-olds. *Child Development, 70*, 1047–1057.

Meltzoff, A. N. & Borton, R. W. (1979). Intermodal matching by human neonates. *Nature, 282*, 403–404.

Morrongiello, B. & Rocca, P. (1989). Visual feedback and anticipatory hand orientation during infants' reaching. *Perceptual and Motor skills, 69*, 787–802.

Newell, K. M. & McDonald, P. V. (1997). The development of grip patterns in infancy. In J. Connolly & H. Forssberg (Eds.), *Neurophysiology and neuropsychology of motor development* (pp. 232–256). Cambridge: University Press.

Newell, K. M., Scully, D. M., McDonald, P. V., & Baillargeon, R. (1989). Task constraints and infant grip configurations. *Developmental Psychobiology, 22*, 817–832.

Piéraut-Le Bonniec, G. (1985). Hand-eye coordination and infants construction of convexity and concavity. *British Journal of Developmental Psychology, 3*, 273–280.

Piéraut-Le Bonniec, G. (1986). Genèse de propriétés des objets chez le nourrisson: propriété physique de concavité et propriété fonctionnelle de contenant. *Psychologie Française, 31*, 73–78.

Pinker, S. (1984). Visual cognition: An introduction 1. *Cognition, 18*, 1–64.

Proust, J. (1997). *Perception et intermodalité. Approches actuelles de la question de Molyneux*. Paris: Presses Universitaires de France.

Revesz, G. (1950). *Psychology and art of the blind.* London: Longmans Green.

Rose, S. A. (1994). From hand to eye: Findings and issues in infant cross-modal transfer. In D. J. Lewkowicz & R. Lickliter (Eds.), *The development of intersensory perception. Comparative perspectives* (pp. 265–284). Hillsdale: Erlbaum.

Rose, S. A., Gottfried, A. W., & Bridger, W. H. (1978). Cross-modal transfer in infants: Relationship to prematurity and socio-economic background. *Developmental Psychology, 14,* 643–652.

Rose, S. A., Gottfried, A. W., & Bridger, W. H. (1981a). Cross-modal transfer in 6-month-old infants. *Developmental Psychology, 17,* 661–669.

Rose, S. A., Gottfried, A. W., & Bridger, W. H. (1981b). Cross-modal transfer and information processing by sense of touch in infancy. *Developmental Psychology, 17,* 90–98.

Rose, S. A., Gottfried, A. W., & Bridger, W. H. (1983). Infant's cross-modal transfer from solid objects to their graphic representations. *Child Development, 54,* 686–694.

Rose, S. A. & Orlian, E. K. (1991). Asymmetries in infant cross-modal transfer. *Child Development, 62,* 706–718.

Ruff, H. A. & Kohler, C. J. (1978). Tactual-visual transfer in six-month-old infants. *Infant Behavior and Development, 1,* 259–264.

Stein, B. E., Meredith, M. A., & Wallace, M. T. (1994). Development and neural basis of multisensory integration. In D. J. Lewkowicz & R. Lickliter (Eds.), *The development of intersensory perception. Comparative perspectives* (pp. 81–106). Hillsdale: Erlbaum.

Streri, A. (1987). Tactile discrimination of shape and intermodal transfer in 2- to 3-month-old infants. *British Journal of Developmental Psychology, 5,* 213–220.

Streri, A. & Gentaz, E. (2003). Cross-modal recognition of shape from hand to eyes in human newborns. *Somatosensory and Motor Research, 20,* 11–16.

Streri, A., Gentaz, E., Spelke, E. S., & Van de Walle, G. (2003). Haptic perception of object unity in rotating displays. *Quarterly Journal of Experimental Psychology* (in press).

Streri, A., Lhote, M., & Dutilleul, S. (2000). Haptic perception in the newborn. *Developmental Science, 3,* 319–327.

Streri, A. & Molina, M. (1993). Visual-tactual and tactual-visual transfer between objects and pictures in 2-month-old infants. *Perception, 22,* 1299–1318.

Streri, A. & Molina, M. (1994). Constraints on intermodal transfer between touch and vision in infancy. In D. J. Lewkowicz & R. Lickliter (Eds.), *The development of intersensory perception. Comparative perspectives* (pp. 285–308). NJ: Lawrence Erlbaum Associates.

Streri, A. & Pêcheux, M.-G. (1986a). Cross-modal transfer of form in 5-months-old infants. *British Journal of Developmental Psychology, 4,* 161–167.

Streri, A. & Pêcheux, M. G. (1986b). Tactual habituation and discrimination of form in infancy: A comparison with vision. *Child Development, 57,* 100–104.

Streri, A. & Spelke, E. S. (1988). Haptic perception of objects in infancy. *Cognitive Psychology, 20,* 1–23.

Streri, A. & Spelke, E. S. (1989). Effects of motion and figural goodness on haptic object perception in infancy. *Child Development, 60,* 1111–1125.

Streri, A., Spelke, E. S., & Rameix, E. (1993). Specific and amodal mechanisms of object perception and exploration in infancy: The case of active touch. *Cognition, 47,* 251–279.

Turkewitz, G. & Mellon, R. C. (1989). Dynamic organization of intersensory function. *Canadian Journal of Psychology, 43*, 286–301.

Walker-Andrews, A. S. & Gibson, E. J. (1986). What develops in bimodal perception. In L. P. Lipsitt & C. Rovee-Collier (Eds.), *Advances in infancy research, Vol. 4.* (pp. 171–181). Norwood, NJ: Ablex.

Wimmers, R. H., Savelsbergh, G. J., Beek, P. J., & Hopkins, B. (1997). Evidence for a phase transition in the early development of prehension. *Developmental Psychobiology, 32*, 235–248.

CHAPTER 12

Intermodal coordinations in children and adults

Yvette Hatwell

The presence of early intermodal coordination in neonates and very young infants invalidates the concepts which, up until the beginning of the 1960s, considered that the modalities were independent at birth and were unified by experience and language (Birch & Lefford 1963). The present chapter will study the evolution of intermodal coordination at school age and in adults, and its manifestation in different situations. In the 1970s and 1980s, the debate opposed those holding the Gibsonian concept of an amodal processing of information allowing immediate intermodal transfer, and those for whom transfer required additional processing which weakened this operation. The interest in this question in children and adults then diminished, as researchers turned towards the newer study of infants and because a less dichotomeous concept of intermodal relations allowed new empirical observations to be better taken into account. Some publications have reviewed these works (Hatwell 1986, 1994), and we will refer to them to avoid repetition.

Three categories of situations involving intermodal interactions will be examined. In intermodal matching, an object (or a property) is perceived by one modality (for example vision), then a recognition test is given in another modality (touch). This allows intermodal transfer to be evaluated, that is the communication of information from one modality to the other. In situations involving simultaneous bisensory functioning, the two modalities apprehend the same object at the same time and must be coordinated in order to coherently estimate the object. In the case of perceptual conflicts, the characteristics of this coordination show the contribution of each modality to the final percept. Finally, in distributed attention situations, the question is to know whether the existence of strong intermodal links disturbs the division of attention between modalities simultaneously activated in different tasks, the activation of one being transmited to the other.

1.   Intermodal matching

1.1   Evolution with age

1.1.1   *Continuity and specificity of intermodal capacities*
Because important interindividual differences have been observed in inter-modal transfer in infants, Rose, Feldman, Futterweit and Jankowski (1998) questioned whether these differences were stable over time and correlate with intermodal performances measured a few years later. A group of 90 children was thus monitored from the age of 7 months to 6 years, and was again tested at age 11. These tests involved spatial tasks of intermodal transfer from haptics to vision (H-V), hearing-vision and vision-hearing transfer (to find out whether intermodal capacities are general or specific to some modalities), as well as IQ and spatial skills. The results showed a certain stability with age of intermodal H-V scores when objects were explored with the left hand (r = .34) between early infancy and the age of 11, but not with the right hand (for the problem of the laterality of hand functions, cf. Chapter 6). A modest but significant correlation (close to .35) appeared with IQ, but no correlation was obtained between intermodal H-V tasks and those involving hearing and vision. The continuity of intermodal capacities with age seems thus specific to the haptic and visual modalities. According to the authors, this correlation (and the cor-relation with IQ) cannot result from spatial aptitudes, as it remains even when the spatial factor is neutralized. The interindividual differences present in early infancy seem therefore to be a precursor of those observed later in life, though we cannot yet explain why.

1.1.2   *Do intermodal capacities improve with age?*
For a long time, it was thought that intermodal transfer capacities improved with age thanks to bimodal experience and language development (e.g. Birch & Lefford 1963; cf. Hatwell 1994). This point of view resulted from the then dom-inant theoretical options (the hypothesis of a radical separation of the modali-ties at birth and their progressive fusion with practice), and of the experimental studies effectively showing that the percentage of correct responses in inter-modal haptic-vision and vision-haptic matching increased with age. However, Bryant's methodological criticisms (Bryant 1974; Bryant, Jones, Claxton, &

Perkins 1968) disqualified the studies (that of Birch & Lefford 1963, and many others both before and after it) which did not include the necessary vision-vision and haptic-haptic control conditions in their experimental design.

When these controls are carried out, it is generally found that the improvements in intermodal performances can wholly be explained by the concomitant improvement in intramodal performances (Abravanel 1981; Hatwell 1986; Jones 1981; Juurmaa & Lehtinen-Railo 1994). As far as we know, only one study gave evidence of real intermodal progress with age, but the study concerned only children aged 5 and 7 years (Stoltz-Loike & Bornstein 1987). Nothing thus allows to assert today that intermodal transfer capacities increase at school age.

1.2 Intramodal equivalences and intermodal transfer

1.2.1 *General characteristics of transfer between vision and haptics*
If, as was assumed by Gibson (1966), the information gathered in a perceptual stimulation is "amodal" (independent of the modalities which sensorially transmitted this information), there should be no difference between intramodal conditions, where stimulus presentation and recognition test take place in the same modality, and intermodal conditions where the modality is changed between presentation and test. However, this comparison is not easy to effectuate when geometric properties are concerned, because haptic spatial discriminatory capacities are generally less efficient than visual ones. It is therefore often observed that intermodal performances are superior to the intramodal performances of the less efficient modality, i.e. the haptic modality (e.g. Garbin 1988; cf. Hatwell 1986). This can be explained by the fact that in the intermodal V-H and H-V conditions, vision plays a facilitating role in the half of the test when it is available, whereas the intramodal H-H condition takes place entirely without vision. When visual and haptic intramodal spatial performances are comparable, sometimes no difference is found between the intra- and intermodal conditions (Garbin 1988; Garvill & Molander 1973) but more generally intramodal performances are superior to intermodal performances (Connolly & Jones 1970; Jones & Connolly 1970; Milewski & Iaccino 1982; Newell, Shapiro, & Carlton 1979). This is not compatible with Gibson's amodality hypothesis (1966) and has been interpreted as evidence of a specific treatment of "recoding" the perceptual data into the code of the other modality (Connolly & Jones 1970; cf. Hatwell 1994), which allows information to circulate between modalities.

Another observation casting a doubt on the amodal nature of spatial information is the asymmetrical character of intermodal transfer. In many studies concerning spatial properties, transfer is easier from haptics to vision than from vision to haptics, in children and in adults (Connolly & Jones 1970; Jones & Connolly 1970; Jones 1981; Juurmaa & Lehtinen-Railo 1988; Newham & McKenzie 1993; cf. Hatwell 1986, 1994). It is as if the transfer of information from the dominant to the minor modality (here from V to H) required a special processing of translation from one code to the other. On the other hand, when the transfer concerns texture, for which touch is as efficient as (if not better than) vision, this asymmetry does not appear.

1.2.2 The role of memory

Intermodal transfer situations raise the problem of storing the data to be transferred and thus of the properties of haptic memory. This memory is more unstable than visual memory (e.g. Connolly & Jones 1970; Posner 1967). However, the most interesting question is to find out how perceptual information is represented in memory. Indeed, intermodal transfer would be disturbed if the haptic organization were very different from that of visual memory. Some studies have looked at the distinction made in vision between explicit memory (or episodic memory, cf. Tulving 1983) and implicit memory. In the first, the subject is asked directly to discriminate between stimuli already presented and new stimuli (recognition task). In the second, memorization is indirectly evaluated via an identification task coming after a priming procedure (Schacter, Cooper, & Delaney 1990). In vision, these two memory types do not process the same information. Explicit memory is semantic and includes meanings as well as the particular physical characteristics of the stimulus. Implicit memory, which is manifested through a facilitation due to past experience, is pre-semantic and extracts the general physical properties of objects through non-pertinent changes. Thus, explicit memory is improved when, in the study phase, the subject performs an elaboration task on the stimulus (for example, indicating its function) whereas it is less effective after a more superficial processing (counting the stimulus horizontal lines). Conversely, implicit memory is sensitive neither to these treatments nor to verbally labeling the objects, and thus does not depend on access to meaning. It is oriented towards object identification, whereas the explicit memory is oriented towards their recognition.

Srivinas, Greene and Easton (1997a) looked at whether these differences reflect the memory basic architecture, or if they are specific to the visual system. They therefore applied these research paradigms to the haptic modality in an intramodal condition. Their results were the same as those reported above, i.e. they found that haptic implicit memory was insensitive to the variations in the depth of processing of the stimulus, whereas explicit memory was improved by a deeper processing such as verbally describing the object.

After having demonstrated the similarity of the visual and haptic memories, the same authors (Easton, Greene, & Srivinas 1997; Srivinas, Greene, & Easton 1997b) examined the differential effects of these two memory types on intermodal transfer between vision and haptics. If visual and haptic representations have the same level of abstraction, then changing modality between presentation and test would have no incidence. The authors' hypothesis was that this would be the case for implicit memory whereas explicit memory, which includes the stimulus specific perceptual aspects, would be affected by modality change. This was actually observed with raised lines geometric drawings and three-dimensional objects: Performances in identification after priming (implicit memory) were the same in intra- and intermodal conditions, whereas performances in the recognition of familiar and novel stimuli (explicit memory) were better in the intramodal condition than in the intermodal one.

It should be noted that in all the other studies on intermodal transfer discussed in this chapter, only explicit memory was tested. This may explain the effects of modality change described above.

2.   Perceptual conflicts in simultaneous bimodal situations

In everyday life different modalities most often work simultaneously. They perceive the same objects and must coordinate their percepts in order to form a single coherent representation. How does this coordination takes place?

Perceptual conflicts are interesting to study in this context because when the data provided by two modalities are decorrelated, intermodal coherence must be restored via perceptual recalibration. During the 1960s and 1970s, the vision-haptic conflicts studied concerned only spatial shape properties and revealed a strong dominance of vision. This dominance was manifested through "visual capture", i.e. a uniquely visual evaluation of the conflicting property, as if the decorrelated haptic value was not taken into account. Further studies showed that the phenomenon may be reversed in favor of the haptic modality in texture conflict and even, in some particular conditions, in spatial conflicts.

2.1 Spatial conflicts

In Rock and Victor's pilot work (1964), subjects felt a square under a curtain and at the same time visually perceived this square through a lens reducing the horizontal dimension of the shape. Therefore, the square appeared rectangular. Them, the participants had to recognize this object from among many others, either visually or haptically. The results revealed a complete visual capture. This means that in the test phase, subjects chose a rectangle corresponding exactly to the visual shape without taking the conflicting haptic data (a square) into account. In later studies controlling some methodological weaknesses present in this first research, results were analogous in 5 to 7-year-old children (McGurk & Power 1980; Misceo, Hershberger, & Mancini 1999) and in adults (Miller 1972), even when subjects were potters and thus were highly trained in the use of touch (Power & Graham 1976). However, the notion of visual dominance has been modulated because in adults the phenomenon is mainly observed when the test is visual. When the test is haptic, a "compro-

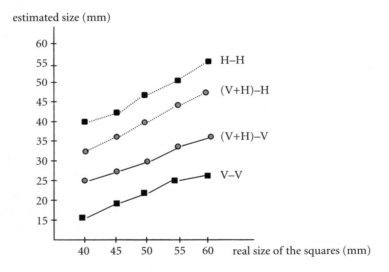

Figure 12.1. Size estimation of squares in unimodal visual and haptic conditions, and in visual-haptic conflict conditions. V-V: unimodal visual presentation of the stimulus, visual test; H-H: unimodal haptic presentation of the stimulus, haptic test; (V+H)-V: bimodal conflictual presentation of the stimulus, visual test; (V+H)-H: bimodal conflictual presentation of the stimulus, haptic test. In the conflict conditions, there is a trend toward visual capture when the test is visual, and a trend toward haptic capture when the test is haptic (adapted after Hershberger & Misceo 1996).

mise" (a sort of mean between the conflicting values) (Hatwell 1986; Hatwell & Cazals 1988) and a tendency towards haptic capture (Hershberger & Misceo 1996, cf. Figure 12.1; McDonnell & Duffett 1972; Misceo, Hershberger, & Mancini 1999) are observed. Furthermore, a compromise (Power & Graham 1976) and even a frank haptic capture (Heller 1983) appear when there is a high discordance between vision and touch. These results show that vision is dominant in the spatial tasks and that, in these situations, haptic information is used only when intermodal coherence is consistently broken.

2.2 Texture conflicts

Results are different for material properties, which is the domain favored by the haptic modality. In a conflicting texture situation with abrasive paper seen and touched, the subjects studied by Lederman and Abbott (1981) gave compromise responses. This means that their evaluation of the conflicting texture was a mean of the visual and haptic texture values. A later study (Lederman, Thorne, & Jones 1986) dissociated the two elements of texture: roughness (a material property) and the spatial density of the grains (a geometric property). A haptic-dominant compromise appeared when subjects were instructed to estimate roughness, whereas a visual capture appeared when subjects were instructed to evaluate the spatial density of the grains. These different recalibrations according to conditions confirm the specialization of touch for material properties and of vision for spatial ones.

2.3 A statistical hypothesis for visual-tactual integration of information

More recently (Ernst & Banks 2002; Ernst, Banks, & Bülthoff 2000) proposed a statistical model to account for the way visual-tactual conflicts are resolved. The general principle on which this model is based on is that the organism tends to minimize the variance of the final estimate. Therefore, the weight attributed to each perceptual modality in a particular bimodal task depends on the variance of the visual and haptic intramodal estimations of the property to be judged. A modality with a low variance (meaning high precision) will have a high weighting of the information it provides, whereas a modality with a high variance (meaning low precision) will have a low weighting. The statistical model implemented by Ernst and Blank behaved very similarly to humans in a visual-haptic task of height comparison. Moreover, it could account for the results obtained in the studies on perceptual conflicts described in the above paragraphs. For example, the visual dominance often observed in spatial conflicts is predicted by the model since the intramodal variances of visual estimations of shape, size, localization, etc. are consistently lower than the corresponding haptic intramodal variances. But when the visual discrimination ability is degraded, as in Heller's (1983) study, tactile capture occurs. On the other hand, when the conflict concerns texture and not space, haptic information predominates over visual information because texture is better discriminated by haptics than by vision.

Taken together, these studies suggest that the integration of visual and haptic information is based on a cooperation in which, at every moment, the most confident modality has a predominant role. This predominant role may be alternately played by one modality or the other, according to the task and the situation.

3.   Attention share in bimodal tasks

In ergonomic situations in which an operator must process several signals at the same time, these signals are sent into the different modalities in order to avoid overloading one of them (generally vision). Thus aircraft pilots, who have to check a great number of visual dials, simultaneously receive auditory and even tactile signals. The same is true for multimodal displays adapted for visually impaired people. These displays generally combine visual signals, when their reception is possible, with auditory and tactile signals (cf. Chapter 17). This raises the problem of the way attention is shared between modalities.

For a long time, studies based on hearing and vision led to consider that attention was specific to each modality. It was therefore assumed that each perceptive system had its own resources of attention and that adding a signal from another modality did not cut into this capacity (Wickens 1980, 1984). This hypothesis was supported by observations showing that very dissimilar concurrent tasks hardly interfere with each other. Thus, performances in a double detection task were better when one task was visual and the other auditory than when both tasks involved the same modality (Treisman & Davies 1973; Wickens, Sandry, & Vidulich 1983). But more recent studies (cf. Spence & Driver 1997) showed that multimodal situations may be more costly than unimodal situations, because focusing attention toward one modality affects how the other modality processes the stimuli.

This intermodal link appears when signals are not located in the same place. Thus, in a cutaneous discrimination test (continuous vs. non-continuous stimulation), Spence, Nichols and Driver (1998) randomly stimulated the subjects' right or the left index fingers. This stimulation was preceded either by visual or auditory priming, and the prime came either from the same side as the stimulated finger, or from the opposite side. Performances were faster and more accurate when the stimulus and the priming were on the same side than the reverse. In the same way, when a visual or auditory stimulus was preceded by tactile priming, performances were superior when the signals came from the same side. Kenneth, Spence and Driver (2002) found in addition that these intermodal links between vision and touch were mapped in the external space and were not dependent on hemispheric activation. This was shown by the fact that when the unseen hands were crossed so that the left hand layed in the right hemifield and the right hand in the left hemifield, the effect of visual priming was higher when the prime appeared in the same hemifield as the tactually stimulated finger than when it appeared in the opposite hemifield. The same was true as concerned the effect of a tactile priming on visual response times. This means that the tactile-visual intermodal links in exogenous covert spatial attention do not reflect a fixed mapping in which the stimulation of one visual field always lead to higher efficiency of a particular hand. Instead, the intermodal effects of cuing remap across changes in the unseen position of the hands (and more generally of posture) implying, according to Kennett et al. (2002), a "modulatory role of proprioception (p.1093)".

Another intermodal effect results from subjects' anticipations, i.e. the probability of receiving stimulation in a certain modality at each test. In a left-right discrimination test, Spence and Driver (1997) varied the frequency of the signals in each modality (75% of visual signals in a task which randomly mixed visual, auditory and tactile signals, or equiprobable signals in a control condition) and asked subjects to orient their attention towards the most frequent modality. When the signal appeared in the expected modality (75%), there was no difference with the equiprobable condition. But when the signal was given in an unexpected modality, transferring attention to the less probable modality had a cost which was manifested by an increase in response time and errors. This cost was greater when the rare signal was tactile (16%) than when it was visual or auditory (8%), whatever the direction of attention reorientation (from vision or hearing towards touch, or the reverse).

The cost of dividing attention between modalities seems to be linked to the extent to which the concerned modalities are trained, as is shown in the comparison of blind and blindfolded sighted people. Kujala et al. (1997) presented to early blind, blindfolded sighted and sighted working in light a detection test involving randomly mixed auditory and tactile signals, all coming from the right-hand side. For auditory signals, responses were faster in the blind group than in the two sighted groups. For tactile signals, responses were faster in the blind group than in the sighted group working in light (no difference was observed with the blindfolded sighted). These results may be explained by the fact that, more often than the sighted in everyday life, blind people experience situations of shared attention between two modalities. For example, in order to get about in the street, the blind must at the same time pay attention to traffic noise and to the tactile stimulations transmitted by the feet and the end of the cane.

The existence of intermodal links in spatial orientation reactions seems therefore well established. As a result, we could hardly consider to-day the systems of attention as independent modules belonging to each modality.

4.   Conclusion

In this chapter, we have examined intermodal matching situations in which information gathered by one modality has to be transmitted to another modality, conflict situations in which data provided by vision and touch are decorrelated, and attention sharing situations between two modalities receiving independent signals.

Visual-haptic matching, which is already possible in infants (cf. Chapter 11), is obviously observed in children and adults too. Real changes with age have not been found in this field, but recent works have longitudinally observed a certain stability of these intermodal capacities and a still unexplained link with IQ. Furthermore, the nature of this transfer depends on the properties considered. For geometric properties (spatial), transfer asymmetry (better performances from touch to vision than from vision to touch) and the often observed superiority of intramodal performances over intermodal ones suggest that this transfer has a cost. This casts doubt on the hypothesis of amodal representation of information suggested by the Gibsons (E. J. Gibson 1969; J. J. Gibson 1966). However, the above concerns only explicit memory, as implicit memory does not seem to be sensitive to modality changes between the presentation and test phases. On the other hand, for material properties like texture, this cost is not observed. The cost thus seems to be linked to the unequal efficiency of vision and touch in the spatial domain.

In bimodal decorrelated situations, spatial perceptual conflicts are generally resolved by a visually dominant compromise, although a few examples of haptic capture have been reported in adults in size conflicts. Furthermore, visual dominance seems stronger in 5 to 7-year-old children than in older subjects. For the material property of texture, a tactually dominant compromise, or even a frank tactile capture, are sometimes observed. This confirms that there is no general dominance of one modality over another. In the case of an intermodal decorrelation, the most efficient modality for the domain considered leads intermodal transfer and recalibration operations, perhaps via a process which recodes data into the directing modality code.

Finally, the solidity of these intermodal links has effects on attention sharing between two modalities. Contrary to what was believed, the attention resources of one modality can be affected by the activation of a second modality. That must be taken into account when displays involving new technologies and intended for the visually impaired people simultaneously emit auditory, tactile and even visual signals.

References

Abravanel, E. (1981). Integrating the information from eyes and hands: A developmental account. In R. Walk & H. L. Pick (Eds.), *Intersensory perception and sensory integration* (pp. 71–107). New York: Academic Press.

Birch, H. G. & Lefford, A. (1963). Intersensory development in children. *Monographs of the Society for Research on Child Development, 28*, 1–87.

Bryant, P. (1974). *Perception and understanding in young children.* London: Methuen.

Bryant, P., Jones, B., Claxton, V., & Perkins, G. (1968). Recognition of shapes across modalities. *Nature, 240*, 303–304.

Connolly, K. & Jones, B. (1970). A developmental study of afferent-reafferent integration. *British Journal of Psychology, 61*, 259–266.

Easton, R., Greene, A., & Srivinas, K. (1997). Transfer between vision and haptics: Memory for 2D patterns and 3D objects. *Psychonomic Bulletin and Review, 4*, 403–410.

Ernst, M. O. & Banks, M. S. (2002). Humans integrate visual and haptic information in a statistically optimal fashion. *Nature, 415,* 429–433.

Ernst, M. O., Banks, M. S., & Bülthoff, H. H. (2000). Touch can change visual slant perception. *Nature Neuroscience, 3,* 69–73.

Garbin, C. P. (1988). Visual-haptic perceptual nonequivalence for shape information and its impact upon cross-modal performance. *Journal of Experimental Psychology: Human Perception and Performance, 14*, 547–553.

Garvill, J. & Molander, B. (1973). Effects of standard modality, comparison modality and retention interval on matching of form. *Scandinavian Journal of Psychology, 14*, 203–206.

Gibson, E. J. (1969). *Principles of perceptual learning and development.* New York: Academic Press.

Gibson, J. J. (1966). *The senses considered as perceptual systems.* Boston: Houghton Mifflin Compagny.

Hatwell, Y. (1986). *Toucher l'espace.* Lille: Presses Universitaires de Lille.

Hatwell, Y. (1994). Transferts intermodaux et intégration intermodale. In M. Richelle, J. Requin, & M. Robert (Eds.), *Traité de Psychologie Expérimentale, Vol. 1* (pp. 543–584). Paris: Presses Universitaires de France.

Hatwell, Y. & Cazals, C. (1988). Conflit visuo-tactilo-kinesthésique et activité sensori-motrice pratique. *L'Année Psychologique, 88*, 7–29.

Heller, M. A. (1983). Haptic dominance in form perception with blurred vision. *Perception, 12*, 607–613.

Hershberger, W. & Misceo, G. (1996). Touch dominates haptic estimates of discordant visual-haptic size. *Perception and Psychophysics, 58*, 1124–1132.

Jones, B. (1981). The developmental significance of cross-modal matching. In R. Walk & H. L. Pick (Eds.), *Intersensory perception and sensory integration* (pp. 106–136). New York: Academic Press.

Jones, B. & Connolly, K. (1970). Memory effects in cross-modal matching. *British Journal of Psychology, 61*, 267–270.

Juurmaa, J. & Lehtinen-Railo, S. (1994). Visual experience and access to spatial knowledge. *Journal of Visual Impairment and Blindness, 88*, 157–170.

Kennett, S., Spence, C., & Driver, J. (2002). Visuo-tactile links in covert exogenous spatial attention remap across changes in unseen hand posture. *Perception and Psychophysics, 64*, 1083–1094.

Kujala, T., Lehtokoski, A., Alho, K., Kekoni, J., & Näätänen, R. (1997). Faster reaction times in the blind than the sighted during bimodal divided attention. *Acta Psychologica, 96*, 75–82.

Lederman, S. J. & Abbott, S. G. (1981). Texture perception: Studies of intersensory organization using a discrepancy paradigm and visual vs tactual psychophysics. *Journal of Experimental Psychology: Human Perception and Performance, 7*, 902–915.

Lederman, S. J., Thorne, G., & Jones, B. (1986). Perception of texture by vision and touch: Multidimensionality and intersensory integration. *Journal of Experimental Psychology: Human Perception and Performance, 12*, 169–180.

McDonnell, P. M. & Duffett, J. (1972). Vision and touch: A reconsideration of conflict between the two senses. *Canadian Journal of Psychology, 26*, 171–180.

McGurk, H. & Power, R. P. (1980). Intermodal coordination in young children: Vision and touch. *Developmental Psychology, 16*, 179–180.

Milewski, A. E. & Iaccino, J. (1982). Strategies in cross-modal matching. *Perception and Psychophysics, 31*, 273–275.

Miller, E. A. (1972). Interaction of vision and touch in conflict and non-conflict form perception tasks. *Journal of Experimental Psychology, 96*, 114–123.

Misceo, G. F., Hershberger, W. A., & Mancini, R. L. (1999). Haptic estimates of discordant visual-haptic size vary developmentally. *Perception and Psychophysics, 61*, 608–641.

Newell, K. M., Shapiro, D. C., & Carlton, M. J. (1979). Coordinating visual and kinaesthetic memory codes. *British Journal of Psychology, 70*, 87–96.

Newham, C. & McKenzie, B. E. (1993). Cross-modal transfer of sequential visual and haptic information by clumsy children. *Perception, 22*, 1061–1073.

Posner, M. I. (1967). Characteristics of visual and kinesthetic memory codes. *Journal of Experimental Psychology, 75*, 103–107.

Power, R. P. & Graham, A. (1976). Dominance of touch by vision: Generalization of the hypothesis to a tactually experienced population. *Perception, 5,* 161–166.

Rock, I. & Victor, J. (1964). Vision and touch: An experimentally induced conflict between the two senses. *Science, 143,* 594–596.

Rose, S. A., Feldman, J. F., Futterweit, L. R., & Jankowski, J. J. (1998). Continuity in tactual-visual cross-modal transfer: Infancy to 11 years. *Developmental Psychology, 34,* 435–440.

Schacter, D. L., Cooper, L. A., & Delanay, S. M. (1990). Implicit memory for unfamiliar objects depends on access to structural descriptions. *Journal of Experimental Psychology: General, 119,* 5–24.

Spence, C. & Driver, J. (1997). Cross-modal links between audition, vision and touch: Implications for interface design. *International Journal of Cognitive Ergonomics, 1,* 351–373.

Spence, C., Nichols, N., & Drive, J. (1998). Cross-modal links in exogenous covert spatial orienting between touch, audition and vision. *Perception and Psychophysics, 60,* 544–557.

Srivinas, K., Greene, A., & Easton, R. (1997a). Implicit and explicit memory for haptically experienced two-dimensional patterns. *Psychological Science, 8,* 243–246.

Srivinas, K., Greene, A., & Easton, R. (1997b). Visual and tactile memory for 2D patterns: Effects of change in size and left-right orientation. *Psychonomic Bulletin and Review, 4,* 535–540.

Stoltz-Loike, M. & Bornstein, M. H. (1987). The role of imagery, language and metamemory in cross-modal transfer in children. *Psychological Research, 49,* 63–68.

Treisman, A. M. & Davies, A. (1973). Divided attention to ear and eye. In S. Kornblum (Ed.), *Attention and performance, Vol. 4* (pp. 1014–117). New York: Academic Press.

Tulving, E. (1983). *Elements of episodic memory.* New York: University of Oxford Press.

Wickens, C. D. (1980). The structure of attentional resources. In R. S. Nickerson (Ed.), *Attention and performance, Vol. 8* (pp. 239–257). Hillsdale, NJ: Erlbaum.

Wickens, C. D. (1984). Processing resources in attention. In R. Parasuraman & D. R. Davies (Eds.), *Varieties of attention* (pp. 63–102). San Diego, CA: Academic Press.

Wickens, C. D., Sandry, D., & Vidulich, M. (1983). Compatibilities and resource competition between modalities of imput, central processing and output. *Human Factors, 25,* 227–248.

CHAPTER 13

Tactile exploration in nonhuman primates

Agnès Lacreuse and Dorothy M. Fragaszy

Tactile perception plays a major role in the investigation of the environment and is universal among animals (Burton 1993). In many mammals, the mouth is the body part most sensitive to touch and the main tool of perceptive exploration. In rodents, for example, the perception of the surroundings relies predominantly on the vibrissae. In primates, the mouth remains rich in tactile receptors and is still largely represented in the motor and sensory cortices, but the differentiation of the anterior limbs into prehensile extremities allows considerable broadening in explorative capabilities. Such advances culminate in the human hand, which has become the main tool of investigation, manipulation and transformation of the world. In this chapter, we first discuss the manual dexterity and manipulative capacities of different species of primates before examining in further detail the manual tactile abilities of nonhuman primates. The last section will be devoted to the problem of the lateralization of tactile perception in primates.

1. The primate hand

Humans belong to the Primate Order, which includes prosimians (e.g., lemurs), monkeys from Central and South America (New World monkeys, e.g., capuchins), monkeys from Africa and Asia (Old World monkeys, e.g., baboons and macaques), hylobates (gibbons and siamangs) and pongids from Africa and Asia (gorillas, chimpanzees, bonobos and orangutans).

The hand is a characteristic of all primates. Anatomically, there are only few differences between the primate hands and the paws of other mammals. For example, the number of muscles in the anterior extremities of a primitive mammal like the opossum is similar to that of man. In fact, even paws can be dexterous (for an example in rats, see Wishaw 1994). Yet, mammals with paws or flippers usually have to use both extremities simultaneously to hold an object. Primates, however, are able to use a single limb to grasp an object and carry it to the mouth. This ability is usually accompanied by stereoscopic vision which allows visual monitoring of the manual actions.

The primate hand and mammal paw differ by three main anatomical characteristics: First, the primate hand is provided with fine skin on the palm and fingers, which reflects a highly developed cutaneous sensitivity. Second, the tips of the manual digits in primates are surmounted by nails, rather than claws, allowing better prehensibility. Finally, the fingers gain some degree of independence, which varies across species. Three groups are distinguished based on the degree of thumb independence (Napier & Napier 1967): (1) Non opposable thumb (Tarsiers, marmosets); all the digits participate simultaneously to prehension; (2) Pseudo-opposable thumb (New World monkeys, except marmosets and spider monkeys); the movements of adduction and abduction are possible but there is no rotation of the metacarpal articulation (3) opposable thumb (pongids, humans and Old World monkeys except colobes). The pulp surface of the thumb is placed squarely in contact with the terminal pads of one or all of the remaining digits. This opposition of the thumb underlies all the skilled procedures of which the human hand is capable (Napier 1993).

Although the hand is built from a structural base common to all primates, it takes on diverse morphologies as a function of the ecological niche in which the species develop (Figure 13.1). For example, some arboreal species that hang during locomotion have very long fingers and have lost the thumb (e.g., colobes).

As Connolly and Elliott (1972) point out, the anatomy of the human hand certainly limits but does not define the prehensile function. The human manual dexterity is better explained by the way manual tasks are organized and controlled by the nervous system rather than by a rapid sensorimotor system or powerful effector mechanisms (Johansson 1996). At the neuroanatomical level, two major developments occur in primates compared to other mammals: (1) the increased reliance on the motor cortex and the corticospinal tract compared to the rubrospinal tract (Kuypers 1981) and (2) the existence of direct cortico-motoneuronal connection allowing a monosynaptic connection between the motor cortex and the spinal motoneurons (Phillips & Porter 1977). This direct access provides greater flexibility compared to the rigid spinal system (Lemon 1993). Motoneuronal connections may play a predominant role in the fractionation of muscle activity and in the performance of relatively independent finger movements (Bennett & Lemon 1996). Indeed, there is a positive

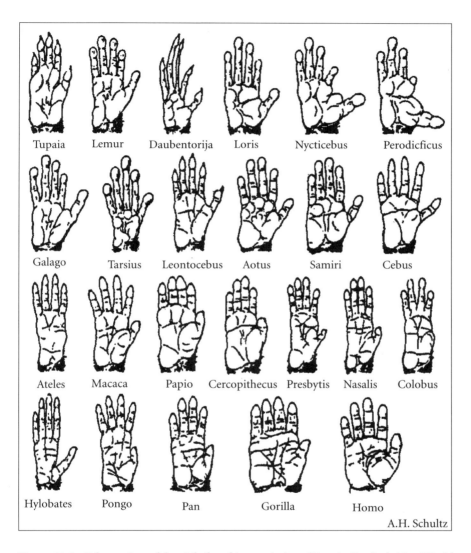

Figure 13.1. Palmar view of the right hand in prosimians (Tupaia-Tarsius), New World monkeys (Leontocebus-Ateles), Old World monkeys (Macaca-Colobus) and hominoidae (Hylobates-Gorilla). The Tupaias are no longer considered as primates (Martin 1990). Drawings from Schultz (1969).

correlation between the number of motoneuronal connections and the manual dexterity of a species (Heffner & Masterton 1975, 1983).

2. Object manipulation

The ability to manipulate objects and to use them as tools not only depends on manual dexterity but also on specific psychological factors (Berthelet & Chavaillon 1993; Fragaszy 1998; Parker & Gibson 1977; Preuschoft & Chivers 1993; Torigoe 1985). Touch is essential to the success of the practical actions of the hand. Examples of fine manipulation in a New World monkey, the capuchin, an Old World monkey, the macaque, and an ape, the chimpanzee, are provided below.

Capuchins are among the greatest tool users after the chimpanzees and humans. They show finger independence and demonstrate different types of fine grip (Costello & Fragaszy 1988). Capuchins have the ability to combine actions, objects and surfaces and perform activities that are rarely observed in other monkeys, such as banging, rubbing, or sliding objects against a substrate (Fragaszy & Adam-Curtis 1991). Capuchins are able to use stones or wood blocks to crack nuts, sticks to inspect inaccessible locations or different materials as sponges (Visalberghi 1990; Westergaard & Fragazy 1987). In Old World monkeys, the use of the precision grip is most remarkable. It allows them to hold an object between the flexed fingers and the opposed thumb, without participation of the palm. An example of its use in natural contexts is social grooming. Tanaka (1995) describes how Japanese macaques remove lice eggs through grooming. They dexterously use a single finger to separate hairs on the grooming partner, scrape a single egg off the hair shaft with the nail of the finger or thumb and then slide the egg off the length of the hair shaft with two fingers. They can also twist the hair and then comb the egg off. Chimpanzees show a wide variety of tool use. They use sticks to fish termites and ants, stones to hit or impress conspecifics, stones or wood blocks as hammers and anvils to pound nuts and use leaves as sponges; they are also able to make tools and can modify the length and thickness of a stick according to the requirements of the task (McGrew 1992). These manual activities require not only a fine control of the fingers but also a highly developed tactile sensitivity.

3.   Tactile exploration

3.1 Learning sets

Manual tactile abilities in nonhuman primates were first studied in the context of learning sets. A learning set refers to the notion of "learning to learn", the capacity to transfer the learning of a particular problem to the learning of another problem. In these tasks, monkeys have to select the positively rewarded object in pairs of objects differing by a single dimension (e.g., the shape). Learning of an initial problem usually facilitates the learning of the subsequent problems. The rhesus monkey (Wilson 1965) and the capuchin (Blakeslee & Gunter 1966) are able to form learning sets in the tactile modality. However, monkeys require more trials to reach the learning criterion at each problem in the tactile modality compared to the visual modality (Carlson & Eibergen 1974).

3.2 Intra- and inter- modal matching ability

In primates, manual actions are typically monitored by the visual system. When grasping an object, the subject receives data from two different systems, tactile and visual, that must be integrated into a coherent whole (Hatwell 1986; cf. Chapter 12). A variety of procedures are used to test intermodal ability in nonhuman primates (Ettlinger & Wilson 1990). Overall, these studies clearly show that chimpanzees (Davenport, Rogers, & Russel 1973; Jarvis & Ettlinger 1977), Old World (Bolster 1978; Cowey & Weiskrantz 1975; DiMattia, Posley, & Fuster 1990; Malone, Tolan, & Rogers 1980) and New World monkeys (Elliott 1977) are able to recognize in the tactile modality objects that they have seen in the visual modality. Only a few studies have investigated intramodal tactile ability in the monkey. Steele and Bauer (1983) report that three rhesus monkeys tactually discriminate the size of different spheres in a similar number of trials as necessary to learn the discrimination in the visual modality. DiMattia et al. (1990), however, indicate that rhesus monkeys require more trials to match objects in the tactile modality or in the tactile-visual modality than in the visual-tactile modality.

3.3 Manual exploratory procedures

Relatively few studies have investigated manual tactile exploration *per se* in nonhuman primates. This is surprising given that manual exploratory procedures in human children and adults (cf. Chapter 5) and infants (Bushnell &

Boudreau 1991; cf. Chapter 4) have been shown to determine, at least in part, tactile performance. In animals, the ability to perform the appropriate movements should also account for the accuracy of tactile perception. Carlson and Eibergen (1974) tested rhesus monkeys in a task involving the tactile discrimination of complex shapes. They found that the monkeys obtained lower performance in the tactile than in the visual modality. Moreover, whereas visual performance decreased as a function of shape complexity, tactile performance was unaffected. Finally, shapes rotated 180 degrees were treated as new in the tactile modality, but as familiar in the visual modality. Interestingly, manual explorations of the monkeys were particularly brief (1 or 2 s) compared to those of humans (14 to 38 s) and their explorations were limited to a small portion of the shapes. In a similar experiment, Jarvis and Ettlinger (1977) observed that manual exploration of chimpanzees were longer and more cautious than that of macaques; the chimpanzees performed multiple comparisons between the target object and the foil before responding, whereas macaques responded very quickly, rarely comparing the two objects. Such descriptions suggest important differences in the way macaques and chimpanzees investigate objects tactually and could reflect actual differences in tactile abilities between the two species. A quantification of manual exploratory procedures would be necessary to test this hypothesis.

With this goal in mind, we compared the manual exploratory procedures used by 21 capuchins and 4 humans in a task requiring the subjects to tactually inspect 12 objects baited with sunflower seeds (Lacreuse & Fragaszy 1997). Tactile investigations were videotaped, and decoded image by image using the definitions of Lederman and Klatzky (1987). Six movements common to monkeys and humans were identified (Figure 13.2) and two movements specific to the capuchins (grasp and pull). The analyses of the manual exploration procedures revealed that (1) the occurrence of specific movement depended on the shape of the object in the two species (2) capuchins and humans obtained a similar performance (3) the major difference between the two species concerned the occurrence of "Contour Following" and "Enclosure". These data indicate that the monkeys used the manual explorations that were most appropriate to the extraction of sunflower seeds. However, the rarity of Contour Following (6 % of all manual procedures) and Enclosure (5 %) compared to their occurrence in humans (31.5 % and 12 % respectively) suggest that the monkeys used a strategy of trial and error, rather than a strategy relying on a mental representation of the object. In support of this hypothesis, the videos clearly show that the monkeys limited their tactile inspection to a very small portion of the objects, usually surrounding the location of the initial contact of the hand on

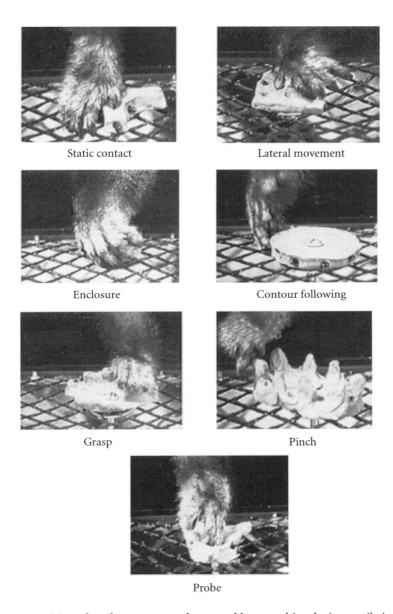

Figure 13.2. Manual exploratory procedures used by capuchins during tactile inspection of clay objects containing sunflower seeds (from Lacreuse & Fragaszy 1997).

the object. Humans, however, started each trial by enclosing and following the contour of the objects in order to gather information on the size and shape of the object to be explored. These findings suggest that monkeys should have more difficulties in processing the spatial properties of objects, such as shape or size, for which contour following and enclosure movements are essential, as opposed to the physical properties of objects, such as texture or solidity, for which lateral and pressure movements are sufficient.

4.   Tactile exploration and manual lateralization

Neuroanatomical and functional asymmetries of the human brain are well documented (Bradshaw 1989; Corballis 1991; Hellige 1993). One of the most obvious expressions of cerebral lateralization in humans is manual laterality, with more than 90% of individuals being right-handed (Corballis 1991). The bias toward the right hand is associated to a left hemispheric specialization for the comprehension and production of language: More than 95 % of right-handers have a left hemisphere specialization for language function (Rasmussen & Milner 1977). Because of this possible association between hemispheric asymmetry and language, manual laterality was thought to be a marker of human uniqueness. We know today that numerous animal species present neuroanatomical and functional asymmetries comparable to those of humans (Bradshaw & Rogers 1993; Bisazza, Rogers, & Vallortigara 1998; Fagot et al. 1997; Ward & Hopkins 1993). Whether these asymmetries are homologous and simply analogous to those of humans remains a matter of debate. Some authors claim that manual laterality reflects an evolutionary discontinuity between man and other primates (Corballis 1991; McGrew & Marchant 1997), while others propose a phylogenetic scenario in which man and other animals are integrated in a unique model of manual lateralization (MacNeilage, Studdert-Kennedy, & Lindblom 1987; Ward & Hopkins 1993).

To study manual asymmetries in nonhuman primates, we can analyze manual preferences through the frequency of spontaneous use of the left or right hand, or the manual performance through the comparison of the abilities of the left and right hand in specific tasks. The tactile modality is particularly interesting for this type of research. First, distal movements are under the control of the contralateral hemisphere in primates (Brinkman & Kuypers 1973). Second, a left hand advantage (right hemisphere) is typically found in humans for the processing of nonsense shapes (Fagot, Lacreuse, & Vauclair 1997; Verjat 1988). Moreover, tactile tasks without the use of vision can be considered as novel or complex for nonhuman primates and these properties favor the expression of manual asymmetries (Fagot & Vauclair 1991).

4.1 Manual preference in the tactile modality

Most studies in nonhuman primates concerned with manual preferences in the tactile modality have used tasks in which monkeys are required to tactually discriminate food items in opaque containers. Several species have been tested in this paradigm, including rhesus monkeys (Fagot, Drea, & Wallen 1991), capuchins (Lacreuse & Fragaszy 1996; Parr, Hopkins, & De Waal 1997), spider monkeys (Laska 1996) and chimpanzees (Lacreuse, Parr, Smith, & Hopkins 1999). Interestingly, both Old World and New World monkeys display a left hand preference to perform these tasks, while chimpanzees tend to use predominantly the right hand (Figure 13.3).

In order to better understand the factors underlying hand preference, we tested 16 capuchins in 4 tasks that differed by their exploratory demands (tac-

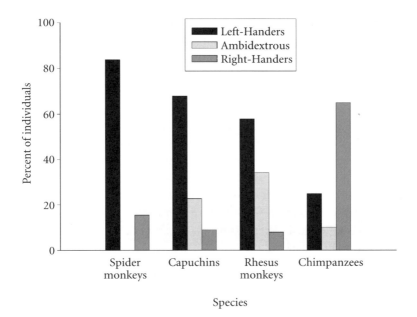

Figure 13.3. Percent of individuals classified as left-handers, right-handers and ambidextrous when performing tactile tasks. Data on spider monkeys from Laska (1996); data on capuchins from Parr et al. (1997); data on rhesus monkey from Fagot et al. (1991); data on chimpanzees from Lacreuse et al. (1999).

tile exploration or simple grasp) and their availability on visual cues (with or without visual control; Lacreuse & Fragaszy 1999). In the two exploratory tasks, monkeys tactually explored objects to retrieve sunflower seeds, with or without visual control. In the two grasping tasks, monkeys reached for sunflower seeds on a flat support, with or without visual control. The capuchins displayed a left hand preference in the two exploratory tasks, independent of the availability of visual cues. However, for the two grasping tasks, the frequency of left and right hand use was equivalent. These results suggest that the exploratory component of the tasks favors the activation of the right hemisphere in capuchins. The right hemisphere could be specialized for the integration of the motor and spatial components of action. Recent data in humans showing greater right hemisphere involvement when manipulospatial processing is required support such an interpretation (Yeary, Patton, & Kee 2002).

4.2 Manual performance in the tactile modality

Right-handed humans typically display a left hand advantage (right hemisphere) to tactually discriminate nonverbal material (Fagot et al. 1997; Verjat 1988). For practical reasons, nonhuman primates have been essentially tested for manual preferences rather than manual performance in tactile tasks, making the comparison with human data difficult. At present, whether or not nonhuman primates display a right hemisphere advantage for tactually discriminating stimuli remains unclear. Although left-handed macaques learn tactile tasks more rapidly than right-handed monkeys, ambidextrous subjects are even better than these two groups (Hörster & Ettlinger 1985). Moreover, lesion experiments have shown that the contralateral hemisphere to the hand used or to the preferred hand is specialized in the processing of tactile information, independently of the hand (left or right) considered (Ettlinger 1988). We have found that two baboons were slightly better with their left hand to perform a tactile discrimination task, but these results need to be confirmed with a greater number of animals (Lacreuse 1995).

4.3 Manual preference, manual performance and manual exploratory procedures

Capuchins tactually exploring objects to retrieve sunflower seeds display a left hand advantage at the group level (Lacreuse & Fragaszy 1996). In order to examine whether this bias provided an advantage, we compared the accuracy and manual exploratory procedures of each hand during tactile inspection of the objects (Lacreuse & Fragaszy 1997). We found that the left and right hands had similar scores and adopted very similar exploratory procedures. Moreover, we failed to find any difference in the manual exploratory procedures used by left-handers, right-handers and ambidextrous subjects. The predominant use of the left hand in the group was therefore not associated with any obvious advantage. Tasks parameters, such as manipulospatial demands, may enhance right hemisphere activation and yield to the preponderant use of the left hand. More research is needed to test the validity of this hypothesis and to examine whether the choice of the left hand becomes advantageous in more complex tactile tasks, such as those involving shape discrimination.

5.   Conclusion

This chapter shows that man, often defined by its remarkable manual ability, is not the only primate that possesses manual dexterity. In addition, nonhuman primates are capable of using the perceptive tactile system to extract the physical and spatial properties of objects. Because tactile tasks induce manual preferences at the level of the group, they probably require the specialized abilities of a specific hemisphere. This makes tactile tasks particularly relevant to the study of manual lateralization in a comparative perspective.

Acknowledgements

I wish to thank Alyssa Volk for her helpful comments on a previous version of the manuscript.

References

Bennett, K. M. & Lemon, R. N. (1996). Corticomotoneuronal contribution to the fractionation of muscle activity during precision grip in the monkey. *Journal of Neurophysiology, 75*, 1826–1842.

Berthelet, A. & Chavaillon, J. (Eds.). (1993). *The use of tools by human and non-human primates.* Oxford: Clarendon Press.

Bisazza, A., Rogers, L. J., & Vallortigara, G. (1998). The origins of cerebral asymmetry: A review of evidence of behavioural and brain lateralization in fishes, reptiles and amphibians. *Neuroscience and Biobehavioral Reviews, 22*, 411–426.

Blakeslee, P. & Gunter, R. (1966). Cross-modal transfer of discrimination learning in cebus monkeys. *Behaviour, 26*, 76–90.

Bolster, B. (1978). Cross-modal matching in the monkey (*Macaca fascicularis*). *Neuropsychologia, 16*, 407–416.

Bradshaw, J. L. (1989). *Hemispheric specialization and psychological function.* Chichester: Wiley.

Bradshaw, J. L. & Rogers, L. J. (1993). *The evolution of lateral asymmetries, language, tool use, and intellect.* San Diego: Academic Press.

Brinkman, C. & Kuypers, H. G. J. (1973). Cerebral control of contralateral and ipsilateral arm, hand and finger movements in the split-brain rhesus monkey. *Brain, 96*, 653–674.

Burton, G. (1993). Non-neural extensions of haptic sensitivity. *Ecological Psychology, 5*, 105–124.

Bushnell, E.W . & Boudreau, J. P. (1991). Haptic perception during infancy. In A. H. Morton & W. Schiff (Eds.), *The Psychology of touch* (pp. 139–167). Hillsdale: Erlbaum.

Carlson, K. R. & Eibergen, R. (1974). Factors influencing the acquisition of tactual random figures discriminations by rhesus monkeys. *Animal Learning and Behavior, 2*, 133–137.

Connolly, K. & Elliott, J. (1972). The evolution and ontogeny of hand function. In N. Blurton-Jones (Ed.), *Ethological studies of child behavior* (pp. 329–383). Cambridge: Cambridge University Press.

Corballis, M. C. (1991). *The Lopsided Ape: Evolution of the generative mind.* Oxford: Oxford University Press.

Costello, M. & Fragaszy, D.M. (1988). Comparison of prehension in squirrel monkeys (*Saimiri sciureus*) and capuchins (*Cebus apella*) I: Grip type and hand preference. *American Journal of Primatology, 15*, 235–245.

Cowey, A. & Weiskrantz, L. (1975). Demonstration of cross-modal matching in rhesus monkeys, *Macaca mulatta. Neuropsychologia, 13*, 117–120.

Davenport, R. K., Rogers, C. M., & Russel, I. S. (1973). Cross-modal perception in apes. *Neuropsychologia, 11*, 21–28.

Dimattia, B. V., Posley, K. A., & Fuster, J. M. (1990). Cross-modal short-term memory of haptic and visual information. *Neuropsychologia, 28*, 17–33.

Elliott, R. C. (1977). Cross-modal transfer in three primates. *Neuropsychologia, 15*, 183–186.

Ettlinger, G. (1988). Hand preference, ability, and hemispheric specialization: In how far are these factors related in the monkey? *Cortex, 24*, 389–398.

Ettlinger, G. & Wilson, W. A. (1990). Cross-modal performance: Behavioural processes, phylogenetic considerations and neural mechanisms. *Behavioral and Brain Research, 40*, 169–192.

Fagot, J., Drea, C., & Wallen, K. (1991). Asymmetrical hand use in rhesus monkeys (*Macaca mulatta*) in tactually and visually regulated tasks. *Journal of Comparative Psychology, 105*, 260–268.

Fagot, J., Lacreuse, A., & Vauclair, J. (1997). Role of sensory and post-sensory factors on hemispheric asymmetries in tactual perception. In S. Christman (Ed.), *Cerebral asymmetries in sensory and perceptual processing* (pp. 469–494). Amsterdam: Elsevier.

Fagot, J., Rogers, L. J., Bulman-Fleming, B., Ward, J. P., & Hopkins, W. D. (Eds.). (1997). *Hemispheric specialization in animals and humans.* London: Psychology Press.

Fagot, J. & Vauclair, J. (1991). Manual laterality in nonhuman primates: A distinction between handedness and manual specialization. *Psychological Bulletin, 109,* 76–89.

Fragaszy, D. M. (1998). How nonhuman primates use their hands. In K. Connolly (Ed.), *The Psychobiology of the hand* (pp. 77–96). London: Mac Keith Press.

Fragaszy, D. M. & Adam-Curtis, L. E. (1991). Generative aspects of manipulation in tufted capuchin monkeys (*Cebus apella*). *Journal of Comparative Psychology, 105,* 387–397.

Hatwell, Y. (1986). *Toucher l'espace. La main et la perception tactile de l'espace.* Lille: Presses Universitaire de Lille.

Heffner, R. S. & Masterton, R. B. (1975). Variation in form of the pyramidal tract and its relationship to digital dexterity. *Brain, Behavior and Evolution, 12,* 161–200.

Heffner, R. S. & Masterton, R. B. (1983). The role of the corticospinal tract in the evolution of human digital dexterity. *Brain, Behavior and Evolution, 23,* 165–183.

Hellige, J. B. (1993). *Hemispheric asymmetry. What's right and what's left.* London: Harvard University Press.

Hörster, W. & Ettlinger, G. (1985). An association between hand preference and tactile discrimination performance in the rhesus monkey. *Neuropsychologia, 23,* 411–413.

Jarvis, M. J. & Ettlinger, G. (1977). Cross-modal recognition in chimpanzees and monkeys. *Neuropsychologia, 15,* 499–506.

Johansson, R. S. (1996). Sensory control of dexterous manipulation in humans. In A. M. Wing, P. Haggard, & J. R. Flanagan (Eds.), *Hand and brain: The neurophysiology of hand movements* (pp. 381–414). San Diego: Academic Press.

Kuypers, H. G. J. (1981). Anatomy of the descending pathways. In J. M. Brookhart & V. B. Mountcastle (Eds.), *Handbook of physiology. The nervous system,* Vol. II, *Motor Control* (pp. 597–666). Bethesda: American Physiological Society.

Lacreuse, A. (1995). Haptic perception in baboons (*Papio papio*): Preliminary evidence for asymmetry in accuracy and exploration times. *Folia Primatologica, 65,* 202–209.

Lacreuse, A. & Fragaszy, D. M. (1996). Hand preferences for a haptic searching task by tufted capuchins (*Cebus apella*). *International Journal of Primatology, 17,* 613–632.

Lacreuse, A. & Fragaszy, D. M. (1997). Manual exploratory procedures and asymmetries for a haptic search task: A comparison between capuchins (*Cebus apella*) and humans. *Laterality, 2,* 247–266.

Lacreuse, A. & Fragaszy, D. M. (1999). Left hand preferences for haptic tasks in capuchins: Role of spatial demands in manual activity. *Laterality, 4,* 65–78.

Lacreuse, A., Parr, L. A., Smith, H. M., & Hopkins, W. D. (1999). Hand preferences for a haptic task in chimpanzees (*Pan troglodytes*). *International Journal of Primatology, 20,* 867–881.

Laska, M. (1996). Manual laterality in spider monkeys (*Ateles geoffroyi*) solving visually and tactually guided food reaching tasks. *Cortex, 32,* 717–726.

Lederman, S. J. & Klatzky, R. L. (1987). Hand movements: A window into haptic object recognition. *Cognitive Psychology, 19,* 342–368.

Lemon, R. N. (1993). Cortical control of the primate hand. *Experimental Physiology, 78,* 263–301.

MacNeilage, P. F., Studdert-Kennedy, M. G., & Lindblom, B. (1987). Primate handedness reconsidered. *Behavioral and Brain Sciences, 10,* 247–303.

Malone, D. R., Tolan, J. C., & Rogers, C. M. (1980). Cross-modal matching of objects and photographs in the monkey. *Neuropsychologia, 18*, 693–697.

Martin, R. D. (1990). *Primate origins and evolution. A phylogenetic reconstruction.* Princeton, NJ: Princeton University Press.

McGrew, W.C. (1992). *Chimpanzee material culture.* Cambridge: Cambridge University Press.

McGrew, W. C. & Marchant, L. F. (1997). On the other hand: Current issues in and meta-analysis of the behavioral laterality of hand function in nonhuman primates. *Yearbook Physical Anthropolology, 40,* 201–232.

Napier, J. R. (1993). *Hands.* (Revised Edition). Princeton: Princeton University Press.

Napier, J. R. & Napier, P. H. (1967). *A Handbook of Living Primates.* New York: Academic Press.

Parker, S. T. & Gibson, K. R. (1977). Object manipulation, tool use and sensorimotor intelligence as feeding adaptation in cebus monkeys and great apes. *Journal of Human Evolution, 6,* 623–641.

Parr, L. A., Hopkins, W. D., & de Waal, F.B.M. (1997). Haptic discrimination in capuchin monkeys (*Cebus apella*): Evidence of manual specialization. *Neuropsychologia, 35,* 143–152.

Phillips, C. G. & Porter, R. (1977). *Corticospinal neurones: Their role in movement.* London: Academic Press.

Preuschoft, H. & Chivers, D. (Eds) (1993). *Hands of Primates,* New York: Springer Verlag.

Rasmussen, T. & Milner, B. (1977). The role of early left-brain injury in determining lateralization of cerebral speech functions. *Annals of the New York Academy of Sciences, 299,* 355–369.

Steele, T. L. & Bauer, R. H. (1983). A method for examining short-term retention of haptic cues in monkeys. *Behavior Research Methods and Instrumentation, 15,* 344–349.

Tanaka, I. (1995). Matrilineal distribution of louse egg-handling techniques during grooming in free-ranging Japanese macaques. *American Journal of Physical Anthropology, 98,* 197–201.

Torigoe, T. (1985). Comparison of object manipulation among 74 species of nonhuman primates. *Primates, 26,* 182–194.

Verjat, I. (1988). La dissymétrie fonctionnelle cérébrale dans la modalité tactilo-kinesthésique manuelle. *L'Année Psychologique, 88,* 83–109.

Visalberghi, E. (1990). Tool use in Cebus. *Folia primatologica, 54,* 146–154.

Ward, J. P. & Hopkins, W. D. (1993). *Primate laterality, current behavioral evidence of primate asymmetries.* New York: Springer-Verlag.

Westergaard, G. C. & Fragaszy, D. M. (1987). The manufacture and use of tools by capuchin monkeys (*Cebus apella*). *Journal of Comparative Psychology, 101,* 159–168.

Wilson, M. (1965). Tactual discrimination learning in monkeys. *Neuropsychologia, 3,* 353–361.

Wishaw, I. (1994). Arpeggio and fractionated digit movements used in prehension in rats. *Behavioral and Brain Research, 60,* 15–24.

Yeary, S. A., Patton, J. N., & Kee, D. W. (2002). Asymmetries in finger-tapping interference produced by mental versus manual rotation of Shepard and Metzler type objects. *Brain and Cognition, 50,* 324–334.

PART 5

Some practical applications for visually impaired people

CHAPTER 14

Braille

Issues on structure, teaching and assessment

Michael J. Tobin, John Greaney and Eileen Hill

1. Introduction

Despite the many technological advances that have improved the blind learner's access to information, the invention by Louis Braille of his puncti-form code has stood the test of time. It is recognized as the world's primary tactile communication system for blind people, and its supremacy and effectiveness are such that Ryles (2000) even reports objective surveys that "indicate that braille readers are employed in significantly greater numbers than visually impaired adults who do not read braille". None of its numerous rivals proved able to match the flexibility of braille, with its capacity to represent all natural languages as well as musical, scientific, and mathematical notations. As with inkprint, new methods of producing and displaying the code are constantly being devised, as exemplified in the report on electronic modes of delivery by Raeder (2000). Similarly, there is no evidence that the rules and structure of the system have reached an endpoint, with "perfection" having been attained. In the English-speaking world, there is a continuing debate, under the auspices of the International Council on English Braille, about the desirability of producing a standardized code. So far, unanimity has not been reached, but something of the complexity of the issues can be gleaned from the overview by Bogart, Cranmer, and Sullivan (2000).

Some understanding of the earlier struggles in the 19th and 20th centuries for the very acceptance of braille can be seen in the title of Robert Irwin's *The War of the Dots* (Irwin 1955), and in Lorimer's scholarly and finely-detailed historical account of the development of the code (Lorimer, P. 1997 and http://braille.org). A shorter account of the early development of the system in France can now be found in "Origins of Braille" (Lorimer, P. 2000).

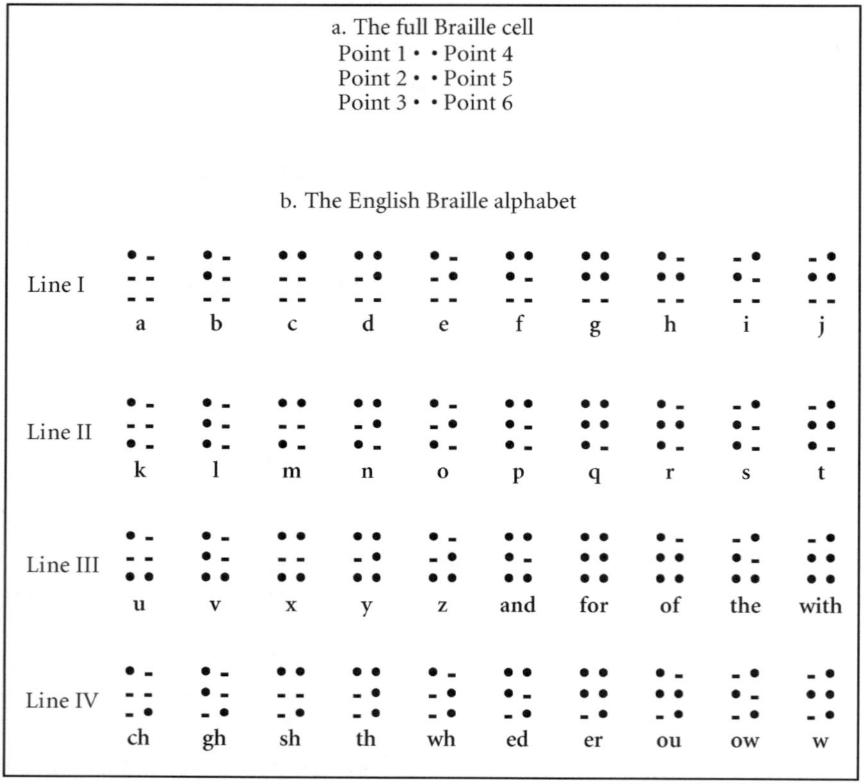

a. The full Braille cell
Point 1 • • Point 4
Point 2 • • Point 5
Point 3 • • Point 6

b. The English Braille alphabet

Figure 14.1. Table of Standard English Braille (first four lines).

Braille poses cognitive and perceptual difficulties for the learner, as brought out in Figures 14.1 and 14.2 which show how the basic unit of the code, the simple six-dot cell, can be elaborated to convey different meanings. Figure 14.1 contains a representation of what is known as the 'Full Cell', with the dots numbered 1, 2, and 3 in the first column and 4, 5, and 6 in the second column. It also shows the first four lines of the Table of Standard English Braille. This is adapted from Louis Braille's original formulation for the French alphabet, and it will be seen that each successive line is constructed from its immediate predecessor in a systematic manner. (At the request of one of his English students, Louis added the letter 'W' at the end of the fourth line as the student thought this would be helpful to blind people who were not French; in the original version, the signs after the letter 'Z' were used for indicating accent signs.) In Standard English Braille, Grade 1, also known as uncontracted

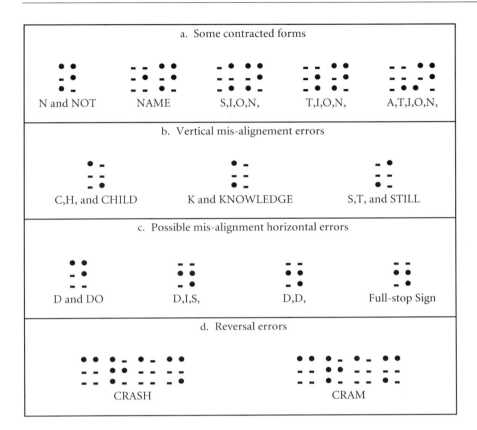

Figure 14.2. Some contracted forms and potential causes of error.

Braille, each letter of the ink-print alphabet is represented by a single braille cell. In Standard English Braille, Grade 2, known as fully contracted braille, ink-print letter-groups and whole words may be represented by single cell and double cell configurations. Figure 14.2 contains a few examples of such contracted forms, and it brings out, also, how the same tactile 'shape' can take on different meanings, giving rise to potential vertical, horizontal, and reversal errors. One shape, made from three dots, can have five 'meanings', i.e. D, DO, DIS-, DD, and the full-stop punctuation sign.

At the basic, physical level, the size dimensions of the cell have not been fully standardized throughout the world, and there are at least two different sizes, i.e. normal and so-called 'jumbo' braille. In the British code, the usual dimensions for the former are: Height of dot, 0.021 inches; distance between centers of dots (horizontal distance), 0.090 inches; distance between centers of dots (vertical distance), 0.100 inches.

Some 1.4 million spaces are saved by fully contracted, as compared with uncontracted, braille in one million words of text (see, for example, Lorimer, J., Tobin, Gill, & Douce 1982). However, mastery of the code entails that readers of fully-contracted English braille have to learn over 200 contractions and abbreviated forms. This cognitive burden is exacerbated by what might be called the perceptual burden and Millar (1997) has referred to this feature of the code when arguing that "the patterns (of braille) themselves lack redundancy" (ibid., p. 248). Failing to perceive a dot, or perceiving a cell as its own mirror-image, or failing to note its vertical alignment, will result in totally different interpretations as illustrated in Figure 14.2. Unlike print, where often a symbol can be understood even when a printing error has been made, a simple reversal of the final sign in braille can change 'CRASH' into 'CRAM'.

Perhaps inevitably the development of braille on a world-wide basis has resulted in various anomalies and accretions that have led to some avoidable problems. Certainly the drive for saving space and for reducing reading and writing time has not always been underpinned by objective research into the frequency of occurrence of the words and the letter-sequences chosen to be represented by contracted forms in braille. In the UK, doubts about the efficiency of the standard code prompted the Lochhead and Lorimer survey (1954) and then in the early 1980's a wide-ranging investigation (Lorimer, J., Tobin, Gill, & Douce 1982). Incorporating, in a meta-analysis, previous studies on frequency of occurrence of contracted forms (e.g. Lochhead & Lorimer 1954; Kederis, Siems, & Haynes 1965), the 1982 Lorimer, J. et al. investigation revealed that the 10 most frequently occurring contractions accounted for half of the total occurrences of the English contraction system, with the last 125 signs accounting "for only 10% of all occurrences" (ibid., Vol. 2, p. 75). Of real significance in terms of space-saving, the first 14 contractions in order of frequency of occurrence perform 50% of the total space-saving against uncontracted braille.

The implications of this particular investigation are that the present content and structure of fully-contracted English braille cannot be claimed to be optimally efficient. If we were to start afresh and use objective, contemporary data on word, syllable, and letter-combination frequency of occurrence, the braille code would be very different. Further support for 'pruning', for cutting down the number of contracted forms, was gathered through a series of nine experiments (using repeated-measures designs) in which the full standard contracted code was compared with 11 possible variants of it.

Six of the 11 modified codes were reductions of the standard code, the number of contractions being deleted ranging from 90 to 189. Three of the modified codes involved the addition of from 11 to 18 new signs to compensate for the loss of space-saving resulting from the removal of contractions. In the other two modified codes, one retained the existing contractions but added 37 new signs, while the second involved a novel use of some signs. The main dependent variable in the experiments was speed of reading.

In brief, the experiments showed that speed of reading in the modified codes "was affected in varying degrees by three factors, viz. increase/decrease of embossed cells, size of learning task, and extent to which Grade 2 orthography was disturbed by code changes" (ibid., Vol. 1, p. 17). Of special interest was the finding that some modified, reduced codes could be read at speeds not significantly different from those achieved by the subjects (all skilled braillists) when they were using the standard code which they had been reading all their life. Also, "where code simplification involves only omission of contractions, it appears that Grade 2 embossed spaces can be increased by about 2% without significant loss of reading speed" (ibid., p. 17). In other words, it is possible to devise a braille code which is much easier to learn, because it has fewer signs and fewer rules, and which does not result in less efficient reading. Here we have an example of the kind of research that can, in principle, lead to changes in the content and structure of tactile communication systems.

However, objective data are not of themselves sufficient to bring about changes. An example of the importance of taking account of personal preferences can be seen in a piece of survey research on the issue of use of capital letter signs in braille (Tobin, Whittaker, Greaney, & Hill 1997). In British braille, it is not the usual practice to indicate that a letter is a 'capital letter', as for example at the beginning of a new sentence, to indicate a proper noun (as in John Smith) or a title (e.g. Archbishop). In the United States, Canada, Australia, New Zealand, and many other English-speaking countries, however, it is the convention in braille that Dot 6 be placed immediately in front of any letter that would be a capital letter in print. The justification for this is that braille should be, as far as possible, an exact replica of print. One of its disadvantages is that it increases the bulk of materials produced in braille. More space is needed, documents are longer, and perhaps more time is taken in the processing of text by the reader. The general move towards greater standardization in all areas of life, towards greater uniformity, led to the Braille Authority of the United Kingdom (BAUK) commissioning researchers in the University of Birmingham's Research Centre for the Education of the Visually Handicapped to sound out the opinions of braillists as to the desirability of making capitalization compulsory in the UK. Of 1,200 respondents, 46% favored the use of the braille capital letter sign wherever a capital letter occurred in print, 12% believed it should be used in certain other designated contexts (e.g. in educational literature), 7% were in favor of a dual standard, and 30% believed there should be no change at all to present British practice. This issue is still unresolved as the opponents of change have been conducting a strong campaign against change, using the media (the radio and the specialist journals) as their platform. What we are observing here is an interesting sociological phenomenon. People's identification with their language and their traditional modes of communication transcends the mere facts or technicalities of the system. The language is the person. Arguments for modifying braille cannot be settled purely on the basis of efficiency. The findings of the Tobin et al. investigation (1997) are still, therefore, the subject of intense scrutiny and, indeed, heated dispute in the UK.

2.   Issues in teaching and learning braille

Given the large number of contracted forms in braille, teachers – whether of congenitally blind children or adventitiously blinded adults – are confronted with the problem of which signs to teach first. Millar (1997) has referred to the advantage, perceptually, of starting the teaching of braille with children by using "letters that differed maximally from each other in dot density" (ibid., p. 257). The problem of the priority to be given to the order in which braille signs are taught has been addressed from a different vantage point by Tobin (1972) who carried out a survey of the vocabulary of young blind schoolchildren. By sampling the spoken and written language of children aged five to eight years, one of Tobin's aims was to present teachers with information about the words appearing most frequently in the everyday language of young learners embarking upon the task of learning to read and write braille. These familiar words were then analyzed in terms of the braille contractions that they would contain. On the basis of this frequency count, Tobin (ibid.) recommended that the new teaching schemes being then devised by teachers should start with contracted forms occurring in the words that were most familiar to the children, an approach that is similar in some respects to that advocated in the United States by Mangold (1982) with her notion of introducing braille symbols by means of a carefully controlled vocabulary, rather than merely via lists of braille contractions that were to be learned in isolation. These recommendations still have an intuitive persuasiveness, but they need to be modified in the light of Millar's suggestion that the introductory signs be as perceptually different from one another as possible. A potential danger in implementing these technical recommendations is that teachers and other writers of texts for very young children may be unduly constrained in the range and originality of the themes and stories that would engage the attention, and the imagination, of these young learners. Striking a balance between these sometimes competing approaches is part of the teacher's professional expertise.

Of course, teaching reading through the medium of braille to the congenitally blind five-year-old is not the same as teaching braille to a newly-blinded 15-year-old. The former is learning to read; the latter has already learned how to read, and is now confronted with the challenge of learning how to do so through a different sensory modality. The adolescent or adult brings to the task a general knowledge base and an understanding of what literacy is that are altogether different from those of the young blind learner. On the other hand, the latter doesn't have any of the psychological, rehabilitational, and re-adjustment problems of the older learner.

In the case of the young learner, the notion of 'reading readiness' is an important factor for the teacher to take into consideration. As with sighted children, an understanding has to be established of what a book is; for example, that it has pages, that it is arranged in an orderly sequence, that it contains information in the form of symbols related to the child's spoken language, etc. Again, as is true for the sighted child, learning to read braille pre-supposes certain levels of cognitive, language, psychomotor, and auditory development. In addition, the young blind learner must be given the opportunity to acquire the ability to make the kinds of precise tactual discriminations that underpin the reading of braille. Harley, Truan, and Sanford (1987) discuss these prerequisite skills and processes, and there are now many practical instructional guides available for teachers and parents.

Where there is still much work to be done is in improving the reading skills of braillists who have mastered more than the basics of the code and who can be justifiably described as competent readers. Unfortunately, as will be discussed later, the reading speeds attainable by touch readers are massively inferior to those recorded for readers of print. One of the major educationally and vocationally handicapping effects of blindness is reduced speed of information processing. All too often, braillists are given little or no formal, structured teaching to become more proficient in picking up information by listening and reading. The assumption seems to be that improvements in these skills will come about as a result of ordinary development and of motivation within the learner. However, investigations reported by McBride (1974), Crandell and Wallace (1974),

Olson, Harlow, and Williams (1975), and Olson (1976) have all shown that significant improvements in speed of tactual reading are possible. McBride has gone so far as to assert "I do not believe we teach real reading in school. I believe, rather, that we teach *slow* reading in school. Real reading is *faster* reading and more in keeping with the way the brain operates. This is true whether the student is blind or sighted." (ibid., p. 12).

As part of the wide-ranging investigation into the structure of braille that has already been referred to (Lorimer, J. et al. 1982), Lorimer reports the results of a programmes of rapid-reading exercises devised by him and used in two schools in the UK. The main aims of the programmes were to lower recognition thresholds for braille signs, and to train readers: To make more effective use of hands and fingers; to make return sweeps to the next line without loss of time; to skim by using context cues; and to eliminate habits that impede efficiency (e.g. regressive and rotatory finger movements, 'mouthing' or vocalizing).

In the first school, using 18 blind boys of superior intelligence (IQ's above 120), the experimental group made a mean 'reading efficiency gain' of 15% as compared with the control group's 3.5% gain. Reading efficiency was defined as follows:

> R.E. = Reading speed (words per minute) x Comprehension Score (expressed as a percentage)
> Example: R.E. = 120 w.p.m. x 60% comprehension
> R.E. = 72 w.p.m

Lorimer also reports that during the course of their training, the experimental group subjects were given informal tests of silent reading speed, and mean gains were of the order of 44%.

In the second school, Lorimer used 22 pupils, with a mean age of 12.1 years and a mean IQ of 97 in the experimental group, and a mean of 13.2 years and a mean IQ of 96 in the control group. The experimental group showed a mean rise from 43 to 79 w.p.m., a gain of some 84%, and reading efficiency rose by 63%. No pre-test had been administered to the control group, but its mean efficiency rate was no higher than 43 w.p.m. Although there are some charges of methodological weaknesses that can be leveled against the Lorimer investigations, it can nevertheless be inferred that the continuation of formal teaching in reading skills is justifiable. Certainly, if adolescents are to be able to cope with the ever-increasing demands of the secondary school curricula, then teachers must recognize the importance of equipping these young people with the reading and other information processing competence to compete on equal terms with their fully-sighted age-peers.

Some measure of the advantage possessed by those who start the learning of braille at an early age is observable in the results of work carried out by Hill, Hill and Tobin (1999). In this investigation, the silent and oral reading speeds of early and later starters were compared. Among the other variables recorded were hand dominance, hand and finger usage, age, age of onset of blindness, and sex. As predicted, mean reading speeds were higher in the silent condition, and substantially higher for those who started to learn braille at an early age. One inference that has been drawn is that there is now a very strong case for continuing with the teaching of higher order reading skills on a systematic basis throughout the whole of the secondary school phase of education.

The teaching of braille to the newly-blinded older learners who were print-readers before the onset of their visual impairment is usually carried out as part of the wider rehabilitation process. For some people, the acquisition of specific new skills, such as braille, and the re-gaining of some degree of independent mobility, can contribute significantly to their overall rehabilitation. One of the problems for teachers is that the teaching of braille cannot be done on a whole class or group basis. Unlike print symbols, braille symbols cannot be put on the equivalent of a blackboard or overhead projector transparency so that their shapes and meanings can be explained to 10 or 20 learners simultaneously. Braille has to be taught on a one-to-one basis, which is costly and time-consuming. Attempts to circumvent this problem are illustrated by Tobin's *Beginning Braille* (Tobin 1988, revised), a 'programmed instruction' system using tape-recordings and braille booklets. These self-instruction materials comprised a linear programme through which the learner progressed in a series of small steps consisting of instruction-activity-confirmation. Learning was under the total control of the individual learner. Each new item in the teaching programme could be studied whenever and wherever the learner decided, and it could be repeated as often as desired.

The research (Tobin 1971) that led to the final version of the programme involved experimental trials of different kinds of content and an examination and measurement of learner variables. The content variables were selected as a result of a survey of the teaching methods used by experienced teachers who specialized in working with newly-blinded adolescents and adults. The survey had revealed two major sets of independent variables. One set was to do with the size of the braille cell (the standard size and an expanded, large-cell version). The advocates of the large cell argued that the tactual perceptual demands of the expanded cell were less severe than those of the smaller, standard cell in the initial stages of learning. Those teachers who opposed use of a non-standard braille cell were of the opinion that different perceptual skills were

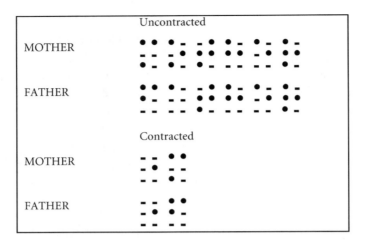

Figure 14.3. Word length in uncontracted and contracted English braille.

involved, and that the practice of using the large cell entailed a subsequent 'un-learning' when the readers changed to the standard format. The other independent teaching variable centered upon the question of starting with uncontracted braille (each letter in a word being represented by a single braille cell) or with the standard set of contractions. The advocates of uncontracted braille claimed that the learning load, but this time the cognitive learning load, was less severe, and enabled beginning readers to make more rapid progress. Again, the opposition argument was to the effect that the use of uncontracted braille would eventually entail 'unlearning' when the readers switched to the standard literary code with its many contracted forms. As Figure 14.3 shows, the words MOTHER and FATHER in uncontracted braille consist of six characters, while in fully contracted English literary braille they require only two.

To take account of the possible combinations of teaching variables (standard size cell, uncontracted; standard size cell, contracted; large size cell, uncontracted; large cell, contracted), two experiments were conducted. In one, 55 blindfolded adolescents were the subjects; in the other, 44 newly- registered blind adults, aged 20 to 80 years, participated. Subjects were randomly assigned to one of the four teaching treatment conditions. A battery of pre-tests was administered to measure pre-braille tactual discrimination ability, short-term memory capacity, and 16 personality traits. On completion of the training, braille reading tests were administered in standard size braille and scores were also obtained on subjects' attitude to braille and their experience of learning braille.

For the blind participants, there was a significant interaction between cell size and grade of braille, with the large cell treatment being significantly more beneficial only when combined with the contracted braille; in fact, the mean score for the uncontracted, large cell group appeared also to be larger than that of its small cell counterpart but this was not statistically significant. The higher performance of the large cell group may be explicable in terms of perceptual task difficulty. More favorable attitudes to their experience of learning braille were expressed by those who had started their learning with large cell braille. Further support for using the perceptually easier, large-cell format, has come from later work, e.g. Newman and his team (Newman et al. 1982, 1984) and Harley et al. (1985).

The high scoring learners had on average obtained higher scores on the pre-braille test of tactual discrimination and on the crystallized intelligence factor of the personality test. The lower scorers on the post-test of braille were also characterized as being lower on the self-sufficiency factor of the personality test. The more introspective, serious-minded learners also performed better, but this is perhaps explicable in relation to the somewhat isolated context of this specific learning situation where there was no opportunity to interact with other learners. The inability to do without such social interaction may be disadvantageous in these learning circumstances for the more extraverted subjects. This necessarily condensed account of the outcome of the experiments suggests, nevertheless, that teachers would do well to try to take into account, and reflect upon, their methods of teaching braille and the personality characteristics of their clients. An unchanging methodology may be easy for the teacher to apply, and in a large-group teaching, lecturing situation it may not be possible to deviate from it. When working with blind people on an individual, one-to-one basis, a more sensitively differentiated approach would be desirable and feasible.

Other factors that may affect the legibility of braille for new learners and experienced braillists are inter-cell spacing, the effects of providing headings, and the actual substrates (papers, plastics) upon which the braille is embossed. In a development of the earlier work, Tobin, Burton, Davies, and Guggenheim (1986) used 18 blindfolded, sighted subjects in an experiment in which the task required the subjects to feel a target braille cell, embossed at the top of a sheet, and then 'read' through the rest of the page "on which a randomized list of braille cells had been embossed ... (and on which) the target appeared four times" (p. 134). Three cell sizes and two spacing conditions were explored, with errors and times being logged. The no-spacing condition "presented formidable difficulties when associated with small and standard size cells", and only the large-cell, no-spacing condition, enabled subjects to attain high levels of accuracy. In the spacing condition, high percentages of accuracy were recorded, with over 60% of targets identified for each size of braille cell. Adequate spacing seems to prevent masking from adjacent cells, while in the no-spacing conditions the shape and textural uniqueness cannot be maintained. The need for teachers and braille-text designers to optimize physical, spatial dimensions is especially important for adult learners in the early stages of mastering this new medium.

Hartley, Tobin, and Trueman (1987) tried to assess the significance of providing headings in braille text since earlier investigations by Hartley (e.g. Hartley & Jonassen 1985; Hartley & Trueman 1985) had shown that headings in printed text for sighted readers aid search and retrieval, but do not so clearly aid recall of the text. In print, headings are often printed in different print sizes and fonts; they lend 'shape' to the page and since they are immediately apprehended by the eye they facilitate search and retrieval. For the touch reader, immediate apprehension is not possible. The whole page has to be scanned by left to right or up and down movements of the hand and fingers to permit location of section headings and other tactile markers. The Hartley et al.'s (1987) experiment comparing headings with no headings and using 24 blind people (median age 59 years, and age-range 17 to 80 years), revealed that while the obtained recall scores were not in fact significantly superior in the headings condition, a majority of the subjects expressed a preference for braille text with headings, making highly positive remarks about their usefulness.

Braille can now be produced in many different forms. When embossed in the traditional, whole-page lay-out, the usual materials are manilla paper (for books and other conventional documents), 'white rag' paper (most often used for printing ephemeral documents such as a braille newspaper), and plastics such as Brailon and Flovic. For some purposes, non-page lay-outs, such as continuous rolls of paper or plastic tape, are available. There are also paperless or 'refreshable' braille outputs, in which metal or plastic pins are activated by electronic or computer-controlled devices. The preference among most braillists seems to be for whole-page, permanent, paper-based systems. Even within this tradition, readers often express strong aversions to some of the standard materials.

To explore this, Cooper, Davies, Lawson-Williams, and Tobin (1985) presented 18 blind adults with short, 200 word prose passages embossed on different kinds of material. Objective measures were provided by manufacturers of such factors as weight, thickness, bulk, strain, burst strength, porosity, and smoothness. After reading the passages, the subjects were asked to indicate their overall subjective preferences among the materials. These evaluations focused upon such phenomena as experience of friction, of stickiness, of static electrical properties, and of readability of the dots. On average, it was found that the heavyweight manilla was most preferred, followed by the lightweight manilla, the white rag, and the Brailon. Two new synthetic materials, Synteape and Tyvek, were not generally very highly regarded, although some subjects did slightly prefer them to Brailon.

Some of the objective measures are directly related to the long-term storage qualities of the materials, their general strength, and serviceability. There is not, by any means, a perfect correlation between these physical properties and the braillists' subjective evaluations. Brailon, for example, was high on thickness, bulk, and burst strength, and was therefore highly durable, and gave acceptable dot definition. Its low porosity gave rise, it is believed, to the readers' adverse criticisms of its stickiness. Perspiration from the fingers would not be so easily absorbed by Brailon. Of course, familiarity and the innate conservatism of readers may be factors influencing their preferences, but the investigators' conclusions were that "it is desirable that engineers should now take account of these subjective factors and try to present braille of higher quality" (ibid., p. 327).

3. Assessment

For assessing progress and for determining appropriate remedial teaching procedures, teachers need objective means of assessing braille competence. An instrument developed in the UK for testing basic ability in reading ability was the Tooze Braille Speed Test (Tooze 1962). This was described by its author as a test of basic perceptual ability. It is not exactly this, since it requires more than tactual perception: It requires rapid and accurate identification and labeling of three-letter words printed in uncontracted, or Grade 1, braille. It consists of 120 phonically regular words, the score being the number of words correctly identified; this score can be transformed into a 'reading age' and into a standardized score with a mean of 100 and a standard deviation of 15. It provides the user with information about a child's familiarity with the elements of uncontracted English braille and of his mastery of simple phonological blending skills.

A rather more searching test of braille knowledge is the Lorimer Braille Recognition Test (Lorimer 1962) which is described as a test of ability in reading braille contractions. A list of some 174 unrelated words is presented to the child, and again the raw score can be transformed into a reading age and a standardized score with a mean of 100 and a standard deviation of 15.

These two tests are essentially 'word recognition tests' and are in no way a measure of the child's ability to read continuous passages of meaningful prose, and then demonstrate an understanding of the story. They do not, therefore, go beyond mere knowledge of the braille code. They do not measure accuracy, comprehension, and speed of reading simultaneously. One of the most seriously handicapping effects of blindness is reduced speed of information processing. The inability of blind readers to compete on equal terms with their fully-sighted peers in terms of speed of information processing puts them at a great disadvantage in their educational and vocational careers. We need, therefore, to be able to measure the extent of this handicap so that appropriate remedial, substitution procedures can be found and implemented.

The University of Birmingham's Research Centre for the Education of the Visually Handicapped has attempted to address this problem by devising and standardizing braille versions of valid and reliable measures of reading accuracy, comprehension, and speed. Lorimer first attempted this with his braille version of a well-known British print-reading test known as the Neale Analysis

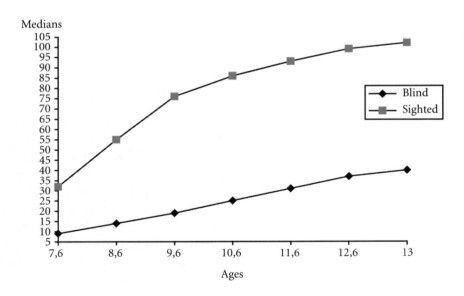

Figure 14.4. Comparisons of print and braille reading speeds. Based upon data contained in Administration and Scoring Manuals of the print version of the Neale Analysis of Reading Ability (Neale 1966) and the braille version (Lorimer, J. 1977).

Table 14.1. Braille readers' increasing deficits in speed of reading over 48 month period; comparison is with sighted normative data.

Testing Occasion	Number of Subjects	Mean Age at Test (in months)	Mean Speed Deficit (in months)
1	36	97	−17
2	33	131	−40
3	34	145	−48

of Reading Ability (Neale 1958; Lorimer 1977). Figure 14.4 brings out something of the disadvantage experienced by the congenitally blind reader. At every stage throughout their primary and secondary school careers, the young braillist is at a massive disadvantage. Of special significance is the fact that the disadvantage grows bigger with increasing age. That this is not a chance aberration, specific to the particular group of children tested by Lorimer, is confirmed by the data gathered in a separate longitudinal investigation of some 120 visually impaired children begun in 1972 by Tobin (1979, 1988). As Table 14.1 shows, the braille readers in that study were repeatedly tested as they pursued their education; once again, the initial gap in speed of reading is relatively small but grows larger with increase in age.

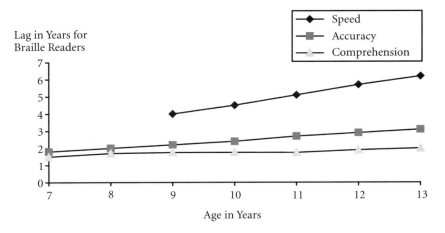

Figure 14.5. Magnitude of differences between print and braille readers. Based upon Greaney, Hill, and Tobin (1998): *Users' Handbook: Neale Analysis of Reading Ability. University of Birmingham Braille Version.* Published by the Royal National Institute for the Blind, London.

Further support for the validity and reliability of these findings comes from another investigation (Greaney, Tobin, & Hill 1998) with another group of braille readers. Figure 14.5 reveals that the 'lag' in reading speed continues to grow. All too often, replication is difficult or impossible in educational research, but here we have three investigations telling the same story. Touch reading places much greater demands upon the learner. Braille's superiority over all rival tactile codes remains uncontested, but it is vital that teachers understand the nature and degree of the severity of the handicap experienced by those who are born blind. The cognitive and perceptual demands made upon the young blind learner are significantly greater than those experienced by sighted children. Short-term memory capacity is placed under greater pressure (information having to be held in store until sufficient information has been received to permit 'closure' and interpretation of the whole word or phrase); extremely fine psycho-motor control is required to ensure smooth left to right scanning and location of the next line; and there has to be the motivation to persevere despite the additional time required for them to decode and assimilate the information. The perceptual window, the width of the human finger, is narrower in touch than in vision.

4. Conclusion

It is clear that 'literacy' for the blind person is not just a matter of converting the symbols of the ink-print alphabet into a tactile form. The punctiform nature of Louis Braille's marvelous invention enables a degree of spatial compression that has not been achievable by any of its many competitors. Nevertheless, the perceptual, learning, and other cognitive demands it makes upon the learner are of levels of severity that warrant further research and development so that the code can be made accessible by even larger numbers of blind people. The existing system of contracted and abbreviated forms has not been based upon objective surveys of the frequency of occurrence of letter groups, syllables, and words. Research has shown that braille codes containing smaller sets of contractions can be devised and can be read as quickly as the standard code, and without any undue increase in the bulk and length of braille books.

Tactual information processing seems to be significantly slower than visual processing, at least in relation to the processing of verbal information, but again, research shows that with carefully structured teaching, the reading speeds of braillists can be improved substantially. Researchers, teachers, and the producers of braille books must have as their goals the optimizing of the system in terms of the code's content and structure, of the ways in which it is taught, and of the physical characteristics of the materials on to which it is embossed.

References

Bogart, D., Cranmer, T. V., & Sullivan, J. E. (2000). Unifying the Braille codes. In J. M. Dixon (Ed.), *Braille into the next millennium* (pp. 160–181). Washington, D.C.: Library of Congress. National Library Service for the Blind and Physically Handicapped.

Cooper, A., Davies, B. T., Lawson-Williams, N., & Tobin, M. J. (1985). An examination of natural and synthetic papers for embossing braille. *The New Beacon, LXIX* (823), 325–327.

Crandell, J. M. & Wallace, D. H. (1974). Speed reading in braille: An empirical study. *New Outlook for the Blind, 68,* 13–19.

Greaney, J., Tobin, M. J., & Hill, E. W. (1998). *Neale analysis of reading ability: University of Birmingham Braille version.* London: Royal National Institute for the Blind.

Harley, R. K., Pichert, J. W., & Morrison, R. N. (1985). Braille instruction for blind diabetic adults with decreased tactile sensitivity. *Journal of Visual Impairment and Blindness, 79,* 12–17.

Harley, R. K., Truan, M. B., & Sanford, L. D. (1987). *Communication Skills for Visually Impaired Learners.* Springfield, Illinois: Charles C. Thomas.

Hartley, J. & Jonassen, D. (1985). The role of headings in printed and electronic text. In D. Jonassen (Ed.), *The Technology of text, Vol. 2.* Englewood Cliffs, New Jersey: Educational Technology Publication.

Hartley, J., Tobin, M. J., & Trueman, M. (1987). The effects of providing headings in braille text. *Journal of Visual Impairment and Blindness, 81,* 213–214.

Hartley, J. & Trueman, M. (1985). A research strategy for text designers: The role of headings. *Instructional Science, 14,* 99–155.

Hill, E. W., Hill, J. F., & Tobin, M. J. (1999). Braille: Oral and silent reading speeds. *New Beacon, 980,* 4–6.

Irwin, R. B. (1955). *The War of the Dots.* New York: American Foundation for the Blind.

Kederis, C. J., Siems, J. R., & Haynes, R. L. (1965). A frequency count of the symbology of English braille Grade 2, American usage. *International Journal for the Education of the Blind, 15*(2), 38–46.

Lochhead, H. M. & Lorimer, J. (1954). *Report of the Survey of the Frequency of All the Contractions of Standard English Braille, Grade 2.* Edinburgh: Scottish Braille Press.

Lorimer, J. (1962). *The Lorimer Braille Recognition Test.* Bristol: College of Teachers of the Blind.

Lorimer, J. (1977). *The neale analysis of reading ability adapted for use by blind children.* Windsor: NFER-Nelson

Lorimer, J., Tobin, M. J., Gill, J., & Douce, J. L. (1982). *A study of Braille contraction. Part 1, Main study.* London: Royal National Institute for the Blind.

Lorimer, P. (1997). A critical evaluation of the historical development of the tactile modes of reading and an analysis and evaluation of researches carried out in endeavours to make the Braille code easier to read and write. Birmingham: Ph.D. Thesis, University of Birmingham, and http://www.braille.org

Lorimer, P. (2000). Origins of Braille. In J. M. Dixon (Ed.), *Braille into the next millennium* (pp. 18–39). Washington, D.C.: Library of Congress. National Library Service for the Blind and Physically Handicapped.

Mangold, S. S. (1982). Teaching reading via braille. In S. S. Mangold (Ed.), *A Teachers' Guide to the Special Educational Needs of Blind and Visually Handicapped Children.* New York: American Foundation for the Blind.

McBride, V. G. (1974). Explorations in rapid reading in braille. *New Outlook for the Blind, 68,* 8–12.

Millar, S. (1997). *Reading by touch.* London: Routledge.

Neale, M. (1958). *The Neale analysis of reading ability.* London: MacMillan Education.

Newman, S. E., Hall, A. D., Ramseur, C. J., Foster, D. L., Goldston, D. B., De Camp, B. L., Granberry-Hager, S. P., Lockhart, J. L., Sawyer, W. L., & White, J. E. (1982). Factors affecting the learning of braille. *Journal of Visual Impairment and Blindness, 76,* 59–64.

Newman, S. E., Hall, A. D., Foster, J. D., & Gupta, V. (1984). Learning a function of haptic discriminability among items. *American Journal of Psychology, 97,* 359–372.

Olson, M. R. (1976). Faster braille reading: Preparation at the reading readiness level. *New Outlook for the Blind, 70,* 341–345.

Olson, M. R., Harlow, S. D., & Williams, J. (1975). Rapid reading in braille and large print: an examinaiton of McBride's procedures. *New Outlook for the Blind, 69,* 392–395.

Reales, W. M. (2000). The art of marketing Braille. The National Braille Press. In J. M. Dixon (Ed.), *Braille into the next millennium.* Washington, D.C.: Library of Congress. National Library for the Blind and the Physically Handicapped.

Ryles, R. (2000). Braille as a predictor of success. In J. M. Dixon (Ed.), *Braille into the next millennium* (pp. 462–491). Washington, D.C.: Library of Congress. National Library for the Blind and the Physically Handicapped.

Tobin, M. J. (1971). *Programmed instruction and braille learning. An experimental and multivariate investigation of some teaching and psychological variables.* Birmingham: Research Centre for the Education of the Visually Handicapped, University of Birmingham (mimeo).

Tobin, M. J. (1972). *The vocabulary of the young blind schoolchild.* Liverpool: College of Teachers of the Blind.

Tobin, M. J. (1988). *Beginning braille. Self-instructional course (Revised Edition).* London: Royal National Institute for the Blind.

Tobin, M. J., Burton, P., Davies, B. T., & Guggenheim, J. (1986). An experimental investigation of the effects of cell size and spacing in braille: With some possible implications for the newly-blind adult learner. *The New Beacon, LXX* (829), 133–135.

Tobin, M. J., Whittaker, J. R., Greaney, J., & Hill, E. W. (1997). The issue of braille capitalisation in the UK: The BAUK survey, 1996. *British Journal of Visual Impairment, 15*(1), 5–9.

Tooze, F. H. G. (1962). *Tooze Braille Speed Test.* Bristol: College of Teachers of the Blind.

CHAPTER 15

The tactile reading of maps and drawings, and the access of blind people to works of art

Yvette Hatwell and Françoise Martinez-Sarrochi

This chapter is dedicated to the tactile apprehension of two-dimensional pictorial material, i.e. maps and raised lines drawings, and to the problems of the access of blind people to the two- and three-dimensional works of art exhibited in museums. Total blindness considerably reduces locomotor autonomy and all the devices rendering easier the navigation in the city are welcome (for a recent review of locomotion in the blind, see Hatwell 2003, in press). On the other hand, in reading braille, the blind are often deprived of the illustrations which accompany ink-printed books. It is thus important to find out whether they could be helped by tactile maps and relief drawings. Is touch adapted to this symbolism? Furthermore, is it possible to make pictorial and sculptural works of art accessible to the blind via touch?

1. Tactile maps

Maps are projective two-dimensional symbolic representations in reduced size of a real space. They give an overview of vast (a town) or reduced (a classroom) spaces. This method of archiving geographical information, over six thousand years old, is interesting as it allows to see things which otherwise could not be seen. Models have the same properties as maps, but are three-dimensional and thus represent the environment via reduced volumes. Rather bulky, but easier to understand than maps, models have inspired less theoretical research and have mainly be used in pedagogy over the last ten years (these models are often exchanged between schools, each "pedagogical set" treating a different theme).

1.1   General map processing

Maps contain spatial data allowing the location of objects (streets, buildings), estimation of distances and directions and the construction of an itinerary from one point to another. But this information is accessible only if the observers have particular perceptual and cognitive skills giving them access to the symbolic codes of maps. Sighted adults having attained of a certain educational level are generally able to use geographical and road maps and, from the age of five, children know what a map is for.

Perceptively, lines and symbols must first be discriminated and the general spatial organization of the figure must be apprehended. Cartographic research studies the elements which make maps readable and how they must be adapted to subjects' perceptual skills: Degree of simplification, scale, line thickness, symbol typography, etc. On a cognitive level, map reading raises numerous problems. The first one is to understand that a tiny, two-dimensional representation symbolizes a large three-dimensional external space. In addition, a map is a representation of space which is itself in space, as it is a material object having its intrinsic geometry. This object, however, represents ("serves as") another space and shares an extrinsic geometry with it through projective correspondence. Using a map thus requires both material properties to be taken into account and access to its symbols. Furthermore, to read a map, one has to project oneself into the map space. Neighborhood plans, with their big "You are here" sign, are supposed to facilitate this operation. But this is the case only if the map orientation is aligned, that is if its top corresponds to the "straight ahead" direction of the observer. Contra-aligned maps (180° rotations) impose a change of point of view and induce "mirror image" type errors, whereas non-aligned maps (rotations other than 180°) induce errors derived from erroneous mental rotation of the display (Levine, Jankovic, & Palij 1982; Rossano & Warren 1989a). After identifying their own position on the map, the observers must locate the goal to be reached, extract the pertinent information concerning direction, distances and landmarks, and hold this information in memory. This requires solid spatial skills and the use of stable reference systems based on external cues.

This analysis of the cognitive load imposed by map reading accounts for the fact that children only acquire this skill towards the age of 8–9 years (Piaget & Inhelder 1947/1967). However, recent studies showed that younger children (5 to 6-year-olds) are already capable of using a map if it is very simplified, contains very visible spatial landmarks and is aligned. Characteristic errors are however observed at this age: Scale change (after recognizing a building in an aerial view, the child identifies a lawn as "a cheese"), symbol reification (a road drawn in red on a map must be read in real life) (Down & Liben 1987; Liben & Down 1989), etc. According to Bluestein and Acredolo (1979), Blades (1991) and Blades and Spencer (1987), sighted 4- to 5-year-olds can locate their own position on a simple and aligned map representing a small space. With three-dimensional models, children from the age of 3 or 4 manage to find an object hidden in a real space after looking at the position of the object in the model representing this space (DeLoache 1989; Marzoff & DeLoache 1997).

1.2   How blind people use tactile maps

The use of maps poses specific problems to the blind. Touch is not very adapted to two-dimensional material (2D). Yet, map reading implies the encoding, processing and retention of such 2D configurations representing a non-perceptible space. In order for tactile maps to be readable, they must thus be partial and simplified representations of the symbolized space (a too detailed map is incomprehensible) but must conserve useful information. Over recent years, technical advances have been made in the production of raised drawings, which allow surface texture and relief height to be varied (raised points lines, linear relief on thermoformed paper, relief molded on vinyl and other materials, cf. Horsfall 1997). Cartographic studies have evaluated the most adapted graphics and codes: Types of line best representing a road, nature of intersections symbols, texture types, map size, etc. (Bentzen 1982; Berlà 1982; Campbell 1997; Easton & Bentzen 1980). In children, perceptual problems in map reading are even more acute than in adults.

On a cognitive level, the first difficulty for the congenitally totally blind who do not have projective space is to understand how the plan on the sheet could represent their three-dimensional space. In a follow-up study of the development of Kelli (a born blind girl) between the ages of 2 and 5 years, Landau (1986) concluded that the capacity to read a tactile map is very precocious (from the age of 4, Kelli was able to use a very simple map to find an object) and does not need to be learned. But this case is exceptional and other observations showed that this capacity is not innate, neither in the blind nor in the sighted. It needs to be learned in order for the child to understand that their hand movements exploring the map give information about the real movements to be carried out in the environment (Millar 1994). Furthermore, Rossano and Warren (1989b) observed in totally blind and partially sighted adults the same difficulties as those experienced by sighted subjects when the map was not aligned.

Using an aligned aerial map of a restricted space, Ungar, Blades and Spencer (1996) found that the majority of early totally blind 6 to 8-year-olds children succeeded in locating their own position on a simple map. In this study, the child was placed in a square space made up of 5x5 tiles 30 cm apart from each other. A braille letter was written on sixteen of the tiles, whereas the others were not identifiable. All were face down and their markers could not be perceived. Firstly, the subject examined a map indicating the spatial arrangement of the marked and unmarked tiles, then traced a route along a line of tiles with the experimenter. Each time the child came across a tile, he/she turned it over and was asked then to indicate its position on the map. At the end of the test, the child retraced the whole route on the map. The results showed a high percentage of success in both the localization task (75%) and the overall reconstitution of the route (81%), and greater ease for routes with numerous markers.

Ungar, Blades and Spencer (1997) also studied the evaluation of the distance between 2 objects among 3 (aligned along a corridor) from the representation of these objects on an aligned map (Figure 15.1). In congenitally blind 5 to 8-year-olds, absolute errors in placing the object in real space were high (69%) but decreased significantly (33.5%) in the 8- to 11- year-olds. In fact, the younger children did not know at all how to operate the scale change ne-

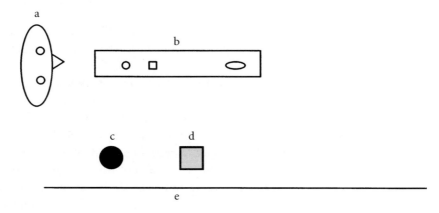

Figure 15.1. Representation of the task of distance estimation on a map. The child (a) holds an aligned map (b) on which 3 objects are drawn in relief. The way to be followed is materialized by a long straight line (e). On the ground, the experimenter has placed two of the 3 objects (c and d) represented on the map (a ball, a cube and a tambourine). The child is asked to place the third object on the ground using the map to estimate its distance in relation to the second object (adapted from Ungar, Blades, & Spencer 1997).

cessary to pass from map to real space. In sighted children working in a visual condition, the observed errors were 46% in 5 to 8-year-olds and 26% in 8 to 11-year-olds. In another experiment, explanations were given before the test. These explanations suggested to the younger children that they make ordinal comparisons between the distances separating the three objects on the map and to report this comparison onto real space. Fractions were explained to the older children. The performances of both groups improved in this condition.

Direction evaluation was also studied by Ungar, Blades, Spencer and Morsley (1994). Six boxes, each containing a hidden object, were arranged in a room. Starting from the center of the room, the child was led towards one of the hidden objects, then taken back to the center. The same procedure was used for the six hidden objects. Then, from the center of the room, the child was asked to orient a pointer in the direction of the objects named by the experimenter. In another condition, the participant was immobilized in the middle of the room and given an aligned map of the overall arrangement of the room and the hidden objects. Then the child was asked to orient a pointer towards each object successively. The performances of the 8- to 12-year-olds congenitally totally blind were consistently higher in the map condition than in the real exploration condition (Figure 15.2). The 5- to 8-year-olds performed errati-

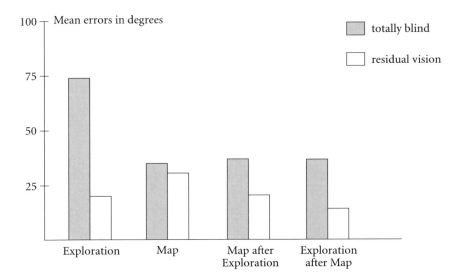

Figure 15.2. Absolute error (in %) in real Exploration, Map, Map after Exploration and Exploration after Map conditions in early totally blind 8-to-12-year-olds and in blind subjects with residual vision (adapted from Ungar, Blades, Spencer, & Morsley 1997).

cally in both conditions. No effect of condition was observed in children with residual vision.

In totally blind adults (occurrence of blindness between birth and 6 years of age), Espinosa and Ochaita (1998) observed better performances when the learning of a new route in a city was done with a map than when it was done through a real locomotion. In another study, Espinosa, Ungar, Ochaita, Blades and Spencer (1998) compared different methods of learning an urban route (2 km) having eight landmarks (either tactile like the texture of the ground, or auditory like the proximity of a school, or olfactory like crossing a garden). All the participants have received "Orientation and Mobility" training allowing travel autonomy. They were first guided by the experimenter along the route, then they walked alone along this route with the experimenter near them (in order to make them secure). Another group walked along the route with the help of a raised map of the routes and landmarks, and a third group walked along the route while the experimenter gave a verbal description of this route. The subjects were then asked to evaluate the distance between two landmarks, and to find a "shortcut" from one landmark to another. The higher performances were observed in the group walking with the map during learning, whereas there was no difference between the other two conditions. This means that only those who could use the map have formed a true cognitive map allowing detours and shortcuts.

Finally, in another experimental condition, totally blind adults learned an urban circuit only with a map. The experimenter guided the subject's finger on the map to indicate the route, and then the subject traveled alone along this route. The results showed no difference between this group and a control group learning the same route by traveling on it without map. This means that, in this study, the map improved performances only when it was added to the direct experience of the travel and not when it was substituted to real travel. According to the authors, the contradiction between this latter result and those obtained by Espinosa and Ochaita (1998) stem from differences in the procedure used in the two studies.

Thus, tactile maps may improve spatial representation in the totally blind, and this from school age. But the maps must be aligned. Indeed, mental rotations are less well achieved by the early blind than by the sighted (Carpenter & Eisenberg 1978; Ungar, Blades, & Spencer 1995), which explains the difficulties of non-alignment in the blind (Rossano & Warren 1989b). The necessity of alignment, especially in young children, shows the limits of tactile spatial representation and suggests that it is perhaps based more on learning a series of local landmarks rather than an overall cognitive map.

2. The identification and production of two-dimensional drawings

Whereas maps transmit only localization information (*where?*), drawings also symbolize *what*, that is object properties (shape, color, texture, etc.). These projective representations resemble the real objects more than maps and are identified very early by the sighted (from the second year of life). On the other hand, the production of drawings is laborious, as it is constrained by the children's motor immaturity, the nature of their mental representations and the inherent difficulty of the projective representation of three-dimensional space which is really mastered by very few adults.

As it seems to be a purely visual activity, drawing was for a long time considered inaccessible to the blind, especially the early blind. Indeed it was so, as there were few means of doing raised drawings. This situation changed in the 1960s when small displays allowing punctuated relief lines to be traced became available at affordable prices (material proposed by the Swedish Foundation for the Blind). A ball-point pen displaced over a special sheet resting on a supple plastic support traces a permanent raised line. This allows the blind persons to check their production tactually, which is obviously impossible when drawing with an ordinary pencil. On the other hand, machines today allow good relief drawings to be printed (by thermoforming or other methods).

Once these technical problems have been resolved, the question was to find out whether these two-dimensional representations were usable by the blind. In fact, these representations resemble the real objects as apprehended by touch far less than usual printed drawings resemble seen objects. In this section, we will examine the studies carried out concerning the drawing of usual objects and the graphic representation of perspective.

2.1 Drawings of usual objects

2.1.1 *The production of drawings*

It is to Kennedy and his partners (Kennedy 1982, 1983, 1997, 2000; Kennedy & Domander 1984; Kennedy, Gabias, & Nicholls 1991) that we owe the most astonishing demonstration of the congenitally blind capacities to draw in relief. According to Kennedy, certain rules of graphic representation, such as masking and featuring of object contours rather than surfaces (the human head represented by a circle, for example) are universal, as they have been spontaneously applied in the pictorial productions of some people blind from birth. Five to six-year-olds often produce the same scribbling as sighted 3-year-olds. However, in spite of these interesting observations, drawing remains difficult for the blind. On a perceptual level, the tactile checking of a drawing during its execution is far less efficient than the visual checking of the sighted, because of the exiguity of the tactile perceptual field, the highly sequential nature of tactile perception and the perceptivo-motor difficulty of following lines with the left index finger while the right hand is in action. Furthermore, and more importantly, the early blind are mostly unaware of the rules for transcribing 3D space into 2D space (Millar 1975). Typical features, such as development (the representation of all the faces of an object, like an unfolded cube), surface filling, errors of orientation, etc. are therefore observed sometimes. These errors will probably decrease these next years because of the generalization of the use of drawing in contemporary methods of teaching the blind at school.

2.1.2   The identification of drawings

More numerous studies have been carried out concerning the identification of drawings of usual objects (a key, a banana, an umbrella, etc.). In vision, recognition precedes greatly the capacity to produce drawings. The reverse is true for touch (Millar 1991): Identifying raised drawings is very difficult. Thus, Magee and Kennedy (1980) observed only 12% success in early blind adults, and sighted subjects working in a non-visual condition were hardly better (30%, Kennedy & Fox 1977). According to Loomis, Klatzky and Lederman (1991), these low performances are due at least in part to the exiguity of the tactile perceptual field. These authors effectively compared the identification of drawings in the tactile and visual modalities in sighted adults by varying the size of this field: In the visual condition, a tunnel reduced it to the dimensions found in the tactile condition when either one or two index fingers were active. With a visual field corresponding to that of one index finger, performances were the same in touch and vision. But when the visual field corresponded to two index fingers, visual performances improved whereas tactile results were unchanged. The capacity of touch to process simultaneous data thus corresponds to the information brought by a single index finger, whereas the capacity of vision is very superior.

The role played by past visual experience was evidenced by Heller (1989). He firstly checked that his three groups of adults (congenitally blind, late blind and blindfolded sighted) had the same rate of success in recognizing geometric relief shapes. He then evaluated his subjects' performances in the identification of drawings (relief contours) of familiar objects. He observed a clear superiority of the late blind over the two other groups, which did not differ. The late blind are advantaged both by their past visual experience, which allows them access to graphic codes and their intense training of the tactile modality. Furthermore, Pathak and Pring (1989) showed that storage of drawings in working memory was difficult in early blind. The performances of early blind participants were lower than those of blindfolded sighted when, after the presentation of three drawings, they were asked to indicate from memory which of the drawings corresponded to a word said by the experimenter. In the reverse situation, where a single drawing was presented and subjects had to choose which of three words corresponded to the drawing, the two groups were equivalent.

Another factor accounting for the difficulty of the tactile identification of the drawings is that relief drawings do not really physically resemble the haptic object. As a result, these drawings poorly specify to what category they belong. By indicating this category in advance (fruit, furniture, vehicles, etc.), Heller, Calcaterra, Burson and Tyler (1996a) obtained 63% of correct responses in blindfolded sighted adults, whereas without this information only 25% of responses were accurate. In this category information condition, the late blind were as successful as the sighted (70%) whereas the rate of success of the early blind was only 37%. The difficulty created by early blindness in drawing identification is thus confirmed here.

However, even the early blind children seem to benefit from illustrations accompanying a text. This was shown by Pring and Rusted (1985) who compared in early and late blind 14-year-olds the retention of a short text including some illustrations (thermoformed relief). The illustrated parts were retained better than the others by the two groups, but unfortunately the authors did not control the duration of presentation which was necessarily longer for the illustrated parts than for the others. It should finally be noted that the late blind once again benefited more from the illustrations than the early blind.

2.2 The graphic representation of perspective

Early blind people are known generally to have difficulty in making spatial inferences (cf. Chapter 8). Could they nevertheless produce and understand drawings representing the different points of view of the same object or group of objects? In adults, Heller and Kennedy (1990) used a simple task to answer affirmatively to this question. These authors presented early and late blind adults with three objects (a cube, a sphere and a cone) arranged on a small board. After haptic exploration, the subjects were first asked to draw the display seen from above or from the side, then they had to recognize the correct drawing of the display also seen from above or from the side. In every condition, performances were superior to chance, and subjects' visual status had no effect. However, Heller, Kennedy and Joyner (1995) later found the early blind to be clearly less efficient than the late blind and the blindfolded sighted in a task in which subjects were asked to indicate where an observer should stand in order to have a certain point of view of a drawn house (seen from above, from ¾ or from the side).

In order to study more directly the representation of perspective by the blind, Heller, Calcaterra, Tyler and Burson (1996b) presented late blind (blindness occurring after one year of age) and early blind adults with a vertical rectangular panel which could be rotated forwards or backwards on its upper horizontal edge. After having explored and drawn in relief the panel fixed vertically (90°), the subjects explored the panel inclined to different orientations and were asked to draw it as it would appear to a sighted person sitting in their place. The blind were instructed to clearly represent the panel angles. As expected, many of the early blind did not understand the task and reproduced a rectangle every time, whatever the panel inclination, whereas the late blind and the sighted applied more or less successfully the laws of perspective. However, when subjects were asked to recognize the inclined panel from among many drawings (instead of drawing it themselves), the early blind improved consistently and obtained the same results as the late blind and the sighted.

In another study on early blind, late blind, low vision (allowed to used their residual vision) and blindfolded sighted adults, Heller, Brackett, Scroggs, Steffen, Heatherly and Salik (2002) studied the production and then the recognition of raised line drawings representing a three-dimensional angle. This angle was made of two wooden boards glued together along one edge and forming therefore an angle either acute, or obtuse, or right. The performances of low vision participants were higher than those of all the other groups, which did not differ.

In another situation, the same subjects were asked to haptically explore a geometrical shape (a cube, a pyramid, a hexagonal prism and a prism with a diamond base), and then to recognize the drawing of each shape among four ones. These drawings represented the shape from four points of view: Frontal view (at the eyes' height), a view from ¾ above with perspective, an orthogonal view from above and a frontal view with convergence lines. Again, the performances of the low vision group were the highest and were significantly higher than those of the early blind. The orthogonal view from above was easier than the others, and the lowest results were observed with the two frontal views.

This set of results show that early blind people can understand certain graphic representations of perspective in very simplified laboratory situations. But when drawings have a certain level of complexity, considerable difficulties appear. This is the reason why those who wish to communicate knowledge about three-dimensional objects to the blind recommend doing so via "orthogonal projection", that is to say via facades or by cut slices (like scanner images of the brain, for example), rather than in perspective (Bris & Morice 1996). The pedagogical material conceived and created for the blind by the Accessibility Department of the *City of Sciences and Industry (Cité des Sciences et de l'Industrie)* in Paris is based on this principle and presents different faces of objects, architectural diagrams (the *Arc of Triumph* in Paris) and biology (the human body) via orthogonal projections.

In conclusion, the representation of external world through drawings is always costly for the early blind. This explains why drawing is very rarely used spontaneously by them. Moreover, visually impaired people manifest sometimes systematic reactions of resistance to what is qualified as "visual colonization" (Michel Bris, documents provided by the *Centre National d'Etudes et de Formation pour l'Enfance Inadaptée* in Paris for the training of teachers specialized in visual deficit). Experimental research and pedagogical practice show, however, that the blind can benefit from the use of drawing, doubtless because of the intense cognitive work and the depth of processing it imposes in order to be understood.

3.   The access of the blind to artistic representations and museums

If the blind have serious difficulties recognizing drawings of usual objects, maps and other transpositions of perspective, can they nevertheless have access to art? Do the efforts made to grasp haptic information allow access to pleasure and to the perception of "beautiful" things created to be looked at?

3.1 Two-dimensional pictorial art publications

Over the last decades, techniques have evolved considerably and have led to multiple attempts to reproduce artistic patrimony works. However, it is very difficult to answer the question "What should be proposed to whom, and how?" Indeed, recent productions of art publications in raised two-dimensional format have been received enthusiastically by some and disconcertedly by others. These difficulties may partially be attributed to the fact that these productions do not take into account either the heterogeneity of the blind public (the receivers), or the nature of the options guiding the publishers' (the transmitters') creation.

Regarding blind people, a distinction must evidently be made between early and late blind. In the former, methods and systems of space representation are organized in an original manner. However, although esthetic properties concern mainly the world of sound and smell in these early blind, encounters with plastic arts may lead them to discover the esthetic aspects of the tactile modality. In the late and particularly the recent blind, the tactile presentation of art works may correspond to the simple rediscovery of a former visual learning.

The theoretical options (and the techniques resulting from them) guiding the elaboration of current research on museum and publishing propositions are partly incompatible. They can be grouped into two categories, one which favors looking for informative tactile efficiency in an educational action, and the other which favors the respect of the artist's intention to share esthetic emotions.

The problem is that, on the one hand, there is a daily necessity of information concerning what is perceptually non-accessible for the blind. On the other hand, teachers and educators try to avoid "verbalism" in the visually impaired people, i.e. the use of words which have no concrete representational base. Therefore, they do not recommend the use of metaphors and analogies in the education of the blind. This fear of verbalism leads to limit the knowledge of the blind to their real and functional environment. As a result, information about art (and not introduction to art) has for a long time remained cautious. This caution is fed by certain specialists in esthetics who declare that "any method likely to allow the blind to understand colors or the contents of a painting is of interest, but is situated in the cultural domain of enriching knowledge and not in the domain of esthetic experience" (Vanbelle 1982). A work like Bonhommeau's one (1979) tries to propose an opening up "towards drawing", but it has mostly been used for illustrating mathematical, scientific or geographical texts. The attempts to enhance tactile efficiency by training is based on these findings. Its supporters concentrate their efforts on information which may be qualified as encyclopedic instead of esthetic, and in doing so they exploit the original aspects of tactile exploration (thus preserving the "cultural originality" of blindness).

For example, in France, the Chardon Bleu Publisher opted for illustrations which presents characters (e.g. *Astérix* by Poncet 1988) as they are drawn by the young early blind. The publication of *Liège 92. Monet au bout des doigts* (*"Monet at your fingertips"*) also showed the authors concern with giving information on the objective and functional contents of Monet's paintings and not on the painted work itself. Each painting is spread over two pages: On one, a schematized transcription of the picture is coded with textures relating to the environment represented (grooves for "water or sea", grid for "vegetation", a smooth texture for "light, sky or reflection", etc.). On the other page, a braille text contains the work identification sheet and a brief enumeration of what is presented on the left page. The book is accompanied by an audio cassette. A voice gives the page numbers and talks about Monet's biography. But if, as Degas said (quoted by Valéry 1938: 129), "a drawing is not a shape but a way of seeing a shape", Monet's impressionist technique which expresses "a way of seeing" and the artist's intention go beyond the illustrated or commented presentation of the work for the blind proposed here.

The raised lines drawings proposed to the blind and severely visually handicapped people by the Louvre Museum, in Paris, are more interesting because they are more adapted to the tactile capacities. These raised lines and textured drawings reproduce only some selected paintings or mosaics in which the representation of perspective and depth is limited or absent in the original work. This is the case of ancient Egyptian art or Greek red and black paintings on vases, which can be easily apprehended tactually by the blind. This initiation to 2D works of arts is inserted in pedagogical workshops in which specialized guides give verbal and practical information about each work.

Another option defends the respect of the artists' intention and their desire to transmit "their way of seeing" in order to share an esthetic emotion. It favors the priority of exchange in the name of the right to universal access to art. This choice governed the publication of works such as *Van Gogh* (Garrandès 1990), *Cocteau envisagé ("Envisaging Cocteau")* (Garrandès 1992), or *Caresser Picasso ("Caressing Picasso")* (Garrandès 1990). In *Van Gogh,* the different tactile surfaces refer to a code of the colors and matters used by the artist. The choice of special papers to be embossed and the exact reproduction of *Picasso's* or *Cocteau's* lines make these books true *objects of art* proposed both to the blind and the sighted wanting "to rediscover the works tactually". They can be accompanied by metaphorical texts (in braille for *Picasso*, read by Jean Marais for *Cocteau*).

The few surveys we were able to carry out with the early blind seem to reveal a difficulty: These art books are not consultable by a blind person without the presence of a sighted guide who directs exploration. The "nice embossing" reduces tactile efficiency ("I couldn't read braille on this paper"), the absence of descriptive commentaries is a handicap for uninformed readers and the fact that lines are not stylized makes understanding difficult. Is this "difficulty" a part of the initiator's intention to privilege communication between the blind and the sighted?

3.2 Discovering three-dimensional works in museums

It is trivial to say that raised lines productions of pictorial or graphic works are transformations, *i.e.* material translations making them available to touch. But what about the tactile exploration of works which, although they were meant to be looked at, can be touched directly? Do these sculptural works imply too a translation when they are explored haptically?

There have been numerous attempts in the past to present three-dimensional sculptures to the blind (cf. Revesz 1950). Because of their material accessibility, it was first thought that no particular adaptation in their presentation was necessary, but the difficulties met in this domain have raised unsolved controversies. This may be illustrated by the testimonies of two blind people representing the two groups evoked above: Borges (1935/1993:350), who was a late blind, described *La chambre des statues ("The Statues Room")* in the following way: "All the figures were round or humped, a blind person could have recognized them via touch alone." On the other hand, Villey (1914/1954:309), who was early blind, claimed in his chapter concerning art that "What is especially striking in a group of blind left to itself is its general indifference to the works of sculpture." We will examine separately the problems posed for sculptors and museum curators, and for the blind.

3.2.1 *Problems posed for sculptors and curators.*

Artists are sometimes reluctant to allow their works to lose what light can bring to the perception of volume: "A bust is not the copy of the protuberances and grooves of a face as they are presented to us: It is their translation through a form which expresses them as they appear transformed by light" (Gimond 1969:23). Furthermore, and above all, curators do not want to let fingers alter heritage works.

This reluctance has led to very varied solutions in itineraries proposed to the blind in museums. Some itineraries are simply marked by braille cards and the visually impaired people can explore haptically the exposed objects. This occurs generally in regional museums presenting everyday objects. Sometimes, for example in Brussels and Paris (Louvre museum, Rodin museum), visually impaired people are allowed to explore haptically 3D sculptures when these sculptures are made of a material hard enough to resist to hand exploration. But very often, specialized rooms offer plaster or resin molded reproductions of the most known works, associated with the intervention of specialized guides (Brussels, Barcelona, Paris, etc.).

3.2.2   *Problems posed for the blind*

For the blind, the first problem concerns texture. The use of gloves (in Anglo-American countries) or the plaster or resin casts (in the Louvre's specialized room) puts off certain blind people because they lose one of the main principles likely to give them esthetic pleasure: The texture of the materials. Indeed, how could stone "veils" (e.g. the tunic in Rude's *La Marseillaise*) evoke the fluttering of a light cloth, when their tactile characteristics are actually more aggressive than the Alps on a geographical relief map? In the same way, in a study proposing Gallo-roman statues to the blind, we observed the difficulty of the (early) blind in accepting that the same texture could represent the face, the hair and the clothes.

The tactile apprehension of shape also poses some problems because, as already seen, touch is much less adapted than vision to this property (cf. Chapter 8). In order to initiate the blind to plastic arts, Eaton (1971) and Fukurai (1974) insisted on the creative activity (modeling) rather than on the strictly exploratory aspect which is considered as random for understanding the work. Difficulties can also result from the artist's technique: A sculptor such as Pompon "satisfies" touch because "details which do not serve to understand volume are suppressed" (Arnold 1938). But a number of blind people visiting the Rodin Museum in Paris "give up" when they discover the works of Camille Claudel because their hands get lost in too much details.

Finally, great difficulties are linked to the encoding processes necessary to interpret the information given by form. Thus, a blind teacher has been delighted to discover facial expressions thanks to a visit to the Rodin Museum and she highlighted the benefit of initiation and explanation of the volumes she was touching in order to discover their meaning. In the same way, the subjects confronted with the Gallo-roman works encountered problems in the recognition of busts when they were greater than one and a half times the real size, which refers back to the problem of changing scale discussed above.

Whatever it may be, 3D sculptural works are more adapted to touch than 2D raised lines drawings depicting paintings. That is why an original method is used in the Museum for the Blind in Bologna (Italy). Some very known paintings, such as the Jocund of Leonardo da Vinci, or the Venus of Botticelli, have been reproduced (and partly simplified) by local artists as bas-reliefs sculptures on a vertical wall. Thus, the shape of the face and body of the Jocund may be explored haptically by visually impaired people guided by a specialized teacher. According to some trained blind adults we questioned, these reproductions give a more correct idea of the true painting than raised drawings and, in addition, they may too lead to esthetic pleasure.

4. Conclusion

In this chapter, we examined the problems posed by the perception of two-dimensional symbolic graphics (maps and drawings) by the blind, especially the early blind, then we enlarged this analysis to include the procedures allowing the blind to have access to works of art.

Maps, which give spatial information, may be useful from the age of 6 to 8 years, provided that they are very simple and above all aligned, so that they do not require mental rotations. But learning is necessary for the early blind to understand the correspondence between the plane space of the map and the three-dimensional space it represents. Raised line drawings represent objects with their properties of shape, size, etc. Contrary to what happens with sighted children, the identification of drawings by the blind is much more difficult than their production. Kennedy (1997) found the same encoding rules in drawings by the blind as in drawings by the sighted (contours and sometimes masking). But very often other rules are observed. Identification (recognizing a daily object in a raised line drawing) is difficult if the category to which the object belongs is not made clear. However, even the congenitally blind people know the effects of changing the observer's point of view, as they are successful in simple tasks adapted from Piaget and Inhelder's (1947) "three mountains" test.

Experimental studies on the blind's use of drawings thus show a certain capacity to exploit this material. Yet, the totally blind rarely draw spontaneously because this graphic mode is not very adapted to touch. Raised maps have a more understandable immediate practical use as they help displacement and thus autonomy. Learning to use them, often laborious, is now a part of training for the young. The number of maps (town and neighborhood plans) available commercially is still small but should develop.

Knowing the difficulties faced by the blind in tactually apprehending information transmitted by two-dimensional supports, how can this population be given access to pictorial art and to the resulting esthetic emotions experienced by the sighted? The solutions which have so far been proposed are still not very satisfactory: The search for tactile efficiency favors the informative aspect over the artistic and emotional aspect, and respecting the artist's intention results in often incomprehensible products unusable by the blind. Sculptural 3D works, which one could expect to be more easily accessible to the blind, pose nevertheless a lot of problems for museum curators and for the blind themselves. Touch, which we have shown in this book that it is an efficient spatial modality however less adapted than vision to space perception and representation, here shows the limits of its capacity to replace vision.

References

Arnold, H. (1938). *Initiation à la sculpture*. Paris: Flammarion.

Bentzen, B. L. (1982). Tangible graphic displays in the education of blind persons. In W. Shiff & E. Foulke (Eds.), *Tactual perception: A source book* (pp. 387–403). Cambridge: Cambridge University Press.

Berlà, E. P. (1982). Haptic perception of tangible graphic displays. In W. Shiff & E. Foulke (Eds.), *Tactual perception* (pp. 364–386). Cambridge: Cambridge University Press.

Blades, M. (1991). Wayfinding theory and research: The need for a new approach. In D. M. Mark & A. U. Franck (Eds.), *Cognitive and linguistic aspects of geographic space* (pp. 137–165). Dordrecht: Kluwer Academic Publishers.

Blades, M. & Spencer, C. (1987). The use of maps by 4–6-year-old children in a large scale maze. *British Journal of Developmental Psychology, 5*, 19–24.

Bluestein, N. & Acredolo, L. (1979). Developmental changes in map-reading skills. *Child Development, 50*, 691–697.

Bonhommeau, M. (1979). *Vers le dessin en relief des aveugles. (PhD, CAFPEADV)*. Paris: Fédération des Instituts de Sourds et Aveugles de France.

Borgès, J. L. (1935/1993). *La Chambre des statues*. In J. L.Borges (1993), *Œuvres Complètes, tome I*. Paris: Gallimard (collection La Pléiade)

Bris, M. & Morice, J. C. (1996). A differentiated analysis of raised line drawings: Proposal for a methodology on their conception. In D. Burger (Ed.), *New technologies in the education of the visually handicapped* (pp. 77–88). London/Paris: John Libbey Eurotext/INSERM.

Campbell, J. S. (1997). A code for reducing figure-ground ambiguities in tactile graphics. *Journal of Visual Impairment and Blindness, 91*, 175–181.

Carpenter, P. A. & Eisenberg, P. (1978). Mental rotation and the frame of reference in blind and sighted individuals. *Perception and Psychophysics, 23*, 117–124.

DeLoache, J. S. (1989). The development of representation in young children. In H. W. Reese (Ed.), *Advances in child development and behavior, Vol. 22* (pp. 2–38). New York: Academic Press.

Down, R. M. & Liben, S. L. (1987). Children's understanding of maps. In P. Ellen & C. Thinus-Blanc (Eds.), *Cognitive processes and spatial orientation in animals and man, Vol. 2* (pp. 202–219). Dordrecht, Netherland: Martinus Nijof.

Easton, R. D. & Bentzen, B. L. (1980). Perception of tactile route configurations by blind and sighted observers. *Journal of Visual Impairment and Blindness, 74*, 254–265.

Eaton, A. H. (1971). *Art not by eye*. New York: American Foundation for the Blind.

Espinosa, M. A. & Ochaita, E. (1998). Using tactile maps to improve the practical spatial knowledge of adults who are blind. *Journal of Visual Impairment and Blindness, 92*, 339–345.

Espinosa, M. A., Ungar, S., Ochaita, E., Blades, M., & Spencer, C. (1998). Comparing methods for introducing blind and visually impaired people to unfamiliar urban environments. *Journal of Environmental Psychology, 18*, 277–287.

Fukurai, S. (1974). *How can I make what I cannot see?* New York: Van Nostrand Reinhold.

Garrandès, C. (1986). *Van Gogh*. Nice: Editions Garrandes.

Garrandès, C. (1990). *Caresser Picasso*. Nice: Editions Garrandes.

Garrandès, C. (1992). *Cocteau envisagé*. Nice: Editions Garrandes.

Gimond, M. (1969). *Comment je comprends la sculpture*. Paris: ARTED, Editions d'Art.

Hatwell, Y. (in press). *Psychologie cognitive de le cécité précoce*. Paris: Dunod.

Heller, M. A. (1989). Picture and pattern perception in the sighted and the blind: The advantage of the late blind. *Perception, 18*, 379–389.

Heller, M. A., Brackett, D. D., Scroggs, E., Steffen, H., Heatherly, K. & Salik, S. (2002). Tangible pictures: Viewpoints effects and linear perspective in visually impaired people. *Perception, 31*, 747–769.

Heller, M. A., Calcaterra, J. A., Burson, L. L., & Tyler, L. A. (1996a). Tactual picture identification by blind and sighted people: Effects of providing categorical information. *Perception and Psychophysics, 58*, 310–323.

Heller, M. A., Calcaterra, J. A., Tyler, L. A., & Burson, L. L. (1996b). Production and interpretation of perspective drawings by blind and sighted people. *Perception, 25*, 321–334.

Heller, M. A. & Kennedy, J. M. (1990). Perspective taking, pictures, and the blind. *Perception and Psychophysics, 48*, 459–466.

Heller, M. A., Kennedy, J. M., & Joyner, T. D. (1995). Production and interpretation of pictures of houses by blind people. *Perception, 24*, 1049–1058.

Horsfall, B. (1997). Tactile maps: New materials and improved designs. *Journal of Visual Impairement and Blindness, 91*, 61–65.

Kennedy, J. (1982). Haptic pictures. In W. Schiff & E. Foulke (Eds.), *Tactual perception* (pp. 303–333). New York: Academic Press.

Kennedy, J. M. (1983). What can we learn about pictures from the blind? *American Scientist, 71*, 19–26.

Kennedy, J. M. (1997). Comment les aveugles dessinent. *Pour la Science, 233*, 76–81.

Kennedy, J. M. (2000). Recognizing outline pictures via touch: Alignment theory. In M. A. Heller (Ed.), *Touch, representation and blindness* (pp. 67–98). Oxford: Oxford University Press.

Kennedy, J. M. & Domander, R. (1984). Pictorial foreground-background reversal reduces tactual recognition by the blind. *Journal of Visual Impairement and Blindness, 78*, 215–216.

Kennedy, J. M. & Fox, N. (1977). Pictures to see and pictures to touch. In D. Perkins & D. Leondar (Eds.), *The arts and cognition* (pp. 118–135). Baltimore: John Hopkins University Press.

Kennedy, J. M., Gabias, P., & Nicholls, A. (1991). Tactile pictures. In M. A. Heller & W. Schiff (Eds.), *The Psychology of touch* (pp. 263–299). Hillsdale, NJ: Erlbaum.

Landau, B. (1986). Early map use as an unlearned ability. *Cognition, 22*, 201–223.

Levine, M., Jankovic, I. N., & Palij, M. (1982). Principle of spatial problem solving. *Journal of Experimental Psychology: General, 111*, 157–175.

Liben, L. S. & Down, R. M. (1989). Understanding maps as symbols: The development of map concepts in children. In H. W. Reese (Ed.), *Advances in child development and behavior, Vol. 22* (pp. 145–201). New York: Academic Press.

Loomis, J. M., Klatzky, R. L., & Lederman, S. J. (1991). Similarity of tactual and visual picture recognition with limited field of view. *Perception, 20*, 167–177.

Magee, L. E. & Kennedy, J. M. (1980). Exploring pictures tactually. *Nature, 278*, 287–288.

Marzoff, D. P. & DeLoache, J. S. (1997). Search tasks as measures of cognitive development. In N. Foreman & R. Gillett (Eds.), *Handbook of spatial research. Paradigms and methodology, Vol. 1* (pp. 131–152). Hove: Psychology Press.

Millar, S. (1975). Visual experience or translation rules? Drawing the human figure by blind and sighted children. *Perception, 4*, 363–371.

Millar, S. (1991). A reverse lag in the recognition and production of tactual drawings: Theoretical implications for haptic coding. In M. A. Heller & W. Schiff (Eds.), *The Psychology of touch* (pp. 301–325). Hillsdale: Erlbaum.

Millar, S. (1994). Understanding and representing space. Theory and evidence from studies with blind and sighted children. Oxford: Clarendon Press.

Pathak, K. & Pring, L. (1989). Tactual picture recognition in congenitally blind and sighted children. *Applied Cognitive Psychology, 3*, 337–350.

Piaget, J. & Inhelder, B. (1967). *The child's conception of space* (translated from: *La représentation de l'espace chez l'enfant*. Paris: Presses Universitaires de France, 1947). New York: W.W. Norton.

Poncet, O. (1988). *Astérix, par Touchtatis*. Lyon: Chardon Editions.

Pring, L. & Rusted, J. (1985). Pictures for the blind: An investigation of the influence of pictures on the recall of texts by blind children. *British Journal of Developmental Psychology, 3*, 41–45.

Revesz, G. (1950). *Psychology and art of the blind*. London: Longmans Green.

Rossano, M. J. & Warren, D. H. (1989a). Misaligned maps lead to predictable errors. *Perception, 18*, 215–219.

Rossano, M. J. & Warren, D. H. (1989b). The importance of alignment in blind subject's use of tactual maps. *Perception, 18*, 805–816.

Ungar, S., Blades, M., Spencer, C., & Morsley, K. (1994). Can visually impaired children use tactile maps to estimate directions? *Journal of Visual Impairement and Blindness, 88*, 221–233.

Ungar, S., Blades, M., & Spencer, C. (1995). Mental rotation of a tactile layout by young visually impaired children. *Perception, 24*, 891–900.

Ungar, S., Blades, M., & Spencer, C. (1996). The ability of visually impaired children to locate themselves on a tactile map. *Journal of Visual Impairement and Blindness, 90*, 526–535.

Ungar, S., Blades, M., & Spencer, C. (1997). Teaching visually impaired children to make distance judgements from a tactile map. *Journal of Visual Impairement and Blindness, 91*, 163–174.

Valéry, P. (1938). *Degas, danse, dessin*. Paris: Gallimard.

Vanbelle, F. (1982). Initiation des aveugles aux arts plastiques par le toucher dans le cadre de la recherche esthétique. *Actes des XIIIèmes Journées de l'Association de Langue Française des Psychologues Spécialisés pour Handicapés de la Vue,* Marseille 1982; (Publication 1989, pp. 32–38).

Villey, P. (1914/1954). *Le monde des aveugles*. Paris: Corti.

CHAPTER 16

Sensory substitution

Limits and perspectives

Charles Lenay, Olivier Gapenne, Sylvain Hanneton,
Catherine Marque and Christelle Genouëlle

A quarter of a century ago, in the preface to "Brain Mechanisms in Sensory Substitution", Paul Bach y Rita wrote:

> This monograph thus risks becoming outdated in a very short time since the development of refined sensory substitution systems should allow many of the question raised here to be answered, and some of the conclusions may appear naive to future readers. (Bach y Rita 1972)

As it turns out, this prediction is far from having been fulfilled: In spite of their scientific and social interest, their real effectiveness and a certain technological development, prosthetic devices employing the principle of "sensory substitution" are not widely used by the blind persons for whom they were originally destined. After a brief recall of the general principle of sensory substitution, we will advance several hypotheses to account for this situation. We will then identify some elements which may favor the conception and, especially, the usability of future devices. To this end, we will focus our analysis on the work of Bach y Rita, particularly well documented, concerning the TVSS (Tactile Vision Substitution System) since the 1960's. This choice is motivated by the extensive and exemplary nature of this research, devoted to the rehabilitation of a handicapped population, as an enterprise which is both technical and scientific in character. We will also present the specific interest of substitution systems employing tactile stimulation, and we will emphasize the essential coordination of fundamental and technological research in this area. In addition, besides their direct utility for handicapped persons, these devices open broad experimental and theoretical perspectives on cognition in general (brain plasticity, perception, intentionality, etc.)

1.   A review of sensory substitution devices

1.1   General functional principles

In general, the so-called "sensory substitution" systems transform stimuli characteristic of one sensory modality (for example, vision) into stimuli of another sensory modality (for example, touch). A sensory substitution system can be decomposed into three distinct components. A *sensor* permits the conversion of a certain form of energy (light, sound, mechanical or other) into signals that can be interpreted by an *(electronic) coupling system* which is then responsible for the coordinated activation of a *stimulator*. The stimulation is generally addressed to the cellular receptors of a sensory organ, and thus consumes electrical energy which can be converted into sound energy (as in the case of visual-acoustic devices) or into mechanical energy (visual-tactile devices). The sensors can be "active", that is to say they can emit and receive signals. This is the case, for example, in devices where the "sensor" component employs a telemetric principle (e.g. laser or ultrasound).

The term "sensory substitution", as such, denotes the ability of the central nervous system to integrate devices of this sort, and to constitute through learning a new "mode" of perception. It is to be noted that *action* on the part of the subject plays an essential role in this process, a point to which we shall return. In other words, sensory substitution can only be constituted and can only function through an ongoing exploratory activity with the sensors. Finally, the access to a mode of perception that is offered by sensory substitution devices after the requisite learning period can be described as "implicit", in other words it makes no call on conscious reasoning concerning the sensations produced by the system of stimulation.

1.2   A non-exhaustive panorama

On account of the relative independence of the three components of these systems, and the great diversity of types of sensors and stimulators which are available at the present time, there are a large number of potential sensory substitution systems, many of which have been realized. In this section, we cannot therefore give a detailed comparative inventory of all such prosthetic devices, even restricting ourselves to the tactile modality. These devices are technically very varied, since their development corresponds to diverse objectives: Aids for handicapped persons, the ergonomics of interfaces, fundamental research or, again, performance in the realms of games or art. This pluridisciplinary aspect means that the literature dealing with this approach is highly dispersed, but the reader may consult several works which present a certain number of these techniques (Barfield & Furness 1995; O.F.T.A. 1996; Sampaio 1995; Warren & Strelow 1985).

It nevertheless seems desirable to give the reader an overview of the "state of the art" in this domain. To this end, we present a table of examples of systems incorporating various sensory modalities. Some of the technologies cited are not complete sensory substitution systems (they are only single components, sensors or stimulators), but these elements are likely, in our view, to participate in the future evolution of these devices. It is to be noted that from the point of view of their technological development, many of these systems currently benefit from the miniaturization of sensors and stimulators. For example, high-performance cameras, of very small size, are now available on the market at low cost (in particular the camera using the CMOS technology); And some research groups are working on tactile stimulation systems which provide high resolution on a very small surface (Exeter Fingertip Stimulator Array; Chanter & Summers 1990). We shall return in what follows to the important role of miniaturization in the appropriation of these prosthetic devices.

1.3   The results obtained with the TVSS

The TVSS ("tactile vision substitution system") makes it possible to convert the image captured by a video camera into a "tactile image". In the standard version, the tactile image is produced by a matrix of 400 activators (20 rows and 20 columns of solenoids of one millimeter diameter). The matrix is placed either on the back (first version), or on the chest, or on the brow (Collins & Bach y Rita 1973). Many technical improvements have been introduced (miniaturization, image definition, electrical stimulation, etc), and this device is still commercially available under the label VideoTact^{TM} (Unitech Research Inc). Finally, it has recently been adapted with a view to being used by young babies (current research by E. Sampaio).

Equipped with the TVSS, blind (or blindfolded) subjects are almost immediately able to detect simple targets and to orient themselves. They are also rapidly able to discriminate vertical and horizontal lines, and to indicate the direction of movement of mobile targets. The recognition of simple geometric shapes requires some learning (around 50 trials to achieve 100% correct recognition). More extensive learning is required in order to identify ordinary objects in different orientations. The latter task requires 10 hours of learning in order to achieve recognition within 5 seconds.

Table 16.1. A non-exhaustive list of various sensory substitution systems. This table also includes single components (sensors or stimulators) which are available for incorporation in this context. Abbreviations: (EM) electromagnetic, (ET) electrotactile, (SMA) shape memory alloys, (PE) piezo-electric, (CA) compressed air, (CG) constraint gauge.

Type	Sensors	Stimulators	References
ETA[1]	5 ultrasound sensors	Stereophonic	Sonic Pathfinder™ (Heyes 1984)
ETA	2 ultrasound sensors	Monophonic	UltraSonic Torch™ (Kay 1965)
ETA/SSS[2]	3 ultrasound sensors	Stereophonic	Sonic Glasses™ (Kay 1974)
ETA/SSS	3 ultrasound sensors	Stereophonic	TriSensor (Kaspa™) distributed by SonicVison[LTD]
ETA/SSS	1 ultrasound sensor	Tactile (EM)	Mowat Sensor (Pulse Data Int. Ltd)
SSS	Video camera	Stereophonic	The Voice™ (Meijer 1992)
SSS	Video camera	Tactile (EM)	TVSS (20x20 tacteurs, Bach y Rita 1963)
SSS	CCD camera	Tactile (ET)	VideoTact™ (1996) Unitech Research Inc.
SSS	Acoustic (micro)	Tactile (EM)	Tactile Sound Transducer (Clark Synthesis)
SSS	Tactile (CG)	Tactile (EM)	EVTS (Orbitec, up to 20 stimulators)
SSS	CCD camera	Tactile (ET)	Tongue Display Unit (Bach y Rita et al. 1998)
	?	Tactile (PE)	Exeter Fingertip Stimulator Array, Chanter & Summers, 1998 (10×10 sur $1 cm^2$)
	?	Tactile (EM)	Tactile Feeling Display, Shinoda et al. 1998
	?	Tactile (SMA)	Form memory activators (Grant et Hayward 1997)
		Tactile (CA)	Stimulation using compressed air (Shinoda et coll., unpublished)
	CMOS camera	?	Low-cost technology allowing high miniaturization of the sensors
	Ocular implant	?	Stimulation of retinal ganglion cells Wyatt et Rizzo 1996
	Cortical implant	?	Schmidt et al. 1996

[1] ETA: "electronic travel aid".
[2] SSS "Sensory Substitution System".

An essential observation is that this capacity to recognize forms is accompanied by a "projection" of the objects which are perceived as existing in an external space. Initially, the subject only feels a succession of stimulations on the skin. But after the learning process described above, the subject ends up by neglecting these tactile sensations, and is aware only of stable objects at a distance, "out there" in front of him. A number of experimental observations confirm this externalization. For example, if the zoom of the camera is manipulated unknown to the subject, causing a sudden expansion of the tactile image, the subject takes characteristic evasive action (moving backwards and raising his arm to shield himself from what is interpreted as a dangerously approaching object whereas in fact the matrix of tactile stimulators is placed on the back of the subject; cf. Bach y Rita 1972:98). According to the accounts given by the subjects themselves, the irritations which can be caused by the tactile matrix are clearly distinguished from the perception itself. Blind persons discover perceptive concepts which are quite new for them, such as parallax, shadows, and the interposition of objects. Certain classical optical illusions are also reproduced (Bach y Rita 1972; Guarniero 1974). The TVSS has also been used successfully in a work situation, by a blind person who was able to perform a certain number of delicate operations on an automatic production line for diodes (for more details, see Sampaio 1995).

However, once the initial flush of enthusiasm has passed, it is legitimate to ask why these devices, first developed in the 1960's, have not passed into general widespread use in the daily life of the blind community. Paradoxically, an analysis of the possible reasons for this relative failure raises some of the most interesting questions concerning these devices. One way of addressing this question is to critically discuss the very term of "sensory substitution", which carries with it the ambiguity, and even the illusory aspect, of the aim of these techniques.

2.   Sensory substitution: A double illusion

2.1 It is not a "sensory" substitution

It is easy to understand, as a means of publicity and marketing, the value of the term "sensory substitution" in order to describe the device developed by Paul Bach y Rita: The device "enables the blind to see". Is this not an accomplishment close to a divine miracle? Nevertheless, the term is misleading and in many ways unfortunate. It implies that the essence of the innovation consists merely in a change in the sensory input, in providing a new channel for the acquisition of information about the world of light. In this case, the device would merely substitute the classical visual input via the eyes, by a hybrid input consisting of the video-camera and the matrix of tactile stimulators. If this were really all that is at stake, the work of Bach y Rita while not negligible, would have only a limited significance. If all that is to be achieved is to create artificial sensory inputs, would it not be better to use a matrix of electrodes directly implanted in the retina (Wyatt & Rizzo 1996) or even in the brain (Brindley 1973; Dobelle & Mladejovsky 1974; Dobelle et al. 1976; Schmidt et al. 1996)? This would make it possible to short-circuit the clumsy detour by the tactile stimulation, and to increase the quantity of information delivered.

However, this would be to miss the real point of Bach y Rita's work. On the contrary, his major discovery is that a mere sensory substitution is of little use. The great merit of his device is actually to demonstrate this very point experimentally. If one presents a blind person with static forms on the tactile matrix (the video-camera is immobile, simply placed on the table), the subject will merely feel a vague tickling sensation or irritation; he will be capable only of very vague distinctions. There will be no question of recognizing or locating external, distal objects:

> The process of perceptually learning to identify these forms with the TVSS is particularly revealing. The performance of all the subjects was never better than chance, even after 60 trials, if (1) the subjects were not able to manipulate the camera, and (2) if they were not given feedback as to whether their responses were correct.   (Sampaio 1995)

On the other hand, if the handicapped person was able to manipulate the camera (movements from left to right, up and down, zoom back and forward, focusing, and the diaphragm), the subject rapidly developed spectacular capacities to recognize forms. He starts by learning how variations in his sensations are related to his actions. When he moves the camera from left to right, he feels on his skin that the stimuli move from right to left. When he uses the zoom, the stimuli "expand" or "contract". After having learned to point the camera in the direction of the target, he discriminates lines and volumes, and then recognizes familiar object of increasing complexity, to the point of being able to discriminate faces.

The work of Bach y Rita is therefore important not only because it is a useful technological innovation, but also because it provides original experimental tools for exploring fundamental mechanisms in perception. These tools make it possible to follow with precision the constitution of a new sensory modal-

ity in the adult. In particular, by providing the means to observe and reproduce the genesis of intentionality, i.e. consciousness of something as external
(the "appearance" of a phenomenon in a spatial perceptive field), these tools
make it possible to conduct experimental studies in an area usually restricted
to philosophical speculation.

From a neurophysiological point of view, sensory substitution opens new
possibilities for studying the extraordinary plasticity of the brain that the use of
these prosthetic devices seems to imply. Tactile sensory input is quite different
from visual input from the retina, and control of camera movements by the
hands is quite different from commands to the eye muscles. Nevertheless, the
brain appears to be able to organize a perceptive world with forms and events
quite analogous to those given in visual perception. Moreover, if the matrix
of tactile stimulators is displaced from the chest to the back, and the camera
held in the hands is replaced by a miniature camera fixed to the frame of some
spectacles, the adaptation is practically instantaneous. The subject recovers a
distal perception in a few seconds. The functional restructuring of the brain
poses fascinating problems for conceptualizing and modeling the mechanisms
of the reorganization of functional neural networks.

On a functional level, these devices put into question the classical conception of perception and cognition based on parallel processing of passively received information. In that conceptual framework, the cognitive system is only
a computational system which receives input information which is then processed in order to produce representations of objects and events; reasoning on
the basis of these representations then, in certain cases, leads to decisions concerning subsequent adaptive actions. It is well known that this conception of
cognition is based on the computer metaphor, and carries the implication that
computers could, in principle, be *substituted* for any other cognitive system. As
a corollary, it is generally considered that the cognitive system is immersed in a
world which contains information, a world which in the last resort *is* nothing
other than information. This conception finds a concrete technical expression
in systems of "virtual reality", with the horizon of entirely *substituting* reality
by a system which delivers sensory input in the form of information which
has been calculated on the basis of a virtual "environment" which includes the
effects of the actions of the subject (Luciani 1996). Thus, in modern technological developments, the current conception of cognition as information processing finds two sorts of concrete manifestations which serve both as a guiding
analogy and as a theoretical horizon: On the side of the subject, the computer as
a system of computation and decision; on the side of the object, virtual reality
as a system for computing the information available to the subject. By con-

trast, when we consider the devices of Bach y Rita as they actually function in practice, it is no longer possible to conceive of cognition and perception as the simple processing of information received from the outside. This radical criticism of the computational theory of mind has hitherto been based on philosophical considerations and certain results in experimental psychology. Here, however, the empirical proof is direct: *There is no perception without action.*

This key idea, that there is no perception without action, finds a particularly vivid illustration in an experiment that we have carried out recently with a substitution device simplified in the extreme: A single photoelectric cell fixed on a finger is connected to a simple vibrator held in the other hand. (Lenay, Canu, & Villon 1997). The vibrator is activated in all-or-none fashion above a threshold in the photoelectric cell; the receptive field is quite wide, corresponding to a cone of about 20° visual angle. Thus there is a single point of tactile stimulation, corresponding to a single receptive field (compared with the TVSS which has 400 points of stimulation corresponding to the same number of distinct receptive fields in the retina of the camera). Nevertheless, after several minutes of exploration, a blindfolded subject who is able to freely move the arm and the hand with the photoelectric receptor is able to succeed in localizing a light source, i.e. to indicate its direction and approximate distance. When the subject achieves greater mastery of the active production of tactile stimulations, he is conscious of the presence of an object situated in the space in front of him. It seems to the subject that the temporal succession of sensations derive from different "contacts" with a single distal object. It is to be noted that the vibrator can be moved to another region of the skin without disturbing this perception of the distal object. In fact, the subject appears to ignore the position of the tactile stimulations (unless he consciously refocuses his attention on that aspect of the situation) to the benefit of an apprehension of the spatial position of the light source. Conversely, artificial stimuli produced independently of the movements of the finger on which the photoelectric cell is placed are not associated with a distal perception, but continue to be perceived proximally at the level of the skin. Similarly, if the movements cease, the distal spatial perception disappears. If the finger is completely immobilized, the tactile stimulation is either continually present, or continually absent, but in either case nothing induces the subject to infer an external distal source. In order for perception to arise, a continual activity is necessary, consisting of oscillatory movements of the hand together with displacements of the wrist in such a way that the stimulation continually appears and disappears.

In a similar vein, in order to enlarge this field of empirical research, we have embarked on a research program concerning the perception of 2-dimensional shapes. This program involves both the technological development of simple prosthetic devices, and the elaboration of experimental protocols concerning the forms of activity which lead to successful perception and recognition of the shapes. Our preliminary results (Hanneton et al. 1998; Ali Ammar et al. 2002; Sribunruangrit et al. 2002) clearly demonstrate that shape recognition is possible with even minimal forms of sensori-motor coupling. A point of interest in this approach is that the perception of shapes takes time, and requires the external deployment of exploratory activity. Precisely for this reason, traces of the patterns of exploration can be easily stored for subsequent analysis. Analysis of these dynamic patterns shows that experienced subjects deploy identifiable strategies, which can and must be learned in order for rapid and reliable perception to occur successfully.

The essential role of action in the progressive emergence of structured percepts strongly suggests that what is perceived, or recognized, does not derive from invariants in the sensory information, but rather from invariants in the sensori-motor *cycles* which are inseparable from the activity of the subject. It is by his action that the subject seeks and constructs the "rules" of constant relations between actions and subsequent sensations. Spatial localization, as well as form recognition, correspond to temporal syntheses of successive sensations in accordance with a rule relating action and sensation. Even if this conception is now quite widespread in research on sensori-motor coupling in general (Berthoz 1991; Gibson 1966; Paillard 1971; Turvey & Carello 1995) and its genesis (Lepecq, Jouen, & Gapenne 1995), a proper definition and/or modeling of the notion of "sensori-motor invariant" remains however to be formulated.

If, as seems to be the case, perception is only possible when the subject can actively master the means of acquiring sensations, it follows that the device of Bach y Rita does not so much achieve a simple sensory substitution, but rather a *sensori-motor* substitution. The richness of the perception depends quite as much on the qualities of the actions (mobility, rapidity, zoom, etc.) as on the qualities of the sensations (sensitivity, spectral width, number of sensors, etc.). This is well illustrated by the astonishing capacity to recognize faces with devices which only give 400 points of sensory input. The face that is recognized results as a higher-level invariant on the basis of changes in sensation associated with active exploration.

2.2 It is not a sensory "substitution"

If one had to persist with the idea of a substitution, the notions of "*sensory-motor* substitution system", or "*perceptual* substitution", would be preferable to "sensory substitution". However, we now wish to argue that the second reason why the phrase "sensory substitution" is misleading and unfortunate, is that what is at stake is not a substitution. The warning came from the visually handicapped persons themselves, who expressed disappointment at the very time when they began to discover this novel mode of access to objects situated at a distance in space. Certainly, these devices made it possible to carry out certain tasks which would otherwise have been impossible for them. However, this was not the fundamental desire which motivated the blind persons who lent themselves to these experiments. A blind person can well find personal fulfilment irrespective of these tasks for which vision is necessary. What a blind person who accepts to undergo the learning of a coupling device is really looking for, is rather the sort of knowledge and experience that sighted persons tell him so much about: The marvels of the visible world. What the blind person hopes for is the *joy* of this experiential domain which has hitherto remained beyond his ken.

Now the problem is that this is not what the device procures. In fact, there are a large number of differences between this artificial coupling device and normal vision: There is no color, a small number of points, a camera whose movements are limited and clumsy, all of which slows down the recognition of a situation. This novel sensori-motor coupling resembles vision in many ways, but the quality of lived experience that it procures is quite different – as can be readily appreciated by sighted subjects who are blindfolded for the purposes of the experiment. The device of Bach y Rita does not produce a sensory *substitution,* but rather an *addition,* the creation of a new space of coupling between a human being and the world. The sensory substitution devices upset the classical definitions of the diverse sensory modalities.

It would be vain to believe that one has alleviated the suffering of a blind person just by giving him access to a sort of information. What is always at stake is the insertion of the person in a world of shared meanings, which depend on a personal history whose coherence must not be brutally shattered. Now what is cruelly missing in this new perceptual modality is what Bach y Rita calls the *qualia,* i.e. the values and the quality of lived experience associated with perceived entities. If one shows a person blind from birth an image of his wife, or if one shows some students pictures of nude women, the disappointment is complete: Their perception does not convey any emotion. But after the event, it is clear that it is the reverse which would have been astonishing. Meaning or emotional significance are not things that are already there, in the world, just waiting to be picked up like a piece of information. Here again, by the failure of its initial ambition, the device of Bach y Rita provides a crucial empirical proof: An isolated subject cannot attribute an existential meaning to objects and events that he perceives simply on the basis of a new perception. Does it follow that something essential is lacking in these devices? Unable to give a "content" to the perception (color, value), they demonstrate what distinguishes natural perception from a simple capacity to discriminate and categorize. There is a striking similarity between these observations, and reports of the absence of emotion and meaning felt by persons blind from birth who recover sight by removal of a cataract. In other words, it is not the principle of sensory substitution as such which is responsible for the impossibility of gaining access to qualia (Gregory 1990).

It is remarkable that in all the observations reported in the literature, it is always a question of a purely individual use of these devices. The user is surrounded by sighted persons, but is isolated in his particular mode of perception. Now it is plausible to suppose that perceptual *values* are closely linked to the existence of a shared history and collective memory, a memory which can only emerge in the course of interactions between several subjects in a common environment. This suggests possible experiments in the future. In any event, it seems to us that the term "perceptual supplementation" is more appropriate than "sensory substitution". This new term implies that these devices do not exactly remedy a deficit, but rather that they introduce perceptual modalities that are quite original.

The sensori-motor coupling devices thus give rise to experimental research into a deep problem, classically restricted to philosophy and psychology, concerning the origin and the nature of the *value* attached to things. A purely intellectual link inferred between a perceived form, and a feeling of pleasure or pain in another sensory modality, does not seem to be immediately sufficient to confer an emotional value to the form in question.

3.   Defining the conditions of appropriation

3.1   Ergonomic constraints

The ergonomic properties, in a wide sense, play an important role in determining the acceptability of these devices. The necessary qualities are in large part dictated by the principles just referred to which condition the success of "sensory substitution". Thus, given the importance of the role of action in the deployment of these new modes of perception, a prosthetic device which hinders the exploratory movements of the subject is to be avoided. This constraint leads to a requirement for developing systems which are light and autonomous. The systems of tactile stimulation which employ electromagnetic transducers do not currently fulfill this requirement. Even though they are very effective and simple to use, in their present state of development they are heavy and require a large amount of energy, so that in order to be autonomous they require batteries which are also heavy. Of course, the difficulties involved in producing a device which is light and autonomous increase with the resolution of the tactile stimulation. In addition, in order to function well as a prosthetic device, the ideal system should be easy to "put on" or to "take off", like the spectacles used by sighted persons. However, the device should also be robust. Since the aim is that the device should integrate the daily life of a person who already has to cope with the anxiety and stress of a partial inadaptation to the environment, it would not be reasonable to propose a system which is fragile and liable to break down.

When it comes to aesthetic criteria, an apparent contradiction arises: The device should lend itself to being "forgotten" by the user and those around him, yet at the same time it should "advertise itself" when the situation requires. A sensory device should be sufficiently discreet so as not to reinforce the handicap, and to avoid the user being perceived as a "technological monster". Miniaturization is not the only solution to this problem; it is quite possible to follow the shape of usual objects present on the site where the device is to be used. For example, a device aimed at providing access to graphic information on a computer screen could advantageously take the form of a mouse. At the same time, even though it may seem to contradict the previous principle, the appearance of the device can also fulfill a symbolic function. The traditional white color of a blind person's cane has the advantage of signaling to others the fragility of this person while undertaking a journey. Finally, another aspect which is important even if it is not strictly ergonomic is the cost of the device. Systems analogous to the TVSS currently available on the market employ advanced technology, and are produced in small numbers, with the result that their cost is virtually prohibitive (45000 $ for VideoTact, the electrotactile stimulation system with 768 points produced by the Unitech company).

3.2 Adaptation to real expectations

It seems to us that the appropriation of a sensory substitution device depends on it corresponding to a real need of the relevant population. We have identified two main preoccupations. The first need concerns the population of visually handicapped persons using computer technology to study, work or simply communicate. The availability of vocal synthesis, Braille keyboards and systems for optical character recognition has until now at least partially fulfilled this need in the case of operating systems (Dos, Unix) which code the information in the form of asci characters. However, the rapid and inexorable development of operating systems which employ mainly a graphical access to computers functionalities is leading to serious discouragement in this population which has already made a tremendous effort to adapt. To the extent that the transformation of graphic or iconical information into the form of tactile stimulation does not present a major technological difficulty, the application of sensory substitution techniques to this area ought to be fairly easy (for example, the Internet site of the Unitech company: http://www.execpc.com/~unitech/winhapt.html).

The second need concerns a wider population. The traditional white cane gives precious assistance in locomotion and avoiding obstacles. However, it does not give access to a distal perception, without contact, of the global scene. A mode of distal perception, ideally coupled with the cane without replacing it, would greatly facilitate the anticipation of movements, for example by making it possible to extract from the environment static or mobile silhouettes of obstacles to be avoided. Other potential applications, such as the access to reading or writing in black and white (such as the Optacon) are less crucial, particularly since they are in competition with proven systems such as braille. It is quite possible to imagine a system which would fulfil conjointly the two needs just described, the reading of graphical information on a computer screen and the distal perception of the structure of a scene. Such a system would have the immense advantage of authorizing a perceptual continuity in the daily life of a visually handicapped person, and would be all the more easily accepted.

3.3 The importance of modes and protocols of learning

Even if the observations reported by Paul Bach y Rita indicate that adaptation to the TVSS can be surprisingly rapid, it is important to remain realistically lucid and to recognize that even the most user-friendly device will inevitably require a substantial learning process. It is revealing that the Optacon device is delivered with an instruction manual which includes a set of progressive exercises which are essential for learning to use it effectively. This manual associates instructions in braille and a corresponding printed figure. The pedagogical quality of the instructions is clearly a key factor in successful appropriation, and is in itself a subject for further research. However, it seems to us that it is also important to take into account the conditions under which the learning is conducted. It is indeed possible that one of the reasons for the relative failure of sensory substitution systems to date lies in the nature of the relation which arises, in the laboratory, between the blind person and the experimentalist who "tests" the capacity of the subject to "see" the objects that are presented to him. When designing a learning protocol, it is important to bear in mind that a sensory device does not give rise to a sort of "degraded vision", but rather to an entirely new mode of perception which should be *shared* by the instructor and the pupil. Using the system should give rise to a *shared* experience, and it is only in this context that one can hope that learning will also produce the attribution of qualia to the percepts.

Finally, we also consider that it would be vain and pretentious to imagine that sighted persons could know, in advance, the best way of learning how to use a sensory device. Thus, the immersion of the system in an appropriate environment will not only make it easier to take into account the experience and the suggestions of the people for whom the system is designed, but may well lead to the emergence of modes of use and appropriation which were not foreseen by the designers.

3.4 The "intrinsic" effectiveness of sensory substitution

When the conditions of appropriation are properly taken into account as just discussed, the intrinsic effectiveness of sensory sensation is, perhaps paradoxically, the point which leaves the least room for discussion. The basic possibility of "sensory substitution" seems to be a very general principle, having its source in the plasticity of the central nervous system and for that reason being relatively independent of the sensory modalities involved. A question does arise as to the incapacity of the scientific community to mobilize for a project which is fascinating and useful (both from the point of view of fundamental research and technological innovation), but which does disturb conventional barriers between academic disciplines.

4.   Touch and sensory substitution

To start with, we will note some of the advantages of a tactile sensory input, rather than auditory input as in a number of existing devices (Sonic Guide, The Voice). The advantages of touch are of three types. Tactile stimulators can be easily dissimulated; the person using the device is thus the only one with access to the stimulation. Secondly, if the tactile stimulations are situated on regions of the skin that are rarely used (the chest, the back of the hand...), they do not interfere with other sensory modalities that are inevitably strongly exploited by visually handicapped persons. Finally, stimulation of the cellular receptors which contribute to the sense of touch make it possible to transmit information *in parallel* to the central nervous system. This parallelism of the sense of touch has been the object of some discussion (see for example Bach y Rita 1972: 15). However, a number of experiments (including those with the TVSS) have shown that this parallelism can be exploited, and that sensory sub-stitution devices are able, via the sensory-motor coupling, to give rise to per-ceptive resolutions superior to those of the material resolution of the matrix of stimulators. This property, shared by "natural" perceptive systems, is called "hyperacuity". By comparison, in the case of an auditory stimulation, it is more complicated to use the parallel properties of the internal ear. The conversion of an image into an auditory event requires the invention of a coupling device capable of recoding into two sound waves (if stereophonic sound is used) the spatio-temporal properties of an image (Meijer 1992). On the other hand, it is theoretically possible to reproduce the topography of a visual image directly on the surface of the skin.

It must nevertheless be noted that, even if these three properties mean that tactile stimulation is probably the best solution for sensory substitution, certain technological obstacles remain to be overcome. Indeed, the two techniques of stimulation that have been used to date have certain defects that are almost pro-hibitive. Electromagnetic stimulatory systems are heavy and consume a large amount of energy. The electrotactile systems produce stimulations that are of-ten felt as "disagreeable itching" on the skin, and furthermore require the use of a conducting gel. However, we may take the risk of sharing the optimism of Paul Bach y Rita; recent developments give reason to hope that these obstacles will soon be overcome. Bach y Rita et al. (1998) are currently experimenting with a system of stimulation in the mouth, which make it possible in parti-cular to dispense with a conducting gel. In addition, there are new alternative technologies with great promise, involving piezoelectric transductors (Chanter & Summers 1998) or alloys with shape-memory (Grant & Hayward 1997). It must be emphasized, however, that the development and optimization of effective stimulators with low energy requirements will only be possible if the physiological characteristics of the sensory receptors involved in touch are taken into account. Thus the electromagnetic systems, usually tuned to a frequency of about 250 to 300 Hz, mainly stimulate in a diffuse fashion sensory receptors with wide receptor fields on the skin. There would be a great advantage in exploiting the great variety in the sensitivity of the different cell-types involved in touch, in order to enrich the transductive capacities of these tactile interfaces (see Shinoda et al. 1998).

5.   Conclusion

As long as one holds fast to a classical conception of perception in terms of the acquisition of information, one will be stuck with the principle that it is always better to have access to more information. In this framework, persons with sensory handicaps will inevitably be considered as defective. We have proposed an alternative conception, in which "sensory substitution systems" are rather thought of as *supplementation* devices which bring about new modes of coupling with the environment. They do not make a difference disappear; rather, they create new differences – and they have applications which are not exclusively reserved for handicapped persons (for example, artistic applications, games, augmented reality, the development of portable and intuitive systems for the detection of heat, radioactivity, etc.). In spite of appearances, it is the classical perception which carries the germ of exclusion since it considers that the problem of handicapped persons lies in a quantitative difference. By contrast, true respect for the world of handicapped persons lies with better knowledge and understanding of the qualitative difference of possible perceptual modes.

Note

The authors expresses their thanks to Clotilde VanHoutte and John Stewart

References

Ali Ammar, A., Gapenne, O., Lenay, C., & Stewart, J. (2002). Effect of bimodality on the perception of 2D forms by means of a specific assistive technology for blind persons. In *Proceedings of the Conference (CVHI'2002) on Assistive Technology for Vision and Hearing Impairement* (pp. 45–52). Grenade, Espagne.

Bach y Rita, P. (1972). *Brain mechanisms in sensory substitution.* New York: Academic Press.

Bach y Rita, P. (1987). Brain plasticity as a basis of sensory substitution. *Journal of Neurological Rehabilitation, 2,* 67–71.

Bach y Rita, P. (1997). Substitution sensorielle et qualia. In J. Proust (Ed.), *Perception et intermodalité. Approches actuelles de la questions de Molyneux* (pp. 81–100). Paris: Presses Universitaires de France.

Bach y Rita, P., Kaczmarek, K. A., Tyler, M. E., & Garcia-Lara, J. (1998). Form perception with a 49-point electrotactile stimulus array on the tongue: A technical note. *Journal of Rehabilitation Research and Development, 35,* 427–430.

Barfield, W. & Furness, T. A. (1995). *Virtual environments and advanced interface design.* Oxford: Oxford University Press.

Berthoz, A. (1991). Reference frames for the perception and control of movement. In J. Paillard (Ed.), *Brain and space* (pp. 81–111). Oxford: Oxford University Press.

Brindley, G. S. (1973). Sensory effects of electrical stimulation of the visual and paravisual cortex. *The Journal of Physiology, 196,* 479–493.

Chanter, C. & Summers, I. (1998). The Exeter fingertip stimulator array for virtual touch: A preliminary investigation. (http://newton.ex.ac.uk/medphys/index.html)

Collins, C. C. & Bach y Rita, P. (1973). Transmission of pictorial information through the skin. *Advances in Biological Medecine and Physiology, 14,* 285–315.

Dobelle, W. H. & Mladejovsky, M. G. (1974). Artificial vision for the blind: electrical stimulation of visual cortex offers hope for a functional prosthesis. *Science, 183,* 440–444.

Dobelle, W. H., Mladejovsky M. G., Evans, J. R., Roberts, T. S., & Girvin, J. P. (1976). "Braille" reading by a blind volunteer by visual cortex stimulation. *Nature, 259,* 111–112.

Guarniero, G. (1974). Experience in tactile vision. *Perception, 3,* 101–105.

Gibson, J. J. (1966). *The senses considered as perceptual systems.* Boston, MA: Houghton Mifflin.

Grant, D. & Hayward, V. (1997). Variable structure control of shape memory alloy actuators. *IEEE Systems and Control Magazine 17,* 80–88.

Gregory, R. L. (1990). Recovery from blindness. In R. L. Gregory (Ed.), *Eye and brain: The psychology of seeing* (pp. 191–200). Oxford: Oxford University Press.

Hanneton S., Lenay C., Gapenne O., Vermandel S., & Marque C., (1998). Dynamique de la reconnaissance de caractères via une interface haptique. In D. Kayser, A. Nguyen-Xuan & A. Holley (Eds.), *Proceedings of the VIIe Colloque de L'Association pour la Recherche Cognitive ARC'98* (pp. 343–347).

Heyes, A. D. (1983). Human navigation by sound. *Physiological Technology, 14,* 68–76.

Kaczmarek, K. A. & Bach y Rita, P. (1995). Tactile displays. In W. Barfield & T. A. Furness, (Eds.), *Virtual environments and advanced interface design* (pp. 349–414). Oxford: Oxford University Press.

Kay, L. (1964). An ultrasonic sensing probe as a mobility aid for the blind. *Ultrasonics, 2*, 53.

Kay, L. (1974). A sonar aid to enhance spatial perception of the blind: engineering design and evaluation. *The Radio and Electronic Engineer, 44*, 605–627.

Lenay, C., Canu, S., & Villon, P. (1997). Technology and perception: The contribution of sensory substitution systems. In *Proceedings of the Second International Conference on Cognitive Technology, Aizu, Japan* (pp. 44–53). Los Alamitos: IEEE.

Lepecq, J. C., Jouen, F., & Gapenne, O. (1995). Sensorimotor organization and cognition in infancy: Some francophone contributions. *CPC – Current Psychology of Cognition, 14*, 121–150.

Luciani, A. (1996). Ordinateur, geste réel et matière simulée. In M. Borillo & A. Sauvageot (Eds.), *Les cinq sens de la création* (pp. 79–89). Seyssel: Editions Champ Vallon.

Meijer P. L. B. (1992). An experimental system for auditory image representations. *IEEE Transactions on Biomedical Engineering, 39*, 112–121.

O.F.T.A. (1996). *Nouvelles interfaces homme-machine. Série Arago, Vol. 18*. Paris: OFTA Editeur.

Paillard, J. (1971). Les déterminants moteurs de l'organisation de l'espace. *Cahiers de Psychologie, 14*, 261–316.

Sampaio, E. (1995). Les substitutions sensorielles adaptées aux déficits visuels importants. In A. B. Safran & A. Assimacopoulos (Eds.), *Le déficit visuel. Des fondements neuro-physiologiques à la pratique de la réadaptation* (pp. 197–211). Paris: Masson.

Schmidt, E. M., Bak, M. J., Hambrecht, F. T., Kufka, C. V., O'Rourke, D. K., & Vallabhanath, P. (1996). Feasibility of a visual prosthesis for the blind based on intracortical microstimulation of the visual cortex. *Brain, 119*, 507–522.

Shinoda, H., Asamura N., & Tomori, N. (1998). Tactile feeling display based on selective stimulation to skin mechanoreceptors. In *Proceedings 1998 IEEE International Conference. Robotics and Automation, Vol. 1* (pp. 680–686).

Sribunruangrit, N., Marque, C., Lenay, C., Gapenne, O., & Vanhoutte, C. (2002). Braille Box: Analysis of the parallelism concept to access graphic information for blind people. In *Proceedings of the Second Joint Meeting of the IEEE Engineering in Medicine and Biology Society and the Biomedical Engineering Society (EMBS-BMES 2002)* (pp. 2424–2425). Houston, USA.

Turvey, M. T. & Carello, C. (1995). Dynamic touch. In W. Epstein & S. Rogers (Eds.), *Handbook of perception and cognition: Perception of space and motion* (pp. 401–490). San Diego: Academic Press.

Warren, D. H. & Strelow, E. R. (1985). *Electronic spatial sensing for the blind*. Dochdrecht: Martinus Nijhoff Publishers.

White, B. W., Saunders, F. A., Scadden, L., Bach y Rita, P., & Collins, C. C. (1970). Seeing with the skin, *Perception and Psychophysics, 7*, 23–27.

Wyatt, J. L. & Rizzo, J. F (1996). Ocular implant for the blind. *IEEE Spectrum, 33*, 47–53.

CHAPTER 17

New technologies empowering visually impaired people for accessing documents

Dominique Burger

1. Introduction

Equal access to documents is a condition of equal inclusion in any modern society. This concerns education, professional achievement, as well as cultural integration or daily life. As a matter of fact, in most cases documents start in a digital form. Both when they are composed manually by their author using a word processor or automatically generated by a software after a request to a database server, electronic documents (e-documents) originate as series of digits in a computer memory. They can be stored in this microscopic form for years, decades or centuries. From this stage, e-documents are processed to be displayed using different rendering techniques: Ink print or screen display, braille embossing or braille refreshable display, for instance.

The tactile alphabet invented by Louis Braille at the beginning of the 19th century is perfectly suited to tactile perception, whose other chapters in this book remind the principles and the possibilities (cf. Chapter 14). Louis Braille had understood that his invention was a necessary condition for the inclusion of the blind at a time where the importance of written transmission of knowledge was about to grow tremendously. The binary coding system invented by Louis Braille rapidly proved to be superior to the large raised letters that were used to produce the first books for the blind in the late 18th century. But could Louis Braille foresee how his innovation would so perfectly correspond to the general evolution of techniques and to the progress of digital solutions to many industrial problems? Could he ever imagine how this simple binary coding system for information was anticipating by one century the advent of information theory? The braille concept was simple and robust as to apply to handy techniques like a slate and a stylus, to mechanic ones like Perkins typewriters, to electro-mechanic embossing, and finally to piezo-electric technology. Nowadays, the tremendous growth of computer desk applications and the Internet make this invention more useful and actual than ever. More than ever, the braille system is a key of the social integration of the blind.

In this chapter we discuss how written documents can be made accessible to the visually impaired using their electronic sources. First, we examine how new technologies can enrich the braille system itself. Then, we illustrate how they can improve the reading of a document. Finally, we discuss the question of adapting documents designed for sighted readers in this new context.

2.   Enriching braille

For around 20 years, many techniques have been beneficial to the braille writing system. Let us remind the most significant improvements of this evolution.

2.1 Electronics

Electronics and miniaturization have made possible to invent electro-mechanical components displaying any braille character. After various preliminary attempts, piezo-electric technology stabilized, around the end of the 70ties. The principle is quite simple: A piece of piezo-electric quartz to which a continuous

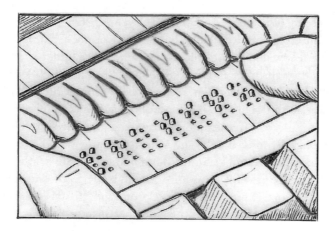

Figure 17.1. Cells of a braille display. On this figure, the raised dots are white and the buttons that are facing the braille cells can be used to point at each braille character. Thus, they can be used to emulate traditional mouse functions.

high voltage is applied modifies its shape with almost no electrical consumption. If the size and mechanical properties of the quartz are correctly chosen, it can move a small rod exactly the height of a braille dot. Six or eight rods compose a braille character. This principle made possible to produce braille cells whose size and weight, electrical consumption, noise and reliability are quite satisfactory. So that the first refreshable braille display could be manufactured with 20, 40 or 80 cells. These devices made accessible computer applications like word processors, spreadsheets, database software, electronic messageries, or even programming environments, and opened new professional opportunities to the blind (Figure 17.1).

A braille electronic display constitutes a small window for reading a document. This is a limitation when compared to traditional braille on paper. On the other hand, it opens new possibilities:

- The number of dots for coding braille has been extended from 6 to 8. This multiplies by four the number of possible combinations. This makes possible to enrich the presentation of braille texts, underlining words, for instance. Electronic display is refreshable or dynamic. This makes possible to produce effects like text blinking to enrich presentation (words can disappear during a short while and reappear);
- Braille becomes interactive, thanks to pointing buttons. Thus a braille display is not only an output device but an input-output device which can be used for entering rapidly information or commands to the computer;
- Text display can be synchronized with auditory of visual information. Thus, braille can be multimedia.

2.2 Speech

Synthetic speech produced by a text-to-speech (TTS) conversion software can be a complement to braille. While braille is stable under the fingers, synthetic speech is fugitive. But is does not need the hands nor the body. It allows to read a text on the fly more rapidly. Braille offers a better restitution of words' spelling. But spoken messages can bring information which is not contained in the braille text. Thus, combining speech and braille can be a solution to the relative poverty of braille for presenting textual data. If this combination respects some rules, reading a text or navigating in a document can be more efficient. It can also alleviate the mental burden of running a software application. Using speech necessitates only a short learning time and the cost of additional speech is minimal if compared to a braille device. In the future, speech synthesizers might be a component of any standard computer.

Also speech recognition progressed during the last decades as to become cheap and reliable enough for simple and usual tasks. Blind people can dictate a text or a command to a software application while controlling the feedback on a braille display.

2.3 Raised line images

Images can be a complement to text and reinforce its meaning. Often, a figure or a diagram conveys a concept more efficiently than a textual description. In some cases, images are necessary. In spite of the many studies done on the subject, there is no realistic technical process to create tactile images dynamically on a refreshable display. Nevertheless, some swell papers make possible to produce raised line drawings at a relatively low cost.

This special paper consists of millions of micro-capsules (containing alcohol) in an emulsion paint-like formula which is spread on to a backing paper. Once an image or diagram is produced, it is pushed through a heater machine. The black areas on the paper then expand in the heater whilst all other areas stay flat, hence creating a raised image that can be read by tactile contact (Figure 17.2).

This technique is quite affordable for schools and universities. Even individuals or family can use it so that raised line drawings can be disseminated in complement to texts in braille much easier than in the past. The image itself can be sent or downloaded as a file on any electronic support or from an Internet server.

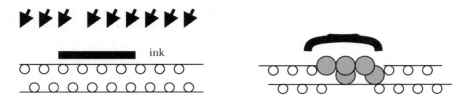

Figure 17.2. Swelling of micro-capsules under heat.

3. Electronic documents

Electronic documents are documents that have been stored in an electronic format on a magnetic memory support, like a disk or floppy-disk, or an optical one, like a CD- ROM. These supports have many advantages over traditional ones, like paper.

3.1 Capacity and size

Currently a CD-ROM can contain more than six hundred millions digits, equivalent to around four hundred thousands pages of a typewritten document. Only a few authors produce such an amount of literature during their lifetime! Moreover, an electronic document can contains text, images, sounds, and executable software, as well. Their costs have decreased tremendously during the past few years. They can easily be reproduced and even produced at home using a family computer, so that individuals can create their personal libraries. Each of us can have in his/her pocket a collection of favorite books to take on the desert island! Let us also consider that a family dictionary once transcribed in braille can take up 10 to 20 linear meters on a shelf, while an accessible encyclopaedia can be read on a CD-ROM, with a lot a computerized facilitating functions for browsing or searching items.

3.2 The reading interface

A computer is necessary to read an electronic document. This computer shall have a reading unit if the document is provided on a physical support or an Internet connection if the document is available from a Web server. It shall also run a software reader. This constitutes the reading interface.

From this point of view, the situation is not very different for a reader with a visual impairment or for a sighted reader, neither being able to read the electronic document directly with the eyes. For a sighted reader, the reading interface is based on a screen display, a keyboard and a mouse, while a blind person will use a keyboard and a braille refreshable display or a speech output. Both of them will need a set of functions for navigating through the document, marking pages or sections, or even annotating it. In some situations, sighted users will need non visual interfaces as well, when driving a car, or consulting an information server over the phone, for instance.

The reading interface performs operations on the document in order to display the requested information. It can be customized to accommodate to user preferences, like the font, the size or the color of the characters. Displaying the text in braille or reading it via a speech synthesizer are nothing more than alternative customization modes. There may be conversions rather performed by the braille display unit or by the TTS software, independently from the reading software. Similarly the choice of the braille code, depending on the language, the abbreviating system, can be set by the end-user as a customization feature. This last option has not to be decided upstream and imposed to the reader as it was the case with embossed braille.

3.3 Standardizing the coding

For around 15 years, standards have progressed considerably concerning computers, input/output protocols, user interfaces and software applications. It also concerns the coding of documents. A document produced using a word processing software in North America can be read elsewhere using another word processor on a totally different computer. There are different types of standardized formats and many tools to convert them to other formats. Converting a document from one format to another is made much easier when the coding respects the logical structure of the document and when the structure and the final presentation are specified separately. Standardization and structuration represent two key issues for the universal access to documents. It is worth mentioning here the work of the DAISY Consortium to promote a standard format matching special needs of people with print disabilities. For the moment the progress toward standardized braille is slow.

3.4 Navigation tools

The reading interface offers functions for navigating in the document. Large electronic documents use hypertext structures making possible to link words or sections between them. For instance, titles in the table of content can be linked to the start of the corresponding chapter. Notes can be linked to given words. These links can be static or calculated dynamically according to the need of the reader. For instance, the definition of a word can be linked to the word when the reader wants to access the dictionary. In any case a mechanism is provided for activating this links. These new techniques to read a document and to navigate through it are extremely useful for visually impaired people, as they provide a solution to the difficult manipulation of traditional braille documents. Moreover, sophisticated operations can be performed by computers like text search, statistics, semantic processing, translation, etc. Blind users may save time in using such possibilities and partly compensate the difficulties encountered for accessing a document globally or skimming it over.

3.5 Internet

The Internet combines the different innovations that brought electronic publishing. It put them to their extreme limits:

The World Wide Web constitutes a gigantic multilingual library with no foreseeable physical limitations. Electronic documents can be downloaded instantaneously from any node of this world-wide network for immediate or delayed reading. The connection cost is low. Books that had never been transcribed in braille or have been published in small number of issues can be made available over the Internet and generate multiple electronic copies.

However, this concerns mainly books in the public domain. For books submitted to copyrights, publishing companies develop new intellectual property right (IPR) management systems. Such systems are still experimental but should contribute to the increase of the amount of documents available on the Internet, and should serve the needs of people with visual disabilities.

The HyperText Markup Language (HTML), which derived from the Standard Generalized Marking Language (SGML), has become a standard for coding Web pages. HTML can specifies standard elements like title, paragraphs, tables, forms, images, using sets of textual tags. Once coded in HTML a document becomes purely textual. Images or multimedia elements receive an address in a universal system of references covering the internal disks of the computer or distant Internet servers, as well. An HTML document can therefore be analyzed or "parsed". The textual elements – which generally convey the main information – can be extracted and displayed in braille or passed to a TTS engine. Graphical elements, like images, figures, movies, or complex tables, can be bypassed or replaced by an alternative comment, if the author has included it in the HTML code.

Free search engines are available on the Web that can locate very quickly information on almost any subject. Their efficiency is getting better and better.

Unfortunately, only a few Web sites are really accessible to people with visual disabilities. One major reason is that their design is based on graphical models. Often the graphical elements have received no alternate description, or information is organized on the screen surface in a too complex hierarchy of frames. Inaccessibility can also simply reflect a general lack of clarity! In order to bring a solution to this problem, the W3C consortium has set up an international initiative called the Web Accessibility Initiative (WAI). The WAI objective is to promote guidelines world-wide concerning the universal access to Web services. Major hardware and software manufacturers take part actively in this initiative. Guidelines are disseminated in several languages. The concern of people with disabilities, especially blind people, is central in this initiative.

3.6 Economical aspects

The technological improvements we have reviewed in this chapter reflect the revolution that affects the publishing world, modifying in depth the way documents are produced, disseminated and read, but also the background of intellectual property. In the near future the economy of publishing will probably change thoroughly. For instance, the costs for duplicating and transporting an electronic document have decreased dramatically. This is even more actual for bulky volumes like braille books. Over the Internet these costs are vanishing, whatever the distance. Moreover, the time necessary for transferring a document becomes negligible. Many newspapers are published on the Web whose electronic issues are available even before the printed ones. Companies have been created for re-publishing rare books electronically at a reasonable cost. Unknown authors can promote their books directly on the Web even before finding a publisher. In the future, the price of documents might be estimated according to the number of megabytes they contain and which have to be transmitted. No doubt that all these changes will also affect the way people with visual disabilities will purchase books and documents.

4. Adapting documents

If the Internet constitutes a gigantic and immediate source of documents, is the adaptation of these documents – done by special transcription centers – still necessary?

Are these centers about to disappear? The answer is no. In fact, the mission of these centers should evolve too. Some activities should be abandoned, some new activities should develop.

Electronic documents – whatever their advantages – will not totally replace paper documents. A braille book provides a type of access to texts which is different and irreplaceable. The physical contact with a traditional book is a part of the pleasure of reading that most readers would not renounce to.

More fundamentally, the adaptation of documents requires the full understanding of the document that no computer but human experts can only have. The adaptation of non linear elements as tables, maths formulas, diagrams and illustrations require a know-how based on a long experience and a good knowledge of users. Nevertheless the Internet encourages the setting up of new co-operative models between publishers, transcription centers, schools and libraries for the benefit of the visually impaired. For instance, unified catalogues of adapted resources have been created collecting the references of books produced in a region or in a country. The electronic files of books can also be centralized and made available on a server for users who want to print them locally. In the future, secured mechanisms should make also possible for individual users to download them and to read them on their own computer system.

The adaptation centers could play a central role in testing multimedia products and Web services. They should assert their accessibility to people with visual disabilities. They would guarantee this accessibility via certificates delivered by experts which would be much reliable than automatic verification tools that are available on the Web.

Finally, these centers could contribute to raise the awareness of Web designers about the special needs of the visually impaired and the international recommendations. They should at least campaign and outreach information, or preferably set up training programmes.

5.   Conclusion

In this chapter we have analyzed how new technologies may improve the access to documents for people with visual disabilities. Certainly, such a significant revolution had not happened since the invention of Louis Braille. This revolution can be summarized in two essential points.

All users, sighted or not, will read information coming from a unique electronic source. There is no need any more to have a double system for producing documents as it has been the case for two centuries, with books produced in braille or large printed by organizations insulated from the publishing mainstream.

The transformation of an electronic document to make it accessible can be performed on a client-computer system equipped with special peripherals (braille printer or display, TTS synthesizer). This computer can be controlled by the end-user who can customize the user-interface and accommodate the document to his/her preferences. Some readers will prefer read large fonts and a certain combination of colors on the screen while others will prefer listen to a spoken text. Some will need a summary or a translation of the content. In this context, a blind user is less distinguishable by his/her visual handicap than by a type of equipment and software installed on his/her computer system.

Probably, this potential will take some time to come to its full realization. But the front lines of the fights for the social integration of people with visual disabilities have still been considerably modified.

The fight for a coherent evolution of the braille writing system, for its adaptation to the needs of a more and more technical world, for its standardization, is an urgent necessity. This urgency is to consider at an international level. National braille alphabets have to be stabilized, published on the Web by recognized authorities and made easily accessible from all over the world. One could object that in many countries several braille systems have coexisted for years and that attempts to unify them have failed most of the time, so that an international initiative should be even more hazardous. In fact, the possibility to personalize the user interface and the flexibility which exists within computers facilitates standardization. It is much easier to agree on standard that comports necessarily arbitrary aspects when the rigidity of a standard can be smoothed through personal adjustments.

The fight for an equal access to information remains fundamental. Today, this right means that the accessibility of electronic documents should be designed as to be accessible by all users independently of the platform they use. This concerns especially the Web documents. This is why the WAI international initiative has been set up by the W3C consortium, in order to produce and promote recommendations world-wide. The respect of these recommendations starting at the design phase can be done at a minimal cost and with general benefits for the final product. Contrary to a widespread opinion, it requests no special feature in the source documents so that it should easily be done for most electronic documents. If this effort were made systematically, the main additional cost for adapting electronic documents would be the cost of the personalized interface. But this interface is also needed for social and cultural integration at school, at work or at home. If we argue a little bit further, we rapidly discover that social inclusion generates richness that covers rapidly the cost of this assistive technology.

In this new context, the right to equal access to information can be defended in advocating the respect of design rules which should be considered as a priority, while the traditional advocacy for special and parallel adaptation centers should be revised.

The techniques we have evoked in this chapter are sophisticated and constantly evolving so that the organizations involved in the production of adapted books have not integrated them yet completely. We hope that this presentation can contribute to clarify some of the many questions raised by technological evolution and that it will help to orient the thoughts and fights in favor of a more inclusive society.

References on the Web[1]

Web Accessibility Initiative: www.w3.org/WAI
DAISY Consortium : www.daisy.org
New technologies for a more accessible society: Braillenet Conference, Paris, 28–29 April 2003
http://www.braillenet.org/colloques/bnet2003/villette2003/prog.htm
Books and electronic school bags for inclusive education of young visually impaired people: Braillenet Conference, Paris 3 May 2002
http://www.snv.jussieu.fr/inova/villette2002/

1. Web links valid on 20 June 2003.

Name index

Subject index

In the series ADVANCES IN CONSCIOUSNESS RESEARCH (AiCR) the following titles have been published thus far or are scheduled for publication:

1. GLOBUS, Gordon G.: *The Postmodern Brain.* 1995.
2. ELLIS, Ralph D.: *Questioning Consciousness. The interplay of imagery, cognition, and emotion in the human brain.* 1995.
3. JIBU, Mari and Kunio YASUE: *Quantum Brain Dynamics and Consciousness. An introduction.* 1995.
4. HARDCASTLE, Valerie Gray: *Locating Consciousness.* 1995.
5. STUBENBERG, Leopold: *Consciousness and Qualia.* 1998.
6. GENNARO, Rocco J.: *Consciousness and Self-Consciousness. A defense of the higher-order thought theory of consciousness.* 1996.
7. MAC CORMAC, Earl and Maxim I. STAMENOV (eds): *Fractals of Brain, Fractals of Mind. In search of a symmetry bond.* 1996.
8. GROSSENBACHER, Peter G. (ed.): *Finding Consciousness in the Brain. A neurocognitive approach.* 2001.
9. Ó NUALLÁIN, Seán, Paul MC KEVITT and Eoghan MAC AOGÁIN (eds): *Two Sciences of Mind. Readings in cognitive science and consciousness.* 1997.
10. NEWTON, Natika: *Foundations of Understanding.* 1996.
11. PYLKKÖ, Pauli: *The Aconceptual Mind. Heideggerian themes in holistic naturalism.* 1998.
12. STAMENOV, Maxim I. (ed.): *Language Structure, Discourse and the Access to Consciousness.* 1997.
13. VELMANS, Max (ed.): *Investigating Phenomenal Consciousness. Methodologies and Maps.* 2000.
14. SHEETS-JOHNSTONE, Maxine: *The Primacy of Movement.* 1999.
15. CHALLIS, Bradford H. and Boris M. VELICHKOVSKY (eds.): *Stratification in Cognition and Consciousness.* 1999.
16. ELLIS, Ralph D. and Natika NEWTON (eds.): *The Caldron of Consciousness. Motivation, affect and self-organization – An anthology.* 2000.
17. HUTTO, Daniel D.: *The Presence of Mind.* 1999.
18. PALMER, Gary B. and Debra J. OCCHI (eds.): *Languages of Sentiment. Cultural constructions of emotional substrates.* 1999.
19. DAUTENHAHN, Kerstin (ed.): *Human Cognition and Social Agent Technology.* 2000.
20. KUNZENDORF, Robert G. and Benjamin WALLACE (eds.): *Individual Differences in Conscious Experience.* 2000.
21. HUTTO, Daniel D.: *Beyond Physicalism.* 2000.
22. ROSSETTI, Yves and Antti REVONSUO (eds.): *Beyond Dissociation. Interaction between dissociated implicit and explicit processing.* 2000.
23. ZAHAVI, Dan (ed.): *Exploring the Self. Philosophical and psychopathological perspectives on self-experience.* 2000.
24. ROVEE-COLLIER, Carolyn, Harlene HAYNE and Michael COLOMBO: *The Development of Implicit and Explicit Memory.* 2000.
25. BACHMANN, Talis: *Microgenetic Approach to the Conscious Mind.* 2000.
26. Ó NUALLÁIN, Seán (ed.): *Spatial Cognition. Selected papers from Mind III, Annual Conference of the Cognitive Science Society of Ireland, 1998.* 2000.
27. McMILLAN, John and Grant R. GILLETT: *Consciousness and Intentionality.* 2001.

28. ZACHAR, Peter: *Psychological Concepts and Biological Psychiatry. A philosophical analysis.* 2000.
29. VAN LOOCKE, Philip (ed.): *The Physical Nature of Consciousness.* 2001.
30. BROOK, Andrew and Richard C. DeVIDI (eds.): *Self-reference and Self-awareness.* 2001.
31. RAKOVER, Sam S. and Baruch CAHLON: *Face Recognition. Cognitive and computational processes.* 2001.
32. VITIELLO, Giuseppe: *My Double Unveiled. The dissipative quantum model of the brain.* 2001.
33. YASUE, Kunio, Mari JIBU and Tarcisio DELLA SENTA (eds.): *No Matter, Never Mind. Proceedings of Toward a Science of Consciousness: Fundamental Approaches, Tokyo, 1999.* 2002.
34. FETZER, James H.(ed.): *Consciousness Evolving.* 2002.
35. Mc KEVITT, Paul, Seán Ó NUALLÁIN and Conn MULVIHILL (eds.): *Language, Vision, and Music. Selected papers from the 8th International Workshop on the Cognitive Science of Natural Language Processing, Galway, 1999.* 2002.
36. PERRY, Elaine, Heather ASHTON and Allan YOUNG (eds.): *Neurochemistry of Consciousness. Neurotransmitters in mind.* 2002.
37. PYLKKÄNEN, Paavo and Tere VADÉN (eds.): *Dimensions of Conscious Experience.* 2001.
38. SALZARULO, Piero and Gianluca FICCA (eds.): *Awakening and Sleep-Wake Cycle Across Development.* 2002.
39. BARTSCH, Renate: *Consciousness Emerging. The dynamics of perception, imagination, action, memory, thought, and language.* 2002.
40. MANDLER, George: *Consciousness Recovered. Psychological functions and origins of conscious thought.* 2002.
41. ALBERTAZZI, Liliana (ed.): *Unfolding Perceptual Continua.* 2002.
42. STAMENOV, Maxim I. and Vittorio GALLESE (eds.): *Mirror Neurons and the Evolution of Brain and Language.* 2002.
43. DEPRAZ, Natalie, Francisco VARELA and Pierre VERMERSCH.: *On Becoming Aware. A pragmatics of experiencing.* 2003.
44. MOORE, Simon and Mike OAKSFORD (eds.): *Emotional Cognition. From brain to behaviour.* 2002.
45. DOKIC, Jerome and Joelle PROUST: *Simulation and Knowledge of Action.* 2002.
46. MATHEAS, Michael and Phoebe SENGERS (ed.): *Narrative Intelligence.* 2003.
47. COOK, Norman D.: *Tone of Voice and Mind. The connections between intonation, emotion, cognition and consciousness.* 2002.
48. JIMÉNEZ, Luis: *Attention and Implicit Learning.* 2003.
49. OSAKA, Naoyuki (ed.): *Neural Basis of Consciousness.* 2003.
50. GLOBUS, Gordon G.: *Quantum Closures and Disclosures. Thinking-together post-phenomenology and quantum brain dynamics.* 2003.
51. DROEGE, Paula: *Caging the Beast. A theory of sensory consciousness.* 2003.
52. NORTHOFF, Georg: *Philosophy of the Brain. The 'Brain problem'.* n.y.p.
53. HATWELL, Yvette, Arlette STRERI and Edouard GENTAZ (eds.): *Touching for Knowing. Cognitive psychology of haptic manual perception.* 2003.
54. BEAUREGARD, Mario (ed.): *Consciousness, Emotional Self-Regulation and the Brain.* n.y.p.